HIGH SCHOOL STUDENTS' COMPETING SOCIAL WORLDS

*Negotiating Identities and Allegiances
in Response to Multicultural Literature*

RICHARD BEACH
AMANDA HAERTLING THEIN
DARYL PARKS

 Lawrence Erlbaum Associates
Taylor & Francis Group

New York   London

Lawrence Erlbaum Associates
Taylor & Francis Group
270 Madison Avenue
New York, NY 10016

Lawrence Erlbaum Associates
Taylor & Francis Group
2 Park Square
Milton Park, Abingdon
Oxon OX14 4RN

Library of Congress Cataloging-in-Publication Data

Beach, Richard.
    High school students' competing worlds : negotiating identities and allegiances in response to
multicultural literature / Richard W. Beach and Amanda Haertling Thein.
        p. cm.
    Includes bibliographical references and index.
    ISBN-13: 978-0-8058-5855-6 (alk. paper)
    1. Multicultural education--United States. 2. High school students--United States--Social
conditions. 3. Group identity--United States. 4. Multiculturalism in literature--Study and teaching
(Secondary)--United States. I. Thein, Amanda Haertling. II. Title.

LC1099.3.B42 2008
373.18--dc22   2007016050

Visit the Taylor & Francis Web site at
http://www.taylorandfrancis.com

and the LEA Web site at
http://www.erlbaum.com

September 5, 2007

Contents

Preface

Until the 1980s, working-class adolescents had little concern about their economic future. They could graduate from high school and take a blue-collar job that paid relatively well and often offered benefits. Since the 1980s, with an economy in which wages associated with low-income jobs have remained flat, with an increasingly global economy resulting in the loss of manufacturing jobs to other countries, with a decline in union membership, and with a diminution in health care and support for schools in low-income neighborhoods, working-class adolescents face a number of serious challenges in contemporary American society characterized by:

1. The emergence of the new knowledge-based economy that is replacing the traditional manufacturing economy and requires students to acquire postsecondary education and to develop flexible, adaptable portfolio identities (Apple, 2001; Gee, 2006; Willis, 1998)

2. High schools with a relatively high percentage of working-class students that emphasize traditional transmission models of instruction associated with physical and intellectual control of students (Weis, 1990, 2004) and, with the implementation of No Child Left Behind testing requirements, instruction organized around teaching for the test (Apple, 2001)

3. Cultural disparities within high schools in which middle-class students' cultural capital affords them the ability to use the high school bureaucracy to serve their needs, whereas working-class students often having difficulty navigating this bureaucracy,

leading them to identify more with the neighborhood and work-place communities (Eckert, 1989, 2001)

4. Increased attendance in postsecondary education yet increased number of remedial classes and high school students who struggle to successfully complete college work because they lack requisite academic skills or cultural capital (Beach, Lundell, & Jung, 2002; Plucker, Wongsarnpigoon, & Houser, 2006)

5. Families in which both parents often have to work in low-wage jobs with minimal benefits, creating difficulty paying for increased health care, housing, transportation, and college costs

6. An increasingly diverse society, while adolescents experience seg-regation by race and class within schools (Tatum, 2003) and in districts across the nation (Orfield & Lee, 2006)

7. Gender disparities in which adolescent working-class females are more likely to graduate from high school and college as well as to obtain employment more consistent with their training than working-class males (Bettie, 2003; Weis, 2004)

8. An increasingly conservative political climate in which politi-cians appeal to White, working-class voters in terms of social conservative issues of gay marriage, abortion, and values, as well as perceived threats to jobs from non-Whites related to wedge, White-backlash issues of affirmative action and immigration (Frank, 2004), creating tensions between White and students of color (Bettie, 2003).

In this book we take the position that, to face these challenges, adolescents need to learn how to negotiate the competing demands of diverse social worlds. They need to learn to be open to entertaining alternative perspec-tives associated with race, class, and gender differences. They also need to acquire literacy practices and academic discourses associated with criti-cal analysis in preparation for college work. And they need to learn how to critically reflect on the limitations of their beliefs and attitudes associ-ated with allegiances to status quo worlds. Finally, they need to learn prac-tices constituting development of socially situated identities (Gee, 1999) that allow them the ability to shift between different careers and social worlds. In all of this, from a sociocultural perspective, *learning* is defined as acquiring ways of knowing and valuing consistent with being certain kinds of persons in certain types of social worlds (Hicks, 1996, 2001).

This redefinition of learning for working-class adolescents challenges prevailing instructional methods in working-class schools that focus on acquiring basic skills based on achievement defined in terms of standard-ized testing — methods that fail to prepare students for participation in a knowledge-based economy that requires flexibility, perspective taking, critical thinking, an openness to cultural diversity, and a critical analysis of how institutional forces function to limit or foster agency to change oneself and the world.

Given the challenges facing working-class adolescents, researchers recently focused attention on working-class students' identity construction related to their ability to acquire certain social and literacy practices valued in different social worlds (Bettie, 2003; Hartman, 2001, 2006; Hicks, 2001, 2002, 2005; Moje, Ciechanowski, Kramer, Ellis, & Callazo, 2004; Phelan, Davidson, & Yu, 1998; Vadeboncoeur & Stevens, 2005). These researchers examine adolescents' identity construction within their participation in social worlds. They also focus on how adolescents acquire certain discourses (Fairclough, 2003; Gee, 1999; Rogers, 2004) or cultural models (Holland, Lachicotte, Skinner, & Cain, 1998) as identity tool kits (Gee, 1996) for participating in certain social worlds. They are particularly interested in the types of practices that serve to foster adolescents' development of agency related to envisioning future selves (Moore & Cunningham, 2006). In some cases, they find that discourses and cultural models of race, class, and gender operating in high schools position working-class adolescents in negative ways, limiting their sense of agency (Rymes, 2001; Weis, 2004; Yon, 2000).

Adolescents in English classrooms also participate in literary worlds in which they construct characters' identities operating in competing social worlds based on their social and literary knowledge. In reading multicultural literature, adolescents are exposed to alternative cultural perspectives that serve to challenge their beliefs and attitudes (Athanases, 1998; Beach, 1997b; DeBlase, 2005). In constructing these text worlds, adolescent readers draw on discourses of whiteness (Trainor, 2002, 2005), class differences (Hemphill, 1999; Hicks, 2005), and gender (Finders, 1997) to construct worlds consistent with those discourses.

Given the need to understand how adolescents learn to critically reflect on their allegiances to social worlds, all of this raises the question of how responding to cultural differences portrayed in multicultural literature serves to challenge adolescents' allegiances to status quo discourses and cultural models. Responding to dialogic tensions (Bakhtin, 1981) between characters requires adolescents to sort through and to judge alternative cultural perspectives operating in a text. Rather than framing multicultural literature as a tool for enhancing tolerance for others, we were interested in how participating in how these dialogic tensions fostered students' shifts in thinking and allegiances to status quo discourses and cultural models of race, class, and gender operating in their everyday social worlds.

Overview

This book reports the results of a study of 14 largely working-class high school seniors' and juniors' identity construction in a high school literature course. We were interested in how they mediated by discourses and cultural models operating in their classroom, school, family, sports, workplace, and community social worlds.

We were particularly interested in studying working-class adolescents' identity construction in the context of a semester-long multicultural literature course. This course was taught in Thompson High School, located in an urban, working-class neighborhood where demographic shifts since the 1970s in the school and the community created racial and social class tensions. Because students were receiving college credit for this course, the teacher and coresearcher, Daryl Parks, provided students with critical analysis strategies and practices associated with college-level work, methods that deviated from the larger school culture of physical and intellectual control (Weis, 1990, 2004). He also employed a critical multicultural approach (Lewis, Ketter, & Fabos, 2001) to challenge students' adherence to discourses of individualism through critical analysis of issues of race, class, and gender differences portrayed in multicultural literature. Through grappling with these cultural differences, students imagined alternative ways of constructing identities that led, for some, to critical interrogation of the forces constituting their identities, particularly in terms of tensions between their largely familiar high school students identities and the identities they assumed as taking this course for college credit.

To understand the influence of the school culture on students, we also conducted ethnographical observations of student practices in classrooms, lunchrooms, hallways, school events, and sporting events, as well as interviews with students about their perceptions of their experiences in their different social worlds.

We also examined shifts in students' literary responses across time in their writing and discussion responses as well as interview data, drawing on critical discourse analysis techniques (Fairclough, 2003; Gee, 1996, 1999; Rogers, 2004) to identify students' use of certain discourses and cultural models as well as amendment of their revising their status quo discourses and cultural models. The book presents seven case-study profiles of students, some of whom did not change in their thinking and some of whom shifted in their thinking.

This book is designed for educators and researchers interested in understanding how adolescents learn to construct and reflect on their identities through responses to literature. It meshes current theory and research on identity construction with specific application of that theory and research to case study profiles and analysis of classroom discussions. The book also provides educators with concrete descriptions of Parks's instructional methods that could be used in literature classrooms to foster critical responses to literature leading to students' reflection on their identity construction.

Organization of the Book

This book begins with a review of current theories of identity construction based on sociocultural theories of learning (Bazerman & Russell, 2003; Cole, 1996; Engeström, 1987), critical discourse analysis (Fairclough, 2003; Gee, 1996, 1999; Rogers, 2004), cultural model theory (Holland et al., 1998), and critical race theory (Bonilla-Silva, 2001; Delgado & Stefancic, 2001). Given the notion of identity construction as mediated by discourses of race, class, and gender, the book also posits the need to move beyond a determinist model of discourses shaping identity construction to consider how adolescents develop a sense of agency (Moore & Cunningham, 2006).

Chapter 2 examines research on how adolescents learn to negotiate identities across the competing demands of school, peer group, family, workplace, and community social worlds (Beach & Myers, 2001; Phalen, Davidson, & Yu, 1998). It describes how the school's high school culture reflects a nostalgic attachment to past values of the local, White working-class neighborhood now coping with a more diverse neighborhood driven by different economic forces. It also contrasts the school culture as mediated by discourses of physical and intellectual control with Parks's classroom world that challenges students' allegiances to status quo discourses and cultural models operating in their other worlds. Finally, it examines how students acquire these discourses in peer-group, family, sports, and community or religious organizations.

Chapter 3 reviews current theories of sociocultural theory of literary response that describe the ways students draw on lived-world experiences to construct text worlds (Blackford, 2004; Smagorinsky, 2001). Chapter 4 proposes a rationale for teaching multicultural literature that goes beyond traditional reader-response approaches of fostering empathy with characters to emphasize the need for students to experience dialogic tensions (Bakhtin, 1981), in responding to multicultural literature (Möller & Allen, 2000; Vinz, Gordon, Lundgren, LaMontagne, & Hamilton, 2000). Students experience characters' tensions given their increased realization of how they may be limited by racist, class-bound, or sexist institutional forces (Kegan, 2000). And students experience tensions in peer interactions based on voicing competing interpretations of literature (Knoeller, 1998).

Based on these theoretical perspectives, Chapter 5 describes Parks's specific methods for socializing students into a college classroom in a high school world, for scaffolding literary and cultural analysis of texts and lived world experiences, teaching literary-critical lenses (Appleman, 2000), facilitating classroom discussions, and challenging students' status quo identity constructions.

Chapter 6 provides case study profiles of two White students, Corey and Michelle, who construct their identities primarily through allegiances to the status quo school culture, limiting the extent to which they adopt a critical stance toward issues of race, class, and gender in the course. These profiles are followed in Chapter 7 by profiles of Devin and Kayla, White students who challenge the status quo school culture through their intellectual participation in Parks's class. These students move beyond a discourse of individualism to engage in critiques of institutional forces shaping portrayals of race, class, and gender in texts and their own lives. Chapter 8 profiles two other students, Kathy (African) and Mai (Hmong), who are somewhat marginalized by the classroom culture, resulting in Kathy's being critiqued by peers and Mai's deliberate stance of not participating in discussions.

Chapter 9 describes classroom discussions of three novels read in the course: *Love Medicine, Kindred,* and *Bastard out of Carolina,* novels that evoked dialogic tensions in students. Having to defend challenges to their status quo discourses and cultural models led some students to examine the limitations of their beliefs and attitudes. In these discussions, the use of writing to prepare for discussions played a key role in preparing students to share their interpretations.

Chapter 10 concludes with a discussion of factors influencing shifts in some students' beliefs and attitudes. Although some students demonstrated little change in their beliefs and attitudes, some began to amend and revise their discourses and cultural models, particularly in terms of critically examining the limitations of discourses of individualism and recognizing the influence of institutional forces. The fact that some of these working-class students demonstrated shifts in their thinking points to the value of providing high school students with instruction that serves to challenge them to think critically about the influence of economic and political forces that often limit their lives and sense of agency.

Acknowledgments

We would like to acknowledge the ongoing long-term support and encouragement of Naomi Silverman for our work on this project, as well as the invaluable feedback on drafts by Thomas W. Bean, University of Nevada, Las Vegas; Cynthia Lewis, University of Minnesota; and Joel Taxel, University of Georgia. We would also like to acknowledge the support, advice, and participation of our colleague Timothy Lensmire in this research project. Also, we wish to thank Rodney S. Wallace for his support for the Rodney S. Wallace Professorship awarded to Richard Beach; this funding was used to support this research project.

CHAPTER 1

Constructing Mediated Identities across Different Social Worlds

Meet Troy[1], a clean-cut, White, working-class, 11th-grade student. In his third year at Thompson High School, Troy already had one foot out the door into the "real world," as he put it. Troy spoke candidly about the past three years: "For me, high school is dumb; it's a waste of time." For Troy, school was a temporary stepping-stone that served as a gateway to the larger world of opportunity. He did not participate in school activities and enrolled in as many college-credit courses as possible via the Post-Secondary Enrollment Options (PSEO) program to save money and to speed his college entrance.

Troy perceived the high school world as unfairly privileging and as marginalizing certain types of students: "If you don't play sports or work on the prom committee, then you aren't cool." He also identified a disparity in the relationship between teachers and the popular students: "There's only like two teachers in the school who are cool with all of the students." Troy also questioned the "fairness" of Thompson's administrators and teachers, explaining that they were more concerned with "giving students a bunch of busy work" than with preparing students for college or ensuring that all students were adequately equipped for success in the real world. Troy's beliefs about school and about the kind of person he wanted to be were bound up in the many competing social worlds in which he participated.

Troy's parents both grew up in the inner-ring suburbs around Thompson. He was two years old when his parents divorced. He attributed the divorce primarily to his father's substance abuse, explaining that both parents "partied a lot when I was young." Though his biological father was not in his life, Troy explained that he learned "not to use drugs" and "not to have kids when you're young" through his father's negative modeling.

While Troy's father struggled, Troy's mother found an entry-level job working for the state government. Over the years, she received government assistance, worked second jobs, took classes, and ultimately completed a degree in social work that allowed her to find stable employment and upward mobility. Troy described her as a "super tough" parent but also cited her as the primary influence on his path to success. He said, "No matter how much I may not like her as a person, she has given me the tools in life to get a little farther than others might."

Troy's mother remarried when he was five, and his stepfather became a key adult in his life. His stepfather worked at a bakery and then a printing press during Troy's childhood. Since his stepfather worked at night and slept during the day, Troy explained that it was a tense environment at home. Troy, however, came to perceive his stepfather as a role model for overcoming life's challenges: "He had kids when he was sixteen. He didn't graduate high school and he has dyslexia. He did drugs, did dumb things. But he taught me that to be a man is to work. If it is 60 or 80 hours a week, you don't cry or whine. You don't get sick, you don't get tired; you just do it."

Troy learned other important lessons in life through his involvement in his community—the East Side neighborhood. His earliest connections around the neighborhood were through athletic leagues in which he played organized football, baseball, and hockey. However, Troy quit these leagues during middle school, explaining that "it got too tough having the neighbors take me and pick me up from practices. My mom could never come to one game."

Troy's other connections to the neighborhood were more problematic. Many evenings found him and his friends running from the police because of the "crazy stuff we did." He noted, "I was a thief when I was younger, a hoodlum. I've seen a lot, been through a lot, been beat up, beat up kids, once beat up a kid so bad I broke my middle finger on his nose, went to juvi [juvenile incarceration] and didn't know how to get out, to stop it."

At age 16, Troy left his parents' home and began to live on his own. He recognized that it is unusual to be self-sufficient at this age but chose to make the best of his current arrangement: "When I got kicked out at age 16, I couldn't say I was a man. But I owned a fridge and air conditioner and vacuum. I've had to work hard all through high school, 32 hours a week. If I didn't go to school, if I didn't do my work, then I knew I would end up being a nobody ... a shift supervisor at McDonalds: I had more potential and the knowledge and the power and the faith to get through things."

Consistent with research that finds that working-class adolescents have strong ties to the local neighborhood community or workplace, stronger often than with school (Eckert, 1989, 2001; Phelan, Davidson, & Yu, 1998; Seitz, 2004a, 2004b), Troy reflected positively on his upbringing and his community. He said, "I take pride in growing up on the East Side because of what I had to come through." He recognized that his neighborhood might be considered "the ghetto" to outsiders, but he saw it as providing him with a definitive set of values. He contrasted his hardscrabble childhood with those of people from more affluent backgrounds: "I think being rich would have turned me personally into a rich bastard. I'd be greedy, have no friends, and have everything."

Troy's development as an adolescent was strongly related to his ties to specific social worlds of his family, neighborhood, church, school, and workplace. As he moved across these different worlds, he was exposed to multiple perspectives on issues related to race, class, and gender—issues such as desegregation, affirmative action, gender wage gaps, immigration policy, antipoverty government programs, and same-sex marriage. Through his participation in competing social worlds, Troy acquired and developed beliefs, attitudes, and practices associated with becoming a certain kind of person (Hicks, 2001).

The Study

Troy was a participant in our research study of high school students' responses to multicultural literature in a class taught in fall 2001 at Thompson High School—a diverse, working-class high school of 1,583 students in a large Midwestern city. Students in this study were enrolled in a College in the Schools course on modern literature that operated in conjunction with a local university through which students earned college credit. Students elected to take this course based on their assumption that they would attend college. However, in contrast to an advanced placement (AP) or honors English class within a tracked system, the students in the class represented a range of ability levels.

Thompson High School was chosen for its diversity—the student body is 39% White, 32% Asian American (largely Hmong), 19% African, 8% Hispanic, and 1% Native American—and because the recent demographic shifts in the school and the community created a unique site for studying racial and social class tensions. Although White students were increasingly the minority in this school, the school and community's long history of a statistical White majority remained discursively intact; Whiteness functioned as the invisible norm against which "others" were judged. The prevailing discourses of athleticism and competition in the school reflected the community's value placed on hard work, competition, and adherence to a controlling authority. Student athletes were often held up as exemplars of the values of hard work and competition in all aspects of life.

The participants in this one-year qualitative research study consisted of 14 11th- and 12th-grade students: eight females and six males. In this group of 14, nine were White, three were Asian American, one was Hispanic, and one was a student of African descent. Two of the 14 students were 11th graders. Of these 14 students, based on information about parental occupations, only two students—the African student and one of the White students—could be characterized as middle class in terms of family income. The other students could be characterized as working class. The research team consisted of Richard Beach, a professor at local university who is White and middle class; Amanda Thein, a doctoral student at the time of the study who is White and middle class; and Daryl Parks, the White teacher of the class that was the focus of this study, who was also a doctoral student at the time of the study. As we will demonstrate, the fact that Parks came from a working-class background was critical to his success in engaging students in responding to multicultural literature.

Much of the previous research on responses to multicultural literature finds that high school students have difficulty interpreting characters' practices because they are not familiar with the cultures portrayed in these texts (Hemphill, 1999; Jordan & Purves, 1993). They also have difficulty interpreting larger cultural or institutional forces associated with race, class, and gender systems, adopting an individualistic stance to interpret characters in terms of their personal agendas and motives as opposed to an institutional perspective in which they interpret characters as shaped by larger social and cultural forces (Beach, 1997a, 1997b; Vinz, Gordon, Lundgren, LaMontagne, & Hamilton, 2000). White students in particular often struggle to see the institutional aspects of Whiteness and, as a result, often impose discourses of White privilege onto their readings of texts (Miller & Legge, 1999; Möller & Allen, 2000).

In this study, we examined students' responses to multicultural literature over a period of six months. We were particularly interested in how the students' responses reflected the discourses and cultural models constituting their identities. Also, we were interested in the ability of students to interpret the cultural differences portrayed in multicultural literature.

In designing the course, Parks selected texts that represented a range of different racial and ethnic groups and perspectives as well as texts that revolve around characters coping with dialogic tensions, including *The House on Mango Street* (Cisneros, 1991), *Bless Me, Ultima* (Anaya, 1995), *Kindred* (Butler, 1979), *Their Eyes Were Watching God* (Hurston, 2000), *Obasan* (Kogawa, 1993), the film *Smoke Signals* (Eyre, 1998), *Woman*

Warrior (Kingston, 2000), *Love Medicine* (Erdrich, 2000), *Bastard out of Carolina* (Allison, 1993), and *A Yellow Raft in Blue Water* (Dorris, 1987).

Parks encouraged exploration around issues of race, class, and gender that were rarely addressed in the larger school culture or in the students' other courses. He employed journal writing and group discussions to foster critical response to the texts in the course, frequently supporting student expression of minority or alternative interpretations to foster dialogic tensions in discussions.

In this study, we analyzed selected classroom discussions, student interviews, focus-group discussions, and an interview with Parks and coded them using NVivo (QSR International, 2005) qualitative software. Employing a grounded theory perspective (Lincoln & Guba, 1985), codes were generated inductively through extensive discussions among the three researchers. We devoted multiple meetings to sharing our perceptions of the transcripts, noting consistent themes related to student identity construction, social practices, discourses, stances, and norms operating in the classroom, school, community, family, and workplace cultures. We generated a tentative set of codes, which were then applied to samples of the data. Comparisons of each of our uses of the codes to analyze the data led to further revisions and refinements of the coding system. A final version of the coding system (see Appendix A) was again used in coding a sample of the data to determine interjudge reliability, and a relatively high level of agreement (more than 75%) was achieved. These codes focused on the frequency of students' use of different discourses and cultural models related to gender, class, race, sports, schooling, historical–cultural contexts, psychology and family, and religion. This analysis identified participants' voicing of discourses, cultural models, and narratives related to various topics, for example, adoption of discourses of individual prejudice or race-talk (Bonilla-Silva, 2001) related to discussions of race.

Constructing Identities across Social Worlds

In conducting this study, we assumed that adolescent identity development is more than simply a matter of an individual's solo projection into adulthood. Individualist models of adolescent identity construction frame adolescent development primarily in terms of their personal traits and behaviors without considering how development occurs through participation in social worlds (Phelan, Davidson, & Yu, 1998; Vadeboncoeur, 2005). These models are reflected in literature units such as "The Individual versus Society," in which students study individual characters such as Holden Caulfield in *The Catcher in the Rye* (Salinger, 1996) as resisting the conformist demands of society. Such models presuppose that individuals exist outside of rather than coterminous with society.

On the other end of the spectrum, postmodern theories of identity positing that adolescents adopt entirely different identities or relational selves across different contexts (Gergen, 1994) fail to consider how in enacting or improvising certain versions of the self (Moje & Helden, 2005), adolescents may still subscribe to certain consistent beliefs or value stances that transcend particular contexts (Erickson, 2004).

Adolescents do not simply construct their identities on their own; they construct their identities through their participation, competing social worlds of peer group, family, school, community, and workplace (Beach & Myers, 2001; Phelan, Davidson, & Yu, 1998). In this socialization, they learn particular race, class, and gender practices associated with being perceived as certain kinds of persons in certain social worlds. Troy acquired gendered practices of masculine assertiveness and resistance to authority through his experiences in his family, sports, and workplace worlds. At the same time, he also acquired practices in his working-class worlds related to resentment toward middle-class norms prevailing in school and workplace worlds.

The purpose of our study was to examine how adolescents construct their identities through their participation in social worlds, including participation in worlds portrayed in multicultural literature. We began with the premise that identity construction is mediated by discourses and cultural models acquired through participation in social worlds and in text worlds. For example, from their experiences in working-class family and school worlds, students acquire certain discourses of race that shape not only their own identity construction but also their interpretations of characters' identities. Rather than perceive these students' identities as fixed entities, we explored the ways their identities continually shift as students take up, revise, and amend discourses of race, class, and gender across the time and space of various social worlds (Holland & Leander, 2004; Leander & Sheehy, 2004).

Understanding adolescent identity construction therefore requires analysis of the particular race, class, and gender practices operating in particular social worlds. Based on previous research on identity construction through membership in subcultural groups (e.g., *jocks, burnouts, preps, rednecks, punks* [Eckert, 1989, 2001; Willis, 1977, 1998]), it is important to examine how adolescents' practices associated with these group memberships vary across different worlds. Rather than simply identifying Troy as working-class rebel who resists the school culture, understanding his identity requires analysis of how his practices vary across his peer group, family, school, and workplace worlds. Troy's perceptions of the value of schooling and the need to persist against overwhelming odds likely stems from the influence of his mother and stepfather, as well as Parks, the teacher of the multicultural literature class that we studied.

Qualitative researchers have also moved away from assigning traits to adolescents based on the reasoning that if X adolescent is of Y type, he or she must have Z traits (Gutierrez & Rogoff, 2003). For example, it could be argued that if Troy is a White working-class male, then he will probably be less likely to enjoy reading or discussing literature than do females. Applying these static, essentialist categories such as *White, working-class male* limits our understanding of the ways adolescents learn to engage with others in communities. For example, through participation in particular communities or social worlds, a White, working-class male may acquire certain practices that challenge stereotypes of that person as uneducated and racist. These essentialist categories are particularly problematic when applied to students of color based on individual traits, for example, that African American male adolescents lack motivation to achieve in school (Gutierrez & Rogoff, 2003).

Identity Construction as Performing Different Versions of the Self

Rather than apply these static labels of identity traits, researchers have studied identity construction as performing different versions of the self in specific social worlds (Bennett & Fabio, 2004; Bettie, 2003; Moje, Ciechanowski, Kramer, Ellis, & Callazo, 2004). Drawing on performance theory (Schechner, 2002), these researchers examine how adolescents' perform different versions of the self in response to challenges of specific social situations or the dictates of social worlds (Bettie, 2003; Erickson, 2004). Rather than simply learning to follow rules, adolescents employ practices that serve to define their footing (Goffman, 1981) or agency in specific situations or events related to how they want others to perceive their identities. As Erickson (2004, p. 148) noted, "People must have ways of telling one another who they want to be regarded as being, for the purposes of that particular moment in the encounter."

In these performances, there is always a tension between bottom-up, innovative attempts to circumvent norms or dictates versus the need to conform to norms and dictates operating in specific contexts. Adolescents will vary in how they enact these tensions. As Lewis and Moje (2004, p. 1984) noted, "At times these enactments may cause tension, but at other times seemingly contradictory enactments may sit perfectly well with an individual, precisely because the relationships, times, spaces, or activities make room for such enactments without tension, without crisis, and without pretense." In the multicultural literature class we studied, there was an ongoing tension between performing new practices associated with critiquing some of the racist and sexist practices operating in the larger school and neighborhood culture versus the need to maintain these norms given students' allegiance to the school and neighborhood. Some of our participants began to critique those racist and sexist practices, whereas other participants were less likely to adopt such a stance. A primary focus of this study is an exploration of the tensions between these practices and discourses as they are performed by the class as a whole and by individual students.

For example, one of our participants, Michelle, wrote a story for the school newspaper based on her knowledge of regular alcohol use by athletes. The school athletic director objected to the story, creating tensions for Michelle between her gender performance and her allegiance to the school culture.

Michelle's identity as an outspoken female student and as a reporter led her to adopt an agentic self (Kashima, 2002) who exposed the hypocrisy of the presumable drug-free male athletes in the high school. In doing so, she negotiated a tension between challenging the status quo norms of male athleticism and acquiescing to the norms of the school culture. She opted to challenge the status quo by drawing on her knowledge of what one does as a reporter within the traditions of journalism and freedom of the press—uncover information that may be unpleasant to others. In resisting her assigned gender discourse Michelle also challenged the discourses operating in her school.

On the other hand, in other contexts, Michelle subscribed to relatively traditional feminine versions of her identity associated with getting married after high school and continuing to work with her boyfriend/future husband at a local fast-food restaurant. In these contexts, she valued the role of wife and worker. And, within the classroom world, she rarely challenged the male students' attempts to dominate discussions but was assertive in arguing with other female students.

Michelle therefore adopted different versions of the self depending on the activity and worlds in which she was engaged (Lewis & Moje, 2004). In participating in the activity and role of reporter, she adopted somewhat different practices and stances than in her family, workplace, or classroom worlds. It is therefore important to examine identity construction as varying across different contexts. Thus, "identity is the outcome of activity instead of its precondition. All identities are constantly evolving over time in the constantly changing social interactions of communities that one participates in" (Roth, Hwang, Goulart, & Lee, 2005, p. 233). Rather than define organizations and individuals as separate from each other—often assumed to be at odds with each other—Roth et al. (2005, p. 259) argued that it is important to examine organizational identities as a "structural feature of organizational life." They wrote, "Who someone is, which is always inferred from his or her actions, is mediated by the organization of which he or she is part; but the identity of organization is inferred from actions, which only human subjects do enact" (p. 260).

Identity Performances Mediated by Discourses and Cultural Models

In examining how our participants constructed their identities in different social worlds, we therefore focused on how participation in these worlds was mediated by identity tool kits (Gee, 1996), including discourses and cultural models of race, class, and gender (Bonilla-Silva, 2001; Hicks, 2002, 2004; Rogers, 2003). Understanding Troy's ambivalent relationships with his family requires an understanding of the discourses of working-class life that constitute his own and his family members' beliefs and attitudes.

Discourses

Identity performances are mediated by different discourses—ideologically based ways of knowing and thinking (Chouliaraki & Fairclough, 1999; Fairclough, 2001, 2003; Gee, 1996, 1999; Reisigl & Wodak, 2001). Discourses serve to represent events, subjects and actors, or time and place in ways that reflect certain value assumptions or ideological orientations (Fairclough, 2003). As Fairclough (2003, p. 124) noted, "Different discourses are different perspectives on the world, and they are associated with the different relations people have to the world, which in turn depends on their positions in the world, their social and personal identities, and the social relationships in which they stand to other people."

Discourses position participants to adopt those practices most valued in a particular social world. Lawyers, for instance, adopt a legal discourse to define their identities in ways that position themselves as experts in legal proceedings. Doctors adopt a medical discourse to position themselves as authorities in a hospital world. In school worlds, students are positioned to adopt a certain habitus (Bourdieu, 1977, 1984) associated with certain practices, discourses, and dispositions valued in that school as social fields (Bourdieu, 1984). McLeod and Yates (2006, p. 90) defined *habitus* as "the embodied accumulation and effects of dispositions ... and 'ways of being,' including orientations, values, and ways of comporting oneself, and it formed in interactions with 'social fields.' Fields are structured contexts of institutions' rules and other relations that form a differentiating hierarchy that shapes these processes and practices and determines what counts as valuable capital."

Based on tracking 26 students in four Australian high schools over their time in these schools, McLeod and Yates (2006) analyzed the socializing influences of the different school ethos or cultures on students' identities. They cited the example of a female student, Gillian, from a middle-class background who attended one of the four schools, an elite private school called City Academy. In the beginning of her school career, Gillian worked hard to acquire the cultural capital that her wealthier peers already possessed. They defined *capital* as "a confident and casual relation to dominant knowledge, know-how and distinctions, an easiness with elite cultural forms, 'good taste,' a less deferential attitude to class and privilege, a kind of liberalism that values the diversity of individual" (p. 94).

Gillian had difficulty making friends and was aware of her uncertainty about appropriate practices in the school. At the same time, she began to voice the prevailing discourses operating in the school related to tolerance toward differences. But, at the same time, she expressed a lack of tolerance toward unemployed people regarded as lacking the motivation to work. By her senior year, Gillian no longer positioned herself as an outsider; she displayed an increased sense of poise and self-confidence associated with the prevailing ethos of the school that values "being nice" (McLeod & Yates, p. 97). McLeod and Yates (2006) attributed her acquisition to "being nice" as representing her strategic need to become a valued member of City Academy, which "prizes tolerance for all its students, for them to be nice to 'others,' and fosters a marketable, middle-class successful femininity for girls, encouraging them into appropriate professional careers" (p. 99). McLeod and Yates's research reflects how schools as social worlds function to socialize students to adopt certain identities. Students at City Academy "were actively acquiring a sense of themselves as a 'portfolio' person: one who was self-conscious about representing a range of achievements and activities beyond examination results as part of what they had to offer in negotiating the world beyond school" (p. 227).

It is also the case that students are socialized to adopt certain identities within particular classes within a school, classes that foster certain practices and dispositions that may or may not coincide with the school culture. In her research on an AP high school literature course, Rex (2002) identifies how the teacher of the course adopted certain orienting discourses of academic achievement to position her students to adopt the habitus of college-bound, upper-middle-class, pre-English majors. These practices included the use of analytic or abstract language associated with literary critical analysis as well as display of positive dispositions toward school contrasted with the practices of resistance found in lower-track classes. Some students with cultural capital consistent with the teacher's orienting discourses responded positively to the teacher's positioning, adopting practices associated with being an AP literature student, whereas other students lacking cultural capital were not able to adopt those practices and were less successful in the course.

Within the world of Thompson High School, we identified a prevailing discourse of athleticism that served to position both Troy's and Michelle's identities. This discourse of athleticism celebrated competitiveness, training, and discipline as positive moral values and markers of success in the school. Although Troy, as a White working-class male, was expected to subscribe to this discourse, he resisted this positioning because he was critical of the larger school culture as "dumb." Similarly, in her school newspaper critique of athletes' alcohol use, Michelle challenged the notion that athleticism fostered positive moral values, a resistance that reflected her own beliefs and attitudes about her gendered identity in the school culture. In this study, we are particularly interested in how discourses such as the discourse of athleticism at Thompson are manifested through larger discourses of race, class, and gender.

Discourses of Race   As critical race theorists argue, discourses of race function to place people in hierarchical social categories and then to assign meanings to groups based on economic or political power in ways that serve to maintain and justify these hierarchies (Bonilla-Silva, 2001; Delgado & Stefancic, 2001; Fine, Weis, Powell, & Wong, 2004).

Students often adopt a race-talk discourse of color-blind racism to avoid being labeled as *racist* (Bonilla-Silva, 2001). This discourse of color-blind racism moves away from blatant individual expression of bigotry to the establishment of more subtle acts of institutional racism. Color-blind racism is mediated by language use in statements of denial such as "Everyone is equal, but ... " or "I am not prejudiced, but ... " or in arguments such as "I didn't own slaves, so I'm not a racist" or in denials of structural nature of discrimination as reflected in critiques of affirmative action programs (Blum, 2002; Wiegman, 1999). In focusing on individuals' perspectives and in denying historical fact, this discourse fails to examine the forces of institutional racism (Reisigl & Wodak, 2001). Pollock's (2004) study of talk about race in a high school found that students and teachers adopted this color-blind discourse to celebrate the school's diversity but had difficulty addressing the inequalities in the school related to racial difference, assuming that all students are the same (Lewis, 2000). This discourse of color-blind racism therefore functions as a means of avoiding any implication that Whites are directly or indirectly responsible for economic inequality related to institutional racism. It substitutes a focus on the idea of everyone is the same, assuming that racial conflicts and inequality would be solved if everyone just got along better.

A Discourse of Whiteness   Within discourses of race, a discourse of Whiteness functions to define White students' identities in terms of positioning them as privileged members of social worlds. In some high schools, when White students are in schools with diverse populations, they are more likely to examine issues of racial difference than White students in a majority White school (Perry, 2002). Such was not the case at Thompson High School. Even though White students were in the minority, the historically White discourses and practices on which the neighborhood and school had for so many years been grounded continued to function as the invisible norms against which others were judged. These discourses reflected the value the community placed on competition, adherence to discipline, and self-control associated with a discourse of athleticism. At the same time, since graduates of the school could at one time readily attain manufacturing jobs upon graduation, the school culture valued form over substance (Weis, 1990) in most of its academic preparation of students.

However, as the community became more diverse in the 1980s and 1990s, the school population also became more diverse with an influx of Latino, Asian American, and African American students. This demographic shift posed a challenge to the prevailing, largely White culture of the school. As we document, White members of the school community nostalgically clung to the idea of their school as largely White by resisting the increasing diversity of the school through framing the practices of students of color in negative ways.

Both staff and White students in the school had difficulty knowing how to address issues of race, often attempting to avoid the topic or evoking a color-blind discourse of race, one suggesting that there is no compelling need to have to critically examine race and differences associated with racial constructions. This stance was evident in one student named Sarah's discussion comments explaining that her White suburban relatives adopted racist perspectives because they rarely interacted with people of color. Sarah described how she imagined a White student coming from a largely White suburb might react to the diversity at her school:

Sarah: If someone from [a largely White, middle-class suburb], they're so used to that. I think they'd kind of freak out. And that's what I think about fish and salt water. You know, the ones that can't survive here.

Parks: What do you think they'd freak out about?

Sarah: Like I was trying to think.... Just the whole diversity. I mean people get weird about that like my family that lives out in like out there and they live you know like they go to like just basically all White schools and then they're like, "Oh, do you have these people?" It's like, "Yeah, they're just like people like us. They act like they're not human, and I think they'd kind of like freak out if they came here.

Sarah addressed the issue of Whites' racial perspectives but framed race vaguely in terms of "the whole diversity." She evoked a metaphor of fish and water to describe peoples' relationships with their social worlds, assuming that once people are detached from their culture, they cannot survive. And in describing her relatives' perceptions of people of color as "these people," she recognized their inability to differentiate between racial differences but did not interrogate the limitations of their global labels. While distancing herself from what she perceived to be her relatives' racist perspective, she evoked an alternative perspective of color-blind racism—explaining that her relatives lack the ability to see people of color as "human," or "people like us." She therefore framed racism as an issue of her sheltered relatives' lack of cultural exposure to people of color, as opposed to an issue of larger institutional forces of housing or employment practices that created all-White suburbs. She also failed to interrogate her own use of color-blind racist discourses, assuming that her urban identity anchors her as nonracist.

An alternative perspective to this color-blind perspective is that of critical multiculturalism, which examines race as constituted and constructed through ideologies of difference. In a critique of traditional multiculturalism, West (2002, p. 28) notes that multiculturalism often fosters an accommodation to diversity rather than examining race as "an 'ideology of difference' (Said), as a genealogy of difference, as one of the most historically fundamental politics of 'othering.'" In contrast, a critical multiculturalism associated with critical race theory focuses on challenging the larger institutional forces shaping political ideologies of difference (McCarthy, 1994). Critical race theory posits that racist practices operating in schools such as tracking and testing reflect dominant discourses of culture and schooling. In contrast, critical race theory calls for a commitment to social justice and a focus on students' lived experiences expressed through narratives, family history, scenarios, and biographies (Solorzano & Yosso, 2001).

In analyzing discourses of Whiteness adopted by our participants, we were interested in explaining the affective appeal of these discourses and cultural models in ways that go beyond simply equating racism with racist language use and White identity; the notion that, because these students are White and are using racist language, they are adopting racist discourses and cultural models. Trainor (2005) argued that one limitation of critical discourse analysis (CDA) is that it presupposes that speakers intentionally employ language to serve their own interests relating to fostering or maintaining power. This application of CDA can lead to judgments of students as being racist or not that fail to explain the affective appeals of racist discourses:

> CDA tends to sponsor a view of language (and in turn, a view of Whites) as promoting political beliefs that serve the speaker's (political) interests and intentions. Racist language, in this view, equals racism on the part of the speaker. Such a view of language and language users encourages critical teachers and researchers to see White students in morally dichotomous and, hence, reductive terms, as good or bad, innocent or racist. (p. 153)

Trainor (2005, p. 162) posits the need to examine discourses of Whiteness as more than simply reflecting a political stance to examine it as "persuasive rhetoric—rhetoric that appeals in multiple domains, that resonates privately and means publicly, that expresses emotion and forwards politics at the same time." She analyzed the affective dimensions operating her college sophomore students' responses to the Ralph Ellison's (1994) short story "Battle Royal" about an African American male who is duped into engaging in a boxing match with other African Americans at a White men's club under the belief that he was attending a function at which he would be awarded a college scholarship. Trainor identifies a number of ways in which students used "White talk" to "see themselves as strong and powerful agents operating within a stable, predictable community" (p. 153)—a rhetorical construction that goes beyond race to appeal to the need for "ideals about health, strength, power, and agency" (p. 154). In responding to the story, one student, Amy, adopted a discourse of individualism to argue that the main character's willingness to engage in the boxing match demonstrated that "'if you stick to your dreams, anybody can make it, even if they have to go through that. You can't let other people hold you back, and you can't let obstacles get in your way'" (p. 155). At the same time, in a follow-up interview, Amy noted that the story reflected a condemnation of racist practices "'people today, society, today, would be like, society would not tolerate something like that happening'" (p. 156). Trainor posited that Amy identified not with individual characters but with stances and positions associated with "people today" and "society"—an appeal to the positive ideals of "strength and power" associated with society, reflecting "an understandable resistance to feeling helpless" (pp. 156–157). Trainor argued that Amy's discourses of individualism that ignore the racist aspects of the event were coupled with "an emotional desire for strength and control" associated with allegiances to an anti-racist contemporary "society" (p. 156).

Trainor (2005) also found that students reacted negatively to text portraying the complexity of racial difference due not necessarily to a racist stance but also to their sense of a need for social order. She cited the example of a student who publicly posited that "'Mexicans have less respect for property'" but then who, in an interview, explored the problematic nature of making generalizations about groups, including his own generalization, a reflection that involves more than simply a racist perspective (p. 160). And Trainor noted that in discussions of White privilege and affirmative action, students' rejection of a focus on racial difference reflected a rhetorical appeal not to White privilege but to the need for a sense of a coherent community that requires a "desire to 'get past racism'" (p. 161). For Trainor, understanding the emotional appeal of discourses of Whiteness requires going beyond perceiving it as simply about "self-interest, power, or gain" to perceive it as reflecting "ideals and values that racist discourse taps and solidifies" (p. 163). She also noted, as we have with Thompson High School, that a discourse of Whiteness is associated with the emotional ideals of "strength, order, and community [that] are embedded in almost every aspect of school culture, from sports activities to hall passes to grading and authority relations" (p. 163). Such analysis may then lead educators to "help students honor their deeply held commitments to ideals like community and strength, while simultaneously finding ways to move beyond the White talk that expresses them, creating new rhetorics and new ways of understanding in the process" (p. 163).

Understanding Troy's perspectives on race requires an analysis of his emotional stances about race that go beyond simply labeling him as a White, working-class male who uses racist language in some contexts. For Troy, the increasing diversity of the school evoked ambivalent feelings. He regularly cited the need to better understand the constructions of the groups that shaped his identity. In a journal entry, he posited a desire to engage in discussions of race, even as he shared his unquestioned stereotypes of others:

Racism to me is the biggest problem in America. One that we don't want to discuss, why? Because them's is fightin' words. I ask why can people hate each other so much because of the color of skin. I don't think its skin. It's attitude, at least for me. Black people seem to have attitudes, either we're discriminating or whatever else automatic opinions of Whites. Hispanics always seem to be cocky and think they can do whatever they want. And Hmongs are always in groups starting fights and 10 are beating up 1 person—these are stereotypes, but sometimes the truth hurts. I'm curious of what Blacks/Hispanics and Hmong have to say about Whites and their attitudes.

These words demonstrate the complexities at work in Troy's inquisition into racial discourses. First, he acknowledged the reality of racism as a national problem, while recognizing that "we" cannot discuss such concerns because the topic is so loaded that it could lead to violence. Next, he shifted from race as constituted by color of skin to an attitude that may exist within the individual, adopting a discourse of color-bind racism (Bonilla-Silva, 2001). As he explained his perception of the truth about the stereotypes of groups that surround him in the school, he was aware of his own use of stereotyping but still failed to examine those stereotypes. Though he purported to know what Black people think about discriminating Whites, he also wanted to understand more fully those attitudes and perceptions in relationship to the White group of which he is a part.

Troy drew on discourses of race as well as class in a discussion about affirmative action in which he wondered aloud about how race plays out in his world:

> I don't like how everybody thinks that just because I'm a White male that I have more power, per se, or that I can do more things in life; it's not really that way anymore. It's like, it costs me if I want to go to a good school, $30,000, and it costs somebody else maybe $5,000, because they are of color they get scholarships. They get all these … they get a bunch of help and just like, I mean … is it MEP [Multicultural Excellence Program] … Like, there is always field trips with school and stuff for MEP to like go places and do things and all of these opportunities, but you don't ever see "White Persons for College" (WPFC) going to college. You don't see that.

Troy argued that even though others perceived him as having "more power" because he was White, he was in fact unfairly treated due to reverse discrimination of affirmative action programs. In this familiar critique of affirmative action, what is important is how that complaint is framed in terms of race intersecting with class. In citing issues of tuition costs, availability of scholarships, and field trips, Troy argued against the notion of White privilege when, in fact, the same complaints about college tuition are often voiced by working-class non-White students facing double-digit tuition increases and lack of aid due to state-government budget reductions. Troy's identity construction was therefore mediated by his subscribing to discourses of White privilege associated with resentment again affirmative action programs.

Discourses of Class Discourses of class are associated with adopting a particular habitus, or dispositions and practices associated with class status and acquired tastes (Bourdieu, 1977; 1984). Discourses of class were central to our participants' identities because most of them identified themselves as working class, frequently distinguishing themselves from their suburban middle-class peers, whom they believed perceived them in negative ways and as living in dangerous, urban, ghetto settings.

Previous research on burnout working-class high school students found that these students adopted practices of language, dress, and social interaction based on resistance to the jock, middle-class, bureaucratic school culture (Eckert, 1989, 2001). However, because Thompson was a largely working-class high school, there was no prevailing middle-class culture against which students could define themselves. Therefore, our analysis goes beyond a working-class versus middle-class binary to examine how students align themselves to more specific subgroups within a high school. In an ethnographic analysis of 12th-grade working- and middle-class females in a Central Valley California high school, Bettie (2003) delineated the categories used by students to construct differences in class-based performances and practices associated with differences in terms of race and family economic situations: *settled living*, supported by relatively secure jobs, higher pay, and health benefits; and *hard living*, supported by less stable jobs, lower pay, and no health benefits.

Students in these different groups were assigned to certain tracked classes in the school according to their class background. Given their assignments to largely vocational classes, the working-class females often engaged in performing identities through "the rituals of girl culture" (Bettie, 2003, p. 55) by adopting practices of resistance to academic demands and prep, middle-class practices. Bettie (2003) explained that working-class performing girls who expected to take on adult responsibilities such as working and raising a family immediately following high school often chose a more sexually provocative older look in their hair and makeup. Conversely, middle-class performing girls who expected to attend college were more likely to embrace a younger, more innocent look since college in many ways delays adolescence for several more years. Finally, Bettie (2003, pp. 61–63) suggests that demeanor in terms of accepting or rejecting school culture is related to acceptance of being positioned by adults as adolescents or the rejection of this positioning in favor of taking on adult roles and dispositions and therefore resisting school authority.

At the same time, girls in this study did not necessarily adopt the class-based practices valued in their homes. Some females from working-class homes engaged in passing as middle-class preps, and some females from middle-class homes engaged in passing as members of cliques resisting prep subcultures. This led Bettie (2003, p. 50) to recognize the need to examine school practices as representing performances mediated by class discourses:

> Girls who were passing, or metaphorically cross-dressing, had to negotiate the "inherited" identity from home with their "chosen" identity at school. There was a disparity for them between what people looked like and talked like at home, and their own class performance at school and what their friends' parents were like. As I came to understand these negotiations of class as cultural (not political) identities, it became useful to conceptualize class not only as a material location, but also as a performance.

Contrary to the preconception of performance as creating a false impression or front, Bettie's (2003) notion of identity as performance points to the importance of learning to deliberately adopt language, dress, practices, and dispositions that mark a person as being a certain kind of person of a certain social class within a certain context. For instance, some of Bettie's middle-class, Mexican American participants masked their middle-class dispositions and practices when interacting with working-class Mexican American peers so that they could maintain their racial solidarity with their peers within the school culture, solidarity associated with their valuing Mexican American working-class values.

Understanding identity performances therefore requires an understanding of the purposes for adopting a certain version of the self in particular contexts constituted by particular discourses. Troy's identity as working-class was shaped by his experiences growing up in a hard-living, working-class family that struggled to achieve stability even as Troy entered his teenage years. From his family, he acquired a need to value instrumental, practical aspects of schooling. He also acquired a commitment to hard work and an avoidance of complaining about one's lot in life. As reflected in his critique of affirmative action, he subscribed to a discourse of self-sufficiency that is not dependent on government support. From his incarceration, he also acquired a sense of distrust of law enforcement and the legal system. On the other hand, based on his mother's need for welfare assistance during her divorce, he recognized the need for government support to help people get on their feet. And from his experiences with sports, he recognized the value of group cooperation, noting that "there is no 'I' in team" based on seeing "how a group of people can work together in accomplishing things."

Discourses of Gender   Rather than essentialist, binary notions of male versus female, current gender theorists posit that there are multiple practices constituting what it means to be male or female that are not exclusively associated with discourses of masculinity or femininity (Blackford, 2005; Connell, 1995; 2001).

Gendered identity practices are often highlighted by construction of spaces as gendered in which certain performances of masculinity or femininity are highlighted (Rowan, Knobel, Bigum, & Lankshear, 2002). In her analysis of elementary school children's playground practices, Thorne (1993) noted that when children play together on the playground, biological differences between being males or females did not matter in terms of how they were interacting with each other. It was only when the teacher asked them to line up according to boys and girls that the children started to take up gendered practices associated with being male and female.

Discourses of Femininity   Girls have historically struggled in school settings to take on active as opposed to passive roles, in part because of the dichotomization of males and females such that boys must behave in certain ways to be accepted as true boys, whereas girls must behave in different, opposite ways to be seen as true girls. According to Davies (2003, p. 8), "The male-female binary is one of the most basic metaphysical constructions. It is an unquestionable base or first principle on which so much else rests." This male–female binary unfolds in the socialization of boys and girls through creating expected, normalized behaviors for each opposing gender. For example, boys are expected to be active, whereas girls are expected to be passive; boys are expected to be rational, whereas girls are expected to be emotional, or irrational.

Discourses of gender often intersect with discourse of class to define what it means to be academically successful. Working-class girls in particular often choose to remain strategically silent (Hartman, 2001) rather than to risk their good-girl images through expressing opinions in the classroom. Conversely, middle-class girls are often more comfortable expressing opinions in class, in part because these discourses are supported at home (Finders, 1997; Walkerdine, 1990).

Discourses of Masculinity   Masculine gender identity is often constructed in opposition to femininity or homosexuality and is constituted by discourses of competition, domination, lack of emotional expression, and allegiance to the workplace (Barker & Galasinski, 2001; Young, 2003). Connell (1995, 2001) argued that the hegemonic form of traditional masculinity remains the prevailing cultural model in society, positioning an equally hegemonic form of traditional femininity as the binary opposite. However, Connell (1995, 2001) noted that masculinity contains contradictions and is capable of being contested and transformed. Lesko (2000, p. xvii) explained, "Masculinities must also be understood as profoundly intertextual: That is, masculinities are constructed, performed, and revised across knowledges, symbols, styles, subjectivities, and norms including distinctive racial, ethnic, and sexuality components. Masculinities are composed as much by knowledge as by willed ignorances."

These contradictions are related to how performances of masculinity can vary across different contexts. As Barker and Galasinski (2001, p. 30) noted, "Men might be held to be tough, heterosexual, stoic, action-oriented and work-directed. However, men can also be verbally and emotionally expressive, inwardly reflective and homosexual with a balanced view of the relationship between paid work and personal recreation."

One of the key gendered spaces is that of the masculine peer-group culture in which adolescent males need to display male prowess associated with male bonding (Connell, 1995, 2001). As we document, the males in our study consistently supported each others' perceptions in classroom discussions in an attempt to mutually assert their collective opinions, particularly when challenged by some of the assertive females.

Cultural Models

Cultural models serve to define hierarchical value systems in which certain social practices (e.g., being self-sufficient) are valued over others (e.g., not trying hard enough) (Holland, Lachicotte, Skinner, & Cain, 1998). Thus, in adopting or acquiring identities in a social world, cultural models help people determine which practices are more valued than other practices based on achieving objects related to success, love, equality, work, or family relationships (Holland & Eisenhart, 1990). D'Andrade and Strauss (1992, p. 30) described these objects as "master motives—for things like love and work, which instigate action with no more ultimate goal in sight." These objects are linked to more specific schema, scripts, or knowledge associated with achieving that object, for example, a schema of focusing on profits over people. As Gee, Allen, and Clinton (2001, p. 720) posited,

> Cultural models tell people what is typical or normal from the perspective of a particular Discourse ... [they] come out of and, in turn, inform the social practices in which people of a Discourse engage. Cultural models are stored in people's minds (by no means always consciously), though they are supplemented and instantiated in the objects, texts, and practices that are part and parcel of the Discourse.

As we noted, one of the prevailing cultural models operating in many school cultures is that of the autonomous individual who should assume responsibility for his or her actions (Bellah, Madsen, Sullivan, Swidler, & Tipton, 1996). Thus, being a complete individual is equated with being independent from constraints or forces, whereas being an incomplete individual is equated with being dependent on institutions or communities (Jung, 2007). In schools, the ability to act on one's own or to be self-disciplined is highly valued; lack of self-discipline is equated with an inability to control one's self and one's emotions (Jung, 2007; Sadowski, 2003). As the next chapter discusses, Thompson High School reflected adherence to a cultural model of control associated with self-discipline, order, and hard work.

This cultural model of control builds on another deficit cultural model that perceives people of color as stuck in a culture of poverty perceived to be inferior to White, middle-class values (Bonilla-Silva, 2001; Bruch, 2003; Hooks, 1992, 2000). Such a deficit model is based on a hierarchy that values rules, order, certainty, and structure over unwarranted expressions of subjective perceptions, tensions, and collective political action (Mayo, 2004). As Barnett (2000, p. 16) noted, "Discourses of 'Whiteness' establish themselves as the norm through their reliance on particularly forms of 'rationality' ... a term that highlights another attribute often credited to 'Whiteness,' it's dependency on rules, order, and formal institutional structures."

Troy subscribed to a cultural model of self-control as necessary for him to achieve success. He argued that given his working-class background, it would be easy for him to assume that the system is stacked against him achieving success. He therefore believed that he needed to subscribe to a mental game in which he believed that he would be successful: "If you're poor, you start to get a bad attitude that you can't make it, and you'll never do it. Your mental game isn't what it should be."

Students' cultural models shaped their interpretations of texts such as *Their Eyes Were Watching God* (Hurston, 2000), which portrays the evolution of Janie, an African American female, through several marriages in which she develops a sense of agency as not being dependent on men. Dan, a White male athlete, adopted the cultural model that White people work harder than Black people. When asked to write about who could be considered the Whitest character in the novel, he selected Janie's second husband, Joe Starks, for a variety of reasons: "Joe carries himself awfully high for a Black man in most people's opinion. He has dreams and hopes and is in the process of making those dreams come true instead of sitting out in the fields and dreaming." Dan suggested that for a Black man to carry himself high connotes Whiteness. In addition, working toward the fulfillment of dreams appears to be part of Dan's notion of White identity. He also equated Joe as a hard-working person who takes charge and controls situations in opposition to Blacks who are perceived as lazy: "Before Joe had come along the town was filled with lazy people with nothing to do and when Joe arrived the city he acted like a White person and put himself in charge and started to make the town into a place that he wanted to live in."

Developing Agency through Individual Choices

In examining the influence of different discourses and cultural models constituting our participants' identity construction in different social worlds, it is important not to adopt a deterministic stance—that our participants had little control over the influence of these discourses and cultural models. We believe that adolescents can and do make choices in their lives that reflect their commitment to certain beliefs and attitudes that represent a sense of agency reflecting their sense of self-determination and self-reliance. Moore and Cunningham (2006) found evidence of adolescents' agency in their personal decisions and choices that reflect the fact that they went beyond the environmental factors shaping their lives to choose certain options representing their commitment to certain beliefs and values. Drawing on Giddens' (1979, 1991) social enactment theory, Moore and Cunningham posited that "people both produce and are products of their social environments. The central message here is that people simultaneously (a) decide how they will act, (b) are influenced and limited in their decisions by their contexts, and (c) contribute to contexts that influence and limit how they will act" (p. 135).

At one point in his life, Troy faced a difficult decision. Having served time in a juvenile detention facility for the crimes he had committed, he had to decide what to do with his life: continue to engage in a life of crime or apply himself to finishing high school and attending postsecondary education. Because he was living on his own after age 16, he also did not have the support of parents to help him; he had to turn to other resources to help him define some direction for him in a way that reflected his sense of agency. As we noted, he realized that he did not want to work at McDonalds for the rest of his life and chose to focus on his studies, a decision that reflected a rejection of the beliefs guiding his past identity as a criminal and a sense of his future self as a college student. This sense of self-reliance created a precarious situation for him because he had to work to support himself: "I can't get sick or I won't be able to make my bills." At the same time, out of this struggle to survive, he acquired an appreciation for others facing the same dilemma: "You don't know what somebody's been through until you walk in their shoes."

Moore and Cunningham (2006, p. 136) perceived agency as reflected over time as adolescents "negotiate links among their past, present, and future selves. It becomes apparent when people orchestrate their own and others' voices across time." Based on Bakhtin's (1981) notion of dialogic voices, Moore and Cunningham posited that agency develops through social experiences and relationships in which adolescents experience tensions between others' authoritative voices and the "internally persuasive voices [that] have been created in previous internal dialogues; they are voices the self has found convincing" (ibid.) related to their allegiances to school, family, peer, workplace, and community worlds:

> When the voices contributing to inner conversations are dialogic, they are respected and consulted diligently.... As youth internalize various views of themselves from their interactions, the begin to compare, contrast, and play with them, seizing opportunities for combinations and modifications. They eventually take on and act out identities that position themselves in various ways. In some cases these actions foster academic identities; in other cases they are impediments. (p. 137)

Troy's talk and writing reflected a range of different voices that influenced his sense of agency related to his belief in a future self as a college student. The fact that he has a steady, romantic relationship with a girlfriend in college means that he often talks about her college experiences, experiencing the voice of an older college student as someone he admires: "She's a great girl."

He also acquired an internally persuasive voice through his active participation in an evangelical Christian church group. The group to which he belonged did not meet in a single building but instead held Bible studies in homes and events in both urban and suburban churches. He cited spiritual changes and friends as important to his emotional stability. Through his experiences with the church, he acquired an emergent discourse of faith and religion in his life: "Without God, I would be nowhere." Troy spoke particularly of mission trips that he and youth-group members took to inner-city Chicago to assist impoverished residents as impacting his faith and stability.

One of the limitations of experiences with institutional religion is that it can foster unquestioning adherence to authoritative voices that dominate internal dialogues at the expense of acknowledging their personal or alternative perspectives (Moore & Cunningham, 2006). Although Troy professed a strong beliefs in some of the religious tenants of his church, he perceived the value of his participation in the church more in terms of the social relationships he developed with others in the context of discussions about their leadership gifts and purity in their dating relationships: "The older I get, the more I realize the power and the miracles that come out of the relationships." He contrasts his sense of faith as emerging through dialogic relationships with a more classic notion of a "God with a lightening bolt waiting to strike you if you mess up," a resistance of an authoritative voice.

And because he perceived himself in terms of being a future college student learning to engage in academic discussions, Troy valued the multiple voices operating in Parks's classes in which he identified not only with Parks's voices but also with those of other students whom he found to be persuasive. In discussions, he believed that it is was important to listen to his peers' voices to compare others' perspectives with his own perspective: "Everybody should get at least one or two things in the discussion, you know, participate a little, play the game. But, I think that being a listener is just as valuable as talking, if not more."

Troy therefore developed a sense of agency out of coping with the challenges of life and his capacity to overcome those challenges, something he described as the mental game derived from his confidence in his ability to persevere. Part of this mental game also included acknowledging the voices of others who have faced similar if not more dire adversities, voices associated with his allegiances to his East Side neighborhood.

This belief in the value of agency influenced Troy's interpretations of characters coping with similar adversities and making decisions about their future. One of the novels that students in the course most directly connected to their own struggles as working-class adolescents was *Bastard out of Carolina* (Allison, 1993), a novel that portrays the transformation of Bone, a 15-year-old, White, working-class woman and the illegitimate daughter of Anney Boatwright. The novel recounts Bone's struggle to overcome sexual abuse at the hands of her stepfather, Daddy Glen, while seeking to find a future for herself. Although Daddy Glen is from a wealthy family, he has squandered his money and now is poor, resulting in his need to assert control over Anney and to abuse Bone. Bone struggles with her mother's inability to rescue her from Daddy Glen's abuse but is ultimately saved by her lesbian aunt, Aunt Raylene, who provides an alternative family world in which she achieves some sense of agency. In his analysis of Bone, Troy wrote,

> Bone is probably going to go through life much the way her mom did, and also have the sass of Glenn. Those both equal physical killers to me. But she has a choice, and just can't see it because she's so young. I know she's been hurt and stuff has happened but she has to know that there's always a worse story just the next block over.

In this analysis, Troy noted that Bone was not aware of the fact that eventually she faced a choice associated with the development of a sense of agency for coping with the abuse and adversities. As in his own life, he posited that Bone can develop agency through recognizing that there's always a worse story just the next block over.

However, rather than simply adopting a discourse of individualism in framing his analysis of characters' development of agency, he was also aware of the power of institutional forces limiting the development of agency. After listening to a presentation by an abuse counselor in Parks's class who discussed the significance of sexual abuse on girls and dismal statistics regarding their future success in a variety of arenas, Troy wrote that "all odds are against" Bone achieving success as an adult. However, he later modified his prediction, noting,

> Yes, but she still has a chance. Bone is molested at a very young age, just another hurdle, right? Yes but she still has a chance. I know people who have changed. People who have snorted cocaine and made it. And I know there are hurdles. The probability is like 2% but I support and know, if you try hard enough you can go somewhere, do something.

Troy again cited his belief in the development of agency against adversity, but now with a sense of the difficult odds in facing institutional forces, or what Parks referred to in the course as *hurdles*. In his retrospective analysis of his experience in the course, Troy noted that Parks's use of the hurdles metaphor built on his need to consider the plight of others who are coping with the institutional forces and barriers he faced in his own life:

> The one thing that maybe bored people but that I like a lot was the hurdles analogy ... that he [Parks] used ... and he like drew a line and like, "these are hurdles" and where do you sit on the "race track?" and you know, this is the finish line and that you have hurdles to jump, "where do you think you sit and where do certain races sit?" and here is where he was like, "well, I would argue that African Americans sit here and that Whites sit here...." Or, "you might argue that upper class Whites sit here and that this is the finish line." And that really turned things around, ya know, you understand that people really do have certain hurdles in life, like where they live, the income of their families, siblings, where they go to school, all of that stuff.... That one affected me a lot. That is the one that like changed my opinion about people, about scholarship kind of thing, and ... that is where that plays into that.

Troy found that considering the notion of hurdles encouraged him rethink his focus on individualistic explanations in favor of examining institutional forces related to the need for affirmative action programs, something he had opposed in the beginning of the course.

Troy's growing awareness of these institutional forces throughout the course was reflected in his discussion of the portrayals of Native Americans' difficulties in *A Yellow Raft in Blue Water* (Dorris, 1987):

> Almost like the way a lot of Americans treat Indians now, we don't give them a chance, we say "Oh … they have special fishing rights and hunting," but we are ignorant to realize what we've taken away from those people. What we've abolished through what we call the greater cause, the expanding [nation].

His critique of how Native Americans have been mistreated by Whites who have been characterized as "we" reflected a shift we found in a number of students toward an increasing awareness of the influence of racist institutional forces. As we hope to demonstrate in this book, this shift toward institutional critique provides students such as Troy with an increased awareness of how institutions and social worlds function and how, within those institutions and social worlds, they can develop agency.

The Significance of This Study

We believe that it is important to understand how adolescents learn to entertain alternative perspectives through responding to dialogic tensions portrayed in literature. In an increasingly diverse society, adolescents need not only to acquire tolerance for diverse perspectives but also to learn to critique the institutional forces perpetuating racism, class inequality, and sexism that work against openness to diversity.

Fostering adolescents' understanding of diversity remains a challenge in today's relatively conservative cultural and political climate. The increasing segregation of society has resulted in fewer opportunities for adolescents to interact in diverse settings; one study found that only 20% of a national sampling of adolescents had opportunities for interracial interactions (Elbert, 2004). Adolescents who operate in relatively homogeneous social worlds are less likely to be exposed to alternative cultural perspectives that serve to challenge their beliefs and attitudes (Perry, 2002).

When it comes to cross-racial relationships, more adolescents (70%) than teachers (54%) agreed that students who share similar racial backgrounds stick together in school (Hyland, 2005). Adolescents appear to hold less promising views of racial interactions, with only 28% of the students surveyed rating relations between students of different races as excellent, compared with 34% of teachers (Hyland, 2005). Though 23% of teachers reported often or sometimes hearing or seeing conflicts between students of different races, including fights, 40% of students acknowledged often or sometimes witnessing such behavior.

Students are also reluctant to publicly discuss issues of race, class, and gender difference. In one national Harris Interactive survey, only about one third of students indicated that they often or sometimes discuss race relations within their schools during class discussions (Reid, 2004). An observational study of 72 students in six California high schools found that, contrary to their stated beliefs on surveys, they were uncomfortable talking with students of color about issues of race given lack of knowledge or a fear of making comments perceived as racist (Lewis-Charp, 2003). And the effects of these discussions may depend on students' openness to changing their perspectives. In this survey, only a third of White students indicated that classroom discussions influenced their thinking, compared with almost half of Black students and a majority of Hispanic students (Reid, 2004).

White students such as those in our study are also reluctant to grapple with the historical realities of racial injustice. In one study, White students frequently denied the significance of the history of racial conflicts in America as a means of avoiding any collective accountability for past institutional racism (Lewis-Charp, 2003). Analysis of these students' discussions in their social studies classes found that students focused primarily on a limited number of events such as slavery, the oppression of Native Americans, and the civil rights movement without analysis of larger collective efforts designed to address these issues—perspectives that might challenge students' beliefs about individuals and meritocracy. And these events were analyzed primarily from a Eurocentric perspective, reifying an *us versus them* binary. As a result, students in the study "viewed history as disconnected from present-day realities and people of color as 'victims.' These perceptions, in turn, led to attitudes that students of color were mired in history and that they couldn't get over the injustices suffered by their ancestors" (Lewis-Charp, 2003, p. 282). Within this context, White adolescents perceive racism primarily in terms of a discourse of color-blind racism (Bonilla-Silva, 2001). They either deny or downplay racism or frame racism in individualistic as opposed to institutional or systemic terms (Raby, 2004).

In our study, we were particularly interested in studying working-class adolescents because we wanted to explore the ways that economic and political developments have influenced their cultural and political tolerance for diverse perspectives. Although working-class people from the 1930s through 1970s were bolstered by increasingly powerful unions and experienced significant wage increases, as we noted in the Preface since the 1980s working-class wages have remained flat. Based on data from the Congressional Budget Office, from 1979 to 2001, after-tax income for the top 1% increased by 139%, whereas incomes for the middle fifth bracket rose by 17% and for the bottom fifth by only 9% (Scott & Leonhardt, 2005). Despite the necessity of a college degree to acquire a well-paying job, reductions in state spending on public higher education have meant that fewer lower-income students can afford to go to college given rises in tuition costs and the potential for incurring debt through student loans (Scott & Leonhardt, 2005). Moreover, reductions in government support for K–12 education, employment training, health care, public transportation, and worker-rights legal enforcement have adversely affected working-class people.

Conservative politicians have exploited White working-class people's anxieties through a divide-and-conquer strategy of placing the blame for these economic challenges on people of color and by focusing on social values related to issues such as abortion or gay marriage (Frank, 2004). And in opposition to government-support programs launched during the New Deal and 1960s, these politicians have increasingly framed these challenges around discourses of individual motivation and morality rather than collective, communal efforts to foster social justice and equity. Moreover, neoliberal, market-driven discourses have framed urban schooling as failing in terms of a lack of accountability to test scores, resulting in a focus in urban, working-class schools on more traditional test-preparation pedagogical methods, often undermining working-class students' engagement with their learning (Anyon, 2005). These neoconservative and neoliberal policies privilege White middle- and upper-middle-class practices and discourses as the norm against which working-class students are judged. As a result, these students are often perceived as deficient or failing for not acquiring and embracing those practices and discourses (Doane & Bonilla-Silva, 2003; Roediger, 2002).

Underlying these policies is the loss of a sense of the larger social good and community represented in the New Deal and Great Society legislation. This collective commitment to enhancing the good of all citizens has been replaced by a focus on private individual choices in schools, neighborhoods, and community activities. This shift reflects discourses of individualism and liberal humanism that assume all Americans have equal chances for success. These discourses mask the practices of institutional racism that systematically exclude non-Whites from labor unions due to lack of antidiscrimination enforcement in the Wagner Act, from mortgages from the Federal Housing Authority and the Veteran's Association, from support for entering higher education from the G.I. Bill, from opportunities to vote, and from fair trials in the justice system (Brown, et al., 2003).

Divide-and-conquer political messages highlight differences in terms of race in ways that mask commonalities between working-class Whites and non-Whites. Bettie (2003) found that students were more likely to define themselves and others in terms of race or gender than class differences. Working-class Mexican American and White students therefore did not acknowledge certain economic issues they shared as working-class people. As a result, discourses of race or gender can trump discourses of class in the construction of social hierarchies in schools so that students perceive their group allegiances primarily in terms of race and gender as opposed to class. This suggests the value of helping students understand how the often invisible forces of class shape their own and characters' identities.

Gender Differences

In addition to the value of understanding the influence of discourses of race and class on identity construction, we also believe that it is important to understand the influence of discourses of gender on identity construction, particularly in terms of the development of agency. One factor related to success in college is the extent to which students bring not only requisite prior knowledge but also a habitus (Bourdieu, 1977; 1984) associated with being a successful college student, a habitus constituted by middle-class discourses and cultural models often associated with the propensity to employ analytic and literary critical reading practices valued in the College in the Schools program but not necessarily employed in working-class homes (Gee, Allen, & Clinton, 2001). We were therefore interested in the extent to which the working-class male students in the study, given their interest in attending college, would be able to acquire these practices, particularly because they had not been accustomed to using those practices in their other courses.

There is also the question as to whether low-income male students are motivated to want to attend college. Within the low-income student group, recent research indicates that low-income males are less likely to attend college than low-income females. Contrary to the notion of a boy crisis, more males are now attending college than in the past (Mead, 2006). However, high-income-class (i.e., families earning more than $97,500) males under age 24 are actually attending at a slightly higher rate than high-income-class females, but low-income-class (i.e., families earning less than $32,500) White and Hispanic males are less likely to attend college than was the case in the past (American Council on Education, 2006). One reason the study cited for this gap is the increase simply in the number of low-income White and Hispanic females, leading to a decline in the percentages of males attending college from 48% in 1995–1996 to 45% in 2003–2004. It also may be the case that sharp increases in college tuition at public universities create financial barriers for students to attend college (American Council on Education, 2006).

The desire to attend and do well in college may stem from the perceived need to obtain a college degree to achieve financial success. However, students may also develop an interest in attending college because they become interested in the kinds of intellectual activities that are valued in college, for example, an interest in study of literature. Developing this interest in intellectual activity requires a certain degree of commitment to work, a commitment that some research suggests differs by gender. One survey of 90,000 students indicates that college males devote less time preparing for class and more time relaxing or socializing than college females (Indiana University Center for Postsecondary Research, 2005). Another University of California–Los Angeles study of 17,000 students found that males were more likely to not complete homework on time or skip classes than females (Mead, 2006). Researchers attribute some of these differences to the females' perception that given gender disparities in the workplace, they need to work harder whereas males may assume that they can still succeed without having to work as hard (Lewin, 2006; Mead, 2006). High school females may also have higher aspirations to prepare for college than high school males; one study indicated that 62% of 12th-grade females planned on graduating from a four-year college compared to 51% of 12th-grade males (Freeman, 2004).

It may be the case that students experience in largely working-class high schools do not provide the intellectual preparation that motivates them to want to attend college (Bettie, 2003; Eckert, 1989, 2001; Yon, 2000). In our study, a student like Troy represents an example of a working-class male who demonstrates an interest in and commitment to engaging in academic work associated with studying literature. We believe that understanding what engages Troy as well as the other working-class students in Parks's class provides some insights into how to enhance the quality of the high school experience to engage students in the kinds of practices that serves to prepare them for college work as well as to assume the identities associated with being a college student.

Learning to Develop Identities in the New Economy

Studying working-class students' identity construction is also significant given the challenges they face in adopting to the new economy. In that new economy, people are no longer expected to establish a long-term relationship with the same company or business. Rather, they are expected to acquire short-term experiences and resources from short-term relationships in a range of different workplaces. Learning to move between and to adapt to these different workplaces requires the ability to readily shift their identities by drawing on a range of resources and institutional connections.

For Gee (2004, 2006), adopting to these shifting demands of the new economy requires the ability to develop the identities of shape-shifting portfolio people who can construct their identities from the social and cultural resources available to them: "A person today is invited to see him or herself as a portfolio of skills, experiences, and achievements, something like a walking resume" (Gee, 2006, p. 166). Continually developing these portfolio identities allows people to "recreate themselves and prepare for multiple jobs—indeed multiple careers—across their lifetimes" (ibid.).

Gee (2004, 2006) argues that high schools such as Thompson High School often do not provide their student with these shape-shifting identity practices that are readily available to upper-middle-class students outside of their school worlds—opportunities to engage in summer internships, travel, or organizations or social clubs or to learn to network through family connections, practices often not available to working-class adolescents. Based on comparisons of upper-middle-class and working-class females (Gee, Allen, & Clinton, 2001), Gee (2006, p. 174) posited that in their perceptions of the world, upper-middle-class adolescents are "focused on knowledge claims, assessment, evaluation, their movement through achievement space, and the relationships between the present and future," necessary ingredients for developing shape-shifting portfolio identities. They are also directly aligned with the norms, values, and goals of their family, peer, school, and community worlds, alignments that provide them with the resources for shape-shifting practices. In contrast, the working-class adolescents' perceptions reflected a focus on more immediate social, physical, and dialogic interactions and fewer instances of alignment with the norms, values, and goals of their family, peer, school, and community worlds involved in building allegiances to adult worlds. They are therefore "immersed in a world of action and feeling untied to vaunted futures of achievement, transformation, and status" (p. 182). In terms of the development of agency (Moore & Cunningham, 2006), this focus on immediate social relationships does not prepare students for envisioning themselves in future contexts associated with participation in adult worlds. As was the case with some of our participations, students therefore become stuck with their allegiances to their fixed roles in their status quo worlds without entertaining the potential for development of agency in future worlds.

Gee's (2004, 2006) research suggests that working-class students, who can no longer rely on traditional blue-collar employment opportunities that were available to their parents, face enormous disadvantages. His research also included analyses of the students' high schools, which, as the next chapter describes, were similar to Thompson High School in their focus on traditional transmission instructional models, adherence to rules, and a lack of intellectual exploration. Nor do these schools provide working-class students with "the realities of the high-tech, global, fast-changing world they would enter" (Gee, 2006, p. 183). In contrast, the schools attended by the upper-middle-class students emphasized "conceptual understanding, self-expression, and self-presentation" (p. 182).

As this book demonstrates, we believe that Parks's class deviated from the prototypical working-class high school world like that of Thompson High School by providing students with some of the practices and dispositions associated with operating not only in the new economy but also in a diverse culture. Though not all of the students acquired all of these practices and dispositions, Parks's class provided some students with some tools to assist them in developing agency. Given the fact that working-class students rely on their school to provide them with the tools for coping in the new economy—something that upper-middle-class students can acquire from outside of school—it is important to understand how instruction within a working-class high school context may actually provide students with these tools.

Summary

In this chapter, we argued that identities are highly fluid performances mediated by discourses and cultural models as tools operating in certain activities or social worlds. We also argued that students are not simply determined by these discourses and cultural models but that they also exercise choices in constructing their identities in terms of developing agency—a sense of themselves as becoming certain kinds of persons over time.

As Troy illustrates, many working-class students are coping with the challenges of poverty, family conflicts, crime, instability, and lack of resources. On the other hand, Troy, in contrast to some of Gee's (2004, 2006) findings, aligned himself with some adult worlds of the church, which provided him with some sense of agency.

As we will demonstrate, through responding to the multicultural literature in Parks's class, some of the high school students in this study began to move away from their allegiances to status quo discourses and cultural models to adopt alternative discourses and cultural models associated with developing agency. In the next chapter, we explore the ways identities may change through the acquisition of these discourses and cultural models as tools for constructing identities.

We believe that it is important to examine how these sociocultural processes of identity construction function in a literature class because we need to understand how students apply discourses and cultural models to construct text worlds. Through constructing these alternative worlds in classroom discussions and in writing, students experience dialogic tensions leading them to imagine alternative ways of constructing identities in different text and lived worlds (Blackford, 2004).

In Chapter 2, we discuss the ways identity construction varies across different competing worlds. In Chapter 3, we formulate a sociocultural theory of literary response that describes the ways readers draw on their allegiances to different social worlds in interpreting texts. Chapter 4 then focuses on a central theme of this book: how dialogic tensions lead to perspective taking and interrogation of status quo discourses and cultural models.

In Chapter 5, we describe the methods employed by Parks in providing students with critical analysis tools for analyzing texts and in challenging students' status quo identity constructions.

Chapters 6, 7, and 8 contain case-study profiles of individual students that illustrate their different allegiances to different social worlds and through their responses to literature. The two White students featured in Chapter 6, Corey and Michelle, construct their identities primarily through allegiances to the status quo school culture. In contrast, the two White students described in Chapter 7, Devin and Kayla, begin to take up, to revise, and to critique some of dominant discourses and cultural models they had acquired in their social worlds. Two students of color featured in Chapter 8, Mai (Hmong) and Kathy (African), who are somewhat marginalized by the school culture, voice their concerns about Whiteness as the norm in the school.

Chapter 9 describes the dialogic tensions in classroom discussions, which led some students to interrogate their beliefs and attitudes related to their race, class, or gender identity construction. The book concludes with Chapter 10, which describes some of the changes that occurred in students' beliefs and attitudes as a result of their participation in the course, along with implications for teaching multicultural literature.

---

[1]Participants are identified with pseudonyms throughout.

CHAPTER 2

The Social Worlds Constituting Students' Identities

In Chapter 1, we argued that identity construction and the development of agency are mediated by discourses and cultural models operating in social worlds. In this chapter, we describe the different social worlds constituting the students' identities and performed within with the social world of community, school, family, and the workplace. Through participation in social worlds, adolescents acquire certain social practices and perspectives that define their identities as members of these worlds. They perform different versions of their identities depending on the demands of these differing social worlds (Moje & Lewis, 2001).

Adolescents are therefore continually negotiating their identities by assuming different practices across different spaces (Beach, Lundell, & Jung, 2002; Harklau, 2001; Phelan, Davidson, & Yu, 1998). The ability to negotiate the competing demands of different worlds requires an *intercultural literacy*, defined as "the ability to consciously and effectively move back and forth among as well as in and out of the discourse communities they belong to or will belong to" (Guerra, 1997, p. 258). When worlds are perceived as incongruent, students may perceive these borders as insurmountable barriers between worlds, particularly when they assume they lack the social or cultural capital (Bourdieu, 1977, 1984) valued in academic worlds.

In our study, we were interested in how students adopted and negotiated identities across the competing demands of the different worlds or spaces of Parks's classroom, community, school, family, and workplace. As they enter into an institutional setting or social world, adolescents bring certain givens related to defined race, gender, and social class categories. These givens are what Koole (2003) described as brought-along practices that people import into worlds as opposed to brought-about practices constructed through interactions and positionings in a world related to developing agency tied to future selves.

As they move between different worlds, adolescents recognize that their brought-along practices may not always be valued in a particular world, requiring them to adopt new, brought-about practices. For example, a popular student who assumes that she has some social status in a school context may enter into a peer group in which school status has little bearing, requiring her to renegotiate her status through how she interacts with peers in the group. Her peers may consider that her brought-along status of being popular in the school carries little weight with them, so she needs to adopt brought-about practices valued in that peer group.

Social Worlds as Constructed Figured Worlds

All of this reflects the fact that these social worlds are not entities "out there"; rather, they are constructed through adolescents' performances in these worlds based on familiar, prototypical traditions, roles, and practices associated with particular worlds. We have found the concept of *figured worlds* (Holland, Lachicotte, Skinner, & Cain, 1998) useful in understanding how social worlds are constructed. Holland, et al. (1998, pp. 41–42) described figured worlds as "historical subjectivities, consciousness and agency, persons (and collective agents) forming in practice." They attributed four characteristics to these figured worlds:

- Historical phenomenon, to which we are recruited or into which we enter, which themselves develop through the works of their participants ... [they are] processes of traditional of apprehension which gather us up and give us form as our lives intersect them ...
- Social encounters in which participants' positions matter ... some figured worlds we may never enter because of our social position or rank ...
- Socially organized and reproduced; they are like activities in the usual, institutional sense ...
- Populated by familiar social types and even identifiable persons ... the identities we gain within figured worlds are thus specifically historical developments, grown through continued participation in the positions defined by the social organizations of those worlds' activity (p. 41).

Within figured worlds, participants are positioned to adopt certain identities as "culturally imagined types such that others and, even the person herself as least temporarily, treat her as though she were such a person" (Holland & Leander, 2004, p. 130). Worlds serve as "spaces for authoring," in which one authors or positions oneself in a world, often based on making or constructing new worlds that serve as figured worlds accommodating reconstructed selves (Holland, et al., 1998, p. 272).

For example, in a study of the figured world of romance in a college setting, female college students acquired practices of debriefing social events, flirting, or language use associated with dating and heterosexual relationships (Holland & Eisenhart, 1990). They also acquired discourses and cultural models for categorizing males' and females' practices based on a hierarchical system of roles associated with appearance, sophistication, and interpersonal skills. Although women in the study came to college with serious academic aspirations, in their junior and senior years they became less interested in academics and more interested in their romantic relationships. They also learned to recognize the significance and value of social practices constituting their identities in this figured world

> in which particular characters and actors are recognized, significance is assigned to certain acts, and particular outcomes are valued over others. Each is a simplified world, populated by a set of agents (in the world of romance: attractive women, boyfriends, lovers, fiancés) who engage in a limited range of meaningful acts of change of state (flirting with, falling in love with, dumping, having sex with) as moved by a certain set of forces (attractiveness, love, lust). (Holland & Eisenhart, 1990, p. 52)

College females learned to perform identities consistent with prototypical roles within the figured world of romance. Being a popular female involved learning practices of socializing, networking, and gossiping with peers in ways that establish one's reputation as being popular.

Positioning of Identities in Social Worlds

Participants in social worlds are also positioned in terms of becoming new versus full-fledged, veteran members of a social world (Lave & Wenger, 1991; Wenger, 1998). This movement into worlds initially begins with peripheral practice through centripetal participation (Lave & Wenger, 1991; Wenger, 1998) and then moves toward full participation as mature members of worlds are perceived as valued participants in those worlds. Veterans of the world of romance socialized novices on strategies for attracting males in late-night debriefing sessions (Holland & Eisenhart, 1990).

In our study, because the students were enrolled in a course for which they were receiving college credit as high school students, they were on a peripheral trajectory that involved acquiring certain academic practices associated with being a college student. Although they were not participating physically in an actual college world, they were exposed to practices associated with being a college student. For example, in writing journal entries and papers, students had to learn to develop their arguments not only by providing supporting evidence but also by entertaining alternative perspectives and counterarguments, strategies consistent with the genre of argumentative writing valued in first-year college composition courses. This represented a challenge for some of the students in that they were accustomed to writing relatively short essays or taking multiple-choice tests.

The challenge with participating on a peripheral trajectory is that one does not have full access to membership in a new community. The students in our study were not on a college campus interacting with college students and attending only college classes. Few of their parents had attended college. Attending only one college course provided them with minimal, peripheral access to what it meant to be a college student. Though they were exposed to classroom activities typically involved in college-level courses, they remained in a high school culture. Consistent with previous research on the transition from high school to college (Beach, Lundell, & Jung, 2001), they struggled to assume a new, unfamiliar identity of being college students when they had little exposure to that world. In conducting this study, we were therefore interested in how students were repositioning their practices and discourses consistent with becoming college students.

As we noted in our discussion of the development of agency, students acquire a sense of agency by emulating adults and peers who position them to adopt certain identities within social worlds (Leander, 2001, 2002; Wortham, 2001, 2006). These positionings project identity expectations from one figured world onto another world. For instance, when a teacher asks a misbehaving student whether that student "acts this way at home," the teacher applies assumptions about appropriate practices in the home world to the school world to position the student in a negative manner (Leander, 2004, p. 190).

Over time in the classroom world, these different positionings can thicken so that a person becomes increasingly defined, labeled, and celebrated or marginalized within a social hierarchy (Holland & Lave, 2001; Kehily, 2005). Wortham (2006) traced how a ninth-grade female student in an English class, initially positioned as a good or normal student, was increasingly positioned as a disruptive outcast by teachers and students given cultural assumptions about cooperative classroom group work, a thickening that served to alienate her in the classroom.

In this study, we examine how the students' identities in the classroom were continually being positioned by each other around discourses and cultural models of race, class, and gender differences. In spatial terms, those with power or agency to act often assume center stage, positioning those with less power or agency to the margins (Roth, Hwang, Goulart, & Lee, 2005). When certain groups assume center stage, people in the margins resist by taking up alternative practices and create their own center, transforming what was the center into the margins (Roth, Hwang, Goulart, & Lee, 2005 p. 42). In our study, a group of White, male students often assumed center stage in the discussions by voicing discourses of masculinity, competition, and individual achievement—discourses privileged within the school and community. Some of the female students in the study—such as Kayla and Kathy, who were marginalized by the male students' attempts to control the floor—challenged the male students by formulating alternative discourses. In reaction to these challenges, these males reacted negatively to challenges to their center-stage positioning by attempting to marginalize students such as Kayla. As these positionings began to thicken over time, Kayla was perceived by the class as an outspoken misfit who was off base in her opinions.

In contrast to some of the other females in the class, these females were willing to reject the school culture's privileging of male domination because they were less aligned to the school world. They perceived themselves more in terms of future identities as college students and therefore had less allegiance to the high school world.

However, the lack of support for these discourses by more popular female students left these discourses largely unexamined by the class on the whole. Similarly, as we explore further in Chapter 9, several Hmong female students felt alienated by the White students' domination of discussions, as well as Parks's focus on challenging these students' sense of White privilege. This sense of alienation was one that these students also experienced in the larger school culture and one that led them to often remain silent in classroom discussions rather than to challenge this domination.

The World of Thompson High School

Our participants' identity constructions involved negotiation of various positionings within the school world. To study this school world, Amanda Thein conducted ethnographical observations of student practices in classrooms, lunchrooms, hallways, school events, and sporting events and also interviewed students regarding their perceptions of the school culture and their identity construction in that culture (see Appendix A for descriptions of her research methods). She was particularly interested in identifying the social practices, institutional norms, and community traditions constituting the school culture as mediated by various discourses and cultural models as well as how these aspects of the school culture mediated identity construction. She was also interested in instances in which students displayed agency in resistance of the school culture.

Parks engaged in community ethnography through observation of community events, interviews with community residents and school alumni, interviews with school administrators, and research into previously written community histories. He also attended sporting events held at the school to better understand the relationship between the school and community.

The Changing East Side Neighborhood

The culture of Thompson High School is shaped by the culture of the surrounding community: the East Side neighborhood. For some 120 years the neighborhood surrounding the school has been the landing point for a variety of historically European immigrant groups. New arrivals were drawn by the proximity to the nearby river with its growing capital city, the burgeoning industries and mills within walking distances of their homes, and the supportive, tightly knit cultural enclaves that were emerging within the neighborhood.

Employment opportunities grew along with the populations. By the middle of the 20th century an ironworks, a nationally distributed brewery, an expanding mining and chemical products company, and an expanding small-business sector provided the economic structure required for the community to prosper. Immigrants who arrived in the neighborhood were upwardly mobile and built larger homes along the bluffs toward the city center or up the hills toward the lake on the city's eastern limits.

In the past 30 years, the East Side community has undergone major transitions. The economic decline in the industrial sector in recent decades played a large part in these transitions: Factories closed; large homes were subdivided and turned to rental properties; and the influx of new racial and cultural groups from at home and abroad have brought uncertainty into the community's sense of coherence. Many longtime resident families, who could trace several generations within the neighborhood and who enjoyed economic freedom, moved to the flourishing suburbs east and north of the city.

Long the home of immigrants, this East Side community continues to attract immigrants, now from Vietnam, Thailand, Laos, and Mexico. Domestic immigration to the state and neighborhood has also risen as African American and Latino citizens move from other urban centers of the Midwest and South seeking greater opportunities for their families and themselves. Within the city itself, gentrification and rising rental prices in other neighborhoods have pushed more low-income people into the East Side community.

The downturn in the economy of the East Side neighborhood has affected the community in a number of ways. The lack of adequate employment in the East Side neighborhood has created a strain for residents—especially women—not only in their financial situations but also in their family situations. Women in the East Side community are no longer primarily homemakers. Most also work long hours in low-level service jobs. This is particularly the case for the many single mothers in this community who raise their children on their own. As we demonstrate, changes in economic situations for women also affect how girls construct their identities and their expectations for the future (Weis, 1990).

Thompson Today

As the East Side community has undergone change, as previously noted, so, too, has the population of Thompson High School. The student body had been 39% White at the time of the study in 2001, 32% Asian American, 19% African American, 9% Hispanic, and 1% Native American. Of the student population, 64% qualified for free or reduced lunch; of those students, only 41% graduated in four years. Thirty-four percent of students received additional assistance in English language instruction, with 29% with a home language of Hmong. Despite the high diversity of the school, only 12% of the staff was non-White.

In 2002, the graduation rate was 80%; however, only 48% of Asian Americans, 50% of Hispanics, and 35% of African Americans graduated in four years, compared with 63% of Whites; only 41% of those receiving free or reduced lunch graduated in four years. Only a small percentage of students in the class of 2002 planned on attending four-year colleges. Of the 1,583 students in the class of 2002, only 142, or 11%, took the ACT test for college admissions.

Thompson's statistical profile suggests that economic and demographic transitions were not easy. Despite a lack of jobs for those with high school diplomas only, a small percentage of students who graduated from Thompson attended college. Students of color were much less likely than White students to actually graduate from Thompson, much less attend college. In this chapter we outline some of the ways that White, working-class discourses from the community's past continued to impact the culture of Thompson High School, even as the school encountered dramatic changes.

Discourses of Form and Control

Having grown up in a working-class community that values hard work over intellectual pursuits, many students at Thompson adopted a short-term, utilitarian perspective on education and schooling, with relatively low expectations for the intellectual benefits of their education (Seitz, 2004a, 2004b). This perspective on education is consistent with previous research on working-class high schools. Weis (1990) found that neither students nor teachers or administrators at the working-class school she studied were actually interested in the substance of learning but rather only with the form of learning: "They simply hoped to get through school and receive the diploma that they have come to view as valuable" (p. 30). According to Weis (p. 33):

> This disengagement coexists with a more positive valuation of education than previous studies have uncovered among White working-class youth, particularly males. The more positive valuation plays itself out, however, largely in terms of student participation in the maintenance of the appearance of order and a willingness to "hand something in" in order to pass courses and be, ultimately, "average" at best.

Weis (1990) also noted that this emphasis on form over substance pervaded the culture of the school and manifested in administrators demanding that teachers put forth the appearance of teaching in certain ways and with certain organization, whereas the substance of their pedagogy was never discussed or observed. She stated, "... Administrators engage in a ritual form of control over teacher labor that does not necessarily affect the selection, organization, or treatment of knowledge—in other words, its content or substance, except insofar as the ritual may suggest that only the form or appearance is important" (p. 93). The result is that both teachers and students saw school and school knowledge as utilitarian and highly routinized. Weis pointed to examples of teachers telling students exactly how and what to write in their notebooks and of students failing to ask any questions of the teachers or each other except those needed to clarify instructions. This utilitarian perspective on schooling served to value a carefully controlled intellectual and physical environment above other aspects of the school experience.

Intellectual Control of Students   Whereas students in advanced courses in middle-class schools are often encouraged to engage in critical, creative thinking as prerequisite experience for college work, previous ethnographic research on working-class high school cultures suggests that working-class high schools tend to operate under the assumption that students of color, will behave in inappropriate ways and therefore need to be closely monitored and controlled, often only serving to further provoke deviant behavior as resistance to controlling regimens (Bettie, 2003; Eckert, 1989, 2000; Gee, 2006; Rymes, 2001; Yon, 2000).

Little of the instruction observed at Thompson encouraged independent, critical thinking regardless of the ability or achievement level of the students. In most of the classrooms, students sat in rows and recorded the information that teachers dictated. Additionally, students often seemed uncomfortable when given freedom to think critically and speak openly, reflecting their familiarity with a passive, teacher-directed environment.

In one case a teacher was observed attempting to hold an open discussion on J. D. Salinger's (1996) *The Catcher in the Rye*, in a regular-level, 11th-grade English class. Though students seemed quite excited about the prospect of this discussion, they had little experience with this type of intellectual and physical freedom to speak. Thus, the discussion was less than successful as the following excerpt from our field notes demonstrates:

> There is a discussion beginning between Ashley, in the back of the room, and James in the front of the room. They discuss whether having several conversations in your head (as Holden does) means you are crazy. Ashley is arguing that it does not. Students quickly begin jumping into this debate, but the debate becomes a series of loud conversations between a few students—everyone is talking over each other. The teacher has to stop the discussion. James then tries to talk again and then Ashley tries. Each time they get started students begin talking loudly amongst themselves. The teacher lets it go on for a few seconds each time and then tries to regain control and calls on a student to speak.

For the more academically motivated students in this school, students' lack of experience in engaging in academic discussion led to frustration. Kayla, a student in our study who was critical of the lack of academic rigor at Thompson, noted, "It's so easy here, and I get bored. ... Well, I mean I like it 'cause I don't have homework and different things like that. I still learn, but in a sense I feel like my, my brain, my knowledge power that I have in a sense is going to waste. I mean, I could be learning so much more."

As we discuss in subsequent chapters, Parks's multicultural literature class was a deviation from much of the larger school culture. As a course for which students were receiving college credit, Parks consistently challenged students to engage in critical thinking through journal writing, discussions, and drama activities. For students like Kayla, who was looking forward to going to college, this class was a welcome alternative to the school culture. On the other hand, as we document in this book, for students who were more wedded to the school culture and who were unaccustomed to engaging in critical thinking, this class was a challenge, requiring them to acquire new practices to succeed.

This lack of congruency between Parks's class and the school culture reflected a larger lack of congruency between the school culture's intellectual control and the world of higher education reflected in the activities employed in Parks's course. These activities are discussed in more depth in Chapter 5.

Physical Control of Students and Facilities   At Thompson High School intellectual control of students was congruent with a larger culture that physically controlled students and facilities. Thompson High School was a highly controlled culture with continuous monitoring of student behavior and enforced regulation of closed-campus rules. This sense of control was reflected in the neatness and cleanliness of the facilities. The floors were spotless, classroom desks were in neat rows in most classrooms, and students were expected to clean up after themselves in the cafeteria and in the classroom. As an assistant principal said in response to a comment on the cleanliness of the facilities, "This is what a real urban school is like. It's not *Dangerous Minds* around here."

This perceived need for physical control of students and facilities was evident in our observations of two annual Winter-Fest coronation ceremonies at which the royalty for the winter dance were crowned. The ceremonies were steeped in school tradition and were carefully managed by administrators and teachers.

Both of the ceremonies we attended were held during the middle of the school day. Students were released from their classes to attend. Attempts to control the student body and the building during the coronation ceremony included a most striking incident in which the doors to the gymnasium where the festivities were held were guarded by all-male Reserve Officers' Training Corps (ROTC) students dressed in full regalia and carrying swords. The actual job of these ROTC students was to make sure that anyone entering the gymnasium wore a button.

To attend this event, all students had to purchase a button for a dollar. Students who did not attend were supposed to report to selected classrooms throughout the building to watch films or do homework, but many students who did not want to attend the assembly simply left school. The selling of buttons was perceived to be an effective way to allow students who did not support such school ceremonies to remove themselves from the assembly, diminishing the disruptions that might have occurred. Those who did not attend the ceremonies were disproportionately students of color.

This effort to control who attended the coronation ceremonies appeared successful. During both years of our observation, students in the audience displayed little resistance to this traditional popularity contest. Any parent or outsider to the school walking into the gymnasium to watch this event might have assumed that the entire student body was unified and represented at this event. The reality was that students who did not support this school tradition were encouraged not to attend and were therefore not given the opportunity to revise or amend such school traditions to better fit the changing values and desires of the student body. As this scenario suggests, discourses of control at Thompson were enmeshed in discourses of race that assumed that students of color lack control; discipline in the form of suspensions were often administered disproportionately according to race. Though suspension data were not available for 2001–2002, for the following year 23% of African American males compared with 12% of White males and 16% of African American females compared with 7% of White females were suspended—about twice as often for African Americans as for Whites. While it is difficult to attribute reasons for differences in these suspension rates, they may reflect attitudes toward African American students operating within the larger school culture that led to their being suspended at a higher rate than was the case for White students.

Discourses of Race and Social Class

The Thompson High School hockey team's annual pancake breakfast provided a striking example of the ways past and present racial and social class discourses from the East Side neighborhood and the school community intersected and gave rise to tensions. Although the breakfast typically drew a large number of alumni, the year we observed the gathering was a particularly important year for the event. Hundreds or even thousands were expected for the retirement of a hockey player's jersey, along with the celebration of a state championship hockey team from the 1950s. Thompson's principal took the stage amid the applause of those present. She framed the culture of the school in this way: "Two words to talk about our community: *tradition* and *pride*. No matter how the school and community change around, these are the two words that guide us. We are about tradition; we are about pride; this is Thompson High School, and we are about hockey!"

Underlying this celebration were discourses of *achievement* and *hard work* that reflected a nostalgic equation of hockey with the school's past when it was largely White.

This linkage of a hockey tradition as a White male sport to the school and the neighborhood reflects a political discourse of authenticity associated with physical hard work in opposition to what is perceived to be an intellectual, bureaucratic middle-class discourse associated with the knowledge economy (Frank, 2004). It also reflects discourses of masculinity, individualism, and self-achievement that presumably served these alumni well in the past.

This nostalgic appeal also masks the economic stagnation of working-class Whites that has led to increasing tension between Whites and people of color. Roediger (2002) argued that, given the loss of well-paying jobs for low-income White males since the 1980s, these males have increasingly defined their class identity in terms of racial polarization and resentment toward Blacks and Latinos whom they view as scapegoat targets for job losses. Although White males could previously support their families through well-paying manufacturing jobs, once they lost those jobs they could no longer define their identities in terms of supporting their families, a loss of their cultural status and prestige. Given this loss of status, they then needed to define their sense of superiority through "othering" Blacks and Latinos as inferior. This othering takes the form of White males distancing themselves from what they perceive to be low-level slave-labor work done by Blacks and Latinos. And they define achieving middle-class status in terms of not being or living near Blacks or Latinos.

Consistent with the ways White, working-class people define their identities in terms of opposition to non-Whites, White students at Thompson High School often defined themselves in terms of racial difference so that discourses of race trumped discourses of class (Bettie, 2003).

From 1970 to the time of our study, Thompson went from being 94% White to one in which Whites composed only 39% of the school's population, a shift that itself fostered racial conflict within the school and the community. In the following exchange, Corey, a popular, White, male senior whose mother attended Thompson and who has lengthy roots in the community, talked about the demographic changes that have occurred at the school:

Thein: Have you ever talked to her [his mother] about the way the school might have changed since she was a student here?

Corey: Yeah she, there wasn't as many, you know like racial, it was more White dominant, I guess you could say, so yeah, and my mom's more concerned about that. I know she doesn't want my brother coming here. I don't think my brother wants to come here anyway; he's gonna go to North [another area high school] I think. And I know for sure she won't want my sister coming here, but ...

Thein: She thinks it's becoming dangerous?

Corey: Yeah, I think she does, but I, not really super dangerous, but to where she doesn't want to make my brother and sister go here.

Corey's sense of discomfort in talking about issues of racial diversity, as well as the apparent anxiety that his mother felt from the demographic changes, were common among White students at Thompson.

Observations of the cafeteria during lunch periods offer further examples of social and racial stratification among students at Thompson. With very few exceptions, students clearly organized themselves into racial groups (Tatum, 2003). According to one student, Ron, the most popular White students sat in the center of the cafeteria, whereas other racial and social groups sat on the periphery. He explained that the popular students sat in the middle and that the regular students sat together on the sides. He said the Asian students sat together, "unless you're cool," in which case particular Asian students might have sat in the middle. When asked why the popular students sat in the middle, he said, "That's the middle of everything, and that's where they've always been."

A similar pattern was often seen in observations of classrooms where students were allowed to choose their own seats. The following excerpt from field notes provides a striking example:

> In the middle row of the class there are four White, blonde girls. In the row to the left of the middle row there are two White, blonde girls in the front two seats. Next back there is an African-American girl, next are two Asian boys, and furthest to the back is an African-American girl. The row to the right of the middle has another blonde White girl in the front seat, followed by a White boy, Angela and Kayla (both White), another White girl and a White boy. The row closest to the door seats all Asian and African-American students.

In this classroom most of the White students sat in the three middle rows and in the front seats, gaining the majority of the teacher's attention, whereas most of the students of color sat off to the sides or toward the back. Again, students interacted very little across racial groups.

There are a number of possible explanations for these patterns of in-school segregation at Thompson by race. Tatum (2003) posited that such segregation is rooted in students' needs for a comfortable, safe space in which they are more fully understood and able to participate in a shared sense of supportive community. But the fact that there was little interaction between racial groups may perpetuate a vicious cycle of sorts that inhibits students from establishing peer relationships across racial groups—relationships that could have served to break down segregation. However, a larger factor may have been the lack of a discourse of class that would have served as a bond between the shared challenges facing both working-class Whites and working-class people of color (Bettie, 2003). Lacking this discourse of class, students turn to the more familiar discourse of race as the primary frame of reference for defining peer differences and relationships (Keating, 2004).

Because many White students at Thompson defined racism as the expression of racist comments, a discourse of prejudice (Bonilla-Silva, 2001), they did not perceive themselves as participating in institutional or systemic racism. These students were also resentful of the economic advantages afforded their middle-class suburban peers (e.g., parental support for going to college). This resentment of their middle-class peers paralleled their resentment toward Thompson students of color whom they perceived to be receiving similar financial scholarship support. In both instances, these working-class White students understood themselves as marginalized.

It is also the case that the White Thompson students voiced ambivalent perspectives about race, a finding consistent with Yon's (2000) and Lewis-Charp's (2003) results. Some of this ambivalence stemmed from the disparity between espousing idealized beliefs about race while at the same time experiencing difficulties in everyday social interactions with students of color. Some of the White students at Thompson, like students in Yon's (2000) study, perceived themselves as lacking any distinct cultural or physical identity markers, so they assumed that they were part of a cultural norm, as opposed to "others" who displayed such identity markers. These markers—such as language, dress, and gestures—emerge in physical interactions and therefore represent a challenge to students' idealized beliefs about race.

In maintaining a sense of control over the facilities, the students, and the traditions of the school, the school community in many ways resisted the cultural transformation that comes with shifting demographic groups. Though struggling to become a place of true diversity, Thompson was still rooted in White culture and White traditions that had been in place for generations. Groups that were relatively new to the school became peripheral factions and were only slowly becoming engaged in the mainstream student culture. Thompson may have been a demographically diverse school, but interactions between racial groups often remained minimal or superficial, as was the case in the broader community.

Because this focus on physical control associated with perpetuating a discourse of Whiteness transferred to intellectual control in the form of transmission classroom instruction, the students in the school were not receiving the resources associated with acquiring shape-shifting identity practices (Gee, 2004, 2006). And given intellectual control over students exploration of alternative perspectives, there is little focus on learning to entertain diverse cultural perspectives associated with living in a highly diverse society.

Discourses of Masculinity and Athleticism

Discourses of form and control, as well as White working-class discourses of meritocracy and hard work, all supported a school culture in which discourses of masculinity and athleticism were highly valued. For students at Thompson, participation in football, hockey, and baseball was the most direct means for gaining social status and power within the school and the community on the whole. Though students of color were active members of other athletic teams—basketball, soccer, track, volleyball, badminton— these sports were not afforded the status of those sports associated with the school's traditions.

For high school males, one of the most important identity markers for performing masculinity is the physical display of the body (Connell, 2001, 2005; Newkirk, 2002; Ng-A-Fook, 2003; Nixon, 1996). Schools, which Connell (2001, p. 34) described as "masculinity-making devices," seek to control and limit physical display of the body in the classroom or school, whereas training in sports focuses on specific ways of asserting power, aggression, and control outside of the classroom space. Participation in sports, particularly football and hockey, is equated with masculinity, an identity construction mediated by discourses and narratives of violence and toughness (Burgess & Skinner, 2003).

The discourse of physical control that mediated social practices at Thompson was consistently linked to a discourse of athleticism, as well as a cultural model in which competition, self-discipline, achievement, and physical prowess were highly valued (Barker & Galasinski, 2001). These discourses and cultural models manifested in the prototypical narrative: hard work, training, and an unselfish team effort result in winning the game. The school administration often evoked variations of this narrative to equate the world of sports with school by assuming that self-discipline acquired through sports directly transferred to self-discipline in other activities. One of the participants, Corey, a student involved with football, hockey, and baseball at Thompson, equated self-discipline in sports with self-discipline in school:

> I think kids kept themselves in line during football season themselves, just 'cause they knew we could go far. And then baseball, baseball's like, it's not as conditioning as like football or hockey; you're not moving as much and so it's kind of, not a lay-around sport I guess, I mean you don't work as hard, it's kind of a more relaxing

sport, more fun, I mean still, you still gotta stay disciplined if you wanna play. You can't be going out, getting in trouble.

The administration also frequently acknowledged popular athletes as representing the kinds of social practices it admired. Students involved in athletics at Thompson were supported not only on the field but also in the positions of leadership at school. In describing his relationship with the school principal, Corey said, "I know Ms. Jones likes sports players a lot 'cause she thinks they're like role models throughout the school. So I think that's really, there's a big bond between the sports players and Ms. Jones."

Athletics was also Corey's means of gaining social power and status, both in the school and the community: "I think it makes you better known, like, like um they always announce your name during the game and people know who you are, they get to know who you are at school and, I mean, I think you're better known when you play sports, just like you're more popular, so yeah, throughout the community too, 'cause a lot of kids, they play hockey and little kids come and skate with the older kids, and they'll ask for your autograph and stuff."

Corey adopted a highly compliant stance toward the physical control and values operating in the school. The world of sports provided students like Corey with a strong sense of status and certainty about their self-worth. In the case of Thompson High School, the congruency between the world of athletics and the world of school allowed students like Corey to move seamlessly between the two worlds constituted by shared discourses of athleticism and a cultural model the valued self-discipline and intellectual control (Weis, 1990; 2004).

In terms of the development of agency, being an athlete in the school certainly served to bolster some of our participants' self-confidence through the capacity to display competence to their peers and coaches (Griffin, 1998). Though acquiring this self-confidence might lead students could envision themselves in the future as successful college athletes, none of the athletes in our study made references to playing sports in college. One limitation of adherence to a discourse of sports is that it precludes envisioning oneself in the future in more academic or intellectual terms. In focusing on the immediate here-and-now world of peer competition, it does not afford a vision of the future self-aligned to academic or adult worlds that require different types of practices and dispositions. And as we discuss in the case of Corey in Chapter 6, adherence to a discourse of athleticism reifies a belief that individual competition and meritocracy deter students such as Corey from adopting some of the institutional critiques employed in the course, critiques that athletes such as Troy began to adopt. Moreover, as we discuss in Chapter 6, students such as Corey readily adhered to authoritative voices associated with top-down mandates and rules without entertaining alternative internally persuasive voices (Bakhtin, 1981).

Discourses of Femininity

Though the culture of Thompson High School reinforced traditional working-class roles for White male students, students of color and female students experienced more room for ambiguity and questioning in their negotiations of identities (Budgeon, 2003; Griffin, 1989; Weis, 1990, 2004). Many girls at Thompson could not be easily categorized into identities based on social groups, racial groups, or even in terms of dress or demeanor. However, our research suggests several broad stances that girls at Thompson often appropriated in defining their identities.

The Jocks The most popular girls at Thompson, like the most popular boys, tended to be White, and they tended to be involved in athletics. In fact, these girls often self-identified as *jocks*. One such jock at Thompson, Molly, identified herself as a member of the popular group because she played softball, hockey, and soccer. When asked how a new student at Thompson might gain access to her group of friends, she said, "Play one of the sports we play, and we'd have to like her, she'd have to be cool, but we like all kinds of people. As long as they're cool."

Molly was in many ways typical of female jocks at Thompson. These were the girls who were both friends and girlfriends with many of the popular male athletes. Unlike membership in popular groups at many middle-class schools, membership in this group did not appear to be contingent on wearing trendy clothes or having expensive haircuts, perhaps because such expenses were not practical for most girls at Thompson. Rather, girls like Molly and her friend Kim often came into their morning classes wearing sweatpants and Thompson sweatshirts or T-shirts representing one of the sports they played, athletic shoes or flip-flops, and wet hair. Conspicuously, these girls often did wear makeup with an outfit like the one just described. This suggests that these girls created this natural, sporty look in a purposeful way as a signifier of class and identity performances. These girls also did not typically dress in sexy or revealing clothing. If they dressed up on game day or for a school celebration, they may have worn short skirts and tight shirts, but dressing in provocative ways did not appear to be a significant part of their performance as popular girls. Likewise, these girls did not appear to be, on the whole, striving for model-thin figures. Rather, they were proud of their athleticism and their physical fitness.

The particular athletic teams for which these jock females played is also of note. Whereas competitive, contact sports have become more popular sports for girls in general, noncontact sports such as cheerleading, dance, gymnastics, and tennis remain popular sports for girls at many high schools. Although many of these sports were offered at Thompson, it is clear that competitive, team-oriented, contact sports (e.g., soccer, hockey, softball) were those in which girls must participate to be part of the jock group. There are several purposes that playing these types of sports may have served for these girls. First, these sports mirror those played by high-status boys at Thompson. Being involved in similar sports may have been a means of gaining solidarity with these boys. Additionally, since highly competitive, contact sports played by male athletes were those most valued by the school and the community, girls may have hoped to gain equal status through playing similar sports.

Girls who identified as jocks often expressed contempt for other girls who were outspoken or argumentative in class. In one Thompson classroom, Molly described her extroverted classmate Vickie: "She's so negative, which just bugs us so much 'cause we're not like that at all, like we agree with people most of the time or we like, we appreciate their opinion and what they say and we're not so critical of everybody." In this quotation Molly did not suggest that she actually disagreed with the opinions that her classmate expressed—in fact, they shared quite similar opinions. Rather, it is the demeanor of outspoken girls that Molly disliked; it was important to Molly and many other jock-identifying girls that they present a positive, cooperative performance at school. For girls who were willing to speak out in class, their mere rejection of acquiescence was a rejection of feminine norms at Thompson. For example, Michelle, a senior in our study, often spoke out in class to disagree with the opinions of another female student. Though Michelle's opinions were in no way transgressive—in fact, they supported the status quo discourses in this classroom—her demeanor in aggressively disagreeing with another student positioned her as outspoken and atypical among girls at Thompson.

For both male and female athletes who were wedded to this jock culture, Parks's class represented a challenge to their need for a definitive sense of status and self-worth related to a sense of certainty operating in their sports worlds. These students sometimes resisted challenges to this sense of certainty from the dialogic tensions in Parks's class. Thus, for these athletes, the worlds of sports and school were congruent, but for the worlds of sports and Parks's class, they were incongruent, creating a challenge to their familiar school identities.

The Ghetto Girls   Whereas jocks were understated in their appearance, the other dominant group of girls at Thompson, often referred to by jocks as the *ghetto girls,* consisted of girls who dressed, styled their hair, and wore makeup in much more sexually provocative ways. These girls, who typically did not participate in jock sports, were often perceived by their fellow students as using their sexuality to gain social status, especially through sexual relationships with boys.

While it is tempting to assume that girls who appear more sexually provocative use sexual capital to gain status with their peers, we draw from Bettie (2003) to suggest that this performance is less about gaining status through sexual relationships with male students and is more about a sense of empowerment that comes with a performance of a less adolescent and more adult gender identity. Additionally, this gender performance is largely bound to girls' performances of social class identities. Bettie notes that the way girls dress and wear makeup is not only about performances of gender or race but also about social class. She explained that working-class girls who expect to take on adult responsibilities such as working and raising a family immediately following high school often choose a more sexual provocative, older look. Conversely, middle-class girls who expect to attend college are more likely to embrace a younger, more innocent look since college in many ways delays adolescence for several more years.

Cultural Models of Romance Mediating Competing Life-Path Narratives

Though many male students at Thompson were strongly defined in terms of masculine discourses of hard work and individual meritocracy, female students at Thompson, like the female students in Weis's studies (1990, 2004) were often more willing to question the prevailing discourses of femininity, such as the much debated culture of romance, constructing multiple narratives for their futures beyond high school.

McRobbie (1978) suggested that because working-class girls realize that school will be of little use to them in attaining well-paying jobs, they instead reject school culture and create a counterculture that values sexuality and romance. Holland and Eisenhart (1990) disagreed with this analysis and instead proposed that the culture of romance is an oppressive, patriarchal culture that college girls in their study tend to fall back on as their college grades and ambitions slip.

This notion is complicated by research by Weis (1990, 2004) and Griffin (1989), who proposed that as working-class girls see economic instability and divorce in the lives of their families and friends, they come to the conclusion that men cannot be relied on for financial stability. In envisioning their future identities and agency, these girls often expect to marry, yet they see marriage as an inevitability and not necessarily as a positive, romantic venture (Bettie, 2003). Likewise, these girls understand that in an unpredictable world, they must find ways of being responsible for their own financial stability (Budgeon, 2003). This is consistent with

Greer's (2004, p. 148) theory of flexible moral realism, which suggests that working-class women interpret lived and text worlds through a stance that is flexible in terms of understanding women's negotiations of relationships. In this stance women are realistic about the difficulties of marriage and other relationships and focus on the notion that despite mishaps, moral and ethical lapses, and other struggles, it is still possible to find resolution and maintain a sense of happiness.

Working-class girls negotiating their identity constructions within the cultural context of Thompson High School defied any simplistic notions of how the culture of romance operates. Many girls at Thompson negotiated competing cultural models of romance related to what it means to be a woman after high school. Whereas some girls clearly expressed romantic notions about relationships or marriage, many expressed ambivalent notions about their future roles and relationships. Thus, in terms of developing a sense of agency based on future roles, these females lacked a sense of themselves in the future, in contrast to other females in our study such as Kayla, who had a clear sense of herself in the future as a college student, a vision that served as an incentive to relish participation in Parks's course. It may also be the case that, as working-class students, they are more focused on interpersonal relationships and conflicts as opposed to achievement in adult worlds (Gee, 2004, 2006). However, working-class students may also have difficulty defining agency in terms of future selves because of all of the uncertainty and economic contingencies they face in their daily lives, in contrast to upper-middle-class students, who can readily chart a well-defined scenario for their future of college, graduate school, and professional identities associated with the resources available to them (McLeod & Yates, 2006).

When asked about her vision of her future life, Davie—a White, academically successful junior who was involved in theater and band at Thompson and who lived with her mother and stepfather—talked extensively and in great detail about college and career goals with no mention of her long-term boyfriend. When directly asked about her thoughts on marriage and children, the following dialogue ensued:

Davie: Possibly getting married, I don't know if I want to have kids. I've already taken care of my sister for the past three years ... and I'm only five years older than her so ... I was sitting there changing her diapers when I was five. Definitely can handle kids, it's whether I want any. 'Cause everyone's always like, "Oh, I want to have a baby," and I don't want to have a baby. I'll have a 13-year-old that knows how to do stuff for themselves, but I won't have a baby.

Thein: And what about your boyfriend. Do you think you'll stick with him?
Davie: Probably, just 'cause we have so much in common.

Davie represents the many girls at Thompson who expressed ambivalent and even conflicting ideas about their goals and expectations for life after high school. Davie seemed to visualize her future through the lenses of two distinct cultural models. The first culture model is a typical middle-class model in which she would attend college and have a career rather than a job. In employing this cultural model, Davie constructed a life-path narrative for herself that included getting degrees in music and in law enforcement from two different schools and then beginning a career in an area of the state several hours north of her current neighborhood.

The second narrative, about which she talked very little, is a more typical working-class cultural model in which she would marry her high school boyfriend and live in the local neighborhood. Davie in no way discussed the ways in which she might negotiate the divide between these two paths. Rather, she seemed to function while holding these two competing and incongruent narratives in her mind at the same time. These competing discourses and narratives about her future identity as a woman suggest that Davie did not position herself solely in a figured world of romance, nor did she reject traditional ideas of marriage outright. Instead, Davie positioned herself in a complex space in between several possible identities.

A Jock Female's Cultural Model of Romance   Of the females we studied, the jock females were most directly aligned with the culture or figured world of romance. For example, Molly constructed a clear life-path narrative that included attending college at the state university, marrying before she turned 26, and having two or three children. She and other jock girls at Thompson were able to visualize and plan for futures that play out in idealized, middle-class ways based on their involvement with middle-class, pop-culture figures. Through involvement with these figures and storylines, working-class girls at Thompson learned the cultural models and narratives for success in middle-class social worlds. For women, these models include romanticized notions of marrying someone from college, having both a career and family, and living a comfortable suburban existence. Therefore, it makes sense that the more a girl performs a middle-class identity, the more she may have romantic ideas about middle-class relationships and lifestyles, suggesting a relationship between gender and social class practices.

This analysis problematizes research suggesting that working-class girls fall more easily into romanticized notions of family and marriage than middle-class girls (Holland & Eisenhart, 1990; Walkerdine, 1990). We do not suggest that these girls were not interested in romance but that in a culture such as Thompson where futures were uncertain, many working-class girls performed a variety of different and often conflicting narratives through which they mapped their lives. These girls were flexible and realistic (Greer, 2004) about the courses their lives may take in a world where economic situations change quickly and where life can take many unexpected turns. They recognized that the traditional narrative scenario of moving into a pink-collar job or marriage after high school may be inconsistent with their aspirations, requiring them to entertain options (Budgeon, 2003).

In summary, at Thompson High School the figured world of romance did not appear to serve as a means for gaining power through a rejection of school culture. Rather, the girls most involved in this world of romance tended to be those who already had a great deal of social status in the school and the community.

However, as was the case with the athletes' sense of certainty afforded by their allegiance to the school culture, these females' allegiance to the world of romance was challenged by some of the portrayals of problematic relationships and marriages in the literature read in the course.

Family Worlds

As previously noted, the students' family worlds consisted primarily of working-class families whose values were congruent with the working-class urban neighborhood and school worlds. Though some of these families were struggling financially, they were strongly allied to the traditions of the school such as the Winter-Fest event and the hockey team's pancake breakfast as representing the values of White, working-class families.

In contrast to this congruency between the family and school worlds for White students, for many Hmong students in the school, family worlds were highly incongruent with the school world. This incongruence stemmed from a wide cultural disparity between Hmong culture rooted in a clannish, agricultural culture of Southeast Asia, from which they fled due to their support for the Americans in the Vietnam War and the urban, industrial and service economy of the Midwestern city to which they migrated. In the Hmong culture there is a strong emphasis on multigenerational family structures and clan system; it is often the case that different generations live together in the same household (Tatman, 2004). At the same time, there are often cultural tensions between these different generations as younger generations adopt more contemporary American values and elder generations maintain native values (Tatman, 2004). And

Hmong students experience tensions between language use and cultural norms operating in their home versus school cultures (Hawkins, 2004).

Many Hmong high school females marry at a relatively young age. Rather than assume that their practice of early marriage is simply a matter of their patriarchal home cultures, Ngo (2002) found that female Hmong college students perceive early marriage as an expression of their opposition to the ways in which they are marginalized in the school culture. Ngo (2002) argued that assumptions about Hmong females' practices as reflecting home cultural difference reify the conception of culture as static and fixed as opposed to continually being transformed and reinvented through relationships and new challenges, as evident in shifts in different generational practices in the Hmong culture. She found that for some Hmong females, early marriage was a means of establishing their own independence from highly restrictive parental controls and parents' desire to keep their daughters within extended family networks. Ngo also noted that the notion of cultural difference is often used as a means of rationalizing students' academic difficulties in schools based on a deficit model that avoids acknowledging the marginalization of these students in the school's culture in which students are judged negatively for not conforming to the White norm.

As they acquire American values associated with female autonomy, Hmong females face conflicted allegiances between remaining in and supporting their families versus establishing their own identities as distinct from their families. Townsend & Fu (2001) sited an example of a young Hmong immigrant girl who wanted to go to college to pursue a nursing career; her brother was willing to pay for her expenses, encouraging her to follow her dream. However, her mother was against the idea, wanting her daughter to stay home and help with the family until a marriage could be arranged. Faced with conflicts between their American and home culture, Hmong females may believe that there is no middle ground—that to embrace one cultural standard is to totally reject the other. Given these competing demands, Hmong females are often confused about acceptable gender roles.

White teachers often perceive Hmong females as victims of their sexist home cultures who need to be saved from that culture to be successful in school (Lee, 1996). Teachers also judge Hmong students as not achieving the stereotypical role of the model minority (Lee, 1996), a construction based on negative comparisons with African American students as low achieving, culturally deficient, and unmotivated. One teacher at Thompson noted that in simply looking around a typical classroom at Thompson distinctions between traditional Hmong girls and with-it Hmong girls are obvious. She said, "Just looking at the girls' hair will tell you so much.

Those girls with the really long hair and no makeup? Those girls are very traditional Hmong girls. The girls with the shorter hair and clips and stuff—I mean that is huge."

At Thompson, Hmong girls did appear to occupy several different social positions. In one 11th-grade classroom that we observed, two distinct groups of Hmong girls developed, sitting at opposite ends of the classroom, rarely interacting with one another. The girls in the back of the classroom blended in well with the norms of the class; they participated occasionally in class discussion and answered when called on. However, the girls who sat in the front were much more outgoing and were some of the most outspoken and opinionated students in the class. Several of these girls still wore long hair but often wore it in curls or clipped up in contemporary styles. Additionally, they wore clothes that were not only trendy but often times also were revealing.

Though these with-it Hmong girls outwardly performed identities that fit well with the culture of the school, they typically remained detached from high-status girls at Thompson. For one thing, Hmong girls who were involved in sports tended to play tennis or badminton; they were typically not involved in the sports that jocks or the larger community value. Whereas with-it Hmong girls worked hard to fit into school culture, they were also often expected to perform roles as traditional Hmong daughters at home. As such, domestic responsibilities left little time for school social functions or extracurricular activities. Lee (2002) also pointed out that most high school cultures make little effort to support Hmong girls who choose—or are encouraged by parents—to be involved in Hmong culture, family duties, and even early marriage outside of school. Though some of the Hmong girls in our study were on prom committees, student government, or even the student newspaper, most still felt quite disconnected from school culture on the whole and noted difficulties in crossing between home and school, even though the school sponsors both an Asian Student Club and the Hmong Women's Circle.

Hmong male high school students often adopt a hypertough masculine image consistent with White masculinities to counter stereotypes of Asian males as reserved and not masculine (Lee 1996, 2001, 2002, 2004, 2005). Lee (2004) found that Hmong students perceive Whiteness as the norm in their school against which they as a group were constructed as the culturally different other and that they were very much aware of this negative positioning in the school culture. For Lee (2004, p. 125), looming behind these perceptions is the discourse of Whiteness:

> Youth of color must negotiate schools designed around pervasive, yet often dangerously invisible standards of Whiteness. The echo of

Whiteness is present in classrooms, hallways, and most experiences that define students' educations. Whiteness sets the standards for appropriate femininity and masculinity, and Whiteness helps determine the definition of an educable student. Although many students are able to resist and survive, the fact that they must endure these racial inequalities suggests that there is still much work to be done to disrupt racial inequalities in our schools.

Hmong families and students have a strong respect for public education and for teachers as authority figures (Vang, 2003, 2005). This perception of the teacher as the authority figure may lead some students to be reticent about expressing thoughts perceived as challenging that authority. In their home cultures, girls are taught to be silent and are uncomfortable in speaking out in public (Townsend & Fu, 1998, 2001). Females who are outspoken, especially in public, are judged either as having no manners or as being too flirtatious or seductive. With this as a cultural context, many adolescent girls are hesitant to speak up in classrooms.

Lia, an outspoken girl from a traditional Hmong family, who was a student in another class at Thompson, spoke at length about her struggle to be both a good daughter and a good student. The following exchange highlights some of the competing roles that Lia occupied:

Lia: When I'm at school, you can't do the things that you do at home 'cause it's two totally different places ... here, I do as much as I do at home, but different things, 'cause at home you have chores and you come to school and you have homework. And then you have to try to do your best here at school then you try to do what your respective role is as a girl at home 'cause that's how it is in our culture and stuff.

Thein: So what do you think your role is at home as a girl?

Lia: (brief pause) When I try to read books, my mom doesn't really like the fact that I, you know do it, cause she doesn't really understand that cause all I'm expected to do is work, work, work, cook, clean, watch the kids, and when I spend a lot of time in my bed just reading it's like, then it's I'm a bad daughter and I'm just kind of slacking off on my duties and stuff.

Thein: Mm hmm.

Lia: So when I try to read, I just try to read when nobody's home.

Thein: Is there a lot of time when nobody's home?

Lia: Not a lot.

Thein: Do you read like at night, before you go to bed?

Lia: Um (pause), the only time when I think that I read is when I'm assigned books because I know that those are what I have to do.... And other than that, I just try to do what I can, like what I'm expected at home and stuff.

Lia also explained that even though she appeared friendly with the girls she sat with in class, none of these girls were friends outside of school, either with her or with each other. According to Lia, the only time she felt she could talk on the phone to school friends was when she had homework questions. Additionally, she said that any free time she had was taken up by her two jobs or helping her parents with their janitorial work.

Lia's story is an example of the difficult border crossings that many students faced at Thompson, especially Hmong students who, like Lia, wanted to fit in with the dominant culture of the high school yet wanted to respect and participate in traditional Hmong beliefs, values, and lifestyles in their home lives—many of which conflicted with the values and norms of the Thompson High School community. However, as we found in our study, some of the Hmong students began to entertain alternative versions of the self that helped them negotiate tensions between these conflicting worlds.

Workplace Worlds

Many adolescents devoted considerable time working to obtain spending money or to provide additional family income (Schneider & Stevenson, 1999). About 80% of the students in our study worked in addition to their high school studies and extracurricular activities. Of these students, several students such as Troy averaged more than 30 hours a week at their jobs, with the median being closer to 12 hours per week. Given the lower socioeconomic status of the community, these students worked in part-time jobs at a nearby gas station, in a clothing store at a suburban mall accessible by bus route, at a Dairy Queen, doing telemarketing, doing lawn service, and at a nearby nursing home. Most of these jobs were entry-level, minimum-wage service jobs that involved minimum training, no benefits, few role models, and routine operations involving limited cognitive demands. Though not all students perceived this work as related to their future careers, many enjoy working because they were given some degree of autonomy and spending money (Schneider & Stevenson, 1999).

The discourses and cultural models of these workplace worlds of punctuality, self-control, order, and deference to authority were quite congruent with discourses of the participants' school, family, and community worlds. The workplace tended to be a world that reinforces rather than challenges both social class and gender norms for students in the Thompson commu-

uent Worlds   On the other hand, when the discourses and cu... odels of worlds are incongruent, participants experience tension... the competing worlds. Some of the students of color, particularly ...hong students, were excluded from the world of the school and ... class, creating separate peer-group worlds defined by race, some-...we discuss in more detail in Chapter 5.

...is the case in Bettie's (2003) study, discourses of race served to medi-...fferences between working-class students of color and White work-...lass students, with less recognition of commonalities between these ...bs based on social class. Within the social world of the school, the ...value afforded to nostalgic perpetuation of Whiteness associated with ...ourses of control and individualism created a hierarchy in which the ...es of non-White students were given lower status.

...hough the worlds of sports and school were congruent, the world of ...rts and school and Parks's class were less congruent. Though intel-...tual control associated with transmission models of instruction and ...e learning prevailed in many of the classes we observed, Parks's class ...ployed constructivist learning approaches that deviated from instruc-...nal methods in other classes. For some of the White students whose ...entities were aligned with the world of sports and the school culture, this ...reated tensions, requiring them to acquire new practices.

And though the worlds of the community and the school were congruent, the world of the school and the world of higher education were somewhat incongruent. With only a small percentage attending four-year colleges, many students were not acquiring practices of constructivist learning valued in college. And many students were not aware of the kinds of practices valued in college. As a course offering college credit, Parks's class served as a transitional peripheral learning community (Wenger, 1998) designed to bridge the gap between the high school and college worlds.

Faced with these incongruent worlds, the students in our study varied in their ability to grapple with dialogic tensions between these incongruent worlds. As we discuss in this book, students like Corey who were wedded primarily to school and sports worlds had difficulty negotiating the conflicting demands of incongruent worlds. Other students such as Kayla who were less wedded to a limited number of worlds were more open to grappling with incongruent worlds.

How then do students learn to negotiate differences between incongruent worlds? In the next chapter, which discusses the literary response process, we discuss how grappling with the dialogic tensions portrayed i... literature may assist students in grappling with dialogic tensions in the... own lives.

nity. Based on his father's experiences, Troy expressed a begrudging acceptance of having to work without complaining about that work associated with the traditions of being a working-class male. Troy noted that he learned to live on his own from his father the need to work as a means of survival. Another student, Devin, echoed his father's attitudes of having to cope with an unsatisfying job working in the post office when he described his own job: "I hate my job and my boss."

On the other hand, there were tensions between workplace worlds and school worlds. Some of our participants had difficulty completing homework assignments on time given demands of extensive work hours, results consistent with research finding that high levels of work have adverse effects on academic performance (Schneider & Stevenson, 1999). From their experiences in service and fast-food restaurant jobs, adolescents often acquire a premature cynicism about the value and nature of work related to one's identity and aspirations (Schneider & Stevenson, 1999). In perceiving work as a necessary evil, these students look elsewhere for ways to display competence and agency: the world of sports. At the same time, they import from this world of sports a nose-to-the-grindstone discourse that serves as a rationale for enduring tough, unfavorable conditions. However, not be recognized for their competence in these low-level jobs leads to negative self-images and low self-worth (Schneider & Stevenson, 1999).

Many girls at Thompson participated in a familiar working-class discourse of women as caregivers for home, family, and community. Aside from the many child-care duties that girls regularly had in their own homes, common jobs for girls at Thompson were working in day-care centers and in nursing homes and tutoring younger children. The discourses of caring that were acceptable for girls in this community were reinforced by girls' employment in care sectors, which in turn influenced their identity construction and trajectories for the future.

Molly is an example of a girl who constructed her identity largely through a discourse of caring. Molly worked about 30 hours a week in a nursing home as a dietary assistant. She described her perceptions of her job as follows:

Molly: I'm in dietary.
Thein: So what do you have to do?
Molly: Um, we just serve 'em drinks and bring 'em their food or supper and then just clean up after 'em. That's about it.
Thein: And do you like it?
Molly: Oh yeah. It was hard at first 'cause you see 'em dying and sick and it's kind of scary, but after a while you get really used to it and you like get to know 'em. It's kind of, you get so attached though,

> like I just had a resident that died a week ago and his name was
> Melvin and he was like a nice person, and it's just hard. When
> somebody dies it's like, whoa.

Thein: Yeah, I bet that's hard.

Molly: It's really hard. I mean you get kind of used to it.

In addition to her work at the nursing home, Molly was also involved in Big Brothers/Big Sisters working with a young girl who was abused by her father. She also helped her mother during the summer in her job as a paraprofessional working with elementary school students with behavioral disorders. Molly said that she felt she was good at working with students with behavioral disorders because she was "used to the nursing home and people being like that."

Finally, in thinking about a career beyond high school, Molly made it clear that caring for others was her first priority in the kind of job she will choose. She explained,

> I narrowed it down to the things I really want to do cause I just love
> kids and I have so much experience like working with nurses and
> doctors cause I work in a nursing home, so I'm really used to doing
> all that stuff. Or I wanna be in the NICU [neonatal intensive care]
> unit. Work with little kids, little babies. I don't know, but I also want
> to be a psychologist 'cause I love helping people. People always come
> to me with their problems.

For Molly and many students at Thompson, high school employment was not just about temporary jobs that end as high school culminates. Rather, their employment was often precipitated by discourses learned in community and family, and in turn, employment frequently reinforced those discourses and became a primary means for students to define their identities.

Negotiating between Congruent Versus Incongruent Social Worlds

In studying identity construction within different social worlds, we were curious as to how acquiring practices and discourses or cultural models in one world transferred to use of practices and discourses or cultural models in another world (Beach, Lundell, & Jung, 2002; Phelan, Davidson, & Yu, 1998). If certain practices and discourses or cultural models in, for example, Parks's class, serve to assist students in operating in a college world, then these worlds could be defined as congruent. On the other hand, if the practices and discourses or cultural models operating in, for example, the school world did not assist students in, for example, Parks's class, then these worlds could be defined as incongruent.

Identifying instances of incongruity acr(
explain why students may have difficulty ente
given the fact that their experiences in other
for successful participation in that world. Othe.
dents indicates that participation in certain pe
studying is not a high priority serves to unde
pation in college worlds (Beach, Lundell, & Jung
switch to peer-group worlds in which shared stu
course content is perceived to be important, then t
between peer-group worlds and college course wor

On the other hand, negotiating differences betwee
can create dialogic tensions that serve to foster stude
extent to which the worlds of Parks' classroom, commu
and workplace were congruent varied considerably ac
our study.

Congruent Worlds

Overall, the working-class community and school worlds
given their shared discourses and cultural models that
alism work, competition, and Whiteness. Likewise, the
our study moved seamlessly between their world of sports
world because they shared discourses of athleticism and a c
that values self-discipline and intellectual control that limit
and independent thinking of students (Weis, 1994, 2004). For
there was congruency among the worlds of romance, family, a
class aspirations for success in sports and college. And there w
ency between the emphasis on control and compliance in both
and the school and community worlds.

Given the congruency between these worlds, many of our Whit
pants adopted relatively similar brought-along versions of the self
2003) across these different worlds. Many of the White students
transfer the practices valued in their homes to the school world. Th
athletes in the study assumed the same practices in both their spor
school worlds. And some of the females in the study assumed similar
tices of caring in both work and family worlds.

Although there are certainly positive aspects for congruency betw
worlds, a high level of congruency between worlds poses little challenge
adolescents. They do not need to negotiate boundaries or barriers requi
ing them to adopt different versions of the self or acquire intercultural li
eracies (Guerra, 1997). Facing few dialogic tensions in their lives, they have
little incentive to step outside these worlds to critique their limitations and
to experiment with alternative versions of the self.

Incongr
tural m
betwee
the Hr
Parks's
thing
As
ate di
ing-c
grou
high
disc
valu

sp
le
ro
e
ti
i

CHAPTER 3

Responding to the Influence of Social Worlds on Characters and Readers

A literary poetics of inquiry accords us the reflexive possibility of considering tension, ambiguity, layered meaning, the concreteness of place and historical relations, the saliency of emotional life.

Hicks (2005, p. 214)

I cannot say with any accuracy which parts of my perceived sense of self have been developed by events that actually happened to me in my face-to-face encounters with humans and which have emerged from my identifications with fictional characters.

Sumara (2002b, p. 59)

In Chapters 2 and 3, we argue that identity construction and the development of agency are constituted by the processes of negotiating differences among competing social worlds of peer group, school, community, and family—worlds mediated by competing discourses and cultural models—as well as by different narrative versions of experience. As a result, students can move seamlessly across worlds where discourses and cultural models support each other, whereas they may experience tensions when these discourses and cultural models conflict. Thus, some of our male athlete participants such as Troy could move easily between their peer-group world of sports, mediated by discourses of masculinity and individual achievement, and the Thompson High School world based on these discourses. In contrast, some of the students of color in our study such as Lia were caught between valuing the discourses of their family and community worlds and discourses of the school world.

We ended Chapter 2 questioning how students can learn to grapple with these differences between these competing worlds as part of developing their own beliefs and attitudes, what Bakhtin (1981, p. 384) described as "ideological becoming." As we hope to demonstrate in this book, a key part of identity construction involves formulating responses to dialogic tensions operating in competing social worlds—worlds that can be negotiated both in lived experiences and also in the alternative cultural spaces of multicultural literature.

As we noted in Chapter 1, identity development over time involves sorting through the multiple conflicting voices operating in one's life to develop internally persuasive voices consistent with one's beliefs and attitudes (Bakhtin, 1981; Moore & Cunningham, 2006). In responding to literature, students experience characters' coping with tensions between authoritative voices and internally persuasive voices associated with their development. They experience dialogic tensions between competing voices in texts reflecting allegiances to different discourses and cultural models. For example, in responding to *Hamlet*, students experience Hamlet responding to his father's (i.e., the ghost's) voices demanding revenge for his murder, voices conflicting with other characters' voices that deny that a murder has occurred, or voices urging caution in seeking revenge. They experience Claudius's authoritative voice demanding that Hamlet defer to his power as the new king of Denmark and Hamlet's development of counter-voices reflecting his moral outrage with Claudius's deeds. Students must then determine whose voices are consistent with their own voices in terms of their beliefs and attitude. In aligning themselves with Hamlet's voices, they experience his moral perspective on Claudius's immoral authoritative voice.

When students respond to literature, they experience voices reflecting or double voicing (Bakhtin, 1981) institutional discourses and cultural models—for example, the institutional voices of business, the military, science, religion, or politics. These voices often take the form of authoritative voices against which characters voice their own resisting personal perspectives. When students identify with these characters' voices, they may experience resistance to institutional discourses and cultural models.

In responding to multicultural literature, students experience voices reflecting alternative cultural perspectives that compete with their own cultural perspectives. For example, in responding to *Love Medicine* (Erdrich, 2000) and *A Yellow Raft in Blue Water* (Dorris, 1987), students experience the voices of Native American spirituality and relationships with nature that differ from Eurocentric discourses and cultural models. They then experience dialogic tensions between their familiar discourses and cultural models and those operating in text worlds.

Through this experience of dialogic cultural tensions portrayed in multicultural literature, students develop an awareness of a multicultural perspective. As Fishman and McCarthy (1995, p. 75) argued, "Individuals do not belong to single clearly identifiable cultures.... We know from our own experience that there is no such thing as monoculturalism. There is only multiculturalism, for each of us, for all of us."

And for non-White students, responding to multicultural literature serves to legitimatize the value of their own cultural identities. An analysis of the responses of 308 Australian students in grades 7–10 to a multicultural literature anthology found that students of color were more likely to respond positively to multicultural texts than White students, even when the characters' racial identities were different from their own (Amosa, 2004).

However, reading multicultural literature in and of itself does not necessarily foster dialogic tensions. An additional key factor in fostering dialogic tensions is the nature of the instruction employed. As we describe in Chapter 5, Daryl Parks employed a range of discussion, writing, and drama techniques to foster students' exploration of dialogic tensions in responding to literature. He asked students to critically reflect on the influence of discourses and cultural models on characters in text worlds, reflections that transferred to reflection on their own lived worlds through what Bleich (1998, p. 60) described as a "reflexive ethnography ... students are reading literature as culturally heterogeneous, as comprehensive in its perceptions of its own society and its potential application to our societies."

All of this suggests a need to move beyond traditional reader-response theories of literature instruction to a sociocultural theory of literary response (Faust, 2000; Galda & Beach, 2001; Lewis, 2000, 2001; Schweickart & Flynn, 2004; Smagorinsky, 2001; Sumara, 2002a, 2002b). Traditional reader-response pedagogies focus on meaning as evolving from a transaction between an individual reader and a text in a social context, as opposed to assuming that there are correct meanings embedded in the text (Karolides, 2000; Probst, 2004; Rosenblatt, 1970, 1978). In contrast, sociocultural theories of response focus not on readers and texts as unique entities but on how readers, texts, and contexts are mediated by what West (2001) referred to as ideologies of difference through engaging in "literary anthropology" (Sumara, 2002a, p. 238). These theories also focus on how readers learn to adopt alternative cultural perspectives through grappling with the dialogic tensions portrayed in texts. As Hicks (1996, p. 221) noted, "Reading involves a set of cultural practices, as integrally embedded within webs of relationships as any other social act of being and knowing."

One key limitation of traditional reader-response pedagogy has been a focus on fostering personal connections between readers and characters (Probst, 2004). By defining similarities in race, class, or gender identities, teachers have assumed that students would empathize or identify with characters' situations (Barak, 2003). This involves a three-step process of identifying with characters as individuals: (1) identification of one's own gender, class, or race identity; (2) identification of the "other" character in a text; and (3) articulation of a synthesis between one's own identity and the identity of the "other," leading to further understanding and tolerance (Easton & Lutzenberger, 1999, p. 276). For example, a White female student may respond to the portrayal of an African American female character such as Janie in *Their Eyes Were Watching God* (Hurston, 2000) by noting how they are "the same" in terms of sharing similar feelings and experiences despite differences in race, leading her to posit that "we are all the same" regardless of racial difference.

Immersed in this approach, students may perceive characters simply as individual persons or personalities, failing to recognize the fictional, language-based nature of texts that reflect larger ideas and beliefs. Gass (1971) argued that treating characters as individual persons shifts attention away from the fact that readers are constructing characters as linguistic entities in ways that represent ideas and beliefs, as opposed to personalities who could walk off of the page. Gass noted that novels could be interpreted as complex networks of ideas and beliefs related to larger thematic meanings as opposed to simply portraits of characters. Constructing characters as simply unique, individual personalities detracts students from focusing on discourses and cultural models shaping those characters.

In this approach, students may assume that they are interpreting a text from the perspective of being a certain essentialist type—as a White or woman, then they may assume that they cannot understand the text. Hum (2006, p. 462) cited the example of one of her students: "Once a young, male graduate student of Spanish descent, in response to my general inquiry to a class, responded, 'I'm not sure what I'm supposed to get out of the reading. I couldn't relate to it because I'm not Chinese.' As an afterthought, he added, probably in response to my frozen expression, 'And I'm not a woman.'" Hum noted that readers may adopt subject positions associated with either a localism stance, which focuses simply on the local, particular details of a text, or a universalism stance, which focuses on "the commonalities we all share as members of the human race" (ibid.). Both of these stances serve to either reify or deny racial difference. By focusing simply on local difference in specific cultural practices, for example, how Chinese characters behave as distinct from American characters, readers may simply apply and reify prototypical notions of Chinese versus American identities (ibid.). Or, by framing difference in terms of shared humanity, readers adopt universalistic notions of difference, assuming that they can relate to characters whose emotions and practices are similar to their own, a reflection of color-blind racism that ignores institutional racism (Bonilla-Silva, 2001). In adopting a universalistic stance, students assume a cultural model of race as simply a matter of individual choice.

Hum (2006, p. 465) called for an alternative approach that involves "ways of reading that highlight disjuncture and instability" by analyzing characters in terms of both their past cultural origins and their present practices in local and shifting contexts. She also argued for readers to reflect on "how we participate in essentializing discourses that stress cultural homogeneity, that naturalizes the apparent transparency of meaning. We must also recognize the taken-for-granted-ness in our attitudes, particularly these reductive, normalizing tendencies. Thus, we must interrogate and destabilize the terms we privilege" (p. 466).

Another problem with encouraging students to simply empathize with characters is that this practice assumes that students can actually appreciate or understand what it is like to experience certain cultural or historical phenomenon. Lewis (2000) argued that it may be impossible for White students to equate their experiences with those of characters who experience institutional forces of racism. To assume that contemporary students can genuinely identify with the experiences of being a slave, for example, is simply naive given their lack of understanding of historical and institutional forces at work in racial relationships. In her critique of the limitations of privileging aesthetic identification with texts, Lewis argues that White students need to recognize that they are not likely to identify with characters who are the targets of racism. As she notes (p. 263),

> For readers who are outsiders to these experiences of racism, an aesthetic reading is not about identification, but about understanding how the text works to position particular readers as outsiders. This position deepens the understanding of the characters' lives as separate from the reader's own in important ways. In disrupting the reader's inclination to identify, the text heightens the reader's self consciousness and text consciousness in a way that should not be viewed as less aesthetic than a more direct or immediate relationship between reader and text.

At the same time, White students often resist the assumption that they are incapable of understanding racism, because such students often see racism as a matter of individual prejudice rather than systemic oppression. They assume that critiques of Whiteness refer to them as individual Whites, as opposed to participants in institutional operations and practices of Whiteness (Trainor, 2002, 2005). In their analysis of college classroom discussions, Maher & Tetreault (1997) noted repeated instances in which White students perceived themselves as individuals, while describing people of color in terms of group membership. They framed the notion of White privilege in terms of their individual power as Whites, as opposed to an institutional force, framing Whiteness "as a self-justifying or self-excusing marker of relative personal privilege and no more" (p. 327). These perceptions of people of color as members of groups only served to reinforce the notion of Whiteness as the norm with "other" groups outside that norm.

Given these White students' attitudes, one frequent justification for teaching multicultural literature is that exposure to multicultural literature will make Whites more sensitive to the plight of racial others (McCarthy, 1994). However, there is little empirical evidence to supports the claim that responding to multicultural literature will foster racial tolerance. In a carefully designed study examining the influence of White middle-school students' studying and responding to several texts in a multicultural literature unit taught by an award-winning teacher, Dressel (2003) found that, although the students were engaged in reading the texts, they did not increase their understanding of people from minority cultures, nor did they grow in self-understanding, as measured by a series of attitude scales. Although these results may be attributed to a variety of factors such as the students' ages, the survey instrument, or the duration of the study, these results may also be attributed to the likelihood that racial attitudes are shaped by family, peer group, or community experiences during the course of a lifetime more so than by studying literature in the course of a few weeks or months.

Learning to Interpret Characters and Selves as Constituted by Institutional Forces

Rather than assuming that teaching multicultural literature will lead to a change in students' racial attitudes, one alternative justification for teaching multicultural literature is that by discussing how characters are constituted by institutional forces shaped by discourses of race, class, and gender, students may begin to critically examine how their own identities are shaped by these discourses. As they track characters' shift from a first-person subject to a third-person object perspective (Kegan, 1994) in which they are increasingly aware of how institutional forces are limiting their agency, students experience the impact of discourses of race, class, and gender on characters' identities. At the same time, rather than simply perceive characters and themselves as social prototypes totally controlled by institutional forces, students may also recognize how characters acquire agency through

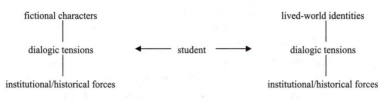

Figure 3.1 Noting relationships between characters and institutional–historical forces in texts and lived worlds

exploring the ways that discourses and cultural models limit their development, leading them to collective action to change the system.

We therefore perceive multicultural literature as providing students with an understanding of the historical dimensions of how characters gain power through grappling with dialogic tensions by participating in collective action, perceiving characters as historical agents involved in historical struggles. As Holland and Lave (2001, p. 29–30) noted,

> Subjectivities and their more objectified components, identities, are formed in practice through the often collective work of evoking, improving, appropriating, and refusing participation in practices that position self and other. They are durable not because individual persons have essential or primal identities but because the multiple contexts in which dialogical, intimate identities make sense and give meaning are re-created in contentious local practice (which is in part shaped and reshaped by enduring struggles.) ... Persons-as-agents thus are always forming themselves in collective terms as they respond to the social situations they encounter locally and in their imaginations.

Recognizing the historical forces operating on characters' lives may then transfer to students' perceptions of how their own social practices and language use are shaped by these forces. As illustrated in Figure 3.1, through noting the dialogic tensions between characters and institutional forces in texts, students may then note dialogic tensions between their identities and the forces shaping those identities. These dialogic tensions (Bakhtin, 1981) stem from characters' and people's negotiations of the competing demands of different worlds as described in Chapter 2. As Bakhtin (1981) demonstrated in his analysis of Fyodor Dostoevsky, Charles Dickens, and others novelists, literary texts highlight these dialogic tensions through the use of heteroglossia—the use of characters' double voicing competing discourses in a text world. Characters' double voicing highlights the dialogic tensions in characters' language by implying tensions between meanings associated with the characters' language and meanings associated with authorial intentions that imply a more critical stance on the characters' language use. As Bakhtin (1981, p. 324) noted, double-voiced discourse "serves two speakers at the same time and expresses simultaneously two different intentions: the direct intention of the character who is speaking, and the refracted intention of the author." When the male characters in *Their Eyes Were Watching God* describe their perceptions of females, they are voicing a patriarchal discourse associated with their allegiances to a male-dominated culture. At the same time, Zora Neale Hurston is implying her critique of those discourses by portraying the ways these discourses limit the male characters' relationships with women.

In our study, students' perceptions of characters coping with dialogic tensions related to institutional and historical forces transferred to their perceptions of the tensions associated with the decline of a traditional blue-collar economy that began to erode during the 1980s and 1990s through their internalization of their parents' and grandparents' voices and language evoking these past traditions. Drawing on Bakhtin (1981), Holland and Lave (2001, p. 15) noted that people identify with past generations' voices and language: "the words of the other may eventually become personalized into one's own. One gains a feeling for their complexity and life, their meaning for one's self. In these cases, the other becomes indistinguishable from the 'I for myself,' or rather part of one's self becomes an incorporation of the other."

By learning how past generations' language use reflected certain historical perspectives, students in our study began to perceive how their own language use reflected current perspectives. This understanding led them to comprehend differences between how their grandparents looked at the world and how they look at the world, leading to an appreciation of how historical forces shape people.

How Multicultural Literature Invites Awareness of Institutional Forces

Kindred

One way that multicultural literature invites readers to focus on the influence of historical and institutional forces is by contrasting characters' perceptions and practices across different worlds. Dramatizing the differences between the same character's perceptions and practices between different worlds focused the attention of readers in our study on the differences between these worlds. For example, one of the books our participants read was Butler's (1979) time-travel novel, *Kindred*. The main character in the novel, Dana, an African American woman, moves between the institution of slavery in 1820s and racism operating in the world of 1970s Los Angeles. In her travels, Dana encounters distant relatives, including her great-grandparents: Alice, an enslaved African American woman, and Rufus, a White slaveholder. Though she finds that Rufus actually professed strong feelings of love for Alice, she also discovers that Rufus raped Alice. In her visits to the past, Dana is harassed by Rufus, and his father, Tom Weylin, the plantation owner. Not only does Dana struggle with exploring her racial identities rooted in the 1820s, but she also struggles with being in an interracial marriage in the 1970s. Through her time-travel experiences, Dana recognizes that history and the heritage of slavery have a profound influence on her current identity as a contemporary African American woman. She perceives herself as the object limited by the historical forces of slavery. This return to the past is itself a biographical counternarrative that serves to mediate the construction of her memory as well as her present identity. Rushdy (1993, p. 137) described the role of biographical narrative in constructing Dana's identity through linking past memories with the present to create an ongoing narrative:

> Dana provides the possibility for that narrative—which would give her a sense of selfhood by returning her to and re-engaging her with the past—when she employs her memory: "I closed my eyes again remembering the way I had been hurt—remembering the pain" (p. 10). Within the parameters of her recollection, as presented in the novel's seven chapters, we receive the study of Dana's unique relationship to her slave-holding great-grandfather Rufus Weylin. Dana's memory, then, acts as a framing device to constructing the story of her relationship with her ancestor.... Her memory is a performance of history, a performance of such potency that it incorporates her into the past, leaving "no distance at all" between her and the remembered events.

In reading about her experiences of slavery, participants in our study relived Dana's experiences of slavery not simply as an historical event or morality tale but as an experience fraught with complexities, contradictions, and silences that persist in 1970s Los Angeles. In experiencing Dana's testimony, students also learned how distortions, disparities, and silences about events reflect larger institutional forces at work, for example, how the historical records of slave ownership Dana uncovers about her past are silent about the morality of slavery.

The students in our study came to understand Dana's experiences in these two different worlds as reflecting differences in the discourses and cultural models operating in those worlds. For example, Troy noted that "people were a lot more racist back then … saying things like 'educating slaves is illegal' and 'it's not the intention of the Lord.'" The time travel genre allowed Troy to think of past and present discourses in sociocultural, institutional terms.

One of the students in the course, Mitch, analyzed the influence of the history and the culture of slavery on Dana's identity and on her relationships with others. From his experience with the novel, he learned that it was important to frame explanations of characters' actions in terms of historical forces:

> Rufus rapes Alice and sells slaves, but who is responsible depends on your definition of self. If you think that a person is only a product of their history and environment, then "his" actions were beyond "his" control. This idea about the relationship between a person and their culture is one of the main points Octavia Butler is trying to make. Dana is given a unique non-objective perspective that causes the reader to see the invisible cultural forces that shape everyone.

Other students examined the tensions related to the function of language in the two time periods in mediating identity relationships between Rufus and Dana. Troy noted,

> Rufus gets mad at her for not saying "master" to him. Or not saying like Master or Hey Master or I don't even know what they said back then "Master." Then he says something like "you want me to call you 'Black?'" And then they go on and like get in a fight about it and he says, "Nigger" and all these other good words, or bad words back then, but good then, or whatever. But then he like, but then Rufus goes, "it's not for me, it's for my dad." So, that kind of surprised me that it was for Rufus and not more for the fact that his Dad … That implies to me that Rufus isn't a racist little guy. Which then in turns means that he could get together with Alice if he is not racist.

Troy noted that Rufus uses these categories to mark power in his relationship with Dana as consistent with the norms of the time. At the same time, he noted that in the context of their own local relationship, Rufus is using language to give the impression to his father that he is in control of Dana, an awareness of how language use also functions within a local context to challenge the discourses operating in the larger historical context.

The time-travel genre also invited students to debate how characters should be judged—whether characters should be judged according to moral principles that transcend certain historical periods or whether they should be judged according to the norms operating in a certain period. Mitch noted that Dana is bringing her contemporary norms of the 1970s to judge characters of the early 1800s: "Dana is a product of her environment in the future, but when she's taken back in time, people like her do not exist. Civil rights and feminist ideas were not heard of, so it would not be reasonable to expect people to understand why she 'acts White' and 'dresses like a man.'"

The students grappled with questions about whether certain moral principles transcend sociocultural, historical contexts. This was especially true as they considered the actions of Rufus in the novel, a character who purports to love Alice, a slave, yet ultimately rapes her. Troy noted that Rufus loves Alice, yet he cannot fully free himself from cultural practices of the day, though he tries. For example, he cited the instance in which Rufus begs Alice not to leave the plantation knowing that she will be killed, a deviation from the cultural norms. Troy stated, "For a White guy to beg a Black woman in 1825 to not go—that's some serious stuff." Troy also argued that it was important to consider how Rufus was "raised and brought up ... in a world that shows no good, but represented evil." He identified a tension that Rufus felt associated his resistance to the voices and language of his parents. Troy stated, "You are the mirror image of your parents. You use words like them and believe the same things as they do." In contrast to Mitch, who framed the tensions in the novel in terms of cultural differences, Troy perceived these tensions in terms of morality. He noted that after Rufus's father kicks Dana in the face, Rufus "shouted, 'you didn't have to do that.'" Troy argued that these instances demonstrate an intrinsic awareness of countercultural morality at work in Rufus despite his later actions.

Other students posited that certain moral principles transcend historical periods, arguing that Rufus is unquestionably wrong in raping Alice. Sue asked:

> How can he be so good when he knows he can lay with and have them to get what he wants ... an example would be his selling of Sam because the two [Sam and Alice] were flirting and Rufus got jealous ... he treated Dana like a dog who fetched things for him and followed is every command. She wanted to exist, so she put up with him. How can any normal person do that?

Students also examined difference in gender attitudes in the competing worlds of *Kindred*. In applying a feminist lens (Appleman, 2000) to the novel, Devin noted in his journal that during slavery, "women have little or no rights. And no rights if you're a Black woman ... (except for kids and marriage which meant little because they were probably sold off for profit anyhow). You were a possession used for sex and work. And if you didn't pull your weight, you were whipped."

Devin wrote that even the wife of Tom Weylin, Margaret, had little agency in this world: "She really doesn't do anything but be bitchy and whine all day. [She] really wasn't good at anything and couldn't or wouldn't read very much. Women were taught to be possessions, not people."

In another instance, Kayla took note of the fact that when Dana is first attacked by a White man during her time travels, she fights back, using self-defense tactics that women would neither know about nor have the agency to use during slavery. Kayla explained that this was a point of contrast and tension between Dana's contemporary gender norms and the gender norms of the antebellum South.

Much of high school literature instruction involves formalist analysis of literary features related to uses of figurative language or characterization and story development techniques. Though this instruction is important, students in the study were going beyond simply analyzing an author's uses of literary language and techniques as matters of literary form to examine how characters' language use reflects dialogic tensions associated with competing discourses and cultural models. As Dickson (2006, p. 735) noted, "Approaching a piece of writing as discourse typically means that you are interested in the historical or cultural 'character' of the rhetoric; you are interested less in the writer as an individual plying her/his verbal gift than as a subject of a particular time and place cobbling together a communication with what's available to them." Students also examined how characters are limited or constrained by certain discourses or cultural models operating in competing social worlds. For instance, students examined how Janie, in *Their Eyes are Watching God*, is constrained by a discourse of patriarchy, while simultaneously coming to understand how Janie's use of vernacular dialect served to establish her sense of power.

The House on Mango Street

By contextualizing the characters' language use within larger historical and institutional forces, students in our study understood these characters as agents struggling to make changes. For example, in *The House on Mango Street* (Cisneros, 1991), the main character, Esperanza, a Chicana, moves to a poor Latino Chicago neighborhood at age 12 and experiences the challenges of growing up as an adolescent in the neighborhood, including sexual assault. Esperanza begins to develop competing perspectives on the poverty and crime afflicting the social world of her neighborhood. On the one hand, she is ashamed about her own status as someone from that neighborhood, particularly in her school world, a sense of shame that she writes about at school. On the other hand, she admires some of the women in the neighborhood who represent a sense of agency in the face of poverty and crime. Given her sense of a future self outside of the neighborhood, she later decides to leave the neighborhood but then later returns to assist those women that she admires.

The fact that Esperanza uses her writing to reflect on her experiences mirrors Sandra Cisneros's own development as a writer; she grew up in a similar Chicago neighborhood. Through her writing, Esperanza experiences a shift to a third-person perspective in which she perceives herself as the object of the racism and sexism in her neighborhood. The students therefore experienced her internally persuasive voices (Bakhtin, 1981) in opposition to being the object of the authoritative voices of discourses of masculinity associated with sexual harassment and control of women in the neighborhood that had positioned her to adopt the identity of a sexually alluring female. They perceive her developing a sense of agency through her use of a reflective language related to the development of a critical perspective on her neighborhood. For example, in response to her descriptions of how much of the neighborhood's poverty is due to racism and the fact that Whites have left the neighborhood, Troy noted that "this quote suggests 'White flight'—the hint of racism in a Latino community."

In some cases, students in our study perceived the depictions of text worlds as challenges to their discursive traditions—particularly those related to White, blue-collar masculinity. For example, though Troy was critical of the racism operating in the Mango Street neighborhood, he was less critical of the patriarchal discourses operating in the neighborhood, which he perceived as stereotyping on Cisneros's part. He pointed particularly to portrayals of older men kissing the younger girls in the Mango Street neighborhood: "[The author is] pointing out that a lot of men tend to be aroused by younger girls and that some are 'pigs.' Not all nice men are nice. Suggests that the book has a sort of negative outlook on men as portrayed as egotistical and macho."

Troy resisted what he perceived to be generalization about males in the novel, resistance that reflected his adherence to a discourse of masculinity. Thus, students may adopt a critical stance for certain topics but may resist adopting a critical stance on other topics that challenge some of their bedrock discourses.

Thus, through responding to novels such as *Kindred* and *The House on Mango Street*, students experience dialogic tensions between voices reflecting competing institutional forces. In responding to *Kindred*, students experienced tensions between the world of slavery and the contemporary world of color-blind racism. By interpreting Dana's identities in these two opposing worlds, students examined how she is shaped by discourses and cultural models operating in these competing worlds, as well as how she develops internally persuasive voices to reject the authoritative patriarchal voices operating in her world. In responding to *The House on Mango*

Street, students perceived Esperanza as caught between allegiance to her neighborhood world and envisioning her future self outside of that world. As with Dana, they also perceived her resisting the authoritative voices of masculinity and racism, resistance that leads her to develop a sense of agency as a future self who adopts a feminist, antiracist identity.

Love Medicine

Students' willingness to adopt critical stances also varied across the different novels, variation due in part to the interest in and knowledge about the kinds of institutional forces operating in these novels. One novel that fostered a high level of critique of institutional forces was *Love Medicine*, by Louise Erdrich (2000), which portrays the lives of six generations of four Native American families in North Dakota from the period of the mid 1930s to the mid 1980s. The families contend with marital strife, death, alcoholism, poverty, and political harassment but at the same time succeed in raising families and coping with a political and justice system that works against them. Though this text was one of the most challenging texts that students read in terms of textual features, theme, and narrative structure, students consistently cited it as one on the most engaging books they read in the course.

One reason that this novel fostered students' awareness of institutional forces was that the students were already aware of differences between their own and Native American cultural practices given their exposure to the relatively large urban and rural Native American population in their state. They were therefore peripherally aware of some of the issues facing contemporary Native American populations: lack of government support for reservations, inadequate health care, low rates of high school student retention, few employment opportunities, as well as high rates of poverty, alcoholism, and suicide. Students also drew parallels with their own experiences in negotiating the social and cultural worlds in *Love Medicine*. For example, Devin noted similarities between the poverty he witnessed on a trip to Juarez, Mexico, and the widespread poverty in the novel. He also noted that alcohol use in his own family often led to conflicts and fights at family gatherings, much as it did in *Love Medicine*.

Students who saw disparities between their own values and the values of Native American characters noted the dialogic tensions between the White and Native American cultures operating in the novel. For example, they identified tensions between the competing worlds of Catholicism and Native American spiritual and mystical beliefs. Mitch cited the example of the character of June, who "seemed to drift out of her clothes and skin with no help from anyone." Students also noted how symbolic images of water reflected a spiritual cultural model that differed from their own cultural models. Dan noted that he "began to look at the water in the novel as being some sort of deity whether it was god or some other Native American god. And throughout the rest of the reading for the day I began to look at water like that."

In responding to the novel, students cited instance of tensions between their prototypical notions of Native Americans derived from popular culture and their own experiences with Native Americans or portrayals of Native Americans in the novel. Dan described his experience of meeting Native Americans on a church mission trip to Wyoming, in which he discovered that Native Americans he met differed from his expectations:

> Just kind of like how Indian people were and how I thought of them and how I know them from actually being there and how different they were from what I thought. I thought that they were kind of like, like they enjoyed telling stories all the time and they were all really silent. But, like, everybody we talked to didn't like telling stories and they talked about everyday things and why were at the place and stuff like that.

In a journal response to *Love Medicine*, he summarized the historical narratives in the novel:

> The stories that many Indian people tell now are about how the natives ruled the land then the White settlers kicked them out and drove them west by force and bloodshed.... Louise Erdrich is helping to bring out this problem into the public eye so that hopefully someone someday will notice it and do something about it.

By adopting the language of "how the natives ruled the land then the White settlers kicked them out and drove them west by force and bloodshed," Pat double voices a Native American discourse that interrogates the historical position of Whiteness.

At the same time, students also observed tensions within the Native American culture regarding characters' commitment to spirituality. Contrary to the Hollywood portrayals of Native Americans as highly spiritual, some students discerned that many of the characters display little spirituality. Sue noted that "there are only like two people who are actually traditionally spiritual and that would be Eli and June. So, I think that it shows that Native Americans are more modern than like they are enacted on TV."

Students also noticed the marked differences in the operation of the justice system for Native Americans and Whites. They cited the example of Gerry, a Native American character who experiences an unfair trial when Native American witnesses slated to testify for him do not show up at the trial or are intimidated by the prosecution. Devin said that "it's hard to stand up for yourself when you are surrounded (outside of your own 'country') by Whites and they control you." Devin also noted that even though Native Americans have their own land, the government continues to take that land and to undercut their attempts at economic development.

The students also examined issues of Eurocentric historical representations of Native Americans they acquired in their history courses in which, as Mitch said, "Native Americans are seen largely as an obstacle to Western settlement ... the history books and White people generally don't know much about the status of Native Americans."

Thus, the competing perspectives portrayed in *Love Medicine* invited students to view text worlds consistent with Native American cultural models. Through constructing these text worlds, they began to reflect on some of the values constituting their own lived worlds, leading them to examine the limitations of their notions of Native American culture and history. They also explored dialogic tensions between Native American cultural beliefs and their Eurocentric beliefs, leading them to condsider how culture shapes identities.

Bastard out of Carolina

Another novel that fostered awareness of institutional forces was *Bastard out of Carolina* (Allison, 1993), described in Chapter 1. Allison (1994) noted that the novel is based on her own experiences coping with negative perceptions of working-class "White trash" people in the South. In writing about her experience of moving from Greenville, South Carolina, to a new junior high school in Florida at age 13, Allison recalled that she realized that she had been perceived by others as "White trash": "The first time I looked around my junior high classroom and realized I did not know who those people were ... I also realized that they did not know me. In Greenville, everyone knew my family, knew we were trash, and that meant we were supposed to be poor, supposed to have grim low-paid jobs, have babies in our teens, and never finish school" (Allison, 1994, p. 20) (cited in Hicks, 2005, p. 214).

As Allison left her childhood home and moved to Florida, she was able to reinvent herself, no longer limited by the class discourses shaping her previous identity. Baker (1999) noted that Allison critiques middle-class discourses positing that working-class people are poor because they lack motivation or schooling, further marginalizing working-class people. Baker pointed to a scene in *Bastard out of Carolina* in which Bone reflects on her mother's numerous attempts to obtain a birth certificate without *Illegitimate* stamped on it: "'Mama hated to be called trash, hated the memory of every day she'd ever spent bent over other people's peanuts and strawberry plants while they stood tall and looked at her like she was a rock on the ground' (3–4)" (p. 5). This portrayal depicts Bone's recognition of how middle-class discourses constructed the category of "White trash," which contributed to her mother's sense of inferiority. Baker noted that Bone's transformation derives from her resistance to these middle-class discourses that position her as inferior, as well as her support from her Aunt who "does not merely speak an oppositional discourse; she embodies it in her own living" (p. 6).

Whereas the students in our study were accustomed to reading novels about characters from cultures that differed from their own, this novel portrayed White, working-class people who led lives that were sometimes similar to their own. However, even though these characters were comparable to some students in terms of demographics, these students often found that the experiences of sexual abuse and class resentment depicted were very different from what they had previously experienced. Still, for many of our participants this novel represented worlds that were somewhat familiar. Though they would never be able to understand what it would be like to be a slave through responding to *Kindred* (Lewis, 2000), many of our participants could understand Bone's emotions of despair and hope as related to class differences. In describing her purpose for writing the book, Allison (1994, p. 14) said that she was driven by

> the need to make my world believable to people who have never experienced it is part of why I write fiction … I know that some things must be felt to be understood, that despair, for example, can never be adequately analyzed; it must be lived. But if I can write a story that so draws the reader in that she imagines herself like my characters, feels their sense of fear and uncertainty, their hopes and terrors, then I have come closer to knowing myself as real, important as the very people I have always watched in awe.

Based on their reading of an interview with Allison (Pratt, 1995), students analyzed the ways that social class systems could work in both the life of the author and the lives of her characters. For example, Mitch posited that Allison lived a similar life to Bone in her early exposure to the harsh realities of life and little social support to cope with these realities. He noted, "She didn't have rape crisis centers." He also noted that for both Allison and Bone, reading books provided alterative versions of the self—that, for Allison, "reading gave her a feeling of self-worth—that she was 'despised.'" Mitch saw reading as affording Allison a "the 'possibility of justice,'" which, he said that Bone acquires from "gospel music, because it suggests God can forgive, but he can also judge. I would guess that in both their worlds, things were so unfair, the idea of fairness and justice are profound."

From their own experiences with being labeled or perceived in negative ways by their middle-class suburban peers, students identified similar negative positioning of Bone in terms of middle-class discourses. Devin noted that Bone's mother

> makes a big effort to not be identified as "trashy," but Bone still picks things up and starts believing she is. Late on page 82, her mom's explaining to Bone: "we're not bad people. We're not really even poor." But Bone sees "we know what the neighbors called us, what Mama want to protect us from. We knew who we were." This is where she first makes the distinction between who she's "suppose to be" and who she "is" in terms of her social class.

Mitch also noted how discourses of class differences created tensions for Bone and for Daddy Glen. He tracked Bone's increasing awareness of the disparities between her working-class life and her relatives' middle-class life, creating a sense of "envy of her cousins' new dresses, their horses, and other excesses she couldn't enjoy." He argued that Daddy Glen is similarly envious of his family's current status because he "came from a wealthy family, so he doesn't think he's 'good enough' because he's tried to live up to expectations." Kathy argued that once Daddy Glen lost his wealth, he would then be perceived as a failure because "instead of climbing up the ladder you keep coming down, so, that's the hardest part I think. Everybody else have nothing to lose in life, but, some people do." And Devin posited the influence of money on his loss of social status. He said, "He's desperate … he needs attention and love … he can't hold a job. Money changes people."

From this analysis, students began to perceive the impact of institutional forces of class differences in limiting Bone's family's potential for development within this class-based system, a critical step toward critiquing the influence of institutional forces. Kayla noted that given the family's poverty, they "start behind … they haven't even had the chance to progress at all, just being born into that, they're starting behind everyone else." This led to disagreements between students as to whether Bone could transcend these class barriers. On the one hand, Troy perceived himself as limited by the same barriers confronting Bone: "If the fan belt breaks on my car. Or I've got to buy groceries and pay rent, and my car bill because my check wasn't in the mail … Like Bone I'm tired like her, I'm always tired, and you just try to keep up." He argued that these barriers can be overwhelming: "she's got hurdles and they're just a little too high for her to jump and that she'll be stuck in the situation forever, or grow older and marry the same sort of man [as Daddy Glen] … [with] all those hardships, how can she make it?" On the other hand, Mia disagreed with Troy, arguing that "she's

strong and she has a mind of her own ... she has a very powerful imagination and this is a positive thing." These competing perspectives reflect
dialogic tensions in students' own lives between a discourse of economic
determinism—that people are ultimately constrained by class differences
and a belief in an individuals' ability to transcend class differences. Given
their own experiences as working-class students, some students experienced dialogic tensions between the realization that the class system works
against them and the need to believe in their own ability to succeed in spite
of this system.

Summary

In this chapter, we have described a sociocultural model of literary response
as an alternative to traditional reader-response models that focus primarily on individual reader's subjective experiences with texts. A sociocultural
model posits that readers construct texts worlds mediated by discourses
and cultural models operating in those worlds (Smagorinsky, 2001). In
constructing these text worlds, students examine the institutional forces
shaping characters beliefs and practices, leading them to reflect on the
institutional forces shaping their own lives.

Four of the novels read in Parks's class—*Kindred, The House on Mango
Street, Love Medicine,* and *Bastard out of Carolina*—highlight the influence of social worlds on characters' beliefs and practices. Combined with
Parks's instruction that encouraged a focus on institutional forces, these
novels invited students to reflect on how social worlds shape characters'
beliefs and practices. In responding to the time-travel structure of *Kindred,* students contrasted Dana's identities in the world of slavery and her
contemporary world as they reflect differences in the discourses and cultural models of race. In responding to *The House on Mango Street,* students
experience how the discourses of racism and sexism limited Esperanza's
agency and how she developed a sense of agency in resisting those discourses. In responding to *Love Medicine,* students explored alternative
discourses of spirituality, poverty, and historical racism associated with
Native American culture. And in responding to *Bastard out of Carolina,*
they examined the influence of class difference on Bone's sense of agency.
From constructing these text worlds, students then reflected on the discourses and cultural models that constitute their identities in their own
social worlds. Therefore, the process of constructing institutional forces in
text worlds then transfers to the process constructing institutional forces
in the students' social worlds.

In this chapter we focused on how reading and discussing multicultural literature can foster an awareness of institutional forces in both text

and lived worlds. The next chapter examines how students may then adopt a critical stance toward these institutional forces through responding to multicultural literature.

CHAPTER 4

Critiquing Social Worlds through Grappling with Dialogic Tensions

Identity emerges within complex systems—which include the sub-human, social collectives, and the more-than-human. Emergent identities also influence the contexts and systems in which experience occur.

Davis, Sumara, and Luce-Kapler (2000, p. 176)

In the previous chapter, we argued that, through negotiating tensions in the competing social worlds of multicultural literature, students can learn to go beyond simply responding to characters as individual persons and can move toward constructing characters as constituted by larger institutional forces. Once students identify the influences of institutional forces on characters and themselves, it is important that they then critique problematic aspects of these forces in shaping characters' and their own beliefs and practices. In this chapter, we explore the ways students in our study went beyond simply identifying these institutional forces to critiquing the influences of these forces on characters, leading them to consider such influences on their own identities.

From Liberal Humanism to Critical Multiculturalism

Learning to adopt a critical stance toward issues of race, class, and gender differences involves moving beyond examining discourses of individualism toward an examination of differences that are constituted by institutional forces. Adopting such a stance means moving from a discourse of liberal humanism to a discourse of critical multiculturalism (Ketter & Lewis, 2001; Lewis, Ketter, & Fabos, 2001). As we mentioned in previous chapters, liberal humanism frames issues of difference through a color-blind discourse of racism that suggests "we are all the same" and fails to consider institutional aspects of racism (Bonilla-Silva, 2001). This discourse presumes that racial conflicts stem from racial groups' inability to understand and empathize with different races (Ketter & Lewis, 2001; Lewis, Ketter, & Fabos, 2001, p. 319).

Conversely, a critical multicultural approach frames racism not as a matter of attitudes of individuals but as a function of systemic oppression (Ketter & Lewis, 2001; Lewis, Ketter, & Fabos, 2001). In this approach, individuals reflect on how their constructions of worlds are shaped by discourses and cultural models in ways that limit or promote change (Ketter & Lewis, 2001). Daly (2005) described such a shift as she recounted how the racist practices in her family and her own schooling in the 1950s in North Dakota shut down discussions of racial difference. She recalled that despite the diversity of her classmates:

> Politeness dictated that these ethnic and racial differences should not be mentioned. Such politeness is, as I understand in retrospect, repressive; for one thing, it gave so-called Whites considerable strength of numbers: all those who claimed a White identity did so over and against an Africanist presence. I also learned in school, through an all-White, male literary canon, that Whiteness was the norm. At the same time, because we studied mostly English writers, not Norwegians—Shakespeare, not Ibsen—I learned that the English were, supposedly, superior to Norwegians. This knowledge was conveyed through silences, since our teachers or parents were too "polite" to say such things aloud; therefore, I also learned to keep secret my thoughts on such matters. In short, the silent curriculum in my school taught me that while I was inferior to certain Whites, I was nevertheless part of a superior race. (p. 223)

Rather than openly expressing her emotions about this racial positioning in this culture of silence, Daly both suppressed these emotions as part of being a nice, popular girl, and she projected them onto African Americans. In her testimonial reading, she also discussed how her White identity shaped her responses to British literature in ways that served to reify the superiority of Whiteness within her culture.

Like Daly (2005), students in our study said that they rarely discussed issues of race or White privilege in any courses other than Parks's literature course. Thus, they were largely unaccustomed to engaging in critical

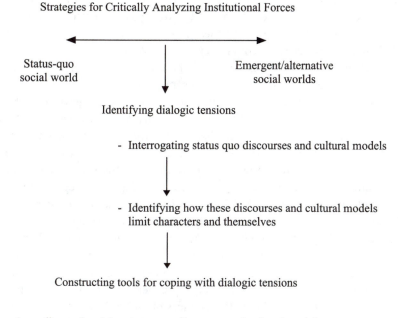

Figure 4.1 Strategies for critically analyzing institutional forces

analysis of institutional forces such as White privilege. During the course of our study our participants learned strategies for engaging in such critical analysis. In this chapter, we describe three basic strategies (illustrated in Figure 4.1) that students used to critique status quo institutional forces portrayed in literature and operating in their own lives: (1) identifying dialogic tensions between status quo social worlds and emergent social worlds; (2) constructing tools for coping with dialogic tensions; and (3) amending and revising status quo discourses and cultural models.

Identifying Dialogic Tensions between Status Quo and Emergent Social Worlds

Recognizing and critiquing the limitations of status quo institutional forces operating in social worlds involves focusing on the dialogic tensions or contradictions created by these status quo forces. Status quo worlds are constituted by what Bakhtin (1981, pp. 136–137) described as authoritative discourses reflected in authoritative voices constituting dominant institutional rules, religion, or traditional authority figures that are opposed to change by voicing internally persuasive discourses that draw on everyday experiences and voices. People and characters experience tensions and contradictions when they adopt these internally persuasive discourses to challenge authoritative discourses, creating dialogic tensions.

Students in our study experienced these dialogic tensions in reading about characters who are caught in contradictory allegiances to competing worlds with contradictory purposes or objects (Engeström, 1987). For example, Esperanza in *The House on Mango Street* (Cisneros, 1991) is caught between wanting to escape her neighborhood world of fixed gender and economic roles yet also feeling compelled to return to the neighborhood that she hopes to change through challenging these fixed gender and economic roles. As Sue noted, characters such as Esperanza represent "a lot of people who broke through the barriers to come back to help their own."

Janie in *Their Eyes Were Watching God* (Hurston, 2000) is caught between having to find and keep a husband for economic survival within a patriarchic social world and developing her own sense of agency as an independent woman. Dana in *Kindred* (Butler, 1979) is caught between understanding her ancestors' heritage by experiencing slavery in a past, historical world and coping with instances of racism inherent in her contemporary world. Bone in *Bastard out of Carolina* (Allison, 1993) is caught between living in a dysfunctional, abusive family and trying to find some alternative world that gives her a sense of hope.

Third-Space Theory of Social Change

From the perspective of third-space theory (Gutierrez, Baquedano-Lopez, & Tejeda, 1999; Soja, 1998), these tensions emanate from conflicts between first-space versions of worlds, or what might be considered the top-down idealized versions of the family or neighborhood social world, and second-space realities of family life or neighborhoods rife with conflict. Third-space worlds represent a bottom-up negotiation between first-space idealized constructions of worlds versus second-space realities and complexities in worlds. Though the students in our study did not explicitly learn to employ this theory, we found it to be useful in analyzing their awareness of disparities between idealized institutional discourses and cultural models versus the complex realities that challenge these discourses and cultural models.

Third-space theory posits that the idealized discourses and cultural models of worlds or institutions—evident in, for example, city planners' concepts for neighborhood redevelopment rarely pan out in reality because they do not take into account the second-space complexities of everyday life—that people in neighborhoods do not always behave in ways that city planners think they do (or should) behave in their idealized plans.

In our study, the students noted tensions between first-space dominant, hegemonic cultural models and the second-space realities of coping with those models. For example, in response to a journal prompt, "What race, gender, appearance, height, religion, sexual preference, or weight would provide the easiest life," Paul, a Latino student, wrote:

> I think the easiest life would probably come from a tall, skinny, straight, Christian, White male. All the other groups are discriminated against like females, minorities, fat people, and homosexuals. [The former] is a model of what every American citizen should be. However, it's not always easier. Minorities are encouraged to be more successful these days in our nation. They receive more money for college and are more easily accepted, so in some ways it is easier but in other ways it isn't. Nobody has an easy life.

Paul contrasted the cultural model of the ideal American citizen with the second-space complex realities of his own life as a Latino student who, despite what he perceived to be some advantages to being a Latino student, posited the difficulties of not being considered an ideal American citizen.

Tensions between top-down idealizations and bottom-up realities result in people learning to create or improvise alternative third-space worlds. Such improvisations were often portrayed in the social worlds of the diverse novels students read in Parks's course. For example, in both *Love Medicine* (Erdrich, 1984) and *A Yellow Raft in Blue Water* (Dorris, 1987) there are dialogic tensions between the first-space Catholic Church's idealized missionary agendas for saving Native Americans versus the second-space realities of Native American's poverty, resentment of American government genocide, and traditional Native American religious beliefs. Out of these tensions emerge some highly compromised alternatives portrayed in the novels in which some practices of the Catholic Church actually assist the Native American characters, whereas in other cases they enable abuse and control of these characters. As mentioned in the previous chapter, when one of the Native American characters in *Love Medicine*, Gerry, is put on trial for beating up a White man, there is a tension between the first-space U.S. justice system that ideally provides for justice for Native Americans and the second-space reality that Native Americans can find little justice in government courts.

We found third-space theory useful for our analysis because it provided a means for understanding students' analysis of conflicts between idealized and actual institutional forces. For example, in responding to Gerry's trial, students argued that he would be convicted because no one—not even his Native American peers—is willing to defend him publicly. However, if he attempts to elude the justice system, he faces even more dire consequences. Given this contradiction, rather than blame Gerry for his dilemma, the students turned their attention to critiquing the systems creating these contradictions. For example, in a discussion of Gerry's trial in *Love Medicine*, Kelly noted:

> During the trial of Gerry. It wasn't a very good trial and it kind of shows, I mean that besides like all the stuff that was said and everything, but it was just like how they were talking about how they held the trial during pow-wow times and it was like and all of his witnesses were gone and they didn't have phone numbers and stuff. I don't know, it seemed really biased to me ...

Parks: ... Talk about that: "biased."

Jill: It's they didn't say anything about the judge, but the people, like the White guy that he beat up, the cowboy had all of his witnesses and that they had names and phone number and addresses and that the native American people didn't, and that they were gone and they held it during pow-wow time when they are definitely gone and they are off someplace else doing like their cultural stuff. I don't know, it just didn't seem fair. They were ... well, he had witnesses, but they couldn't find them and the one that he did have wasn't a very good one. It just didn't seem fair at all.

Parks: Oh, that the course system was biased against Gerry? Not getting a fair trial?

Jill: Yeah, I don't think it was a fair trial. If it was me in that position, I would want people to read this book because it shows how the court system is biased against Native Americans.

In discussing this trial, Jill identified dialogic tensions between how a fair trial should operate and how the trial is actually biased against Native Americans, noting that the testimony in the trial excluded Native American witnesses. She therefore framed the tensions not just as interpersonal conflicts but rather as associated with institutional racism toward Native Americans based on a justice system that perpetuates White privilege.

Jill's identification of competing cultural systems was a significant move away from a focus on the culpability of individual actors. She recognizes that the official first-space notions of fairness operating in the legal system do not apply to Native Americans, leading her to identify contradictions between the notion of a just legal system and Gerry's unjust, biased trial that functioned to perpetuate the system of White control operating in the social worlds portrayed in *Love Medicine*.

A related shift in perspectives occurred in a six-year study of a group of eight middle-school teachers who discussed multicultural literature in a book-club setting within the context of a rural, largely White Iowa community (Ketter & Lewis, 2001; Lewis, 2004; Lewis, Ketter, & Fabos, 2001). In the beginning of their book club, most of these teachers adopted what we previously referred to as a discourse of liberal humanism, in which characters that differ by race, class, and gender were constructed as individual people who were perceived to share the same values. For example, one teacher, Barb, responding to a Black character mistakenly shot by the police, framed this shooting as resulting from the characters' own actions, as opposed to the influence of a racist institutional structure. This teacher adopted a color-blind racist discourse that assumes that skin color is an arbitrary marker of identity. This discourse was also evident in her use of a classroom activity in which students stood in a circle and revealed the skin color of their arms to demonstrate that none of them was actually White in color. The researchers noted that Barb's responses reflected her positioning within her largely White community's culture in which Whiteness was the normative, hegemonic discourse.

On the other hand, some teachers, over time, moved toward adopting a discourse of critical multiculturalism and were more likely to explain characters' actions in terms of larger institutional forces related to race, class, and gender differences. For example, Barb, who framed the shooting of the Black character in individualistic terms, momentarily shifted to consider the fact that if the character had been White, then the police might not have shot him, a perspective voiced by other participants that considers race as the key factor in explaining the shooting.

Our participants voiced a related awareness of how governmental institutions employed power to limit or repress change. In reaction to a discussion of East St. Louis in excerpts from Kozol's (1992) *Savage Inequalities,* Sue posited that the use of police in that community was designed to protect status quo interests and to "protect wealth. In this way, they used their power to serve those with money and keep those without in prison. This is a repressive force, because it hinders change." She also noted that because there are two justice systems—"one for the not poor and for the poor"—the poor had little protection against the police force.

The students also identified a number of tensions between first-space notions of the ideal or normal family and the portrayals of dysfunctional families in the novels. Sue said that she initially considered the Weylins, the slave owners in *Kindred,* to be normal but then realized that they were dysfunctional and "not normal because of the way that Mr. Weylin wanted Rufus to take control of the plantation or whatever. Martha Weylin ... had issues too, like just the fact that I think Mr. Weylin slept with a slave ... So that family was really twisted too. I mean none of the other books were the families perfect too. There was always something."

Kathy posited that the same power tensions operate in Dana and Kevin's marriage, noting that when both Dana and Kevin return to the plantation Kevin receives preferential treatment and does not object to their living arrangements:

> He's put into like this huge room, and Dana's the cook in the slave quarters, and when it first happened he doesn't have a problem with her going there to and he says you know, "Come in my room and stuff," so why doesn't he just say, "Oh no, she's gonna stay with me."

Analyses such as this can lead students to interrogate their own notions of what constitutes a first-space ideal or normal family. Based on their experiences with characters' competing perspectives regarding what could be considered normal, they challenged idealizations of families, where, as Kayla said, "There is nothing wrong and nobody ever fights. Nobody is mad at each other but is just happy." She noted that though others may perceive a family to be normal, as was the case with the Boatwrights in *Bastard out of Carolina*, "there is always something wrong significantly with one person at least." Arguing that "there is no such thing as a Beaver Cleaver family," Michelle argued, "You need some problems in order to have a healthy family. Because if you never fought, it just wouldn't be right you know."

Students also explored the idea that once a character assumes that her dysfunctional family represents the norm, she may then believe that there is little hope to change her family. Kathy explained that because Bone has few role models of success in her life, she may believe that her abusive family is normal. She said:

> Her mom and her aunt and like nobody, she has not seen anyone who has actually made it out of everything. So, people have it that way where their whole family, I mean, you have relatives who have come back to the same life and you're thinking, "Oh, I'll never get out" like, after a while it just become the norm. You don't want nothing else but just to be where you are. You say, "I will be happy where I am." So, I'm not going out there and coming back again.

Students also debated the influence of single-parent families on characters. Sue argued that in *A Yellow Raft in Blue Water*, which portrays three different generations of Native American women—a substitute grandmother (Ida) who raised Christine to cover for the biological mother and Christine's daughter (Rayona)—"they are single parents; that is why they are so dysfunctional. It is not a stable family … Christine never knew her father and Ida is stuck in this situation where like her son she you know had to deal with a son that just passed away." Drawing on her own experiences with a single mother, Kayla argued that single-parent families are not necessarily dysfunctional, noting that much of their success depends on economic factors.

The students also discussed how the class system functioned to limit characters. As Mitch noted, Bone was continually positioned as "White trash," a category that marked her as "the other" in juxtaposition to the middle class. In these discussions students critiqued institutional uses of language to perpetuate status quo practices. For example, Dan highlighted the rhetorical uses of categories in a book excerpt (Reiman, 1995) about class differences and the justice system in which the wealthy receive shorter prison sentences at better facilities even as they are sentenced less often:

> The fact that someone's economic status determines how they get "punished" is a complete and utter travesty. In the article, rich people who commit crimes are called 'white-collar criminals (p. 89), which is an obvious degradation to people who consider themselves white-collar. Being associated with the word "poor" just appalls people who look at the "poor" as criminals. Same goes with "white-collar criminals."

In his analysis, Dan analyzed how categories such as *poor* and *White-collar criminals* mediate perceptions of criminals in ways that privilege the wealthy over the poor within the justice system. Examining how these categories privilege certain groups over others led Dan to understand how language functions to perpetuate this system.

Students also identified how these idealized notions and categories are constructed by institutions. In responding to *Bless Me, Ultima*, (Anaya, 1995) they argued that the characters' notions of gender differences were related to norms and beliefs in the Catholic Church that served to privilege males over females. For example, Sue noted that in the novel:

> Women are expected to be strong and faithful believers. The men on the other hand can basically do whatever they want and everyone would say that's okay…yet when the women don't follow church rules or they don't go to church at all, they are branded as evil and witches. When men don't go to church, they aren't called evil or a witch, they are called non-believers. I think that it's just wrong for the people to judge the women more harshly than they would judge the men.

Sue's analysis points to disparities between the first-space idealized expectations for all members of the Catholic Church and the second-space reality that men often do not follow these expectations yet suffer none of the social consequences faced by women who do not follow these expectations.

Students noted that these disparate expectations created some third-space resistance to these various contradictions. For example, students noticed that Ultima, a central character in the novel, does not conform to the traditional gender role expectations for women, creating her own third-space resistance by drawing on both female and male social practices. In the novel, Ultima is an elderly healer and spiritual mentor for Antonio. Though she is not recognized as legitimate by the Catholic Church, she draws on both Catholic and indigenous spiritual beliefs and attends church on a regular basis. She teaches Antonio the importance of an open-minded tolerance for others. Dan said the following about Ultima: "Ultima is like a priest: She falls between gender roles. She is free to play the role of the man in times of conflict and trouble. She is like a gender-free role model for both men and women who long for change."

In this analysis, Dan posited that because Ultima falls between gender roles, she can play the role of the man. She functions as an alternative to the traditional gender roles in the novel, serving as a third-space option for men and women who long for change in the ways these role definitions limited their lives.

These students therefore recognized how idealized notions of family, social class, and gender roles functioned to limit characters' development of agency. In the case of Ultima, they also recognized the fact that characters are sometimes able to entertain alternative third-space practices that challenge such idealized notions.

Identifying second-space tensions through writing and discussion of text worlds often provided students with tools for identifying tensions in their lived worlds. Kathy argued that when her family moved to the United States, it was her understanding that being middle class was the norm. In a discussion, she then posed the question, "What does it mean to be a middle-class person? I really don't get it. Does the person have one car less than the other person [upper] who is not middle class? I don't get it." Kayla responded by defining "middle-class" as "making ends meet to live … comfortably." However, Michelle complicated these conceptions by noting that middle-class people begin with certain advantages that poor people lack in terms of acquiring higher education. She argued that being middle class functions as an exclusive versus inclusive notion given the difficulty that those outside of the middle class have accessing higher education.

Some of the students noted contradictions between the idealized discourses of Thompson High School as devoted to achievement and the realities of the lack of intellectual challenge in most classes. Kayla criticized the limited academic opportunities at Thompson High School as a world limited by a focus on control and discipline. She was therefore highly engaged with Parks's course, which offered college credit and hoped that she could be admitted to a competitive college, despite her perception of her high school courses as providing inadequate preparation for college. In comparison to her former suburban high school:

> I think Thompson as a whole is a really easy school ... and I get bored ... I feel like my, my brain, my knowledge power that I have in a sense is going to waste ... going from here to out there was a big jump you know. I had to work so much harder out there, and yet I mean it was still not extremely hard, it was just regular hard I guess [laughs]. And then I come back here from out there, and it's so easy. It's like easier than before because I had to come up to a certain level.

For Kayla, Parks's course represented a third-space compromise that provided her with some preparation for college work despite the limitations of her other classes. Kayla could have simply blamed herself for being bored with high school. Rather than focusing on herself, Kayla focused on the limitations of the high school's institutional practices in limiting her potential.

Analyzing the Influence of Institutional Forces on Characters and Students

In analyzing the influence of idealized first-space institutional forces on characters, the students recognized how these forces were operating to limit characters' sense of agency. This involved tracking characters' growing awareness of how their potential development was being limited by institutional forces, leading them to take action against these forces.

Shifting from First-Person to Third-Person Reflection

One way of defining this growing awareness is in terms of a shift from first-person to third-person reflection in which a person perceives herself as not as an subject operating in an institution but rather as an object constructed and limited by status quo systems (Beach & Spicer, 2004; Kegan, 1994, 2000). For instance, Kayla was able to perceive herself as the object of a system that is limiting and contradictory when she stepped back and recognized that she needed to succeed in high school to attend college, even though her high school courses were not providing adequate college preparation. As Roth, Hwang, Goulart, and Lee (2005, p. 91) noted:

> This stepping back constitutes a conversion from a direct, unmediated relation with the lifeworld to an indirect, objectifying, and objectified relation (Buber, 1970). The conversion is constituted by the change of view from the first person to a (quasi-) third person; that is, it is constituted by a change from the mere experience of resistance

of an individual subject to the idealized perception of a contradiction from a generalized and generalizing perspective of the collective.

Engeström (1987, Ch. 3, p. 8) described this shift as moving from perceiving the self as subject to the self as object shaped by a system: "What was 'subject'—the self experiencing the contradictions—becomes 'object'—a stance through which the object system is seen as containing the subject within it. The person gains an awareness of whole systems of activity in terms of systems' past, the present, and the future." This shift in perception from first-person subject to third-person object often serves as the basis for portrayals of character's narrative development in literature. Characters are often initially congruent with their social worlds but, in perceiving themselves as the object of those worlds, become increasingly aware of the limitations of those worlds. Shifting from subject to object leads them to consider and possibly to challenge the discourses and cultural models constituting their identities, leading to construction of new worlds and a rearticulation and resituation of the self (Lewis, 2004).

Kegan (2000) illustrated this shift from subject to object in literature with the example of Henrik Ibsen's (1992) *A Doll's House*. In the play, Nora's husband's, Torvald, attempts to maintain control of his wife, reflecting his allegiance to patriarchic systems and traditional family roles in the late 1800s. In the beginning of the play, Nora assumes a subservient, childlike identity. However, after a series of miscommunications and misunderstandings that lead to her husband forbidding her to visit her own children, Nora begins to perceive herself as object of the patriarchic system. Unable to accept such an arrangement, Nora tells her husband that she is leaving him. Torvald then implores her to recall her "sacred duties...toward your husband, and your children" (p. 61). She replies, "I'm no longer prepared to accept what people say and what's written in books. I must think things out for myself, and try to find my own answer" (ibid).

Kegan (2000, p. 67) argued that this is more than simply Nora "changing her mind." Nora has come to "a new set of ideas about her ideas, about where they even come from, about who authorizes them or makes them true (ibid.). In this sense, she is no longer subject to others' definitions of sacred duties. These changes also involve more than simply adopting a different way of knowing. They involve "being someone different—the Nora at the end of *A Doll's House* who has the temerity to call her 'sacred duties' into question" (p. 68). Nora recognizes how a patriarchic system, as mediated by Torvald's patriarchic discourses and cultural models, positioned her as subordinate as the object of that system.

In recognizing themselves as the object of systems, characters also realize how they are positioned by dominate authoritative voices to assume subordinate roles undermining their sense of agency. In Nora's case, deconstructing Torvald's authoritative voices constituting patriarchic discourses and cultural models leads her to develop internally persuasive voices (Bakhtin, 1981) based on defining her sense of agency as an independent female (Kegan, 2000).

However, many of the characters the students encountered lacked Nora's ability to perceive herself as positioned as objects by her social worlds, leaving these characters unable to challenge status quo institutional forces. These characters then remain stuck in status quo worlds with no way of challenging or changing those worlds. Sue noted that in *Kindred*:

> Rufus was going through so much because he didn't, he was stuck between two worlds through Dana and his father and like he didn't know what to do—how to accept slavery but not accept slavery because he is White and says that and well just society in the 1800's being racist was just expected. But he was stuck between Dana's world and he didn't know what to do so.

On the other hand, some of the characters were able to challenge status quo forces. Students were aware of Bone's increasing resistance to dominant patriarchic discourses. They also noted that she was increasingly aware of how class hierarchies repressed her and her family. In his analysis of the novel, Mitch noted the power of such systems in both Bone's life and that of Daddy Glen. In a journal entry, he noted how Bone becomes aware of her family's poverty:

> Bone recognizes that her family is more poor than the other people at church and school ... On p. 66, she says, "just for a change, I wished we could have things like other people, wished we could complain for no reason but the pleasure of bitching and act like the trash we were supposed to be," her mom making a big effort to not be identified as "trashy," but Bone still picks things up and starts believing she is. Later on p. 82, her mom's explaining to Bone, "we're not bad people. We're not really even poor." But Bone says "we knew what the neighbors called us, what Mama wanted to protect us from. We knew who we were." This is where she first makes the distinction between who she's "supposed to be" and who she "is" in terms of her social class.

Mitch charted how Bone moves from a first- to a third-person awareness of the effects of poverty and the negative perceptions of others on her identity, leading him to make the distinction between who she's supposed to be in idealized middle-class cultural models as opposed to who she is: poor. He inferred that Bone is aware of how these notions of class differences position her in negative ways.

Mitch also considered how Daddy Glen perceives himself and is perceived by others as a failure because he was born into wealth but moved backward in the town's social class hierarchy by marrying into the Boatwright family:

> Daddy Glen complains, "nobody wants me to have nothing nice." Daddy Glen is basically an outcast because he associates with the Boatwrights [Bone's family] … I think the difference between Daddy Glen and Bone is Bone has lived in poverty since birth and so she as a default sees herself as poor, and Daddy Glen came from a wealthy family, so he doesn't think that he's "good enough" because he's trying to live up to expectations.

Finally, Mitch argued that Daddy Glen realizes he is a victim of the class system but that, given his lack of power within the larger system, he asserts his power within his family through abuse of Bone—turning his anger inward to his family rather than challenging the system. As Mitch noted, "He's got to find a way to deal with his frustration, so he turns to the only thing he knows to empower himself, and that is to victimize Bone."

Mitch therefore framed his analysis of these characters not simply in terms of individual traits and beliefs but also in terms of institutional forces of class differences. He attributed some of this critique to his brother, who he said helped him "see poverty as a problem of society. I don't think of poor people so much as I do poverty and the injustice inherent in it." The fact that Mitch perceived individuals not simply as poor but rather as shaped by poverty and the injustice inherent in it represents his ability examine the influence of institutional forces.

Constructing Tools for Coping with Dialogic Tensions

As students shift from first- to third-person perspectives and are able to identify the institutional forces contributing to tensions in text and lived worlds, they need to acquire tools such as alternative third-space discourses, cultural models, and narratives that will allow them to cope with these tensions. Engeström (1987, p. 11) cited the example of Huck Finn, who, as a vagabond in a small, segregated town, is friends with both the middle-class Tom Sawyer, and also with the Black slave Jim, symbolic representations of two competing systems creating contradictory allegiances for Huck between "the private freedom of the individual vagabond and the public unfreedom prevailing in the vagabond's immediate cultural context." Huck could simply continue to operate as an individual vagabond in resistance to Tom Sawyer's middle-class world, or he could address the moral issues of slavery and racism operating in that world. In escaping on the raft with Jim, Huck faces another choice between having to lie to those pursuing escaped slaves to protect Jim, and his moral obligation to support Jim's attempt to become free, creating a double bind. Caught in this contradictory situation, Huck creates a new, alternative system by imagining an alternative narrative in which he saves Jim. He also employs language to trick those who are attempting to capture Jim and himself. Engeström noted that through these actions, Huck is creating a new activity of "radical moral anarchism" involving "a deadly serious moral and existential struggle" (p. 14). Huck is therefore employing the tools of discourses and narratives of racial integration to reject the segregated society and to construct a new, alternative world.

In responding to the novels in the course, students in our study noted instances in which the characters in the novels employed their own tools for creating new, alternative identities and worlds. For example, in *Their Eyes Were Watching God*, Janie suffers from subjugation to the domineering Joe Starks, who regularly silences and marginalizes her. As Joe ages and becomes ill, he also becomes more controlling. In a central scene that takes place in the store Joe and Janie operate, Joe publicly chides Janie for her incompetence and her aging body. However, Janie retaliates by telling the male customers Joe is impotent, a counternarrative that leads to Joe's public humiliation. Later, addressing Joe at his deathbed, as did Nora, she tells him that she rejects the role of being his obedient wife. After Joe's death, she establishes a relationship with Tea Cake, one that provides her with a genuine experience of agency in a marriage relationship.

Janie's rejection of Joe represents a rejection of a patriarchic system in which she had to marry Joe to survive. The students noted that Janie married Joe even through she did not necessarily love him, given the economic necessity of marriage in a patriarchic system. They also noted that Janie eventually realizes that having to marry simply for economic necessity positioned her as the object of this system, leading her to an alternative need to establish a marriage relationship based on love.

The students also noted how characters create new, alternative worlds through the use of literacy tools such as reading or writing. In discussing a transcript of an interview with *Bastard out of Carolina* author Dorothy Allison (Strong, 2001), Mitch noted that both Dorothy and Bone turned to books as a means of coping with poverty, reading that provided them with alternative narratives for coping with their impoverished home environments. He noted that Bone's mother's in the novel encouraged her to read: "Mom didn't make me save for clothes, but let me spend as I pleased mostly on secondhand books...." (Allison, 1993, p. 56) He also cited Allison's discussion of the way that reading led her to see the need to address the possibility of justice for even the poorest segments of society.

Mitch also cited the ways in which music and the messages in gospel lyrics served as tools for Bone to redefine her identity "'because it suggests God can forgive, but he can also judge.' The language and messages of gospel music provided Bone with an alternative world in which ethics and morality can exist, a world in which justice can prevail, allowing Daddy Glen to be judged negatively and her Aunt Raylene to be judged positively." Similarly, Pat described how music functioned as "a metaphor for Bone and her secret ambition … to sing through all of the crap in her life and have everyone hear her while she is doing it."

Students also described the ways reading assumed as a tool for change in *Kindred*. They noted that Tom Weylin encouraged Kevin and Dana to read to his son but opposed the idea of having his slaves learn to read because, as Michelle noted, "He doesn't like 'my slaves will be educated,' cause it said earlier in the book if you have educated slaves they get away more easily by writing passes for themselves." Kayla also argued that Weylin was not only resentful of the fact that Dana was a reader but also that his wife was also a reader, which meant that "she had more power in some different way than him."

Just as students described characters' uses of tools to challenge and change social worlds, they also cited instances in which they used certain tools to change their own worlds. After living on his own, spending time in juvenile detention, and having little contact with his father, Troy found a supportive environment in the church that "showed me that there are infinite possibilities in life and that more than anything knowledge is power." Troy explained that his faith was not about following a religion or rules but was about more honest relationships with others and with God: "The older I get, the more I realize the power and the miracles that come out of the relationships." Such an alternative space allowed Troy to find increased hope in the midst of tough situations. He said, "I'm more honest," and he emphasized truth and love for other people, dispositions he practiced during numerous mission trips with his youth group friends.

Amending and Revising Status Quo Discourses, Cultural Models, and Narratives

From engaging in critical analysis of institutional forces over the six-month period, some students in our study began to amend or revise some of their status quo discourses, cultural models, and narratives, as opposed to adopting totally new discourses and cultural models.

As we discuss in more detail in Chapter 6, some of the students demonstrated little change in responding to the dialogic tensions in literature, in part because they were strongly wedded to their status quo discourses and cultural models. The adherence that these students had to status quo discourses may have been related to their emotional attachment to or desires for certain discourses. In our study, the students who resisted change were those most likely to subscribe to familiar, monologic discourses of masculinity and femininity that afforded them with a sense of certainty, mitigating against their need to amend or revise these discourses. Alcorn (2002, p. 98) argued that people who adopt certain definite, bed-rock, fixed discourses are not likely to be changed through rational debate or competing discourses; they may only change if they desire some change in themselves: "A new discourse will effect a change only if the subjects desire and make use of this discourse. Real change requires not the discourse production of new knowledge [as discourse] but a certain mobility in desire."

For Alcorn (2002), desire creates a dialectical conflict related to a demand for a better symbolic representation of the world and one's identity. This dialectical conflict stands in opposition to what Lacan (1978) described as the master discourse—the need for an authority figure in the form of political or religious leader, for example, who provides people with a sense of certainty. One of the subjective appeals of a master discourse is that it provides a ready-made alignment to a community of similarly devoted members. People then define their identities as loyal followers of the leader or authority figure who fulfills their desires for an identity constituted by a set of nondialectical, fixed beliefs.

In our study, we were particularly interested in how and why some of the White working-class males such as Troy and Corey subscribed to discourses of individualism and meritocracy reflected in their opposition to affirmative action and political correctness. One explanation of their adoption of these discourses is the larger emotional appeal of a master discourse of Whiteness in opposition to threats to the assumed power of White males in politics, business, and other segments of society (Keating, 1995, 2004; Roediger, 2002). Based on her research on White college students' resistance to discussing race, Trainor (2002, 2005) argued for the need to examine the emotional appeal of a discourse of White privilege, an appeal related to both the "rational and the irrational, the conscious and the unconscious, thought and feeling" (2002, p. 637). She cited a study of White college students (Gallagher, 1997) that demonstrates the emotional appeal of a Whites-as-victim theme as a rallying cry for group identification with others who share this discourse (Trainor, 2005).

As previously noted, during the past 40 years, conservative politicians have adopted political appeals to White working-class males' anger over the presumed loss of jobs due to affirmative action programs (Frank, 2004; Roediger, 2002), whereas the actual cause of the loss of well-paying jobs is related to a shift of manufacturing jobs to other countries, the decline of unions, the lack of job training, stagnate wages, and reductions in employer health care (Frank, 2004).

Analysis of the 2004 Pew data on political attitudes pointed to sharp gender differences for people the analysts identified as Libertarian—people who oppose government intervention in economic areas (Keeter & Smith, 2006). Within this group, 59% are males, whereas 41% are females; many of these males are young people who did not graduate from high school. A 2003 Quinnipiac University Poll found that 55% of males versus 44% of females oppose affirmative action; in the state of New Jersey, 68% of Whites oppose affirmative action compared to 21% of Blacks (Quinnipiac University Polling Institute, 2003). These survey results indicate that the appeal of opposition to affirmative action programs is relatively high for White males, suggesting the emotional appeal of a discourse of individualism in opposition to discourses of collective political action.

Trainor (2002, 2005) argued for the need to recognize the emotional appeal of these discourses of White privilege as tools for diverting attention from the realities of the economic system. In our study, students who demonstrated little change consistently adhered to a discourse of White privilege. One reason for their steadfast allegiance to this discourse was its emotional appeal as reifying their sense of power, which they perceived to be under threat by affirmative action programs. Given these potential threats, these students gravitated toward emotional appeals voiced in their family and community about the need to protect themselves from affirmative action programs. For example, Corey, a White male, voiced opposition to affirmative action programs because, since he wanted to go into law enforcement, his understanding was that he would be discriminated against in getting a job because of affirmative action mandates to hire people of color.

The students who resisted entertaining alternative discourses and cultural models often responded positively to the sense of monologic, definitive certainty inherent in the notion that, given their White privilege and status, their positions must be the correct positions (Barnett, 2000). Students such as Corey therefore had difficulty entertaining counterevidence challenging the institutional racism and advocating for affirmative actions programs. For example, when noting that police officers were more likely to release minority drivers without a ticket at much higher rates than White drivers, Corey saw these statistics as evidence of reverse discrimination against Whites rather than the practices of police officers stopping persons of color without valid reasons.

On the other hand, as we discuss in Chapters 7 and 10, other White males such as Devin and Troy, as well as White female students who subscribed to discourses of individualism and meritocracy toward the end of the course, began to challenge the appeal of the master discourse of Whiteness. Through discussions of how different characters were positioned by dominant discourses limiting their sense of agency, these students began to challenge some of the ways institutional forces function to limit people's agency in lived-world contexts, for example, noting how African Americans in East St. Louis or Native Americans in these students' state are limited by systemic forces of poverty and discrimination. They also began to realize the ways White privilege functions in everyday life as a political force. These White students began to interrogate the powerful political appeal of a master discourse of Whiteness, leading them to amend or revise their adherence to discourses or individualism and meritocracy, shifts that point to the value of engaging these students in discussions of characters' challenging status quo systems in multicultural literature.

Summary

In this chapter, we described students' responses to characters coping with dialogic tensions related to their competing allegiances to different social worlds portrayed in literature. For example, in response to *Kindred*, students identified tensions that Dana negotiated between competing allegiances to save her ancestors and combat racism. By defining the norms operating in these novels' text worlds, students were able to go beyond perceiving characters simply as individual persons to focusing on institutional forces shaping their practices.

Once they identified the dialogic tensions facing characters, they then focused on characters' use of tools to cope with these tensions through imagining or creating new, alternative social worlds—tools such as language, discourses, reading, or music—that provide different perspectives on status quo institutional forces.

From discussing characters coping with status quo discourses, cultural models, and narratives, some students began to interrogate, amend, and revise their status quo discourses, cultural models, and narratives. Students who demonstrated these shifts were willing to entertain alternative perspectives leading them to adopt a critical multiculturalist critique of institutional forces related to race, class, and gender differences, resulting in shifts in understanding of issues such as affirmative action.

Shifts in students' language use, as well as in their ability to take perspectives and to voice alternative discourses, suggest the value of instruction in multicultural literature in leading students to interrogate their status quo beliefs and attitudes. Though they may not have demonstrated consistent shifts in their beliefs and attitudes (Pace, 2003), they did learn to focus on how institutional and historical forces shape characters' and people's lives. And from grappling with dialogic tensions in texts, they learned to be more open to adopting different perspectives in analyzing issues in their own social worlds.

All this suggests that experiencing dialogic tensions and alternative perspectives in literary worlds can lead to shifts in allegiances to status-quo discourses. However, the shifts students in our study were able to make were fostered by more than simply reading the literature. They were also fostered by various activities employed by Parks as well as challenges from peers in discussions.

In the next chapter, we describe Parks's use of instructional techniques to foster dialogic tensions in the classroom. To illustrate the influence of these techniques on students, we provide some case-study descriptions of students in Chapters 6, 7, and 8. Some of these students demonstrated little change, whereas others experienced greater shifts. And in Chapter 9 we discuss how dialogic tensions between students in classroom discussions served to foster change.

CHAPTER 5

Parks's Methods for Teaching Multicultural Literature

In the previous chapter, we discussed the ways students in our study experimented with adopting different stances and roles in a course on multicultural literature. In this chapter, we explore the techniques employed by the teacher, Daryl Parks, in not only fostering students' responses to multicultural literature but also in socializing high school students to assume the identities of college students engaged in critical analysis of literature. In any classroom community of practice, the teacher assumes a central role in helping students acquire new practices and discourses through modeling and scaffolding these practices (Edelsky, Smith, & Wolfe, 2002; Wenger, 1998). Parks played a somewhat unusual role in that he mentored students operating in a relatively controlled, traditional high school world to adopt unfamiliar, new identities associated with being college students. And he also assumed a key role in helping students with little experience in critical literary analysis to acquire such approaches to analyzing literature. Further, given the challenges of entering into alternative cultural worlds in responding to multicultural literature, Parks provided students with ways of understanding different cultural perspectives as constituted by discourses and cultural models of race, class, and gender.

Parks's Participation in the College in the Schools Program

One of the major problems with teaching multicultural literature from a critical perspective is that even though many teachers may subscribe to the value of multicultural education, many White teachers lack the training or commitment to engage students in critical analysis of issues of race. One survey by Harris Interactive found that although teachers believe the integration of schools is important, only 44% of White teachers believe that diverse classes improve student learning, compared to 67% of Black and 54% of Hispanic teachers (Reid, 2004). White teachers were also less likely to critique the school and teachers in contributing to the achievement gap between White students and students of color. Rather, they were more likely to attribute this gap to families or individual students, while Black and Hispanic teachers attributed the gap to low teacher expectations and lack of access to challenging coursework (Reid, 2004). And White teachers often also equate academic ability with a middle-class background, whereas a working-class background is perceived to create obstacles to achieving academic success (Morris, 2005).

Even when teachers attempt to address issues of diversity in the classroom, they experience difficulty fostering productive discussions about issues of race, class, and gender difference (Kumashiro, 2000; Tatum, 2003). One study of a White, male university instructor who employed a multicultural curriculum that included the sharing of narratives about race found that his students' racist perspectives ossified during the course (Fishman & McCarthy, 2005). One reason for this was the instructor did not share reflections on his own White biases; he also did not contextualize the students' stories in terms of the contemporary debates about race and White privilege.

In contrast to teachers who lack training in multicultural literature instruction, it is important to note that Parks's teaching methods described in this chapter were the result not only of his experiences in his teacher education master's program and his work in a doctoral program but also of his participation in the College in the Schools (CIS) program at the local university, which sponsored the program and the course. Because the students received college credit from this university, the university believed they needed to ensure that instructors of the courses they sponsored were receiving support in college-level methods of teaching. We describe the specific aspects of this program because we believe this program represents the kind of in-service program that could better prepare high school literature teachers to address some of the issues associated with teaching multicultural literature identified in this chapter.

To participate in the CIS program, high school teachers are interviewed by university faculty and, if approved, are appointed as teaching specialists at the university. Teaching specialists need to have a minimum of three years of teaching experience, graduate-level course work in literature, and a familiarity with and interest in multicultural literature. Course instructors are encouraged to teach multicultural texts chosen from a list of recommended books (see Appendix B); instructors can also select other alternative books.

As part of the program, instructors attend meetings during the year and an intensive training program in the summer organized by the university faculty coordinator, who is a literature professor in the university's English Department. Instructors receive articles and resources on teaching multicultural literature at these meetings. In reflecting on his participation in this program, Parks noted the value of receiving literary critical analysis articles about the texts he was teaching as well as essays appropriate for use with his students.

Challenges Involved in Teaching Multicultural Literature

In teaching multicultural literature, teachers like Parks face a number challenges in attempting to foster high school students' critical analysis skills. One challenge in teaching multicultural literature is that students often assume, based on previous experience, that multicultural literature is being used to further an agenda of addressing students' assumed prejudices (Blake, 1998; Fecho, 1998; Kumashiro, 2000; Smith & Strickland, 2001; Vinz, Gordon, Lundgren, LaMontagne, & Hamilton, 2000). White students may resent what they perceive a challenge to their White privileges and therefore may adopt race-talk discourses to avoid being perceived as racist (Beach, 1997a, 1997b; Bolgatz, 2005; Trainor, 2002, 2005). As previously noted, students are particularly likely to resist such instruction if teachers adopt a human relations agenda designed to enlighten students about the limitations of their individual prejudices or attitudes. Such an agenda reflects a liberal humanism assumption that students' responses to multicultural literature simply reflect individual differences beliefs and attitudes, as opposed to larger institutional forces (Beach, 1997b; Lewis, Ketter, & Fabos, 2001). This discourse that "we are all the same" emphasizes the importance of shared human values and concerns as opposed to examining differences and conflicts related to issues of oppression and racism.

One approach to addressing this issue is to have students, particularly White students, examine how language or narratives are used to keep people safe in specific, local, social relationships. In her teaching, Winans (2005) helped students critically examine assumptions inherent in narratives of color-blindness that reify racism as individual prejudice. At the same time, she remained sensitive to White students' fears about being perceived as racist. Winans's students examined writers' autobiographical narratives about race to highlight the ambiguities and contradictions in their own experiences of constructing and coping with race. For example, in responding to James McBride's (1996, p. 29) *The Color of Water: A Black Man's Tribute to His White Mother,* she asked students to explore the contradictions associated with being the mother of 12 biracial children that are evident in quotes from the text such as the following:

> Mommy's contradictions crashed and slammed against one another like bumper cars at Coney Island. White folks, she felt, were implicitly evil toward Blacks, yet she forced us to go to White schools to get the best education. Blacks could be trusted more, but anything involving Blacks was probably slightly substandard.

In discussing the mother's color-blindness, Winans' (2005) students explored the limitations and contradictions associated with color-blindness, and they discussed how being a White person can be distinguished from White privilege. Noting that McBride's mother was White, the students recognized that she did not necessarily subscribe to White privilege. In her teaching, Winans avoided attributions of

> innocence and guilt [that] offer false resolutions that misrepresent the complexities of students' experiences [by] seeking to understand the consequences of our actions and responding accordingly, then we are freed to explore students' narratives of those experiences rather than facing, confronting, and rediscovering "correct" conclusions. (p. 272)

Another approach to avoiding didacticism involves examining the limitations of a shared we-are-all-the-same discourse often evoked in teaching multicultural literature. In her study of four White teachers' beliefs about teaching multicultural literature in a small rural Minnesota town with largely White students, Leer (2003) found that the teachers differed in the degree to which they perceived multicultural literature as reflecting culturally unique themes as opposed to universal themes of shared humanity. Whereas some teachers focused on cultural similarities, others believed in the value of exposing students to cultural differences. One of these teachers noted that students need to be exposed to alternative cultural perspectives so that they do not lapse into a similarity approach to justify racist points of view and close themselves off from deeper understanding:

> When I teach [*The Lone Ranger and Tonto Fistfight in Heaven*] and talk about Native American culture, students always talk about how "lucky" Native Americans are because they get so many special privileges—free land, they don't pay taxes, lots of casino money, no hunting and fishing regulations. They say, "If we're so similar, how come they get all these benefits that I don't?" (p. 95).

The alternative of focusing on cultural differences requires that teachers go beyond creating an illusionary "safe" classroom space to recognize the need to create a contested space (Powers, 2002). Baszile (2003, p. 31) argued for the need to address racial difference and conflicts given her belief that:

> Racism is not only an institutional phenomena, it also an inter/intra personal one. To act as if my experiences are irrelevant is to allow many students to remain too comfortable, to obfuscate my complexity as a person and to reinforce the idea that race and racism is simply about respecting difference. The question, for me then is not whether to include my experiences, but how do I engage students critically and responsibly. Knowing that I am the first and for many the only encounter with a Black female professor, I have come to understand that I am myself a counter hegemonic text, a living oppositional framework and as such a subject of study by the students.

Without addressing these issues, Baszile (2003) found that her White students resorted to silence for fear of being perceived as racist. This silence was read by students of color as an implicit admission of racism, creating frustrations for these students who then themselves became silent. The result was that none of her participants were willing to publicly address issues of race. Based on an analysis of group discussions of 25 White women, Trepagnier (2001, p. 143) found that:

> With one exception, the participants in this study did not defend White privilege, and yet almost all of them exhibited silent racism ... both silent racism and White privilege emerge from a sense of group position and therefore are characterized by power. They expected that they should not have to reveal knowledge about themselves even as they desired and expected the nonwhite students ... to put it all out on the table, to lay open to scrutiny all knowledge about themselves.... And further, many of the White students thought that they should be able to react with indignation and frustration when the nonwhite students did not yield knowledge about themselves, or at least did not reveal the kind of knowledge that the White students expected.

While students of color may share their experiences, White students' failure to share their experiences with White privilege leaves discourses of Whiteness unchallenged. Keeping silent serves to reify the power of White students, who assume that there is no urgent need to voice their opinions, particularly if those opinions will be challenged by peers.

In reflecting on his role related to interrogating students' discourses of race, class, and gender, Parks recognized the challenges of adopting an agenda perceived by students as attempting to change their attitudes (Beach, 1997b; Trainor, 2002, 2005). Parks was therefore very cautious in how he framed his agenda. "I'm very careful in how I present myself. I know that if I share all of the racism I've seen in society, that many students will shut me out." He noted the difficulty his White students experienced in discussing race:

> The problem is, especially for the White students, as soon as we talk about the topics, I know that they are cringing, and they tell me they are. They don't know how to talk about these things. So, the students who are not White, my classroom is diverse, have much more experience talking about these topics. Much more experience. Afterwards, I talked with a couple of students and bounce this hypothesis off of them. Talked to an African American girl and she said, "Yep, I've talked about this topic many times. I've seen my parents talk about race many times. I've seen my sister...." it's a regular thing.

Rather than attempting to impose his beliefs onto his students, Parks positioned himself as someone who, like his students, was grappling with similar issues of race, class, and gender. As he noted:

> If from day one, I say my whole opinion of how prevalent racism is, then many Whites will see me as trying to shove my personal agenda down their throats. And so I've learned to present myself as one of them which of course I am, but in my understanding and perspective on these issues I see it differently.... So, I tend to sort of present myself as similar to them in understanding these issues and gradually trying to lead them toward the things I see ... hoping they will see it too.

Though some of Parks's students voiced racist and sexist discourses, he avoided labeling or implying that these students were racist or sexist by recognizing the ways these students were shaped by larger institutional forces. Rather than focusing his critiques on individual students, he focused students' attention on the workings of institutional forces shaping characters and their own identities (Reason, Scales, & Rossa-Millar, 2005). And to address the fact that some students were reluctant to publicly express some of their feelings about race, Parks selected quotes from journals and shared them with students as discussion starters without citing students' names (Rich & Cargile, 2004).

Parks was also aware of the fact that there was a strong emotional appeal of a discourse of individualism in opposition to programs such as affirmative action, leading him to recognize the need to challenge that discourse while at the same time valuing students' emotional attachment to that discourse. As Trainor (2002, p. 634) noted,

> We are asked, on the one hand, to respect, even love, students ... and we must, on the other, organize our teaching around attempts to change students. Caught between these two mandates, we struggle to represent Whiteness and White students as perpetrators of injustice who must be taught to disavow Whiteness and as legitimate social actors on whom we must risk "an act of love." I want to suggest that once we confront this contradiction and the ways it delimits how we see mainstream students, it becomes possible to represent and understand encounters with resistant students in less politicized and essentialized terms.

Given the potential for conservatives to exploit White anger, Trainor (2002, p. 647) argued for the need to avoid the use of "rhetorical frames that demonize Whiteness and White students" by recognizing the role of subjective perceptions of racial hierarchies. Parks was aware that these subjective perceptions stem from feelings of stigma and privilege, feelings that vary according to specific social situations or cultural contexts (McDermott, 2006). Based on a year-long observation of working-class Whites and African Americans interacting in convenience stores in Atlanta and Boston, Monica McDermott (2006, p. 56) found that feelings of stigma and privilege vary considerably:

> What racial identity experienced as stigma in one setting could be experienced as privilege in a different time and place. These differential experiences can exist within the same individual, subject to situational constraints in addition to spatial ones. For example, an individual might experience White racial identity as a stigmatized identity at the local level but as a privileged identity when the nation is the frame of reference (Delaney, 2002).

McDermott found that Whites in Boston were more likely to experience a sense of White privilege given their status as Whites with a strong sense of pride in their neighborhood associated with Whiteness. In contrast, the working-class Whites in Atlanta had a lower sense of status and pride in their neighborhood, in which Whiteness was actually perceived as a liability by middle classes in Atlanta, creating a sense of stigma for living in that neighborhood. Given their sense of pride in their neighborhood, the Boston Whites were more likely than the Atlanta Whites to adopt a protective, reactive stance that resulted in what were often misperceptions of threats and challenges from African Americans.

As a working-class person who had been raised in similar neighborhoods to the Boston neighborhood of McDermott's (2006) study, Parks was aware of how perceptions of race can be shaped by these feelings of stigma and privilege, leading him to try to create an egalitarian classroom context in attempt to minimize status differences that result in perceptions or misperceptions of threats or challenges to one's status.

Parks's Methods for Teaching Multicultural Literature

Given these various challenges, Parks adopted a range of teaching methods designed to foster critical analysis of the novels read in the course.

Providing Cultural Background Knowledge for the Novels

In reading multicultural literature, students need to understand some of the characteristics of the cultural worlds portrayed in the novels, particularly cultures about which they have little knowledge. To emphasize the need to understand characters' actions within specific cultural contexts, Parks consistently employed a *fishbowl* metaphor to help students interpret the ways that practices and beliefs are shaped by cultural forces. Early in the course, the metaphor emerged from a journal prompt in which he asked students to respond to the following: "Water is to fish as culture is to people." The crux of the discussion about this journal prompt was the question of whether fish know that they are in water. Once students acquired an understanding of the metaphor, they continued to use it to remind themselves that they were operating in particular cultural worlds. As Parks noted in a journal reflection about a discussion of *Kindred* (Butler, 1979):

> The whole idea of a culture having such profound influence in the lives of its members seems pretty fresh to the students. As we discussed the character of Rufus in *Kindred*, students understood that his culture had shaped him to such an extent that he could not break free of the norms and examples given to him by his father; he felt that rape was a culturally acceptable option but that the love of a Black woman was not. Students keep coming back to the idea of culture as a fishbowl and that there was little chance for Rufus to even consider an outside idea. At the same time, students were quick to note that somehow some individuals in the society were able to transgress the culture and consider ideas like abolition, racial equality, and the like.

In a class presentation, describing the world of the family in *Bastard out of Carolina* (Allison, 1993), Parks talked about the insular nature of the family world for the children growing up in that family:

We've been talking about the fishbowl and fishbowls describe families too, when you grow up in a family, you think that the way your parents parent is normal, that that's how the whole world does it, and you think however your brothers and sisters behave, you think that's normal. And if you have a Grandma and all your uncles and cousins doing the same thing, it all seems normal, so you're sort of stuck in a family culture fishbowl.

In introducing the different novels, Parks provided students with background information about the cultures portrayed in the novels. In teaching *Their Eyes Were Watching God* (Hurston, 2000), he provided biographical information about Zora Neal Hurston's life associated with her different cultural worlds. The students read her essay, "How It Feels to Be Colored Me" (Hurston, 1994), in which she described her experience of becoming aware of being colored at age 13 in Jacksonville, Florida. In that essay, Hurston described how her identity changed when she moved from her hometown of Eatonville to the larger White world of Jacksonville:

I left Eatonville, the town of oleanders, as Zora. When I disembarked from the riverboat in Jacksonville, she was no more. It seemed that I had suffered a sea change. I was not Zora of Orange County any more, I was now a little colored girl. I found it out in certain ways. In my heart as well as I the mirror, I was now a fast brown—warranted not to rub or run. (p. 1426)

The students then discussed the ways Hurston's racial identity was constructed by the external cultural world of Jacksonville in which external discourses of Whiteness positioned and defined her as *colored*. The students also discussed the end of her life in which, despite having published many books, she was penniless and had to work as a maid, a reflection of the status of African American female writers in the larger culture.

In teaching *Bless Me, Ultima* (Anaya, 1995), set in 1940s rural New Mexico, Parks provided students with knowledge of the highly diverse culture of New Mexico and its strong ties to Mexican culture. He described the war between the United States and Mexico that led to New Mexico becoming a part of the United States and how the residents of the state were often caught between allegiances to Mexican and American cultures. He noted the differences between these two cultures related to the influence of the Catholic Church in Mexico on gender attitudes, particularly in terms of the role of the male head of the family.

Focusing on Institutional Forces

In discussing the influence of these cultural worlds on characters, Parks used a racetrack metaphor to illustrate how institutional forces operating in these cultural worlds shaped characters' development. He drew a line on the board representing the racetrack, and, at the end of the line, he wrote *finish line* and the word *success*, defined in terms of financial, educational, social, or career paths. Students then discussed how beginning life at certain locations along the racetrack afforded different groups of people born into a specific race, class, or gender different degrees of status or cultural capital in proximity or distance to the finish line within American culture. Students suggested that some groups had to overcome more hurdles on their way to success than did others. This came to be known in the class as the *continuum of success,* and the metaphor of *hurdles* was frequently referred to in terms of the institutional barriers facing certain groups in attempting to achieve success. Though this metaphor could be interpreted as reifying discourses of individual competition and athleticism, it was used to highlight institutional barriers as a means of challenging students' discourses of meritocracy.

This hurdles metaphor also helped students see that even though there are exceptionally successful people from all walks of life (e.g., students cited Oprah Winfrey and Michael Jordan as African Americans who are very successful in American culture), exceptional people from oppressed groups typically have to jump more hurdles than do Whites. Conversely, this metaphor helped students understand that although they may know a number of White people who are less than successful, this might be due to a social class hurdle that must be jumped, but White people in general have fewer and shorter hurdles to jump than people of color in the United States.

To help students recognize the ways institutional forces shape differences between different worlds, Parks provided students with concrete examples from students' own lives that served to illustrate the relatively abstract notion of institutional forces constituting worlds. For example, after students read an excerpt from Kozol's (1992) description of schools in East St. Louis, Parks sensed that his students were having difficulty understanding the ways poverty in East St. Louis reflected broader social forces. To make this concept more tangible, he went on line and found a home for sale in the East St. Louis community. It was a spacious, brick home with a large fenced yard and two porches with columns. Removing from the description all of the details about the geography and $2,000 asking price of the home, he gave the advertisement to the students and asked them to assess its value. Predictably, the discussions rendered the house somewhere between $150,000 and $250,000, depending on the neighborhood. When he shared the actual value of the house and the fact that the mortgage payments were $11.00 a month, the students were astounded; they could not understand what could make such a home of such little worth. He then explained that the value of the house was a function of the perceived value of the community of East St. Louis—a perceived value that reflected institutional racism in the form of segregated housing, city funding priorities, and real estate redlining practices. Grappling with this concrete example challenged students' status quo discourses of race and class by demonstrating the impact of institutional racism on housing. In reflecting on this activity, Parks noted,

> I think how hard it is to understand activity systems and to think outside of your world. They had read the Kozol piece, still they could not fathom it. Somehow, reading Kozol, though startling, seemed unreal. Considering this house to their lives, seemed real. The point for me was for them to feel the disconnect. To deeply say, "Why is this house $11 a month?" This is a great house! Kayla said, "Can I buy it and move it somewhere?" I want them to consider "How could life be so bad? How could a place in the U.S. be so bad that this house is this price?" They could not understand. That is what I wanted. I wanted to create that sense that my understanding of the world does not make sense in this situation. And, I think it happened.

In their journal writings, many students cited this example of the real estate advertisement as providing them with a concrete illustration of the impact of institutional racism on everyday life.

Interrogating Discourses of Individualism

Discussing the influence of institutional forces led to debates about the degree and influence of discrimination in society. In responding to portrayals of slavery in *Kindred*, some students argued that because they did not participate in past instances of racism, they should not face reverse discrimination in the form of affirmative action programs that discriminate against White students.

In challenging students' arguments related to affirmative action, Parks pointed to contradictions in students' assumptions about a history of exclusion operating in higher education. He created a hypothetical case of low-income or first-generation college families, like the families of many students in the course, receiving more financial aid than families whose income disqualifies them from receiving aid, like many families in the suburbs. Adopting the voice of a middle-class, suburban youth, he asked his students, "Why should I be penalized because my parents were smart enough to go to college and get good jobs?" Because most of the students in the course fell into the low-income category and were more likely to receive financial aid than middle-class students, students began to recognize some the advantages afforded them by government-support programs due to their lower socioeconomic status.

Parks also supported those students who resisted the shared, majority consensus emerging in the classroom. For example, in challenging the classroom consensus that Whites should not be held accountable for past historical events such as slavery, he assigned outside readings such as McIntosh's (1988) essay on White privilege. He then read aloud one of the journal writing responses to the essay: "I can be pretty sure that my neighbors wherever I live will be neutral or pleasant to me because I am White." In response to this statement, one of the students, Michelle, argued that more important than race in building relationships with others is one's behavior and appearance, or "how you present yourself."

A number of White students said that they agreed with McIntosh's (1988) position on White privilege, particularly statements such as "I can speak in public without putting my race on trial" (p. 8) and "I can turn on the television or open up the front page of the newspaper and see people of my race well-represented." They also responded to McIntosh's argument that Whites are oblivious to how race shapes their attribution of motives to others' practices. In reacting to this position, some White students shared stories of being stopped by police because of their age or clothing, not their race. Then, Paul, a Hispanic student, shared his own experience of being stopped by police. Parks then asked Paul, "And we are not saying that it was race, but did it cross your mind that … " Paul then clarified his position, noting, "Yeah, it did …. They said that they thought that we had a gun or something, ya know, so supposedly, that was the reason … " By interrogating the underlying assumption that race was not related to these incidents, Parks pushed students to examine their presuppositions about race and privilege.

Students then cited other instances of discrimination in their workplaces in which people of color were asked for identification whereas Whites were not. As one White, male student, Devin, explained:

> You know, a White guy will come walking in and get something and pay for it with a check, and she won't check his ID; she will just do everything, but then, ya know, a Hmong kid might come in and order or get some stuff and put it on his credit card, and she'll check his ID and everything so, ya know, but people just come up and I'm just "alright, have a nice day" the checks are not clearing, it's not my problem, I just don't like my job so I don't card anybody.

Sharing these experiences helped students recognize how racial perceptions were tied to larger institutional practices associated with law enforcement and workplace practices as opposed to individual prejudices. This recognition was a shift in their stance toward issues of race. One White student, Michelle, noted how she changed her view on affirmative action programs, which she initially resented, because she became aware of how race and culture served to disadvantage some groups "because of their race and their culture and how they grew up and all of the things that they had to deal with that I wouldn't being White." Another student, Troy, said:

> I just thought just because you were a minority you could just get along in life a little easier when it comes to school and stuff like that. Get scholarships and all that other good stuff. And then when we got into it a lot of it kind of changed my whole aspect on it like how I look at that now. The way earlier hurdles and that sort of thing and where you come from and your family situation. So that changed me a lot.

Consistent with a pragmatic rather than a theoretical approach to understanding racism (Henry, 2005), Parks encouraged students to focus on everyday practices to inductively recognize how institutional practices of racial privilege influenced those practices.

Socializing Students into the World of a College Literature Course

Parks also assumed the role of mentor to students in the course in helping them acquire new academic practices consistent with the *habitus* (Bourdieu, 1984) of college students. Socializing high school students into college academic communities of practice involves helping them adopt new practices that differ from their familiar practices operating in high school classrooms (Beach, Lundell, & Jung, 2002; Harklau, 2001).

A central part of this socialization was teaching students in this class to engage in critical analysis—the ability to employ critical discourses such as feminist or literary criticism. This was particularly challenging in working with the working-class students in this course who were often unaccustomed to employing decontextualized analytic language (Gee, Allen, & Clinton, 2001). As we found, students in our study had engaged in little critical analysis in their other courses, so many of them had little experience with employing critical analysis.

The issue of students' academic socialization into critical analysis discourses has often been framed in terms of their need for accommodation into the languages and discourses of the university as members of a discourse community that value academic analysis (Bartholomae, 1985). This model of academic socialization assumes that to succeed in the university, students need to learn to mimic or adopt their instructors' analytic discourses, leading them to abandon their previous, outsider literacy practices.

One problem with this model of an academic discourse community is that it privileges an inclusive, insider status for members of the academy as the language of power (Boyd, 1991). Moreover, the notion of simply imitating instructors' discourses can create a sense of dependency on the teachers as someone to imitate but who does not necessarily want students to assume their power (Boyd, 1991).

Another problem with this model is that it assumes a sense of consensus about what discourses should be valued and imitated. In describing his own role as a high school teacher, Majerus (1996, p. 9) noted that rather than assume a sense of consensus and certainty, he fostered a sense of dissensus based on differences among competing social worlds:

> I must prepare my students to be elastic enough to appreciate the various discourse communities they will need to enter to find success and competence in life. To do that, I realize that I must give them the opportunity to see such a blending of communities as possible, and in fact, desirable. To do so, I must show them the legitimacy of building on their "home language" as we move into "schooled literacy."

Rather than privileging the academic world over students' own worlds, Majerus (1996) acknowledged the importance of recognizing students' allegiances to different worlds, including their home worlds, as providing equally valuable resources and discourses of power.

Hicks (2005) also noted the need to build on rather than marginalize students' home worlds. In a four-year study of her work with a group of working-class sixth graders, Hicks argued for the need for her students to acquire some middle-class discourses and conversational turn-taking practices, while at the same time valuing their working-class discourses and language use. She noted the need to help students recognize the value of their often difficult home life experiences and their literary experiences at school, which provided them with new ways of imagining their worlds. Rather than set up one world as superior to the other, she described her role as helping her students become:

> ... *bilingual—capable* of moving productively between a working-class idiom and the middle-class language and literacy practices of school—has become a leading vision for what critical teaching might achieve .... Working-class girls can also learn to speak, read, and reason as bilinguals, in their case in more than one class-specific voice. But in order for such changes in language and subjectivity to occur, girls must first see a place in the classroom for the *real* as they know

it. Through genres ranging from popular fiction, to rap, to memoir, the girls engaged with the concreteness and complexity of their lives. (p. 225, italics in original)

Parks helped his students move between their own working-class worlds and the world of college literature study by describing and valuing autobiographical experiences in both of these worlds and by explaining how discourses or cultural models of race, class, and gender shaped his identities. In this manner he described how his identity was constructed through uses of language and narratives, reflecting what Jacobs (2005, p. 9) described as the "teacher as text" approach, in which Jacobs, an African American instructor, described his particular experiences with racism associated with popular culture texts. Jacobs encouraged his students to study him as a text whose construction of racism as an African American teacher influenced his interpretation of race in texts. Then, when his predominately White students noted that he may have been biased about his perceptions and therefore racist, he argued that his perceptions represent only one of many different, multiple forms of racism operating in the classroom.

To share how his identity was shaped by discourses and cultural models of class, Parks described to his students his working-class upbringing involving financial destitution, family members' run-ins with the law, the prevalent drug culture of his factory-employed neighborhood, and his struggle to begin working his way through college at age 25. In discussing his own working-class background, Parks established identification with his own students, who perceived him as a "co-author of students' lives" (Rymes, 2001, p. 168)—someone who was able to bridge competing worlds. As Troy noted, "You're one of us, Mr. Parks." Another student described his identification with Parks's working-class background:

If you walked into a room and there is a rich guy and a poor guy, who are you most likely to sit next to? I think you are gonna lean more toward the guy who has something in common with you. I think that is why people get along with you, Mr. Parks, 'cause we're peers and so are you.

In perceiving Parks as "one of us," his students saw him as someone who had a shared interest in their personal lives given his own prior experiences (Borkowski, 2004). Through forging relationships with students and sharing narratives about his experiences, Parks emphasized similarities between his experiences and those of his students. He also maintained close ties with students outside of the classroom as well as shared interests in sports, music, school activities and events. Students therefore trusted Parks and saw him as an example of someone who was proud of his working-class background, positively engaged in the working-class culture of their high school, and also successful in a university culture. Parks served as a role model for many of his students, helping them understand the possibility of coexistence in competing social worlds.

In his teaching, Parks continually addressed questions of identity construction such as, "Who am I? Who are the others around me? How am I seeing things? How are they seeing things? How are they seeing me?" In modeling this kind of identity work for student, Parks shared his autobiographical experiences. For instance, Parks talked to his students about his identity as an avid reader who, in his childhood in a working-class home, used reading as a means of understanding other worlds outside of his home world. He explained in an interview:

> All I can point to is my upbringing and growing up in a poor neighborhood with few options. My mother took me to the library a lot. And, somehow, from the library I would come home with boxes of books. And somehow, ultimately, not easily, I was able to see places outside of my experience. Since I have seen books not as a way of escape per se, but as a way of realizing what is going on in the world, then I try to pass that along to the students, which of course is based on the premise that I feel like my students' understanding of the world and the way it works is limited given the boundaries of their class or life experience.

Consistent with the idea of learning about other worlds through literature, in his teaching, Parks asked students to recognize that these experiences are filtered through narrators' or characters' perspectives on those worlds, perspectives they could compare with their own perspectives as a means of entertaining alternative perspectives or value stances. As he noted:

> In other words, we can't stop time in reality; we can stop time in the text. Then, not only can we stop time in the text and reflect on what is happening in the characters' lives, but everybody in the classroom just had that same life experience in the text, so we can stop the text and unpack what just happened through different people's eyes. In doing that, ultimately, like when we talk about lenses and stuff like that, the goal is ultimately that they can do this in life.

In addition to helping students acquire critical analysis practices, Parks also demonstrated how he operated in a college world as a person from a working-class background: "I thought going to college was just a way to get a better job. I had no way of knowing that it would change my understanding of the world." Central to that transition was his experience of learning to value the intellectual aspects of academic work that transcend the idea of simply being on a college campus and taking college course work. Given these instrumental conceptions of schooling (Seitz, 2004a, 2004b), Parks had to show his students how analyzing literature afforded him some intellectual satisfaction as a worthwhile endeavor. For Wenger (1998, pp. 272–273) teacher–mentors need to help students imagine "who they are, who they are not, who they could be … reinventing the self, and in the process reinventing the world." Wenger argued that teachers also need to go beyond their conventional institutional roles by "just being adults [who] act as members and engage in the learning that membership entails" (p. 277).

In sharing autobiographical narratives about his negotiations of trajectories into academia, Parks faced a challenge common to teachers from working-class backgrounds about how to position himself between close attachments to his family and neighborhood and the often alien, impersonal academic world (Dews & Law, 1995; Ryan & Sackrey, 1996; Shepard, McMillan, & Tate, 1998; Villanueva, 1993; Zandy, 1990). People from working-class backgrounds who have gone to college or graduate school often struggle to negotiate their identities in relationship to their working-class backgrounds. For some, such negotiation demands a rejection or silence regarding their working-class backgrounds or experiences. For others, making this transition involves creating a third space (Soja, 1998) that rejects binary, either–or thinking to consider the benefits and limitations of both working-class and academic worlds.

To provide his students with the experience of the world of college, Parks took them to a session at the same local university he had attended. In this session, a university professor gave a lecture on multicultural literature and students discussed their responses to the lecture in small-group sessions. While on campus, Parks gave the students a campus tour and described his own prior experiences as a student on this campus: "I told them about nearby coffee shops and the types of people who hung out in them. I explained that part of my college success had been sitting in those shops, reading literature, writing poetry, and figuring out what it means to be a college student."

Prior to the field trip to the university, Parks prepared his students for encounters they would have with suburban students who might have stereotyped ideas about urban high school students and about whom his students might also make assumptions. He developed a lesson in which students analyzed how conceptions of race and class differences are reflected in how they label suburban or rural people. Prior to going on the field trip, students discussed and role played prototypical perceptions of rural and suburban life, as well as perceptions of others about urban students.

In describing the suburban students, students frequently referred to class markers, particularly money, as a feature that distinguished them from their suburban counterparts, noting that physical markers such as dress, hair, and speech served to differentiate them from suburban students. At points during the activity, however, students would look over their lists and realize that they were, as one student noted, "doing the same thing to them that they do to us in the inner city." One student, having already explained that she envisioned the rural version of her to be "up early milking cows," declared that such a notion was likely derived from films, not reality. Students became aware that such media images were likely also responsible for their suburban peers' stereotypes of urban students. In their discussions with the suburban students during the university event, they faced questions about "metal detectors in the school building," which do not exist at Thompson, in addition to questions about crime that the other students were certain were part of urban students' daily lives. As students fielded these questions, they confirmed the ways the suburban students' perceptions of their lives matched their own stereotypes of suburban and rural students.

Parks also attempted to construct the world of the classroom as a college class in which he taught in the manner of a college instructor. He explained his role as a college instructor to students by drawing two circles on the classroom floor, one representing their high school world and one representing the university world. By standing in the circle representing the college world, he noted that he would have different assumptions about completing assignments—that they needed to assume their own responsibility for completing their work and that, as is the case with college work, they would not be reminded about deadlines as they were in their other high school classes (Harklau, 2001). To create a college-like atmosphere for the course, students were also expected to have e-mail access and were expected to maintain continuous communication with Parks. Students also were given free time two days a week for reading and writing on their own, a time schedule more consistent with that of a college schedule.

In an interview, Parks described what he shared with the students about his two identities as college instructor and high school teacher as he moved between the two circles on the floor:

"At the college level, they will not explain it to you like this. It will be an assumed; it will be a given. And they will expect that you will know this already, but you don't know it, and that's why I'm telling you. So do not do this again." Then, I say, "Do you understand?" They say, "Yes." Then I step over, one step sideways, and I say now, "I totally understand your situation. I know that you were working late last night." I resume the high school sort of in-touch working-class sort of person. The first example that comes to mind in current practice is a student who keeps coming in late. I explain that at the high school level that simply means a detention. "But there are no detentions here. So, let me explain what message this sends to the professor in the course. It is a message of priorities and of engagement in the course" and things like that. I explain how that is interpreted at the college level as I understand it, versus how it is interpreted at the high school level.

Parks drew on his own college experiences to create expectations for the level of intellectual work in the course. In the interview, he explained how he drew on his experiences in learning the discourse of a college classroom discussion:

> I'll never forget the first time it happened to me in a college classroom discussion. People were exchanging opinions, and I put mine in, and then they asked, "Why?" And I didn't know why. And ... I don't want them [these high school students] to go through that. So, I explain to them the need to know the why of things.... If you're going to say that this character is misunderstood, you can't just say that; you have to know where you got the idea. So I talk about metacognition and thinking about your thinking.

Even though Parks knew that his students would still be operating primarily as high school students, he attempted to socialize them into discourses from the world of college by formulating a set of ground rules consistent with a college classroom.

From listening to Parks's descriptions of negotiating the social and academic worlds of college, students in the course acquired an understanding of the difference between their current identities as high school students and the practices associated with being a college student.

Teaching Literary Critical Analysis

Parks also wanted to provide his students with tools for engaging in a form of literary critical analysis that remains consistent with a critical analysis of institutional forces (Edelsky, Smith, & Wolfe, 2002). Critical analysis that is based on New Critical or formalist analysis of form and language in literary texts often bears little relationship to engaging students in critical inquiry about institutional forces shaping those texts (Beach, 1993). New Critical approaches assume that the meaning of the text is embedded in the text and needs to be teased out by closely reading textual language. By focusing solely on the text, teachers employing these approaches often do not examine the larger cultural and institutional forces shaping the author's or reader's construction of the text (Beach, 1993).

On the other end of the spectrum, as noted in Chapter 3, a reader-response approach that focuses on fostering connections between students' experiences and the text—though a positive approach on many levels—may not lead students to critically analyze how discourses and cultural models mediate the construction of text meaning.

Parks sought to fuse teaching literary critical analysis with criticism of institutional forces by framing texts as constructions mediated both by institutional forces and by students' perceptions of the world. He provided his students with three scaffolding categories for defining the relationships between texts as mediating forces: *text to text, text to life,* and *text to world.* Rather than asking students to simply apply their autobiographical experiences directly to texts, Parks asked them to focus on how their own experiences as texts were constructed or mediated by language and narratives by continually asking them, "How is this world constructed?" in terms of texts—as language or narratives. As he noted in an interview, he had students construct a narrative of their field trip to the university to understand how that narrative mediated the field trip experience:

> I literally have my students create texts, so I'll have them write about their life. So, for example, last week we were on a field trip here at the university, and students went in different directions and did things. The next day, they had to write their lives as text. They became the author. They themselves became the protagonist, and they had to write the story of what happened, not just the external but the internal.

Parks also focused students' attention on the uses of symbols in the novels to reflect the cultural values of particular text worlds. For example, in teaching *Love Medicine* (Erdrich, 2000), he shared his own responses to the portrayal of the character June in the introductory chapter, highlighting the symbolic use of water in reflecting Native American spiritual cultural values: "I also wanted them to consider the idea that the first chapter was actually full of meaning for the rest of the novel, but it didn't make sense at the time. I also wanted them to latch onto a specific recurring theme not only with June but the idea of water and the spiritual inhabitation of beings in the novel." He engaged in this modeling in an inductive manner, working off of the students' difficulties interpreting symbolic meanings. In discussing the novel, students had difficulty understanding the ways that symbolic meaning might play out in a text, for example with the last chapter titled "The Bridge":

Devin: The title of the last chapter is "The Bridge," but it only mentions a bridge in there when they are talking about Henry who says "He thought of diving off the river bank, a bridge." I didn't understand what that was supposed to mean or the significance. Was he trying to commit suicide?

Kayla: Talks about a bridge on 141, too.

Devin: Yeah, that's the one.

Michelle: Albertine talks about it, too.

As part of this discussion (see also Chapter 9), Parks modeled ways of noting the symbolic meaning of water and the bridge in the novel. He cited a quotation from the beginning of the novel related to the symbolic meaning of water and then elicited other examples of how water assumes a symbolic role in other parts of the novel. Though he never explicitly explained the meaning of the bridge, he engaged students in the process of inferring symbolic meanings associated with understanding the Native American cultural world.

Teaching Critical Lenses

As part of teaching literacy critical analysis, Parks also modeled the use of different form of literary criticism associated with feminist, Marxist, cultural, psychological–psychoanalytic, and deconstructionist lenses in responding to the novels (Appleman, 2000). He initially modeled the application of a particular lens by defining key terms and methods involved in using a lens. He then applied those key terms and methods to analysis of a text. To help students compare the differences between these lenses, he employed a jigsaw activity by putting students into groups and asking each group to assume a different lens for analyzing the same text. Then, when the students shared their interpretations in the large group, they could discern the differences between these different critical lenses.

In teaching students to apply feminist and Marxist lenses, Parks asked students to examine how differences between characters' agency is related to differences in race, class, and gender. For example, in asking students to assume a Marxist perspective with *Love Medicine,* Parks asked questions such as, "Who has power within the novel and how are their lives portrayed? Who has no money in the novel and how are their lives portrayed?"

In applying a feminist lens to *Bless Me, Ultima* (Anaya, 1995), Mitch noted how discourses and cultural models of masculinity are shaped by different institutional forces. He said, "Expectations of men differ in the various groups in the story. For the farmers of Luna family are not expected drink and fighting was not expected qualities of a man. They are more quiet and understanding, but men still have the role of proving for the family. The Luna didn't see becoming a priest as womanly because they have different values."

In applying a Marxist lens to *A Yellow Raft in Blue Water* (Dorris, 1987), Devin noted the class status of the Native American characters. He said, "Life on a reservation itself automatically puts you in a lower class ... being born into certain situations or lifestyles puts your closer or further from the goal-line in the game of success."

In teaching students about a psychological/psychoanalytic lens, Parks discussed ways of examining character' actions as psychologically motivated. In applying this lens to *Bastard out of Carolina* (Allison, 1993), Dan examined the forces influencing Daddy Glen:

> Daddy Glen grew up in a somewhat normal home and somewhat normal parents.... He is described as the scapegoat of his family with feet "so fine that his boots had to be bought in the boy's department of Sears Roebuck, while his gloves could only be found in the tall men's specialty stores" (p. 35). The metaphor of his boots being bought in the boy's department could represent the fact that a part of his childhood is still fresh in his memory.

Dan noted that Daddy Glen's strained relationship with his own father may have shaped his behaviors. In a dialogue journal response to Dan's entry, Troy wrote that "Glen was probably abused by his father as a kid, which leaves a fear of him, which also makes Glen think he's never good enough for him."

To adopt a deconstructionist lens, Parks had students examine some of the binary categories operating in a text, categories such as "good" versus "evil" or "White" versus "Black," and the tensions inherent in these binary categories. For example, he noted that in responding to *Bless Me, Ultima*, Pauline examined how the character, Tony, was grappling with the contradiction between a merciful God and the existence of evil. This led her to critique how the binary categories of good and evil created an internal struggle for Tony.

Parks also modeled strategies for analyzing how language use and categories reflect institutional power structures (Appleman, 2000). This led students to attend to interrogating the meaning of key concepts in a text or in their discussions. For example, in discussing the portrayal of Native American reservations in *Love Medicine*, Devin noted,

> We kicked a culture off of its land, but in the history books it's recorded as "settlement." That's what it was, "settlement." But then I ask the question, "How can you settle a place that is already settled?" How can you go into somebody's else's environment and start to build houses and then say that it's "settled?" When someone is already there, living there.

Devin's focus on the concept of *settlement* and *settled* reflected his awareness of how concepts as defined by history books reflect certain ideological perspectives. By noting how language itself reflects certain beliefs and attitudes, the students learned to critically examine the ways language use reflects cultural and ideological perceptions of the world.

This awareness then transferred to students inferring larger symbolic meaning in characters' dialogue. For example, Troy responded to Daddy Glen's dialogue in a quote from *Bastard out of Carolina*: "'Come on, girls.' Glen's voice when he called Reese and me for the picture had had a loud impatient note I had never heard before" (p. 43). Troy noted that "the first time I read that, I was lost in thought. I immediately said to myself, he's abusive." In this instance Troy was able to infer how dialogue functions symbolically to portray characters.

Using Drama Activities

Parks also used drama activities to help students examine how language use reflects cultural beliefs and attitudes. Students created written monologues in which they adopted a character's voice to describe how that character coped with challenges in the novel. Parks asked that each student first describe the character's behavior and then proclaim, "You think you know me, but you don't!" The notion of using speech to reveal a character's underlying traits and attitudes was consistent with Parks's use of an *iceberg* metaphor—that characters' surface language suggests larger, deeper phenomena underneath. Students then read aloud their monologues to the class, leading to discussions about their character's perceptions and actions. Parks described how he modeled a monologue for Daddy Glen illustrating the tension between surface practices and other aspects of his character:

> "From *Bastard out of Carolina*, I'm Daddy Glen. And you think you know me. And you think that I'm a child molester and I'm this and I'm that ...," and then at some point they have to say, "But you don't know me." And then they go on with the other parts of the character's life that is either hinted at or makes sense of ... in other words that the students have to take the way they understand the world and the way that people work in the world, and they have to impose it on the lives of the characters.

In his monologue related to the novel *Obasan* (Kogawa, 1993), about the internment of the Japanese in British Columbia, Paul assumed the perspective of the Canadian government toward the Japanese Canadian people:

> We finally bombed them. We totally wasted them. Now they will surrender and we will win the war. Our country will now be safer. The

Japanese will now know not to mess with us. A lot of people died, but that's the price of war. The ones in our country should also be sent back to their country or rubble. They are the enemy and shouldn't be considered Canadian citizens. They are a danger not only to us but also our kids and their kids. Why have the enemy on our own soil. They will want revenge and they will be more capable of that when they are over here.

In this monologue, Paul assumed an institutional governmental voice that justified its actions against Japanese Canadians. In doing so, he employed a discourse of exclusion through his use of pronouns, equating the government as "us" as opposed to the Japanese Canadians as "them," "they," and "the enemy." In this exercise he learned how language can function to create "we–them" exclusionary binary categories that position people as the "other."

In performing these monologues, students broke out of their conventional classroom identities and experimented with alternative roles. For example, Mai, who was often quite reserved in classroom discussions, became highly engaged when she adopted the role of Tenorio, one of the characters in *Bless Me, Ultima*. As Parks noted:

We all loved her little taped-on moustache and beard. She basically told us everything we knew about Tenorio. I loved when she threw the bird up in the air and said, "Whew, I killed Ultima's spirit guide!" and she spun in a circle with glee. It was like the only time that I saw her carry out what she'd obviously practiced a great many times. It was like her mental checklist said, "When you throw owl, spin and yell to show emotion." It was a great moment of seeing someone slip from complete nervousness into the fulfillment of one of the hundred things she'd practiced.

In other drama activities, Parks had students take characters from the novels and place them into lived-world situations. For example, with the novel *Their Eyes Were Watching God*, students assumed the roles of Janie's grandmother, Janie, and her multiple husbands. Working in pairs, students adopted the roles of these characters and a counselor who would ask them questions about their practices and perspectives. For example, some of the students had previously criticized Janie's grandmother for forcing Janie to marry a man for whom she had no love. When Janie and her grandmother met with a family counselor to explore reasons for their conflict, the grandmother described her experience of slavery, sexual abuse, and poverty that led her to recommend marriage as a form of security. Students explained that though they had read those details in the text, these role-play meetings encouraged them to frame these details in terms of characters' internal motivations for their actions.

Facilitating Discussion

To foster discussion of these various topics and perspectives, Parks assumed the role of facilitator of classroom discussions, modeling strategies for expressing diverse, alternative perspectives. For example, he emphasized the need for students to cite material from texts to support their opinions. Rather than direct students to certain text passages, Parks encouraged students to select their own passages that served to illustrate their interpretations.

In a visit to Parks's class the year after this class, the CIS university faculty coordinator observed Parks's teaching and praised Parks for his patience and trust:

> I was mightily impressed by your ability to sit on your hands (and keep your mouth closed, to mix metaphors shamefully) while they floundered about for the first 10 minutes or so. I've always had the hardest time doing that, so congratulations. When you did intervene momentarily it was with humor and deftness, prodding without criticizing, opening the way for new voices that had been silent without insulting those who had already spoken. I feel sure your students value this tremendously and that they find in your stance the room to risk saying things other teachers might label "inappropriate" or worse.

In discussions, Parks also adopted the perspective of a student who was reading a text for the first time. One of the challenges for literature teachers is that they may have read and taught a book many times and tend to focus on larger thematic patterns they can discern from their multiple re-readings of a text, responding according to what Rabinowitz (1998) defines as rules of coherence. In contrast, students who are reading the text for the first time are often concerned with what Rabinowitz described as rules of configuration, readings having to do with simply understanding events or predicting outcomes.

Parks also tried to promote divergent, alternative perspectives that created dialogic tensions by encouraging a range of different interpretations. As we discuss in more detail in Chapter 9, creating these dialogic tensions served to foster disagreement between students, leading to stretches of sustained discussion around particular topics. He also refrained from voicing his own interpretations, asking students to react to each other's interpretations as dialogue–journal partners to encourage tensions between competing interpretations.

To foster divergent perspectives in discussions, Parks modeled and encouraged students to adopt what could be described as tentative hypotheses, hunches, or passing theories (Kent, 1993) about characters' actions or perspectives (Beach, Eddleston, & Philippot, 2003; Eddleston & Philippot, 2002). Adopting an exploratory, "I'm-not-so-sure-about-this" stance as opposed to a definitive, "this-is-the-answer" stance invited other students to explore these initial hypotheses in extended stretches of discussions. For example, in a discussion of the film *Smoke Signals* (Eyre, 1998), which students viewed after reading *Love Medicine,* students compared the film to the novel, noting that they both deal with the topic of a house on fire:

Sarah: One thing I found like *Love Medicine* was the house on fire. Didn't Lulu run into her house and get out a baby? But the baby was in the house and she went in and got it? Well, actually, he did run in and get Tom's son, Victor, and there was a baby involved with the fire.

Kathy: Like Devin and Sarah said, it's like *Love Medicine*, when they said, "When the Indians go away they don't come back?"

Parks: What do you mean?

Kathy: The kids playing with matches, and you know Lipsha. Ashes are like a combination of something in life. Like you have the matches and then you have a book of them? Like when he said, "Some are children of fire, and some are children of ash." The fire probably symbolizes something.

Parks: What do you think? I don't have an answer in my head …

Kathy: … symbolizes life. It starts bright, but then it is put out; then it ends. Lipsha had things in the ashes.

Parks: Anybody care to join us in playing the "maybe" game? Trying to interpret possible if … Kathy's statement, which does sound symbolic in some way … "some are children of fire, some of ash." Wanna play the maybe game with her idea of the fire burns different colors?

Devin: Maybe it's like, I don't know where I'm going with this, but children of ash and fire are like, if you're born of ash or I mean of fire, it is kind of like Victor. You are kind of more … you are more aggressive. You are more like and athlete or a jock kind of thing. You are a hunter. But if you are born of ash, you are more the medicine man type; you are more insightful and mysterious. You know more about like future, past, and looking at futures and stuff.

In this exchange, the students collaboratively explored the symbolic meaning of the house fire in the film and novel. What is salient about this stretch of dialogue is that the students framed their responses in a tentative, exploratory mode. Sarah started this stretch by posing some questions about what happened in the fire. Kathy then conjectured about the symbolic meanings of fires, noting that "the fire probably symbolizes something," a tentative stance reflected in "probably." Parks then described this exploratory process as the "maybe game," leading Devin to entertain possible meanings for both ash and fire. The fact that Devin framed his speculation with the words "I don't know where I'm going with this" represents his sense of the hypothetical, exploratory nature of his interpretations. Parks therefore created a context in which students felt comfortable exploring their ideas without concern for the need to generate definitive right answers.

In this context, students avoided judging each other. To further encourage students to adopt a nonjudgmental stance, Parks promoted the need for students to distinguish between the ideas being expressed and the students expressing those ideas. He described how he encouraged students to perceive ideas as having a life of their own:

> I ask the students if they can see the idea sitting there. They say yes they can. So I say, "When you respond, you have to respond to that idea, you cannot respond to the source of the idea." So, we begin separating ideas from individuals, which they do not have a lot of experience with. So, then, literally, the students will say, "I do not see student A's idea as that different from student B's idea," and they point to the middle of the room rather than the students. So, there is something there. I don't know what it is, but it seems to be working.

He also suggested to students that with any issue, there are certain prototypical stances on these issues that could be interjected into discussions, stances that are not necessarily associated with any individual person. He described these prototypical stances by using the words "Some people might say":

> I've encouraged students not to use the "I" if talking about a difficult topic but instead to present the "Some people might say." So, practically, in today's discussion, when some students say, "Whites have the easiest life," and the White students are sitting there thinking, "No," then I heard the White students doing it, echoing me, saying, "Some people might say that because they are White that they have to pay for their own college. So that means that their life is harder." And the students distancing or being equipped with the skills to

begin to talk about these things that they've never had the chance to talk about before.

Parks was therefore orchestrating expression of a range of competing perspectives associated with dialogic voices (Bahktin, 1981) related to "some people might say ..."). He then refrained from voicing a clear perspective on these issues, preferring students to experience disequilibrium in relationship to questions. In fact, as will be discussed later, some 10 weeks into the class students would ask him in individual meetings if he would please explain where he was at on all of "this stuff": "You never tell us what you think," explained one student.

After many of the discussions, Parks and Thein, and, in some cases, Richard Beach, would meet to review and reflect on the discussions as part of the research project. Because Thein kept notes about students' talk, they could reference specific instances in the discussion. We believe that these shared postdiscussion reflections had a positive influence on Parks's efforts to lead the discussions. For example, the researchers would note instances of extended stretches of discussion about a particular topic and what prompts or teaching techniques precipitated those stretches. Through reflecting on those techniques that fostered discussions, Parks could then capitalize on the use of those techniques in future discussions.

Using Writing as Discussion Starters

Parks also employed writing as a tool to prepare students for discussions. He framed journal prompts by voicing characters' perspectives. For one journal prompt, he passed out a note from Lulu, a character in *Love Medicine*, that stated, "Everybody around me keeps calling me a 'slut' based on the actions that happened in chapter five. They don't see all of the other parts of my life that you guys have read about. Will you explain to them that there is more to me than just that behavior?" In doing so, he encouraged students to not simply adopt characters' perspectives but to also consider how language, such as the word *slut*, functions to mediate identity construction.

Students wrote in their journals as homework assignments and often engaged in free-writes at the beginning of class. Parks often asked students to pass their journal entries around the circle so that they could read each other's journal reactions as a means of starting a discussion. Additionally, Parks often read aloud or provided students with a list of anonymous quotations from student journals as a means of provoking discussions. For example, in discussing the film *Smoke Signals* (Eyre, 1998), he provided students with anonymous quotations he had culled from students' journals related to the topic of race and asked students to circle the three quotes they perceived to be the most controversial, for example, "White people as a group enjoy an easier life than anybody else in the country." Starting with these controversial quotes fostered a debate between students about the moral responsibility for White Americans' treatment of Native Americans. For example, after he cited a student quote indicating that it is difficult to consider Whites as oppressive to Native Americans when Native Americans are prospering from casino gambling revenues, in response, Shelley, a White student, noted:

> This doesn't make sense; it says that they don't believe that we are unfair in real life; but I think that we are unfair. I mean, one of the quotes on here said, "Number seven, we just kicked them off the land and took it for our own." I mean, we gave away little stupid things in return, but we didn't really do a whole lot for them.

Parks then focused on Shelley's use of "we" in terms of making generalizations about groups:

> Let me speak for the students who aren't going to saying something here. Shelly, you keep saying "we," I mean, I wasn't there. I wasn't alive. I didn't have anything to do with it. Umm ... should I be lumped in with them?
>
> *Shelley*: It's like we as the White culture. I don't mean we (in the room) did it but that we are still stereotyped by that. Like it says here, that, like, "We did this and we did that," but we had nothing to with what our ancestors did, but we are still the ones who have to face the consequences for it ... I don't think that that is right, but what it is talking about is that we, those of sitting in this room right now, are being stereotyped by other people for what our ancestors did. It's not like we didn't do it, but we are facing the consequences for it. And I agree with you, I totally do, that it was totally unfair and we like stuck them in the corner and said like, "This is what you get, and we get everything else." So, it's like, but yet, it's not us that did it.

Shelley argued that contemporary White Americans should not be stereotyped for the acts committed by White American ancestors. Drawing on a previous minilesson in which Parks discussed the relationship between statistical and anecdotal truths about populations, Shelley focused on the use of "we" in terms of making generalizations about groups—a focus on how language categories functions to mediate perceptions of racial difference. Shelley's reference to the "we" as the students in the class who are not responsible for previous actions prompted further debate about the justifications for White settlements on Native American land. By focusing on the "we" category, the students were examining the larger issue of White people's moral responsibility for past actions.

At other times, Parks challenged students' discourses underlying these prototypical conceptions by voicing "orienting" discourses (Rex, 2001, 2002) that contradicted the students' discourses and cultural models constituting characters' identities. The students brought certain discourses and cultural models about Native American culture to their responses to both *Love Medicine* and *A Yellow Raft in Blue Water*. To challenge these discourses and cultural models with some of his own orienting discourses, in the class before starting the study of *Love Medicine*, Parks told students that prior to their arrival to the class he had drawn a scene featuring a Native American on the chalkboard, a picture hidden behind the projection screen. He then asked students to write in their journals about what they believed the hidden picture depicted. Parks described their prototypical perceptions and journal responses: "It is a Native American man usually on a horse. He has long hair. He is physically fit. He is looking in the distance because there is somehow always going to be White people around. He might have a bow and arrow." When asked the sources for their perceptions, the students cited examples of movies portraying Hollywood versions of Native Americans, such as Disney's *Pocahontas,* as common sources of their images. The students then compared these stereotypical images with descriptions of Native Americans in *Love Medicine*, as well as newspaper articles about contemporary Native Americans.

Parks then gave students the following journal prompt:

> If you were a Native American person and you heard that a group of non-Indians (the students in this class) were reading a novel that would likely serve to influence their understanding of your culture and experience, would you want them reading this novel? Would you want me, the teacher, to even introduce this novel to you?

Overwhelming, the students responded negatively—that the novel's depiction of everybody sleeping around and getting drunk just added to stereotypes of Native Americans. Parks continued to push students to grapple with this tension throughout their reading of the novel. Ultimately, students came to identify the character of Uncle Eli as the healthiest, citing his rejection of White culture's influence and his retention of traditional practices. By contrast, students came to understand some of the less healthy behaviors of other characters in the novel as precipitated by oppressive, institutional forces related to White culture and American governmental policy.

Parks also challenged students' stereotypical notions of Native American characters by describing institutional forces shaping Native Americans' lives, noting the high levels of poverty, alcoholism, health problems, and high school drop-outs. He then contrasted some of the stereotypical notions of Native Americans with historical information, including the South Dakota Wounded Knee massacre; the hangings of Native Americans at Mankato, Minnesota; and the violations of treaty agreements with Native Americans by the U.S. government. He also described the wide diversity of different Native American tribes related to differences in their habitats. In his initial reaction to *Love Medicine*, Devin perceived King as an abusive drunk who neglected his child. However, after Parks provided students with background information, Devin adopted a different perspective of King and constructed a role-play presentation of him as shaped by larger economic and cultural forces that undermine his sense of hope for his future.

Mediating Racial Tensions in Classroom Discussions

Though Parks was successful in fostering discussion with most of the students, three female Hmong students in the course—Mai, Pamela, and Sue—were often reluctant to actively participate in discussions. Some of this reluctance may reflect the fact that although students of color constitute the majority in the school, they are rarely acknowledged or listened to by those with social power. Such hesitancy may also be consistent with Southeast Asian cultural norms regarding both gender and the classroom authority of the teacher (Lee, 1996, 2002). Though Parks experienced some measure of success in mediating White students' resistance to interrogating racism, he was less successful in drawing these students into the classroom conversations of race and Whiteness. Moreover, in the discussion of the McIntosh (2006) essay on White privilege, these students openly challenged the assumption that only Whites were endowed with certain privileges—a position at times at odds with McIntosh—but the White students in the class did not take up their perspectives in ways that encouraged their further participation.

When Parks talked with these students individually about their participation at different times in the course, they explained that in discussing issues of race they were fearful of being perceived as biased if they expressed racial solidarity with peers or characters of color. Mai explained that this displayed itself even in small ways: "I wanted to talk about how much I enjoyed the novel *Obasan*, but I feared that the other students would think that I liked it just because it was Asian." Pamela noted that though White students experienced the invisible burden of a fear of being misunderstood as racists, the students of color were fearful of being perceived as saying something primarily in terms of racial allegiance; they feared being seen as doctrinaire or narrow minded. Pamela also noted that, given her outsider value stance, she had "learned how to read the other [White students]." As she noted:

I'm used to being in a group of all Asian people. I'll be hearing the same thing because we see things the same. But to see what a White person has to say about certain issues, like racism ... to see that it really does exist is as hard for them to confront as it is for me.

During Mai's participation in the course, she learned to realize the power of institutional forces of privilege, to the point that she believed that even though she may challenge Whites in the discussion, it was unlikely that they would change their racist value stances.

Recognizing that these students did not have an opportunity to develop this topic, Parks and Thein met privately with one of the students, Mai, a highly motivated student who ranked in the top of her class and had plans to continue her studies the following year at a state university. Although Parks had known Mai for years, her initial questions suggested that she did not understand Parks's objective, distant stance when facilitating the topic of White privilege. She noted that in focusing attention on challenging some of the White students in the class, some of her own and the other Hmong students' perspectives regarding White privilege had not been voiced in discussions. She also expressed frustration about the fact that "you all just talk about this stuff and then act like everything is fine," explaining that institutional racism adversely affects her to a greater degree than the White students in the class. Mai was skeptical about the effectiveness of engaging White students in critique of White privilege, questioning whether this kind of critique would really promote change or whether it might even reify White privilege. And she was frustrated about the fact that the system of White privilege, a system she did not believe would change, positioned her as different.

Mai also implied that Parks was reluctant to directly criticize the White students, explaining that if he was "saying stuff about 'bad Whites' or something, the students will, like, turn on you." Parks argued that he was reluctant to adopt a specific agenda designed to "change somebody in one class ... they have to consider things for themselves." As previously noted, Parks attempted to focus his critiques not on individual White students as racist or sexist but rather on the discourses and cultural models of White privilege (Trainor, 2002, 2005). However, Parks's approach assumes that his students can readily distinguish between critiques of discourses and cultural model and critiques of individual students. He also recognized with McCoy and Jones (2005, pp. 70–71) that changes in his White students' beliefs and attitudes did not necessarily:

... ensure social progress or liberation from Whiteness or racism.... There is no one ideology or pedagogical strategy that can solve racism or Whiteness.... Academia seems to be coherent in asserting how Whiteness disrupts "progress," but we seem to be less clear on what "progress" is and subsequently what our goals in such class-rooms should be.

During discussions, students like Mai were reluctant to publicly critique the White students in the class or to voice their frustrations about the system of White privilege. Parks realized that he needed to adopt a more proactive role in including these students in the discussions and in encour-aging them to voice their concerns.

Comparison of This Class with Other CIS Courses

The kinds of learning that occurred in this CIS course reflects some of the finding from some large-scale survey research on students' and teachers' perceptions of the benefits of taking or teaching CIS courses. In a study conducted in 2003–2004 of 476 students who enrolled five years previously in CIS courses (about half took one course) in 1999–2000, two years before the students in our study took the course, 93% of students indicated that taking the CIS courses improved their academic skills in preparation for college (Wahlstrom & Riedel, 2004a). The students also said that they expe-rienced intellectual stimulation and academic challenges that they had not found in many of their high school courses. One student said, "I preferred the environment where the [CIS] teacher gave us more responsibility and treated us more as young adults who were significantly responsible for our own learning" (p. 10). Of these students, 98.5% attended some form of postsecondary institution; 64% of these students had plans to apply to graduate school.

And a survey of teachers teaching in the program found that the CIS courses allowed students to have a college-level experience yet remain in high school (Wahlstrom & Riedel, 2004b). The teachers also said that participating in the CIS program meetings provided valuable professional development.

All of this suggests the critical importance of professional development programs to support teachers who are teaching multicultural literature (Lewis & Ketter, 2003; Lewis, Ketter, & Fabos, 2001). The fact that Parks could draw on the training and resources available through his participa-tion in the CIS program was a critical factor in the success of his teaching. In Chapter 10, we draw some implications for the importance of preservice and in-service training to teach multicultural literature.

It was also the case that Parks continued to employ the methods described in this chapter in teaching the same CIS literature course again in 2002. As part of her visit to observe Parks's students in 2002 after our study, the university faculty coordinator asked the students in the course to compare the CIS with their other literature courses, including their advanced placement (AP) courses. She cited some of the student comments:

- This is better than AP because there the goal is a test, not learning. This class is challenging and I learn more.
- Everything's totally structured in AP but here we stay involved because there are no ruts or set routines.
- The course is intellectually challenging to think and see myself and the world differently.
- It helps connect with life, and I look at myself in a new light from reading these books.
- We get to hear other people's opinions and to make connections between the text and real life.
- This course prepares us for college really, for taking college classes not just making scores on tests to get into college.
- I can voice my opinions here where in AP we just sit still and work quietly to get ready for the big test. Here we are rewarded for opening up and for listening. It's the difference between closed [in AP] and open [in CIS].
- AP has one answer; here there are no right and wrong answers.
- I've learned to expand my mind and I am getting an edge on college work.
- This course gives literature a life; books here are not presented as a tunnel but as an ocean.
- We are discovering who we are at this stage of our lives and this course really helps with that by showing us who people in the books are who are like and different from us.
- I'll remember and keep lots from this class; AP goes in for the test but then is gone really soon.

Though these comments are from a group of Parks's students a year after the group in our study, these students' comments reflected the difference between the orientation in Parks's class on critical analysis revolving around dialogic tensions and the orientation in the typical AP literature courses on preparing students for the AP exams. These students noted that having to prepare for the exams created an overly structured approach based on formulating interpretations evaluated based on the AP test-scoring criteria. In contrast to a course driven by the need to cover material according to testing mandates, Parks's course was driven by the alternative philosophy of the CIS program, which focuses on the need to foster divergent, critical thinking as important preparation for college work.

Summary

This chapter illustrates the ways a teacher, making explicit his own processes of identity construction, helped his students to negotiate dialogic tensions across competing social worlds in both lived and text experiences. The fact that the students witnessed their teacher sharing his experiences of continually negotiating the competing demands of different worlds provided them with specific practices and tools for exploring alternatives to their status quo identities. This suggests that rather than masking their identity construction to create a façade of neutral objectivity, teachers need to make explicit their processes of identity construction associated with interpreting literature.

In the chapters that follow, we consider the impact that Parks's instruction had on particular students. We examine what kinds of change, if any, occurred for individual students as a result of participating in this course and engaging with this literature. The next three chapters describe six students who demonstrated different degrees of change in their participation in various discourses. These case-study profiles illustrate the ways students internalized some of the practices and tools from the course in constructing their identities.

In Chapter 9, we return to Parks's class and an analysis of the dialogic tensions that occurred in discussions as a result of his fostering multiple perspectives in class discussions. As we demonstrate, through participating in these discussions, some of the six students profiled in the next two chapters, as well as other students in the course, began to interrogate their status quo identities, resulting in a shift in their identity constructions, the subject of Chapter 10.

CHAPTER **6**

Identity Construction Congruent with the School World

Corey and Michelle

In this and the next two chapters, we report on six individual students' identity constructions. These six students are two White males, Corey and Devin; two White females, Michelle and Kayla; and two students of color, Mai and Kathy.

None of these students demonstrated marked dramatic change in their identities during the six-month period of the class; such changes in identities are likely to occur only over a period of years or decades. However, as noted in Chapter 4, we did find some variation in students' reactions to the dialogic tensions operating in the class that may have led them to entertain alternative discourses and cultural models. We were therefore curious as to why some students were more open to entertaining alternative perspectives than other students. As we demonstrate, consistent with the theme of this book, their propensity to entertain change had much to do with their allegiances to their social worlds—the extent to which they were comfortable constituting themselves through status quo versus interrogating the limitations of these status quo discourses. Given the attempts by teachers such as Parks to foster critical analysis of status quo discourses and cultural models, understanding why these efforts succeed with some students but not others has implications for devising critical pedagogical approaches.

We were also interested in examining differences in students' agency in constructing past, present, and future selves. Because students in Parks's

141

course adopted identities as future college students, we were particularly interested in how their perceptions of themselves as college students influenced their sense of agency. For students like Corey and Michelle whose agency was grounded in status quo, present worlds, an identity as a college student may have been difficult to envision. In contrast, students like Kayla and Mai, who envisioned themselves as future college students, were more likely to critique the limitations of their current, status quo worlds.

And given Gee's (2004, 2006) contention that working-class students are more aligned with relationships in peer and family worlds, whereas upper-middle-class students are more aligned with school, community, and adult worlds, we were interested in determining variations in the nature of these students' alignments with different worlds.

We therefore selected six students who represented a wide range in their willingness to entertain alternative perspectives in the course—openness that led some of them to amend or revise their discourses and cultural models. Of these six students, two, Corey and Michelle, demonstrated little or no change in their beliefs and attitudes. Despite their exposure to challenges to their identity constructions, they retained status quo discourses and cultural models in alignment to the institutional forces of family, peer group, and sports.

As we noted in Chapter 1, it is important to consider the affective, rhetorical appeal of these discourses and cultural models of race, class, and gender to adolescents. For Corey and Michelle, their appeal may be related to their need for a sense of community, order, self-initiative, and control—ideals that go beyond simple racism (Trainor, 2002, 2005). We believe that their lack of critical reflection stemmed from their sense of security with the emotional appeals of the discourses and cultural models constituting their status quo worlds of sports, school, workplace, and family, as opposed to alternative future worlds such as the world of college. Because these status quo worlds afforded them with a sense of agency, they therefore had little reason to step outside those worlds or to look critically at those worlds. Their lack of critical analysis of institutional forces shaping their own lives was also evident in their lack of criticism of institutional forces operating in the text worlds they read about in Parks's class. Because they did not step outside of their comfortable, status quo perspectives, they were therefore less likely to engage in perspective taking—a willingness to entertain alternative points of view and scenarios in coping with life.

Corey

Corey, a popular White athlete at Thompson identified strongly with his working-class family background. Corey's father was a self-employed construction worker who bid for construction work with Corey's uncle; his mother was not employed outside the home. Corey would be the first in his family to attend college.

In class discussions, interviews, and journal entries, it was common to hear Corey voicing his family's beliefs, using them to anchor his opinions. This reflected the strong socializing force of the family in shaping racial attitudes around the need for social conformity (Feagin, 2000)—in this case, family members who were uneasy about the increasing diversity of the school. He noted that his mother did not like the increasing diversity and was therefore reluctant to send his younger brother and sister to Thompson.

Much of Corey's identity and sense of agency revolved around his performance as an athlete on the baseball, football, and hockey teams—he was captain of the hockey team. He traced his active participation in sports to the influence of his father as a role model who also played football. He said, "He kind of got me into it, like when I was seven, he'd get me out there."

Corey perceived himself as performing two different identities—one within the world of sports and the other outside the world of sports. In the world outside of sports, he said that he was "probably one of the quieter kids in school, so I'm pretty, I'm shy actually in school, you know what I mean, I talk to a lot of people, but I'm not like, I don't just run into crowds and start talking to people." However, when he was engaged in sports he said, "I change differently, I, I can go after people, I can talk a lot, I talk a lot more during sports, so I don't know, I think people see me as a bigger kid ... I think they see me as a nicer guy." He cited the example of assuming this alternative identity as captain of the hockey team in which he asserted himself in a leadership role:

> Before a game that's all I think about and when I get out there and our team's down, like—hockey, we had an alright team but we lost a lot of games, I just get mad. I was a captain so I gotta say stuff in the locker room. I can say stuff, I can get mad in the locker room and stuff, so it gives me more confidence to—like I know the guys who are in the locker room with me are gonna listen to me, like think about what I'm saying.

Being a school athlete afforded Corey with a high status level in the school and community. He said, "I think you're better known when you play sports, just like you're more popular, so yeah, throughout the community too, 'cause a lot of kids, they play hockey and little kids come and skate with the older kids and they'll ask for your autograph."

His participation in sports was linked to discourses of self-discipline and competition in the school culture. He said,

There's discipline in football so you learn that, but then I'd say hockey there's a lot more discipline … if you do something wrong you're gonna get punished for it. Even at school, he [the coach] finds out about everything. And then baseball, baseball's like, a more relaxing sport, more fun, I mean still, you gotta stay disciplined if you wanna play, you can't be going out, getting in trouble …

When asked about the relationship between sports and race, he argued that athletics are largely color-blind, creating a bridge between all races. He said that when groups in the school congregate with each other, "people group themselves like sports players, I mean we sit, like I don't think, there's some racial, but if you're a sports player you can sit next to somebody who's a different color." Even as Corey explained that students of all races play on the football team, he also acknowledged that hockey and baseball are dominated by White students, whereas basketball is dominated by African American students. He did not perceive this segregation by sport as problematic given his adherence to discourse of color-blind racism that ignores the larger institutional forces, such as the expenses associated with playing hockey, resulting in this segregation by sport.

Discourses of Athleticism and Meritocracy

Corey adhered strongly to a discourse of athleticism linked to discourses of individual achievement, competition, and discipline operating in the larger school culture. As suggested by working-class British adolescent males' football fan club activities (Nayak, 2003), sports functions as a nostalgic substitute for workplace bonding in what were, prior to the diminution of manufacturing jobs, vibrant workplace contexts. These working-class males' obsession with sports and winning appears to serve as a mechanism to avoid addressing complexities and contradictions associated with the declining status of working-class people in England. For Corey, the world of sports provided a codified context based on set rules and clear winners and losers as opposed to the ambiguous complexities operating in other worlds.

Corey therefore adopted a cultural model that explains success and failure in terms of individual initiative and hard work. Because Corey perceived everyone as having an equal chance at sports, he perceived sports as a metaphor, and success in sports as a function of individual motivation and for meritocracy dependent on each athlete's willingness to train and work hard. He also assessed differences in student social groups according to their participation in and attitudes toward school sports. He criticized Hmong students for their lack of school spirit, which he attributed to the fact that these students were less involved in football, hockey, and basketball. He also judged his peers based on their displays of self-discipline—a value operating within a discourse of athleticism suggesting that success in sports requires the ability to maintain control of oneself both in school and outside of school.

This focus on individual competition in athletics can be linked to a discourse of traditional masculinity constituting an autonomous, independent self. This discourse suggests that anyone can succeed if he or she works hard because everyone is judged according to his or her own individual efforts and motivation on an equal playing field (Young, 2004). For Corey, this discourse of meritocracy conflicted with a critical discourse of institutional constraints and barriers associated with Parks's metaphor of *hurdles*, which, from Corey's perspective, was inconsistent with the notion of an equal playing field because it suggests that some people have an unfair advantage over others.

Given his adherence to these discourses of physical and intellectual control operating in the school culture, Corey was celebrated as a role model by school administrators. Thus, in the school culture he enjoyed a strong sense of agency as a star high school athlete constituted by discourses of athleticism and meritocracy. However, in Parks's class, because these discourses were challenged by other students, his social status was also challenged. He therefore often adopted a defensive stance, resisting critiques of athleticism and meritocracy in arguments. In the class, he sat with other male athletes and typically supported their perspectives, often in opposition to female students' assertions. He was particularly critical of Kayla, whose challenges to male domination of discussion irritated him and the other male athletes. He said,

> She will be trying to argue an opinion and four or five people in the class will be like, "No, it's right here in the texts! It says, this is what happens." "No! I think it's deeper than that!" No! It can't be deeper than that! It is the deepest as it will go! She just doesn't know when to call it quits and say okay whatever let's move on to the next subject. That was one of the main reasons people strike out; some people kind of had issues with her.

Corey based his refutation of Kayla's opinions in terms of textual evidence—"it's right here in the texts! It says, this is what happens," as well as in resistance to Kayla's interest in exploring larger symbolic or ideological meanings. His need for objectivity reflected a larger need for a definitive absolutism and certainty associated with a discourse of Whiteness (Barnett, 2000). In this cultural model of a controlled, set world, it is assumed that factual evidence from the text supports a set of definitive truths (Barnett, 2000). Students like Kayla who challenged this definitive notion of the world with dialogic tensions and alternative interpretations—the idea that "it's deeper than that"—were perceived as threatening to Corey's need for certainty.

This need for control reflected a binary of masculine strength set against feminine weakness. Davies (2003) argued that gender binaries position male heroes as physically strong and dominant, set against the weak female, a binary that undermines their openness to complexity and to nurturing aspects of the self (Young, 2004). This need for control is reflected in Corey's perceptions of his role as a physical protector of others whom he perceived as defenseless. He described his role on his hockey team as that of protector:

> I take, not a lot of, I'm not out there to score for my team, I'm out there basically to protect littler guys, so I take a lot of penalties and they put you in the penalty box and the fans are right behind you yelling stuff at you—I mean I like it, I doesn't bother me, I mean actually I like it a lot.

Similarly, in his response to *Bastard out of Carolina* (Allison, 1993), Corey reacted angrily to the character of Daddy Glen who abuses his stepdaughter. He again adopted the role of protector of defenseless people, in this case, Bone:

> This almost made me want to jump into the novel and take this guy's head off. How can you be so sick and twisted to do that to a helpless little girl. People like this make me so protective of my little sister and even my mom.

In class discussions, given his adherence to a competitive discourse of individualism, Corey was critical of government programs such as affirmative action that he believed undermined people's self-initiative and motivation. He consistently argued that affirmation action policies discriminated against Whites both in terms of college admissions and job-hiring practices. He explained his perception that working-class Whites like himself have worked hard to obtain admissions or jobs whereas non-Whites may not have but are still given preferential treatment.

In a journal entry related to affirmative action, Corey wrote that these practices were adversely affecting his chances of becoming a police officer:

> I want to be a police officer, but supposedly nowadays it is not easy to be a cop if you are White. Now it is a lot easier to become a cop if you are a minority. If you are White and you are better than the person next to you and he is Black, the White person might not get that job. Just because that person is a different color.

He also cited what he believed to be instances of reverse discrimination in traffic violations. Drawing from a recent newspaper report that he heard about, Corey posited that White drivers were discriminated against by the police:

> I don't ... really ... because I heard of statistics that a White person is more likely to get pulled over by cops, but a minority gets pulled over then they get off. They don't get a ticket, whereas there is a better percentage of White people who do get pulled over; you are going to get a ticket.

In Corey's model of reverse discrimination, Whites are the victims of their skin color. Though other students in the class cited data supporting the claim that people of color are stopped more frequently without justifiable cause than White drivers, Corey's cultural model of "Whites are discriminated against" left him unable and or unwilling to accept this counterevidence.

His discourses and cultural models of individualism and meritocracy also mediated his interpretations of characters' actions. He explained the successes and failures of characters' actions in terms of the level of their own individual initiative and motivation, as reflected in his explanations of characters' actions in *Bastard out of Carolina*. He argued that Bone's future depends on her own self-initiative: she is responsible for her own fate. As he noted,

> I think she could [succeed] if she stayed in school and went to college after, just like anybody else could. But, I don't know, the things that went on in her life might mess her up a little bit. She might need counseling or something, but I still think that she could get probably get through it. I just think that she has a chance like anybody else. *Anybody* can [his emphasis], if you do the right stuff and work hard your whole life.

Corey also suggested that Daddy Glen's problems were the result of turning away from his family's expectations for him. He explained that Daddy Glen would do better if he began living the way he was brought up in a middle-class family.

> I thought that Glen sort of started off backwards from his family. His family is rich, and he should have an easier life to start off with, but he kind of failed at everything and started going down the tubes, and now he's got to rebuild his way back up. Like, you guys were saying, he didn't follow in his family's footsteps; he kind of funneled down. He's got to just build up and work harder now to get back up to where his family is ... with expectations.

Corey adopted a discourse of meritocracy to argue that Daddy Glen needed to "just build up and work harder now to get back up to where his family is" so that he could regain his middle-class status. Given his adherence to a discourse of Whiteness, Corey did not recognize the ways the White middle-class people in the novel actually discriminated against and stigmatized White working-class people. He therefore did not consider class differences within race—the fact that once Daddy Glen is poor, he faces institutional barriers that mitigate against his efforts to work hard.

Corey also resisted challenges to discourses of masculinity in the texts, a discourse consistent with discourses of athleticism and control. In responding to *Bless Me, Ultima* (Anaya, 1995), he was critical of the portrayal of men in the novel, noting "that the only thing the men do in this novel is eat, work, sleep, and think about sex … this is one of the major reasons why I really didn't like this book as much as others I have read. Men are basically portrayed as pigs and drunks." And in responding to *The House on Mango Street* (Cisneros, 1991), he adopted sexist discourses in a critique of a young female character's attempts to wear provocative clothing:

> I feel that a lot of girls try to dress like they are too old; they should try and look young. You just don't want to look good to have guys look at you all the time. I feel this is why so many young girls get bodily harmed and raped.

In his response to *Obasan* (Kogawa, 1993), a novel set in Canada during World War II, he posed the following rhetorical question in his journal: "Would it be better or not for all the Japanese in Canada to go back to Japan [during World War I] … I ask this because the Japanese are always getting slurs thrown at them in Canada. The reason is if they all went back to Japan would they have more freedom?" In analyzing the racial inequalities in the novel, Corey wrote, "You have to admit that everybody isn't treated totally fairly, but for the most part they are." He then posited that if the character Naomi was living in America today, she would be pleased with what she would find: "Naomi would come to the world of today and look at the Japanese American or Canadian and would be proud. They are very important people of today coming up with a lot of our electronics." This analysis focuses on the actions of the individuals—Japanese Canadians, defined in stereotypical terms, without critiquing systems or institutions shaping their internment.

In a class discussion about *Kindred* (Butler, 1979), Corey described what he would do if he adopted the identity of Rufus, the slave owner's son:

> If I were to go back then I could see myself running a plantation, I mean if I was raised that way, I mean, but I don't, I couldn't see myself

hitting somebody with a whip, especially a girl, I mean how could you just sit there and hit a girl with a whip, tied down, defenseless ... I just couldn't see myself doing it. That's what's hard to think about.

In imagining himself assuming Rufus's identity and moving between different worlds, Corey perceived himself as assuming a masculine role of someone who could not whip defenseless females, a stance that minimizes the role of race. When asked by Parks why he focused on gender rather than race, he noted,

Oh well, I mean, like for, I don't know, I couldn't hit nobody, so I don't think my plantation would be going too well if I was, 'cause all those guys whip everybody just to like discipline them and make them stay in the plantation, and if you run away you get whipped and I couldn't do it, I don't think.

Corey avoided reference to race, except in twice using the pronoun "them," likely rooted in the fear of being misunderstood as racist (Lewis-Charp, 2003). He used sentence fragments and pauses in searching for words about race, a struggle that reflects his difficulty in analyzing issues of race. And in reiterating the fact that "I couldn't do it," he continued to focus on individual choice as opposed to a critique of the institution of slavery.

In summary, Corey performed the collective identities acquired through his allegiances to the worlds of athletics, family, and school that afforded him a strong sense of agency in his status quo worlds (Taylor, 2002). Corey performed Whiteness in his perception of self as nonracialized (Keating, 2004), a resistance to group membership's significance in favor of individuality. Corey preferred a color-blind stance (Bonilla-Silva, 2001) and rejected the structural nature of discrimination except when he interpreted it as being unfair for Whites, as reflected in his attitudes toward affirmative action.

These discourses of athleticism, Whiteness, and meritocracy, and the cultural model of a competitive social hierarchy that he acquired from these discourses defined his identity as self-assured, confident, authoritative, and in control, which mitigates against the potential to explore conflicting subjectivities, ambiguities, and complexities (Davies, 1993; Trainor, 2002). In consistently subscribing to these discourses and cultural models, Corey therefore demonstrated little change in the course as someone who was largely satisfied with his identity allegiances to status quo worlds. He therefore had little reason to step outside those worlds to critique their limitations.

Michelle

Michelle was a working-class, White, female student whose parents, as was the case with Corey, have been a stable influence on her and her brother. Longtime residents in the school's neighborhood, her parents were a classic example of a family in this community that struggles to succeed economically. When Michelle was born, her father was working a variety of jobs: He was a warehouse laborer, an army reservist, a security guard, and anything else he could fit into his schedule. Eventually, he began work with the Veteran's Administration (VA) where he appraised houses and had remained with the VA for 15 years. Michelle's mother followed a similar path. Beginning as a hairstylist, she eventually found work as an entry-level clerk with the Internal Revenue Service (IRS). Her longevity allowed her to move up the ranks, receiving additional training and some college course work along the way. She had remained with the IRS for nearly two decades.

Michelle's parents were not involved in their community or church. "Michelle and I basically hated going to church," explained Michelle's older brother, Bill. "The only time we 'did anything' was when I ushered to work with the kids and when Michelle ran a game booth a couple of times at the Fall Festival." In contrast to some of the other case-study participants, Michelle and her brother were rarely involved in community organizations or activities.

The work ethic displayed by Michelle's parents influenced both her and her brother. At age 16, Bill began working at a local Dairy Queen restaurant and continued to work full time at the restaurant after his high school graduation. When Michelle turned 16, her brother hired her as a part-time worker, and she continued working at the restaurant even after graduation. Bill and Michelle's focus on the need to be employed, despite the relatively low pay, as opposed to seeking postsecondary education, mirrors their parents' need to maintain steady employment and job loyalty. Bill said that this sense of loyalty was "probably why we are both still working at Dairy Queen; we feel like you need to work hard and be loyal to those who give you a break."

Michelle was confident and vocal both in class and in the school in general, particularly through her involvement in the school newspaper. However, during the course, she was hospitalized due to major health problems. In classroom discussions, she consistently voiced strong opinions about texts. However, she was not a typical popular girl at Thompson. She fit in neither with the jocks nor with a group she described as the *ghetto girls,* whose practices of wearing makeup, tight-fitting clothes, or the latest fashion trends she criticized. Given the limited roles available to

girls at Thompson, Michelle solidly rejected both of these dominant feminine roles. According to Michelle,

> I honestly haven't gone to Winter-Fest since I have been here, coro-
> nation I mean. I have not gone to a homecoming thing; I leave, I
> don't go to pep fests ... I don't really care if someone wants to put
> something on their head to say, "Hey look at me, I'm popular!" That
> was not a big deal to me. I always left and every teacher knows that I
> did ... I mean it's just not me.

But although Michelle did not want any part in school sanctioned popularity contests, her social interactions in school and in class suggested a more
complicated picture than one in which she rejected school culture and
norms on the whole. Rather, Michelle did embrace many of the ideological frameworks and discourses operating in her school and working-class
community, including those related to her gender identity. However, her
rejection of typical White female roles at Thompson created more ambiguous and circuitous avenues through which she constructed her identity
within these frameworks. In many ways, unlike Corey, she represents a
case in contradiction and a powerful example of competing discourses in
the identity construction of one student. However, unlike Devin and Kayla,
who are discussed in the next chapter, she did not acknowledge and address
these contradictions in ways that led to change in her thinking. Some of this
resistance to examining contradictions was related to her sense of agency
as constituted by a focus on peer relationships, particularly her future marriage and family. This focus precluded Michelle from envisioning herself as
a college student operating in adult worlds (Gee, 2004, 2006).

Discourses of Individualism and Meritocracy

As was the case with Corey, Michelle drew on the prevailing discourses
of individualism and meritocracy operating in the school culture to construct herself as someone who was principled and self-confident, who
trusted her own instincts, and who was not afraid to hold and express
strong opinions. She also was concerned with performing identities in a
carefully composed, calculated manner as a social chameleon of sorts. She
liked to think of herself as someone who could fit in with any social group
at school but who chose not to be a true member of any of these groups.
She also was not concerned about how others perceived her. She said, "Not
everybody is going to agree with everything you do ... I really don't care
what anybody in this school thinks of me, and I never have." Michelle
found her social power and status in the school through believing that she
had the freedom not to fit in, not to care, and to float between groups. In

describing her close friends and their relationships to the popular students in the school, Michelle said,

> We know all the primary popular people; we just choose not to associate with them—that's how we do it. We get along with them, we can talk to them, we don't have a problem with them, but you see them in the hall and can have a conversation … I bet a lot of people in the school know us. But I don't really care … "

Here Michelle expressed that she not only does not care what others think of her, but she also does not have a problem with others who choose not to conform to mainstream hegemonic student norms at Thompson. However, though Michelle said she did not have a problem with students who do not fit the White, mainstream norm, this does not mean that she believed these students should be accepted by others, nor did it necessarily mean that she even liked such students. The same discourse of individuality and meritocracy Michelle used to explain that she and others were free to do and say what they want she also used to suggest that acceptance into particular social groups at Thompson was an individual choice for each student. Michelle explained that not being accepted into a particular group has to do with how that student presents herself and not with any systemic or institutional forces beyond that student's individual control.

Thus, although Michelle used discourses of individualism in theory, in practice Michelle was extremely concerned with her own ability to fit in discursively with powerful White students in the school. She was therefore agitated by students in her English classroom and in the school at large who did not present themselves in ways that conformed to mainstream White peer culture at Thompson. Thus, she used the same discourses of individualism and meritocracy to give herself and others license to discriminate against certain students, not based on race (e.g., skin color) but based on how individuals presented themselves through practices and performances consistent or inconsistent with status quo cultural norms.

Cultural Model: People Choose Their Social Standing Based on Choices about Their Presentational Style

In responding to issues of systemic oppression, Michelle relied on cultural models assuming that though race, class, and gender categories should not be used to judge others, individuals can and should be judged on actions, dress, and appearance. The following journal prompt, in which students were asked to think about who—in terms of, for example, race, class, gender, or sexual orientation—has the easiest life in America, typifies Michelle's use of this cultural model to dismiss systemic oppression:

If I were to look at it from a race point of view I would have to say that overall it would be easier to be a "White" person. Although a few exceptions would be when it comes to scholarships, it's cultured people, also when it come to a person getting a job cultured is easier ... I don't necessarily think a certain hair color or eye color has to do with an easier way of life. I think it has to do with how you present yourself. Obviously if you dressed like a bum you aren't going to look that good compared to somebody else.

In this excerpt, Michelle proposed that conflicts between different groups are not due to race but to personal behavior and appearance, noting that "I don't think it's necessarily racial ... it's how you present yourself." She suggested that how someone presents herself is entirely a matter of personal choice. This cultural model assumes that particular groups of people are not oppressed institutionally, but rather individuals are rejected based on personal choices. It places the onus for students' social standing on their individual motivation and choice—how they choose to present themselves in certain ways to certain students as opposed to how institutionalized discourses position them as students. Any critical analysis of students' success or failure in the system is focused on individuals' ability to choose as opposed to the institutional practices constituting race, class, and gender group categories.

Michelle's discourses of race reflected her parents' and grandparents' concern with the neighborhood's increasing diversity, which is stereotypically associated with a decline in real estate values (Fine & Weis, 1999). As longtime residents of the East Side neighborhood who devoted a lot of money to upgrading their house, Michelle's parents expressed concerns about the fact that the neighborhood was "going dark." In an interview, Michelle's brother, Bill, said that their grandfather explicitly stated racist perspectives: "My grandpa would actually go up to like, you know, like ethnic people and say negative things right to their face. He wasn't KKK or anything, but he sounded like it sometimes. I imagine that kind of rubbed off on my dad a little bit."

Bill and Michelle perceived their grandfather and father as adopting racist perspectives; however, they did not believe that they had to accept those views. As Bill said, "My dad had a firm belief that his views were his and you need to develop your own; you hear his views, but he doesn't impose them on people." They therefore believed that they could construct their own attitudes about issues of race in their neighborhood and school.

In talking about her own social standing at school, Michelle attributed her status to how she has presented herself to others. In an interview, she explained that students at Thompson choose their social groups during their freshman year by participating in certain sports, dating certain people, and sitting in certain areas of the cafeteria. About herself, Michelle said, "I didn't know what I wanted to do freshman year, so I was absolutely nothing and I still am, but I like that. I'm not crappy; I'm not ghetto, I have my own group of friends, but I am happy."

In identifying herself as "nothing," Michelle described herself as socially neutral—she was able to function in the environment of Thompson without actively identifying with any particular social group. In describing her group allegiances in the school, she said that she identified with a group of people who do not care and who chose to have less prestige in the school than the more popular students:

> I would say that we were like secondary. Like there is a primary popular group that everybody knows and then we are secondary. The group that doesn't want to get to involved and be like totally [Thompson]. And yet we want to be cool, and yeah I bet a lot of people in school know us. But I don't really care.

Here Michelle actually empowered herself by suggesting that she could choose to fit in with popular students and that she was accepted by them but that she made a personal decision not to join them. Additionally, identifying with neutrality at Thompson entailed conforming to the general norms of the White mainstream. Michelle's desired social invisibility is the result of maintaining fringe membership in mainstream, White, popular groups. Without her Whiteness, Michelle would not be afforded this invisibility or nothingness.

In Michelle's cultural model of schooling, she placed a high priority on the value of fitting in to predetermined group categories and practices according to what groups one chooses, with little challenge to the assumptions behind these preexisting race, class, and gender categories:

> I think your younger freshman years are what decides where you fit in totally. And I think a lot of people can say if I hadn't done that as a freshman I wouldn't and I think it's true. You find your little niche freshman year, and that is where you are stuck pretty much for the rest of your four years. You know whether it's a geek or whether it's a band that's where you are going to fit in. You want to be a popular person, then you are going to go out for all the sports. Whether you can get the ball or throw the ball or not. You are going to go for it because that is what you want and that is what determines popularity and culture.

She perceived many of students of color, to whom she referred as *cultured people*—a manifestation of race talk (Bonilla-Silva, 2001)—as not fitting in because they lacked the funds to play sports.

I think that is why cultured people are not totally popular because they cannot afford to play all the sports they can't afford to lift the ball; they can't afford to play whatever. And that is why they tend to make their own groups based off their own popularity. Like, the Asian culture club or whatever, that is why they tend to do that because that is their outlet. Instead of sports or whatever they will have their own clubs and make their own space of popularity that's all 'cause they can't afford stuff like that is what I think.

When we asked Michelle about how race influences social status, she proposed that it did not. Rather, she again put forth that individuals make choices about how to present themselves—she believed that this was how social status is measured.

As does Corey, Michelle expressed resentment about criticisms of Whites by "cultured people." She said,

In cultured people it is like totally different because it is about them and about who they are, like, if somebody was going to sit there and bash on us, I'm sure that we would take offense to it too. I'm not saying everybody is bashing on each other, I just think that it is hard when somebody sits there and talks about your race or your culture … a part of you, pretty much. I think that anybody will sit there and feel uncomfortable with that.

Michelle's descriptions of her interactions with students of color at Thompson further suggest a color-blind stance toward racism (Bonilla-Silva, 2001). In thinking about why she personally knew very few Hmong students, Michelle suggested two possible reasons. First, despite the fact that there were three Hmong students in her English class, Michelle believed that "I don't have any Hmong people in my classes." Second, Michelle attributed her lack of contact with Hmong students to the exclusive social practices of Hmong students. She recognized that these students were rarely seen at school events or activities—at least the ones she attended—but she did not see this as attributable to a lack of practices of inclusion on the part of White students but rather to an exclusivity on the part of Hmong students: the way these students chose to present themselves socially. The following passage demonstrates Michelle's ideas both regarding Hmong students' exclusivity and a general inclusivity on the part of mainstream students at Thompson—again she forwarded the notion that personal choice is at play in school social status:

I don't think it depends on race. I mean for Hmong people I do think it is different. I think they like being in their own group. I don't think they feel singled out but that is what they like. That is what they are comfortable with, you know, that's what they want and if Hmong people wanted more they would go for it … I don't think anybody really is turned down by friends or people. I don't think Thompson tends to turn down people at all. Groups, I mean. Yeah if they were in my class or whatever you can sit by me at lunch …

Her perception that the social status of Hmong students was based on their actions as opposed to racist hierarchies is mediated by a discourse of individualism and meritocracy. She pointed out that groups were not turned down and that individual Hmong students made their own choices to form exclusive social groups. If those individuals were to want more, they needed simply to go for it, presumably by presenting themselves in particular ways consistent with the social practices of mainstream White students.

Interestingly, Michelle did acknowledge the strength of White mainstream culture, particularly in the form of the culture of athleticism at Thompson but, like Corey, perceived sports as an equalizer of races rather than as a domain through which White students maintained power in the school. She believed that African American and Latino students were accepted into mainstream groups on an individual basis, if they chose to participate in White-dominated sports of football and hockey. She cited individual examples of practices involved with these sports to explain why Hmong students' lack of athletic involvement kept them from being accepted:

The Hmong people have no way to bring themselves into it [athletics], which tends to be a big thing at Thompson; they do not have a way to bring themselves in. Black people obviously do, whether it's basketball or football, and that's how [A], he's Black, popular with Black people, popular with athletic people, pretty much with everybody in the school. [G] same way, Black same thing, got in from football. I think that is how the Mexican people did it too. I think football is a big thing for guys and tends to be a White, Black, and Mexican sport. There is no really Hmong sport for people to do or they don't feel accepted.

In reality, Hmong students at Thompson were actively involved in sports; however, they were involved in sports such as tennis or badminton rather than football or hockey—the sports to which Michelle seemed to refer when she broadly referenced sports. Because Hmong students were not involved with sports they could not possibly be accepted by athletic people, by which in the previous excerpt Michelle clearly referred to White students who played football or hockey.

Although Michelle proposed that African American students were often accepted by athletic people in school culture through their involvement in sports—especially in comparison to Hmong students—her attitude changed significantly when she discussed the social behavior of African American students. She expressed annoyance toward African American students for being loud in their hallway behavior:

> They [African American students] are loud, and they drive me crazy all up in the hall. You can hear them halfway down the hall, and it's just like that's rude. You know? I'm not saying I wouldn't talk to them. I don't have any problems with them; it's just annoying, and I wouldn't really be friends with them. I would talk to them and probably wouldn't say anything.

Similarly, Michelle attributed White students' low attendance at the high school basketball games to this loud behavior:

> I personally wouldn't go to a basketball game because I know that the Black people will be so loud. And I would get so mad and would be like, "Shut up." You know, 'cause, not only, I don't care if they are loud and they are cheering or whatever, but they will start talking about stuff and they will get so loud. I am like, "Shut up, shut up." And you get a headache, and you don't want to be there anymore. It is just so loud that I wouldn't even go. I wouldn't put myself through all that headache just to go see a game.

Michelle applied the same rationale used in explaining why Hmong students don't fit in with the popular group to explain the status of African American students in the school. She again set up a construct by which she viewed individual African American students as excluding themselves through their behavior or presentational choices, rather than seeing White students as excluding certain cultural practices of particular racial groups. In the following quote she pointedly stated that being loud is unacceptable with the popular students" "I think they [African American students] still can be accepted but like with the popular people, no. If you are loud, don't even bother … that's just not how other cultures like you to be."

Though Michelle used a cultural model that said, "It's not race, it's how you present yourself" as a means to claim that race was not an important factor in the social hierarchy at Thompson, this cultural model functions within a discourse of color-blind racism (Bonilla-Silva, 2001). As a White student, she seemed unaware of the racial social systems creating hierarchies within the school in which the practices of being White were the neutral norm against which practices such as being loud were judged.

Michelle frequently used this same construct in making sense of characters she encountered in classroom literature. In her journal responses to *Obasan*, she grappled with her beliefs about individual and institutional racism, considering some of the dialogic tensions portrayed in the text. The following journal entry was one of Michelle's early responses related to *Obasan*. In this entry, Michelle adopted a color-blind stance toward racism and the discourse of individualism in which individuals are responsible for how they present themselves:

> The first quote that really caught my attention was "How come you got such a flat face Naomi? Steamroller run over ya?" That quote really stood out for two reasons. One was because of the fact that they even had the guts to say it to someone, and two how Naomi or anybody else never says anything about it.
>
> If somebody were to make fun of you because of your race and facial features you should stand up for yourself and be proud of your heritage. Although in Naomi's world no one that I have seen really stands up for their culture (Japanese). The other quote that struck me as quite weird was when they were talking about how they had to change their names because they were too complicated to remember. Again, as I mentioned earlier I can't believe they wouldn't stand up for their cultural ways. To change something so drastic as your name, that's just crazy, and to me it's unheard of. I could never imagine life being that bad where you would have to change something that is a part of you.

In this journal entry, Michelle reacted in two ways. First, she expressed outrage at the idea that anyone would judge or make fun of another person based on his or her facial features or name. She saw this kind of judgment as racist. To Michelle, facial features and names were equivalent to heritage, or cultural ways. She did not believe that anyone should have to change these things to fit in. However, Michelle's second reaction—outrage directed toward the Japanese characters for not standing up for their heritage—was in and of itself a value-laden, cultural stance. In suggesting that the Japanese characters in this novel should change their reactions to racism, Michelle again demonstrated her use of a cultural model through which she did not see criticism of behaviors and attitudes as racism but rather saw racism as related only to outward appearances.

Despite this early color-blind response to racism in *Obasan*, Michelle did go on to challenge some of her firmly held beliefs as her reading of *Obasan* continued. In the following excerpt from her response journal, Michelle was willing to entertain, if only momentarily, the idea of systemic oppression. In responding to the statement, "White people as a group enjoy an easier life than anybody else in the country," Michelle wrote the following:

> I used to totally disagree with this statement until I read *Obasan*, which completely changed my viewpoint. Now that I look, I agree with that comment if they were relating it to *Obasan*. It is true, Whites do enjoy and easier way of life when it comes to the time of around 1942. It seems as though the Japanese don't enjoy life due to the factors of always being moved and kicked around. The reason I never considered it to be true before was because I didn't really have any picture in my mind where it actually occurred. I guess that proves to me that you can't judge all until you have both viewpoints. I can say for this book that it tends to be true but not necessarily for everybody and everything in life.

In arguing against the idea of systemic racism, Michelle frequently contended that while some racist practices may be perpetuated by some people some of the time, the fact that these practices do not affect all people all of the time means that they are not worth considering as problematic. This journal entry represented a real stretch in Michelle's thinking; she admitted that in reading *Obasan*, she realized that in some cases White people as a group do enjoy easier lives based on their race alone. However, the hedging language that Michelle used carefully qualified her comments—she was clear that she would only entertain the notion of systemic racism in this particular time, place, and situation.

Through reading *Obasan*, she was presented with a scenario in which White people, as a group, have easier lives than other groups of people. In a White, working-class neighborhood like Michelle's, this may well have been true and certainly serves to provide further rationale for the use of multicultural literature in a school such as Thompson.

Discourses of Femininity

Discourses of traditional femininity (Davies, 2003; Walkerdine, 1990) were ever present within the culture of Thompson as well as within the working-class community in which Thompson was situated. Embedded in these working-class discourses were cultural models that suggest that *good girls,* like the jocks at Thompson, are quiet and acquiescent in class (Hartman, 2001; Walkerdine, 1990), whereas *bad girls,* such as the ghetto girls, at Thompson rejected school culture through a culture of romance and sexuality (Holland & Eisenhart, 1990; McRobbie, 1978). Michelle adopted contradictory discourses of femininity. For example, as we discuss later in this case study, Michelle was aware that being outspoken, in and of itself, went against norms for typical feminine behavior at Thompson. On the one hand, Michelle embraced her outspoken nature and rejected what she saw as more typical female performances (Bettie, 2003), such as playing dumb, acting slutty, wearing tight-fitting clothing, and deferring to the opinions of male students. But on the other hand, Michelle's major decisions in life associated with the development of her agency were often tied to her relationships with her male friends and family members, as well as to her relationship with her longtime boyfriend. Likewise, in responding to literature, Michelle often talked and wrote about marriage as a critical factor in the economic stability of women.

In talking with Thein about her perceptions of feminine culture at Thompson, Michelle explained that to be a popular female at Thompson, girls had to play dumb, worry about their weight, dress in tight-fitting clothing, and "act easy"—all with the purpose of attracting male attention. She indicated that she refused to participate in these practices, and, in fact, she was disdainful of girls who were willing to act this way, calling them pathetic. In the following excerpt, Michelle shared her thoughts about girls at Thompson:

> Problem is that a lot of girls at Thompson tend to be slutty. And they tend to act stupid ... Like all the other people who have to act like they have no brain even though they do and that just bothers me. Girls just act so stupid nowadays to be accepted and it's just like you are stupid ... I think that a lot of girls tend like to go to the parties when they are freshman or sophomores whatever and they are invited to them ... I think it depends on how they present themselves. Like if they seem really easy or something, all the guys are going to be like hey yeah you know. They are probably not going to do anything about it, but they will be accepted just because she is easy and that's cool.

In rejecting feminine norms related to appearance and the use of sexuality to gain popularity, Michelle also rejected certain practices associated with involving herself in school events. She refused to attend events like Winter-Fest, in part because those events glorified popular students but also in part because she did not want to dress up for those events. However, it is important to note that though Michelle rejected feminine norms in that she did not participate in practices that would give her sexual capital (Bourdieu, 1977; 1984), this did not mean that she did not care about gaining male attention and social status.

She therefore adhered to traditional feminine discourses and cultural models as mediating her practices in her relationships with her boyfriend and other male friends. Similarly, in responding to literature Michelle was often critical of female characters for allowing men to treat them in certain ways, yet she was not critical of traditional female roles in general. As we discuss later in this case study, in her responses to literature Michelle often talked and wrote about marriage as a critical factor in the economic stability of women.

Although Michelle constructed a somewhat androgynous image for herself in school, her classroom interactions with other students demonstrated that approval by and attention from popular male students was still very important to her. Her cultural model of gender, though rejecting what she perceived to be blatant attempts at sexual appeal, still gave high priority to the value of romance and marriage consistent with Holland and Eisenhart's (1990) cultural model of romance shaping college students' priorities. She was therefore not able to step outside of this cultural model to interrogate the limitations of that model by adopting larger institutional critiques.

Cultural Model: Being an Outspoken Girl Is Stylistic, not Discursive

In constructing herself as the kind of person who spoke her mind and who rejected conforming to expectations, Michelle also depicted herself as someone who did not accept the traditional gendered feminine norms of her school and community, especially as they related to how she presented herself. However, breaking with gender norms for Michelle did not necessarily equate to a generally feminist perspective on life. For Michelle, being opinionated and outspoken on its own was a rejection of feminine norms. For example, Michelle described her previous experience of challenging the school's athletic director as part of writing a story on student athletes' drinking for involvement on the student newspaper as a liberating experience because it gave her the opportunity to be outspoken in unexpected ways:

> I talked to the athletic director about my stories about athletic students drinking, and he got mad at me for writing it and said I was putting this really negative response on our school and I was like no, whatever. I am not going to play like that and I argued with him. I was like no, you know, and he was going to sit there and tell me I was wrong for doing it or something and was like he doesn't know me. I figure he thinks that I am like this little girl and would be like okay, and I am not like that because I am very outspoken and I just told him. I was like I'll listen to your opinion and what you are going to say but I am not going to stop what I think we should do.

Exposing something negative about the male athletic culture at Thompson played a part in why she felt she was seen as stirring up controversy. She perceived the athletic director as someone who viewed her as an acquiescent female. For Michelle, speaking out through the medium of the newspaper was a way of rejecting feminine norms. It is important to notice however, that though Michelle actually criticized the male athletic culture at Thompson in this incident, in general speaking her mind as a rejection of feminine norms did not necessarily include having a nonconformist or feminist viewpoint. In fact, in class discussions, Michelle almost never offered an opinion that would conflict with the opinions of the popular, male students in the class. Rather, in these discussions being outspoken was more about her confrontational style than it was about the substance of her argument. Typically, Michelle was outspoken only in supporting the opinions of the popular, male students in the class. In this manner, she differed from Kayla—whose case study follows Michelle's—who often expressed dissenting opinions.

In the following exchange, Michelle and Kayla, along with some other students, discussed whether Albertine, a character in Louise Erdrich's (2000) *Love Medicine,* was raped or whether she was a willing partner in a consensual sexual encounter:

Kayla: Devin doesn't think so, but I know that I took it that the second time she was raped … Like, she is resistant, and she rolls away and she got as far away from him as possible, and then Devin said, "Well, that's just part of sex."

Devin: Well, I mean if it says she got "as far away from him as possible," you would figure that she would go farther away than the edge of the bed.

Michelle: Like, she would have left?

Devin: Yeah, she would have left the hotel and ran.

Daryl: And where would she have gone as a runaway?

Michelle: She could go wait for another bus to come by.

Devin: She was already a runaway; she might as well have kept going.

Kayla: But they were drunk, so …

Devin: But you said that she wasn't …

Kayla: Yes. Yes. She wasn't "drunk, drunk" but they were drinking …

Devin: That's what I said, but you said, "no."

Kayla: No, I agreed with you after that … [voices are clearly heating up as the recall what must have been a discussion prior to the taped discussion]

Paul: … But it was her first time, though, so she was pretty nervous about it.

Michelle: … She didn't know what to do …

Paul: … Yeah, she didn't know what to do. She just kind of …

Devin: … Kind of went with the flow …

Paul: Yeah, kind of …

Parks: … Anybody else uncomfortable right now, or just me?

Paul: … I mean, she took her pants off and stuff and jumped into bed with him …

Kayla: … the first time …

Paul: … What "first time?"

Troy: Whoa [Kayla: cuz …], so did she get back up and put her clothes back on and jump into bed without her clothes on?

Paul: So, I mean, she obviously wanted to, and she wasn't raped. … She was just kind of nervous about it …

Devin: I think that if she would have been raped, the text would have made more of a reference to it, rather than just using her "back as being like as hard as a board" [Mathew: yeah] as just it … that's just describing part of her body. I don't think that is a subtextual thing that she was being raped …

[students spend a few minutes trying to determine who is narrating]

Kayla: … It's supposed to be like some intimate act, but she rolls away and gets away from him. If she was wanting to do that "intimate act," then why would she roll away when he was trying to express that?

Michelle: But she doesn't even know what she is really doing …

Devin: Even so, she does know who he is because she knows about Lulu and so that might be that she might be feeling disgusted like, "Uh, I can't believe I just did this with a guy that my grandma had an affair with," you know, that's kind of gross. She might have just been disgusted. I know for a fact that a lot of people these days, ya know, always give the excuse, you know, "Oh, I was so drunk" and "I didn't mean to do that and now this happened and we ended up in bed together but I was so drunk." You know, it is kind of like one of those types of things that are the repercussions of drinking.

Kayla: Well, yeah [reading], "after it all happened, near dawn, she couldn't remember where she was …

Michelle: Yeah, she'd been drinking …

Devin: Yeah, yeah, alcohol …

Kayla: Yeah, yeah, I understand, so if she ummm … doesn't completely agree, but sort of agrees or has any resistance while drinking, it is still considered a rape.

In this exchange, as in many other similar exchanges, Devin disagreed with a student with little social power in the class: in this case, Kayla. As in numerous similar exchanges, as soon as Michelle noticed conflict between Devin and Kayla, she joined the argument, not with her own ideas but with lines of reasoning that directly supported or mirrored Devin's argument. In the first few lines of this exchange, Michelle helped Devin construct an argument that countered Kayla's theory. Devin proposed that if Albertine had been assaulted, she would have gone farther away than the edge of the bed. Here Michelle helped Devin to construct this argument by suggesting that Albertine could have gone outside and waited for another bus to pick her up. As the argument against Kayla continued, other popular male students joined in. Paul suggested that Albertine's awkward behavior was due to her lack of experience with sex. Michelle echoed this suggestion twice when she said, "She didn't know what to do" and later "But she doesn't even know what she is really doing." Finally, at the end of this exchange, Michelle repeated Devin's earlier argument: because Albertine had been drinking, she may have regretted her actions but probably was not raped.

From this exchange two important points should be noted. First, Michelle clearly did not take a feminist stance—in fact, the stance she took was quite the opposite—nor did she take a stance that would conflict in any way with the opinions of the socially powerful students in the class. Second, Michelle was pointedly antagonistic toward Kayla, as she was on many other occasions. Kayla's dissenting views were seen by Michelle and the popular male students in the class as both irritating and off base—in fact, we saw Kayla's ideas as some of the most thoughtful and interesting. In the following excerpt from a focus group conducted following the culmination of this class, Michelle provided commentary on Kayla's contributions to class discussion:

> When Kayla talks, I kind of like drown it out, and when Devin talks I actually listen. But when Kayla talks, I'm like, "I'm not gonna listen 'cause I'll get really irritated and start feeling like, "Whatever, shut up." And when Devin talks, it is like he is just so Devin and that's his opinion.

Although Michelle was outspoken in class, she was only outspoken in the context of agreeing with and supporting the opinions of popular male students. Though she was proud of her ability to voice opinions, she expressed frustration with students like Kayla, who truly expressed dissenting opinions. For Michelle, being outspoken countered traditional feminine expectations because such expectations would have girls sit quietly and refuse to argue either in writing or in speaking. However, being outspoken for Michelle did not necessarily mean expressing opinions that would diverge from those of the powerful student in this class; in fact, Michelle clearly disapproved of this practice. This reflects her adherence to the status quo system even though that system does not necessary enhance her agency.

Cultural Model: Women can Find Independence through
the Economic and Emotional Stability of Marriage

Michelle also rejected traditional feminine norms through critiquing the lack of independence that she perceived in some marriage relationships. In writing journal entries in response to the literature read in class, Michelle focused on the roles of female characters in relation to male characters, particularly, portrayals of female independence or lack thereof in the context of marriage. She pointed out that in *Bless Me, Ultima* the women are limited to the role of a housewife, who "cooks, cleans, and does all the family necessities"; teacher; or "girl at Rosie's" (i.e., prostitute). Though Michelle, on several occasions, expressed frustration with these roles, she did not necessarily suggest breaking from these institutions altogether. In her journal response to *Bastard out of Carolina*, she criticized Annie for staying with a man who abuses her children:

> All I can say is I was extremely outraged. I can't believe half of the stuff I read. First of all how could Anney leave her child and go back with Glen? Is she crazy or what? If Glen was psychotic enough to do that with Bone what makes her think he wouldn't attempt to do that with Reese? … For a woman to sit there and tell her child that she is going back to her daddy is really pathetic. She obviously thinks life will not go on without him, and that just bothers me even more. She needs to stay independent and find herself a real man.

In this journal response Michelle judged Anney as pathetic for staying with Glen. However, it is also noteworthy that Michelle did not suggest that Anney strike out on her own, move away from town, or begin a new career. Rather, she suggested that Anney should find independence through finding a better situation with a real man. For Michelle, having the strength of character to hold out for a "real" man rather than a man who abuses his children is equal to independence. Clearly independence did not mean not being married; rather, it meant being involved in a particular kind of marriage. In discussing other female characters in *Bastard out of Carolina*, Michelle further defined her views on female independence:

> All I see is women in the slave type roles again. Always staying at home and cooking/cleaning and watching the kids. We see this throughout the Boatwright family. When Aunt Alma and her husband get in a huge disagreement about him cheating on her, and she

leaves trying to show her independence I think that showed strength because he assumed that it was okay, always saying, "A man has his needs." I mean come on now, it doesn't matter what your needs are, but that's just pushing it a little too far.

Based on this journal entry, a "real man" could also be defined as someone who does not cheat and does not treat his wife like a slave.

However, Michelle also understood that there are other factors to consider in a marriage as well as independence. In particular, Michelle understood marriage as necessary for economic stability. In responding to another situation involving marital infidelity, this time in *Love Medicine*, Michelle expressed more sympathy toward the female character, Marie, largely based on economic realities:

> Why would she go back to him or give him the opportunity to stay with them? In the text it suggests that some of it has to do with Nector's figure as being a man of a high place ... I think it's more that she knows he'll come back to her because Lulu would probably turn him down. She also probably looked at her life and thought what would she do without Nector? How would all the kids be fed and be able to support them all?

Initially, the situation between Marie and Nector did not make sense to Michelle. Again, a bad marriage—where a husband cheats—was against her principle of female independence. However, as she considered the situation further, she was able to understand this marriage in terms of economic need.

This economic aspect of marriage is in fact what Michelle considered first in responding to a journal prompt related to *Kindred* that asked her to weigh her options for how she would react to being sent back in time to the antebellum South. She wrote, "I guess if some rich White guy was into me and wanted to marry me, I would probably jump at the chance to marry him just because I know I would be financially okay ... I would be like any other person and go for the safest way and probably marry the rich, White plantation owner because things would just be easier that way." Before she considered how she might be independent or what her political beliefs might be, she considered what would create the most stability and what would be easier. Perhaps this stability is in fact a form of independence within Michelle's understanding of the concept.

Attitudes toward the Course

Michelle very much enjoyed being in the literature class, noting that it was one of her two favorite classes she had taken at Thompson. She also said that she acquired some new perspectives on the world that "opened up your eyes to stuff you didn't see before and I think we all liked that, you know? I mean we would leave class and go to lunch and talk about everything we were talking about."

However, as evident in her participation, she did not demonstrate marked changes in her thinking or beliefs and attitudes. As she noted, "I don't think a lot of it changed our minds, but it made us look at stuff totally differently." She also posited, "You can't change somebody's mind just by whatever you read. You're gonna believe what you're gonna believe either way basically." Unlike Devin or Kayla, who are discussed in Chapter 7, Michelle did not begin to interrogate institutions shaping her own or characters' practices.

One possible reason for her lack of change was her adoption of a color-blind discourse of racism that mitigates against any larger institutional accountability for one's actions or words. In describing the class discussions, she said,

It didn't matter what race we were, it didn't matter what we had to say and it was just like you could say what you wanted to say and you could talk about anything. We would see both sides but yet still think what we wanted to think you know. We could still have our own opinion but then like see both sides instead of being so close minded. I was like yeah, I see where you are coming from but I am not going to agree with you because this is what I think.

In arguing that "it didn't matter what we had to say," Michelle valued the fact that she could openly express her opinions. However, this thinking also reflects what Perry (1998) described as a multiplist developmental perspective, which goes beyond absolutist perspectives to acknowledge that there are multiple perspectives on an issue but does not critique the relative value of competing arguments against larger belief systems, critiques in which race does matter (West, 2001).

It is also important to acknowledge other factors in Michelle's life that may have contributed to her resistance to entertaining alternative stances to literature. Her indecision about life after high school and some serious medical problems may have led her to seek firm grounding in discourses she already knew and understood. With so much instability in her life, changes in ideological thinking may have proved more than Michelle was able to handle at this point in her life.

Another key factor in her lack of change was that her sense of agency was tied to her status quo worlds of immediate social relationships as opposed to a vision of herself in any future role as a college student engaged in the academic practices valued in the course. Though Michelle considered attending college, she ultimately chose to continue her job at the Dairy Queen restaurant and to marry her boyfriend after she graduated from Thompson. Consistent with her cultural models of marriage, gender roles, and individual choice, Michelle framed independence as being able to choose a marriage that involved economic stability and that did not involve abuse or infidelity. Even though she perceived herself as independent, she constructed her identity primarily in terms of dependency on stable, institutional feminine and marital roles as opposed to through a critique of those roles.

As was the case with Corey's allegiance to sports as a primary institution constituting his identity, Michelle perceived herself as fitting into the more typical role of marriage after high school. And, as was the case with Corey, she adopted discourses of individualism to frame analysis of herself and characters.

Unlike some of the other students, Michelle resisted the invitations in the course to entertain alternative constructions of her identity. This can be explained in part through her adherence to her status quo beliefs and attitudes acquired from her family, workplace, and relationships with her boyfriend. In Michelle's case, though she did perceive the influence of the school's adherence to a discourse of athleticism, the discourses of family, workplace, and marriage trumped any emerging discourses of academic critique that she might have adopted to interrogate her notions of race, class, and gender.

Summary

The profiles of Corey and Michelle reflect two students whose identity constructions were relatively congruent with the cultural models and discourses operating in larger community and school culture. Because they both drew heavily on the discourses of individualism related to race, class, and gender issues in their community, family, and school cultures, they did not embrace or appropriate the institutional critiques facilitated in Parks's class. Corey's strong adherence to a discourse of athleticism was highly valued in the school culture and community. Michelle's adherence to notions of marriage and job loyalty related to economic stability was highly valued in her family and workplace cultures. Given the fact that they both spent far more time in these cultures than in one single semester course, it may be unrealistic to expect that they would be influenced by their participation in the course to an extent that they would experience significant change. This points to the power of the discourses of the larger community and school cultures on students' identity construction compared to the influence of any single course.

Although it is difficult to predict Corey's and Michelle's future development in adulthood, they represent a large segment of America's working-class population who maintain loyal ties to their peer and local community worlds for much of their lives (Gee, 2004, 2006). Although there are many positive aspects to such a commitment, such a focus on the here and now precludes envisioning future selves associated with participation in alternative worlds or transformation of these status quo worlds.

Given their ties to their peer and local community worlds, students like Corey and Michelle valued neighborhood stability, job loyalty, and consistent family ties, all of which are challenged by increasing cultural diversity, shifts to a free-market, fast-track capitalism, and a decline in government support for families and children. Rather than framing these changes as shaped by larger institutional forces, Corey and Michelle, faced with challenges to their cultural models, returned to the very discourses of individualism that are used to justify adoption of a free-market economy and concomitant reductions in government support for communities like their own. Without a larger conception of how institutional forces serve to benefit people, Corey and Michelle may have had difficulty understanding how these forces shaped their lives, their workplace, and their community.

CHAPTER 7

Identity Construction Challenging the School World

Devin and Kayla

Devin

Like Corey, Devin was a popular White male athlete, who often dominated discussions in ways that excluded females and students of color. However, as we demonstrate in this profile, Devin differed from Corey, Dan, and the other male athletes in the course, as well as from Michelle, in that he was willing to critically examine discourses of race, class, and gender constituting his identity and those of the characters' in the texts. Though he was strongly tied to his family and community world, he also possessed a strong sense of agency associated with envisioning himself as a college student who would soon be leaving his family and community worlds, fostering his engagement with the practices and perspectives operating in the course. Given this high level of engagement, Devin actively voiced discourses and cultural models operating in the class that differed from his status quo discourses, a process of appropriating new discourses that led him to engage in some institutional critiques during the course.

Devin was a stocky, handsome, pale skinned, 17-year-old male who weighed more than 200 pounds. Given his stature, it is not surprising that Devin participated in a large number of athletic activities in the school, including standout years on the football team and serving as the captain of the wrestling team. While he was injured for part of his senior year—

the year of the study, he still continued to assume a leadership role on the football and wrestling teams. Such leadership caused other students to vote him as having the "Most School Spirit" in the senior yearbook, a testimony to the widespread popularity he enjoyed in the school and the local community.

Devin also possessed a comic, charismatic personality that put him at the center of many school activities, including regular appearances on the school's morning video announcements' team. In addition to reporting the weather or news, he also enjoyed a recurring role in "Hall Wars," a student-produced video soap opera in which Devin and other students fled and avoided hall monitors through a variety of outlandish pranks. The satiric stance adopted in this video—resisting the discourse of physical control that prevails in the school culture—reflected his willingness to challenge status quo institutional practices.

Devin's Family Allegiances

Devin's family had long been a part of both the neighborhood and the community. He appreciated "having two parents at home"; his mother was a day care worker, recently promoted to assistant director, and his father had worked for the post office for 17 years. Devin believed that neither his mother nor father enjoyed their work.

His parents were strongly committed to supporting Devin's educational success leading to attending college. His mother served as a member of a school district site council group and voiced perspectives on the future of the high school. His father was a regular speaker at the school's career day, in which community residents discussed their vocational aspirations and training. Consistent with Devin's parents' support for his attending college, in his father's presentation at career day he encouraged students to pursue higher education "so you don't just push giant carts of mail on and off the elevator all night" as he did. Devin's father also noted that his supervisor is "some kid, 23 years old, with a college degree," suggesting to the students the value of postsecondary education.

Devin also had an older brother who had been a popular figure at the high school a few years prior to his attendance. "He is the most important person in my life," Devin wrote; at the time of the study Devin's brother attended a state public college a few hours from home. Give his desire to emulate his brother's success in college, he defined his future self in terms of becoming a college student by acquiring the practices operating in Parks's class.

Devin's family was also actively involved in community organizations including a Christian church across the street from the school. There, the family encouraged their children to be active in youth group and community service activities, experiences that had a strong influence on the development of his values related to attitudes toward poverty. He was also active in groups such as Boy Scouts, acquiring his Eagle Scout award during the course of our study.

The supportive relationship of Devin's family within the school community was exemplified through actions such as the placement of a full-page advertisement in the school's yearbook at Devin's graduation, one of only three such ads. On the page, Devin's parents placed six photos documenting diverse aspects of his life and experiences: Devin as a child in the high chair; Devin crawling with his older brother; Devin as a teenager with his arm around a large statue of Snoopy; Devin as a teen playing a guitar; Devin's senior photo, in which he stands wearing his school letter jacket; and Devin and his older brother leaning together on a couch wearing jester-like hats, each containing the initials of their college. These photos represented Devin's multiple roles as son, brother, musician, student, athlete, and comic.

The text on the page reflected Devin's family's perspective on Devin's identity as shaped by religious, family, and community values:

> Through your eyes we see a world filled with possibilities and hope. Through your spirit we are reminded of what is most important in life … how we love and give to one another. People who will share your days will know that they are in the presence of someone very special. You are a wonderful, unique, and enormously talented person with no comparison. You are loving, affectionate, and compassionate. You have the wonderful ability to make people laugh and feel good just being around you. Don't ever forget that you have strong foundation of family and friends who will always love and care for you. We know that God will keep watch over you always and keep you safe.

The support provided by his family provided an identity trajectory filled with possibilities and hope. As he noted, "I view my world as having a lot of advantages … I have a lot of opportunity that I know other kids don't have." Devin planned to attend college with the hope of working in a career involving working with people, a sense of a future self based on a commitment to these values.

This allegiance to his family shaped his interpretations of the role of the family in the novels. For example, in responding to *Bastard out of Carolina* (Allison, 1993), Devin focused on the breakdown of the family system as reflected in Daddy Glen's sexual abuse of Bone as leading to her traumatic, troubled identity construction: "I mean it's a whole lack of trust and loyalty and Bone even says she starts to hate her mother. Kids at the age of 12 aren't supposed to hate their parents, you know. She's got a lot of hate and a lot of feelings that at her age you're not supposed to be exposed to."

Devin was also aware of the economic realities of being in a working-class family; he worked 10–15 hours a week at a gas station two blocks from the school: "I have to work for what I need and want. And so do my parents, we're a working family ... I won't get a free ride, so to speak, to college. I'll have to work for it." His references to hard work reflected his adherence to the same discourses of individualism and meritocracy shared by Corey. Devin used a football analogy to formulate his cultural model mediating his practices: "Life is like a touchdown. You have to drive down the field against opposing obstacles while taking some bumps and bruises in order to get there."

Entertaining Alternative Perspectives and Discourses

Devin was willing to entertain alternative perspectives and discourses in his journal writing and class discussions, frequently shifting his allegiances between a discourse of individualism and a discourse of institutional critique of White privilege and masculinity. In contrast with Corey, he was able to step back from his participation in sports to critique some of the values operating in sports, noting that football is "that elegant sport of violence, anger, and defeat."

Devin's willingness to entertain alternative perspectives and discourses derived from his emulation of Parks's modeling of these practices. Parks therefore functioned as a mentor in helping Devin move from the peripheral world of high school to the world of college work (Wenger, 1998). He described Parks's role as a mentor:

> Mr. Parks, he's in college, he's an English major, and he just knows how to set up, he's been in the teacher setting now for a long time and he knows kind of a sense of what gets kids going, what gets them thinking and what doesn't, you know, and students just simply don't have that type of experience.

He was therefore more open to acquiring the critical stances operating in the course than was Corey, given the value he placed on being critical as essential to assuming the identity of a future college student as demonstrated by Parks's practices in the class.

In literature class discussions, Devin adopted an assertive stance similar to that of Parks. As he noted, "I'm kind of one of those people who likes to jump out and say things. I don't really like to sit back and listen because I usually have a lot of opinions and like to be heard ... I am not afraid to speak my mind to people, and I kind of make the mistake of not knowing when to bite the bullet and just not say anything, but I don't really think it plays a part in class."

Devin was also influenced by his participation in his church activities. On the first day of class, as students introduced themselves to one another and highlighted a summer event or activity, Devin chose to mention his trip to Mexico with a church youth group, a trip in which they assisted in the construction of an orphanage for needy children. He noted the value of "serving others" as the basis for expressing concerns for people and characters he perceived as the adversely marginalized by institutional forces. In doing so, he went beyond an autonomous notion of the self to consider perspectives other than his own as shaping people's attitudes and beliefs. For example, in responding to *The House on Mango Street* (Cisneros, 1991), he reacted to a quotation from the text referring to the fact that outsiders are reluctant to enter the poor Latino neighborhood on Mango Street: "It's sad how many people are afraid to step outside of their comfort [zone] just because they're somewhere they're not used to being. They think everyone is a criminal." In this analysis, he recognized the ways institutional prejudices and stereotypes perpetuate parochial perspectives. In a discussion, he cited an instance in which others apply stereotypes of race to Thompson:

> I actually met a girl from a suburban high school once that thought, she found out I went to Thompson then she asked me, she looked at me, she was real concerned. She went [whispers], "Are there Black people in your school?" I was like, "Yeah there's a lot of diversity," She was like, "Aren't you scared?" [laughter] "Scared of what?" "Don't they like mug you and stuff?" "Nooo. They're regular people, just like you and me. It's just the lack of knowledge that they have over the diversity in public schools is just kind of, kind of weird.

He also valued the need to consider alternative perspectives on certain issues. In a discussion of the binary of good versus evil, Devin cited the need to consider alternative perspectives related to the terrorist bombings of September 11, 2001:

> I think most people in general don't have good or evil; it's just there's a little of both, a little A and little from B. It's not like, I mean there are certain people in the world that certainly have certain opinions and views uh you know that we would disagree on, but who's really to say whether who's good or who's evil cause there's always the opposing side … you take this whole thing with the World Trade Center incident, well you've got us the Americans saying that's the evil in the world, that's the worst thing that could ever happen to anybody, you know? But then you've got to remember there's another side of it

saying, "Well what we did is for a just cause, it's a holy war, all this, so it was a just cause," so there's not really whether we're good or bad, there's just different opinions and views.... We're judging them because of their actions, but we don't really know what their intent, well we kind of know what their intentions were, but then again we don't. But we see ourselves as heroes of the day because we're gonna go and start a war because of our intentions.

His openness to entertaining alternative perspectives proved to be central in his propensity to adopt internally persuasive voices in opposition to authoritative voices (Bakhtin, 1981). Because he was willing to consider another side of an issue, he continually adopted different, alternative discourses during the course, at times momentarily trying them on as temporary perspectives that mediated his interpretations of the texts. For example, in responding to *The House on Mango Street*, he was critical of what he perceived to be the feminist stance toward males in the book:

I don't really like the strong feminist side of this book. The author makes it seem like all men are petifials [sic] who like to engage in sexual conduct with little girls. One example from the text is when Esperanza gets her first job and the old Asian man forces a kiss on her lips. Or when the drunk offers a dollar for the kiss. All men are not like that. On the contrary, in a culture like hers, that is probably common.

Yet he also qualified his critique by noting that Cisneros is attempting to gain the audience's sympathy toward sexual harassment of young females: "At the same time I think the author is trying to make the reader aware and sympathetic toward the little girls and the cheap thrills and life they live." The fact that he qualified his judgment of Cisneros's feminist stance reflects his willingness to question his own perspectives.

In constructing Esperanza's identity as a character, Devin shifted between the discourses of individualism and meritocracy and the discourses of institutional critique, a modulation that occurred throughout the course as he appropriated new discourses. In his journal, he quoted her statement about the fact that she eventually plans to leave her neighborhood: "'One day I will say goodbye to Mango. I am too strong for her to keep me here forever.'" He then noted:

I really like this quote ... it shows determination and persistence. Here you have this little girl with little to no self esteem, she hates her life and the way she lives, but she puts a mind set in her head that she can't be bound and gagged by this world and not be noticed. Instead she breaks the chains and wants to become a somebody. Somebody who people look up to because she did something extrodinary [sic] and went back to help the poor.

In this response, Devin contextualized Esperanza's identity as shaped by the institutional forces of this world that resulted in the fact that she haslittle to no self-esteem. At the same time, he praised her ability to break the chains to become a somebody, voicing the discourse of individualism. And, consistent with his religious values, he attributed her desire "to become a somebody" to the need to help the poor, a reflection of his perceptions of the need to change the status quo.

Devin was also willing to reflect on the limitations of his own perspectives. He qualified his criticism of what he perceived to be critiques of males in *Their Eyes Were Watching God* (Hurston, 2000), noting, "The main chunk of this already worn out battle are the roles of our characters. It's always the same. The men are no good and control their wives and the wife is the helpless innocent victim." At the same time, he noted that "men can be known to be a little controlling but that doesn't go for all of us men," an admission about the limitation of his critique.

Discourses of Whiteness   Devin expressed a strong interest in examining discourses of White privilege, an interest that stemmed from his ethical concern with issues of power and control. In citing McIntosh's (1988) essay on White privilege a second time toward the end of the course, he noted that he was learning to recognize the institutional advantages associated with White privilege that blind people to the need for affirmative action:

> There are people in this world that will give a job because of race and not of skill. We just don't see it because we have unearned advantages of being White. We don't see that because we are brought up this way— "a process of coming to see that some of the power which I originally saw as attendant on being a human being in the U.S. consisted in unearned advantage and conferred dominance … "

He continued, noting that many of his White peers "do not see Whiteness as a racial identity" because of the "way we were brought up and taught was all about the Whites and how 'good' we are. But notice there isn't a whole lot on how poorly we treated others [people of minority]. In a way we are dictators of other cultures. I say this because we enslaved a race for almost 200+ years because we were fat and lazy." So in reality, are we really all that great? I tend to think not. Our privilege system only seems to benefit us."

In the class debate over the issue of affirmative action, Devin challenged his peers'—including Corey—voicing of discourses of individualism and meritocracy as represented in statements valuing individuals' hard work as opposed to affirmative action hiring programs. He argued that such programs were needed given the institutional racism shaping hiring practices: "They said if you work hard for it, you get what you deserve, and that's not necessarily true, because the racism in society is really strong when you try to get a job." He also framed the need for affirmative action in terms of the historical impact of institutional racism "given the history of what we put all of them through. About time we give something back to them."

He drew on this critique of White privilege in his interpretation of the role of Whites in the novels. Though he was not entirely consistent in his stance and would occasionally voice more traditional discourses, in contrast to the other White males in the course he was one of the students in the class willing to entertain new ways of thinking about issues of race and White privilege. In responding to *Their Eyes Were Watching God*, he argued that Whites in the past and present control African Americans:

> Although slavery is over and Black people have their own ways, they are still extremely segregated from the White race. The people have to go down to the Everglades and farm to raise money. Their towns consist of little shacks in mud. Basically, they get the shaft because they are considered free. The White man still has his oppressive hand clutched around the throat of the African American culture.

Similarly, in responding to *Love Medicine* (Erdrich, 2000), he posited that Whites were responsible for Native Americans' dire conditions in their cocreation of a reservation system and by imposing their beliefs onto Native Americans:

> We just kind of came over with all of our oppressionistic views and Catholicism and this is the way to be and this is the way you should be and oh yeah, this land is good for cultivating so I'll tell you what; we have guns and you have spears so we will kick you out of here and give you a crappy little plot of land up north. And, we'll let you sit there for a little while until we need more land, and then we'll take that from you. Then you can live in a more confined area and we'll take some more and then take some more ... It was their land in the first place. We had no right to cheat them out of their own land.

These interpretations reflected his focus on the institutional forces of the segregation and the reservation system constituting the marginalization of African American and Native American characters' identities. In doing so, he perceived the ways these systems employ Whiteness as a discourse to justify their segregation practices. In writing about the reservation system, he quoted from the film *The Matrix*: "Now today, they live on reservations and are being told how to live with Catholic and education oppression. 'We are the plague. We spawn to an area and multiply until everything is consumed and used.'"

At the same time, drawing on his active participation in the church, he reacted to what he perceived to be the negative portrayal of religion in the novel, noting that "the book sees religion as something bad and evil," as embodied in the character of the nun, Leopolda, whose practices undermine his sense of religion as "good, wholesome, and pure." Though he was highly critical of the American government's control of Native Americans in the novel, he had more difficulty coping with the ambiguities associated with institutionalized religion.

Discourses of Class   Devin also drew on his own family's class status to examine issues of class in the novels. He was very much aware of how his family was positioned in the class system, as reflected in his comment, "I know that my family is not like 'well to do,' or anything; we just get what we can to pay the rent." The fact that he double voiced the category "well to do" suggests his awareness of how others may frame his family status in economic terms.

In interpreting characters' practices in *Bastard out of Carolina*, he examined the ways the class system functions to limit Bone's family given their working-class status:

> They haven't even had the chance to progress at all, just being born into that, they're starting behind everyone else. They are just gonna have to ... if they do want to become something, they would have to work harder to get above, like, right from the start it's really hard.

He noted that middle- or upper-middle-class families already have certain advantages:

> It's a lot harder anyways, somebody who is rich is gonna start farther. Like, even in the book, they are talking about "I wanna be rich, I can be rich someday" it says. Like, that is the thing to be. I don't know, when you are rich, you're kind of already there. You don't really have to do anything, you just have to stay there. It is a lot easier to keep things than to make them.

By drawing on discourses of class, he focused on the economic institutional forces shaping Bone's family. He voices some resentment toward the class system in which the rich are "already there. You don't really have to do anything," resentment associated with Bone's increasing awareness of how the class system limits her agency.

Analyzing Characters within Cultural Worlds

Over time, Devin demonstrated an increased ability to move from simply summarizing plots in his initial entries toward analyzing characters' practices in terms of institutional and cultural forces, a shift related to Parks's feedback requesting that he go beyond simply summarizing plots in his journal. In a journal response to *Kindred* (Butler, 1979) about two thirds of the way into the course, he applied Parks's use of the *fishbowl* metaphor to people's relationships to culture in analyzing Dana's relationship to the world of slavery: "It's like she's adopting to different water and learning what it's like to live in a different time." Through the experience of responding to characters moving between different worlds, he analyzed the relationships between cultural worlds and characters' practices constituted by the objects driving those worlds as systems. In his analysis of Rufus's rape of Alice, he condemns Rufus's actions yet considered the influence of his culture upon him in such actions.

> Given our time and what we grew up in, we would consider Alice's rape to be outlandishly wrong and that I said [in a classroom discussion] 'whooping his ass' was well meant and called for. But is Rufus really to blame? He lives in a time where raping Blacks and White superiority was oppressed on youth. It's what Rufus observed as the way of life.

Though Devin struggled with Rufus's actions in that sociohistorical context, days later he revisited the scene in a journal assignment in which Parks asked the students to describe themselves and their lives if they had to survive in the text world and to describe a character from the text if transported into our present world. In doing so, Devin took up different identity perspectives, in this case, assuming the identity of a White supremacist: "I know that just by fact I would probably be a White supremacist, would live on a plantation and probably have slaves. I would have the viewpoint that I was superior to Blacks and that they were subhuman." Devin regularly displayed an awareness of the ways individuals are shaped and constructed by the societal and institutional forces at work in their world.

When describing Rufus's life if placed in the present, he posited the following: "Rufus fits into the present day White trailer trash. He is a drunk and he is a sorrowful abuser that's like 'I'm sorry I beat the daylights out of you honey, but you made me. It's all your fault.'"

Days later, Devin continued to reflect on these moral judgments in relationship to Rufus. Finally, with the book at its end, Devin revisited the question of Rufus's culpability for his actions. First, he wrote of his uncertainty, "Are we really in a position to judge him?" and added, "Now, given our views of Rufus' doings we consider him less than a man, but is he at fault?" Finally, after days of engagement within this dialogue, he defined Rufus as shaped by the plantation system:

> If anyone is to blame, it's his Father Tom. Tom is Rufus' father so he has the most influence. Rufus is a man of his time, he is only doing what is being pushed on him, that everyone else thinks is right. He's a fish in a bowl.... Rufus is part of a tyrannical, oppressionistic system that prohibits the rights of Blacks to do anything but work on a plantation.

In grappling with Rufus, Devin went beyond simply constructing this character in terms of an individual personality with whom he may or may not identify. He ultimately constructed Rufus as functioning in the novel as a symbolic manifestation of a corrupt racist system mediated by a cultural model of White, male hierarchical control.

In all of this, Devin was therefore momentarily taking up alternative discourses and cultural models of institutional critique that challenge the discourses of control and meritocracy operating in the school culture, leading him to amend and revise his status quo discourses and cultural models, something we attribute to Parks's modeling of these alternative discourses and cultural models. We have no evidence that these revisions led to any permanent shifts in his discourses, but we do know that Devin did go on to become a successful college student, success that may have been due to his experiences in Parks's course.

Summary

During the course, Devin was increasingly more likely to interpret characters' actions within the context of larger institutional forces, leading him to critically examine the discourses of race, class, and gender shaping characters and his own identity. One key factor in this shift was his active, often aggressive participation in classroom discussions, in which he challenged others and was challenged by some of the more assertive students, leading to dialogic tensions that fostered his self-reflection. He also emulated Parks's modeling of critical analysis, as evidenced by his increasing ability to apply critical lenses to specific examples from the texts as opposed to simply regurgitating the story. In all of this, Devin momentarily appropriated different discourses, which in some cases he subscribed to, as in critiques of White privilege and governmental oppression, but in other cases only momentarily considered, as in critiques of discourses of gender and religion.

Kayla

An Identity in Transition

> As the bell rang to begin second period geometry, Kayla was working intently on her history homework. She saw me walk in and sit down near the teacher's desk in the front left corner of the room. She smiled and waved and then nudged the girl next to her. She whispered to her and subtly pointed in my direction. I heard a few students asking about my presence. Kayla told them, "She's here to watch me." Throughout the rest of the class period Kayla frequently responded to the teacher's questions, always looking slightly in my direction after answering—she wants to be sure I've seen her.
>
> excerpt from Thein's fieldnotes

Kayla was a White, working-class, 12th-grade girl who was an engaged, thoughtful student, particularly in Parks's class. However, within the larger school community, she had few friends as someone who recently transferred into the school as a junior. Though Kayla was originally from the East Side neighborhood, her parents' divorce took her out of the neighborhood to a White, suburban school for the first two years of high school. Back at Thompson, Kayla lived in a difficult family situation with her brother and her mother and wanted nothing more than to look and act like an everyday, average student at Thompson.

Kayla was motivated and intellectually curious. She also believed that the courses she took at Thompson were not challenging her in the ways she desired. She found it frustrating that her classes held so little rigor that she could complete her homework during lulls in classes, leaving her time to work 30 hours a week for a telemarketing company.

Parks's literature class was one of the first that Kayla found challenging at Thompson. She was eager to read all the assigned texts in the class and even more eager to construct opinions and ideas about the texts through journal writing and class discussions. She hoped that this class was a first look at what college would be like for her—something she talked about with great hopefulness.

Kayla also made great strides to stay involved with activities at Thompson. She was an editor and a photographer for the student yearbook and participated in the daily audiovisual announcements that aired on TVs in every classroom in the building. However, there was a sense that Kayla's heart was not in these activities. She also joined the school debate team. She often did not have positive relationships with other students who participated in these activities, nor was she very excited about her participation. Rather, as someone attempting to adjust to the school culture, she participated because it helped her to feel as though she was a normal student as perceived by her peers. However, as Kayla mentioned several times, the kind of person she wanted to be differed greatly from the kind of person others perceived her to be at school as well as from the kind of person she was at home. Like Devin, Kayla perceived herself as projected into a more academically oriented, postsecondary future, an identity mediated by some of the discourses, genres, and languages she acquired in Parks's class. As the result, she was a person at a very different place in life than the majority of other students described in this book. While those students continued to negotiate discourses that were familiar to them, Kayla experimented with new discourses in an attempt to transform her life as a participant in future communities. In this case study we consider discourses and cultural models that Kayla employed in the process of negotiating and redefining her identity.

Discourses of White Middle-Class Normalcy

Even though Kayla grew up on the East Side, she previously attended Oaklawn, a suburban, middle-class, overwhelmingly White high school for her first two years of high school. She contrasted her experiences and identities in her former school with experiences and identities at Thompson, leading her to question whether the East Side, working-class world she grew up in was normal. As she reflected on her experiences at both schools, she aligned her identity more with the discourses and social practices of the White middle-class world of her former schools than with those of other cultural, racial and social class groups in diverse contexts such as Thompson. By contrasting her experiences in the two schools, she interrogated the limitations of the social hierarchies and segregation at Thompson, while at the same time expressing a desire to conform to the hegemonic discourses within Thompson as a means for appearing normal as defined by her middle-class high school experiences.

In discussing her experiences at Oaklawn, Kayla described an idealized world where students of all races got along better and were more innocent and wholesome than students at Thompson:

> I think that, when there's no diversity like at Oaklawn the people being social with each other, like it's easier in a sense because you're like everyone. I think it's a little more open to be, they're more willing to let you in. I mean there is separation to points but I mean it's not as big here I think cause there was a few you know colored kids and stuff there but they, they were not, I guess, the stereotypically Black person like there will be here. They acted just like a White

person only they had Black skin, so it was just like race, anyways there wasn't really any difference; it was just everyone was together.

In this excerpt Kayla employed a discourse of color-blind racism (Bonilla-Silva, 2001) to suggest that the reason people do not get along at Thompson is that students of color do not act White, but rather insist on acting in stereotypical ways for their races. She suggested that acting White is authentic, whereas performing racial identities is inauthentic.

Similarly, based on a comparison of Oaklawn's middle-class world and Thompson's working-class world, Kayla was uncomfortable with her own working-class identity, especially as it related to her difficult family situation and her workplace. In seeking to transform herself into a person who was normal, happy, and middle class, she used involvement in high-profile activities at Thompson as a means for acting as if she was happy and normal even though she felt alienated from the school culture.

In negotiating her identities across these different school, family, and workplace worlds, she adopted a set of cultural models mediating her current and future projected identities associated with defining a sense of agency as a future college student. A central theme in performing these different identities was her concern with how others perceived her as distinct from her self-perceptions.

Cultural Model: Involvement in Hegemonic White Culture Creates the Appearance of White, Middle-Class Normalcy and Happiness

Kayla was painfully aware of the fact that her home life did not fit into what she considered to be the White, middle-class norm—both her mother and brother struggled with chemical dependency, and money was often very tight. Although many students of all races at Thompson deal with similarly difficult home situations, Kayla held herself to a standard of what she wanted to become and therefore sought to present the face of a happy, middle-class, White girl through involvement with particular school activities that allowed her to be seen by other students in particular ways.

Most students served on the yearbook staff at Thompson to obtain an easy grade in an enjoyable class, to socialize with friends, and to provide good coverage for their friends in the yearbook. However, none of these reasons explain Kayla's involvement with the yearbook.

As an editor and a photographer, Kayla put in long hours and demanded high-quality work from herself and others. This bred resentment on the part of other students who were more interested in the social function of yearbook than the work. Students also resented her close relationship with the adviser, viewing her as a "suck-up." When asked about her relationship with other students on the yearbook staff, Kayla said,

Ruby is probably the only one I like, well that I am good friends with. There's a couple people that I've known for a while, and I'm cool with them, but that's only like three people and so I guess liking three or four people out of 15 that I honestly just can't stand is kind of bad but it's I don't know, it's a real gossipy class so I don't like when people get into all that so I end up not liking them I guess.

She went on to explain that she felt she was often the target of yearbook gossip and made clear that yearbook was not a positive social environment for her unless she was working with Ruby or the adviser. Given Kayla's negative social experiences on the yearbook staff, we asked her more about what she gained socially from her involvement in yearbook. Her response suggested that a large part of being on the yearbook staff was the appearance of being normal and being involved with student life, even if in reality she was a misfit in the class:

The biggest thing is pictures. You get out there and you take pictures of everyone and everything that happens like, you know, Winter-Fest week we take pictures of everything, you know, we take pictures of kids just in class for Spanish or whatever, so I mean I guess it really gets you out there in the school 'cause you have to and I think that's like the biggest thing for that and taking pictures.

Not only did being a member of the yearbook staff help Kayla to perform in a way she imagined was normal, but also as a photographer on the staff she had a legitimate reason to attend the kinds of events that normal students attended without actually participating in these events. For Kayla the appearance of being normal was more important than the substance.

Kayla's involvement with the morning announcements served the same purpose as her involvement with the yearbook. When asked why she wanted to be on the announcements team she said, "I wanted to be on it just to be on the morning announcements actually 'cause I'm kind of interested in video and all that, but not really, like I think it's when you watch them and you see other people up there and they're doing fun things. I wanted to be part of that I guess." As with the yearbook staff, she was not well liked on the announcements crew, either. Rather, she tended to wait until other students signed up to cover stories and then volunteered to work with whoever was left without a partner. When she was not working on an assignment, she sat and completed homework rather than socializing. She rarely suggested her own ideas because she felt that no one would listen to them. Kayla described the rest of the students on the morning announcements' team in the following way:

They're pretty much the like loud popular kids making everything funny I guess like not shy—pretty much just the kids that aren't shy and they want to do everything and be cool on the announcements and so everyone knows who they are type thing, and there's one kid in there and he kind of stands out, but everyone knows who he is again because he stands out so I guess it's that type of thing. There's not really anyone there who isn't like known I guess.

Her involvement on both the yearbook and the announcements teams afforded her opportunities to be seen among popular students in a formal capacity where she could not be rejected.

Kayla was also keenly aware of the importance of her performance in informal social situations, such as eating in the cafeteria. However, she was also aware of her inability to function well in these situations. Rather than being seen as a misfit, Kayla chose to opt out of these situations altogether. In the case of the cafeteria, Kayla knew that there was pressure to sit with certain kinds of people, but she could not sit with those people unless she was accepted by them, which she was not. Rather than subjecting herself to this pressure, Kayla chose not to eat in the cafeteria:

I eat with my friend Crystal. Most of the time we've been coming back to the classroom to work on the yearbook, but when she's not there it's actually kind of sad because I don't have anybody to sit with or to talk with so I normally just come back to the class otherwise and just find whatever open spot I can, which is pretty crummy.

Though Kayla adopted an outsider stance in her daily life, she did so as part of her performance of being perceived as normal rather than as a means of attempting to conform to a peer group. She was aware that she did not fit in with other students and did not imagine that she could change her stance at this late point in her high school career. Performing as a certain kind of person so that she would not be judged negatively made her more aware of the norms constituting the Thompson world. This led her to perceive the school from the perspective of an outsider who was aware of the limitations of that world. Her outsider stance also gave her the confidence to adopt unpopular views on the issues discussed in Parks's class.

This outsider stance was mediated by a discourse of White, middle-class achievement that marked her identity as someone who, projected into the future as a college student, perceived the high school world as only a limited stepping-stone to college. In contrast to Corey and Michelle, who used these discourses to posit that anyone can be successful if they work hard enough, Kayla used more middle-class versions of this discourse to reject many of the prevailing working-class discourses operating in the school and her family. For example, in Parks's class, she was critical of a discourse of athleticism, masculinity, and competition prevalent in the school culture, which often put her in conflict with the male athletes in the class. In the following exchange students discussed the character of Janie in *Their Eyes Were Watching God*. While the other students in this discussion perceived Janie's choices in relationships and marriage through typical working-class stances on marriage (i.e., marrying for money, security, or love), Kayla attempted to understand Janie through trying on less familiar discourses.

Troy: What makes her a woman in the text? Age? Ability to have children?
Michelle: Learning to live without someone to take care of her.
Kayla: She's a woman according to her grandma after she kisses Johnny. But the narration says that she becomes a woman after her dream dies. Where is the connection?
Nell: First she's being told that she's a woman. Then the dream died. You can associate dreaming with children. So that's when she grew up.
Troy: Does Joe even love her? Her grandma tells her she can't be a "player." But isn't that what she's doing? She's letting men run all over her.
Kathy: Her grandma's version of love is to her someone to take care of you.
Kayla: [Quotes the text] It says she knew now that marriage didn't make love.
Devin: Janie goes along with what her grandma said. Joe is the guy with money and a suit.
Mark: She just wants to be more well off. She's looking for love.
Kayla: Do you think she's looking for love in marriage? She knows that marriage doesn't make love. Teacake has to come into the story somewhere, and Joe has to go out. Support doesn't equal love. After you find something real you may find happiness in marriage, but not through marriage.

In this exchange Kayla is arguing that Janie knows that "marriage didn't make love"—that her marriage to Joe was simply for economic survival and support and not love. In contrast to Michelle, who perceives fulfillment through marriage, she distrusts the institution of marriage as not necessarily leading to happiness. Her critique of marriage reflects her own identity as someone who trusts and relies on no one but herself and is preparing to lead a life different from the one she's grown up in.

Cultural Model: Family and Friends Cannot Be
Counted on To Help You Get Ahead in Life

Unlike our other case-study students, Kayla did not typically draw on values acquired in her family or in friendships to negotiate her beliefs or her identity. Her difficult family experiences led her to be critical of her family's practices and to emphasize self-reliance so that she would not emulate those practices. In one discussion of *Bastard out of Carolina,* Kayla told the class that despite her difficult family situation, she hoped that she would not repeat the mistakes of her family. In her journal she wrote about having the same hope for Bone, the young girl in the novel who is sexually abused by her stepfather:

> She doesn't have any family support because it's part of her family that physically abuses her. She does have goals for herself, that's a big plus. "I wanted a miracle in my life. I wanted to be a gospel singer and be loved by the whole world" (141) … If she can be strong and follow her religion and dreams she has a chance to be "normal." I believe that no matter how she ends up she will struggle with her life. Nothing will come easy and anything she does get she will have to work very hard for.

In this journal entry Kayla discussed her belief that if someone's family is jeopardizing his or her opportunity to be normal and happy, that person must become self-reliant to escape the burden of the family's influence. This alienation from her family world differs markedly from the other working-class students in our study. Paul, a senior whose single mother struggles with alcoholism, said that leaving his family to attend college and to move into middle-class worlds would feel like "leaving them in a burning building."

Kayla was also wary of friendships with peers she perceived as trapped by the school culture. She had few friendships outside of school or at work and even limited her friendships within the school. For instance, the only person she talked to in her geometry class was Sally, another senior:

> I don't actually know that much about her. I just talk to her. She's a nice person; she's not like a friend that I hang out with after school. She, I know she was adopted and she's from, like I'm not sure where from actually. I don't actually know that much about her when I think about it. I just know that she's nice I guess.

Though Kayla admitted knowing little about Sally, she did not seem to want to know much. She simply wanted someone to talk to her during her math class.

Kayla similarly avoided relationships with people with whom she worked as a telemarketer in sales:

> I'm on the phone most of the time, but when I make a sale we print out our sale and then you know I go and grab it and I'll pick it up and I'll chat for a few minutes and most of the people there are pretty approachable, they're nice, but then let me think, there's one guy that's, I think 22 and other than that the next youngest person is probably over 40 so I mean there's a big difference that way.

Kayla pointed out that her job required her to be on the phone much of the time but that she did chat with people on occasion. Additionally, she pointed out that because people she worked with are not her age, she did not make friends with them. Kayla's job experience contrasted with some of the other participants' more rewarding ones. For example, Michelle perceived her work at the Dairy Queen as central to her personal relationships. By contrast, Kayla remained disconnected from this work world, assuming that she would be going to college and developing new career goals. Even though she needed the money from her job to support herself, she did not perceive her workplace identity as consistent with the kind of person she wanted to be.

Kayla also had no male friends in school and did not flirt with male students in any of the classes we observed and expressed little interest in any of them. However, she often did dress in tight or revealing clothing that may suggests she identified as an adult working-class woman (Bettie, 2003) who perceived male relationships and high school marriages as a possible inhibitor to her upward mobility.

Ultimately, Kayla did not feel that she really fit in at home, school, or work. In a journal response Kayla explained that she felt she wore a mask throughout most of her life:

> I know that I wear the mask during school to hide things in my home life so that I can be the happy girl who will make a few friends. When I'm at home I hide my school life and my stresses there .... Of course I wish that I could be myself 100% of my life, but sometimes I like wearing the mask if I am forcing myself to be happy.

By appropriating White, middle-class discourses of achievement Kayla adopted a self-reliant stance through which she rejected prevailing family beliefs, protecting herself from high school friendships. In doing so Kayla struggled to find an identity that fit her goals and desires.

*Cultural Model: The Right Kind of Education Is Not Just a Means
to a Well-Paying Job But Can Also Be Transformative*

Kayla also appropriated a discourse of White, middle-class achievement to construct herself as valuing particular kinds of education. As noted in Chapter 4, Kayla was critical of the education she was receiving at Thompson, noting her boredom with her classes.

Given her stance as an outsider, Kayla perceived the school culture as anti-intellectual and utilitarian. She embraced the idea that her education should be more substantive and not just formative in terms of jumping through certain hoops to get a degree (Weis, 1990). For this reason, Parks's class was one in which she believed she was intellectually challenged, a challenge she liked. Additionally, she appreciated the idea of receiving college credit from a major state university as opposed to taking a course at a local technical college.

Through both her experiences at a middle-class suburban school and her participation in discussion on the school debate team, Kayla found herself interested in learning participating in well-formulated, analytical, critical discussions. Though Kayla did not value her involvement with the speech team for its social aspects, she did value some of the strategies of argumentation she acquired through being on the speech team. She perceived this genre of argumentation as mediating her identity as a future college student who is making deliberate choices to develop agency so that she could acquire this identity (Moore & Cunnningham, 2006). As she noted, "You have to jump in and give your opinion and be able to back it up with facts and know what you're doing so I mean you have to be confident about that to get the better score and you have to speak well to get the better score."

Kayla equated this analytic discussion genre with middle-class norms and expectations for critical academic analysis, which she valued over emotional responses or subjective opinions. For example, in a discussion debate over whether Rufus, a White slave owner in *Kindred,* is aware that his actions in raping a slave are wrong or if he is simply engaging in something that was appropriate in this historical time period, she challenged others' positions by citing textual evidence to argue her position:

Devin: It was considered okay for you to just go ahead and do that type of thing 'cause White was considered superiority, they were considered the dominant race, so in his mind, the way his conscience has probably been formed is, "Hey I can go ahead and go have sex with the Black slave anytime I want ... "

Kayla: I don't think it was like that throughout the whole culture though. I mean, the slaves didn't enjoy being raped, and they were in that culture and even when he did do it I still think that he knew he was in the wrong 'cause like …

Michelle: Where does it say in the book that he knew it was wrong, that it felt wrong?

Kayla: It doesn't say anywhere in the book that he felt wrong. I just think there's examples from the text …

Michelle: What?

Parks: If you can, I'm gonna pause there for a minute, are you, do you have some examples in your mind?

Kayla: Yeah.

Parks: 'cause somehow from the book you got the idea that he was wrestling with his conscience or something?

Kayla: Yeah.

Parks: Can you think of what those might have been?

Kayla: Well, like, let me check what page this is one…. Well, yeah, he says, "I'll have her whether you help or not." He's talking to Dana about Alice. Um, "All I want you to do is make it so I don't have to beat her," like right there, like he feels guilty. Like why would he care? You know why would he care about beating her to rape her?

As the debate ensued, Kayla continued to support her point with examples from the text while the rest of the class disagreed with her. She got the final word in this discussion by bringing up one more example that she discovered while other students continued talking:

Kayla: On page 154, this is like right after she had her amnesia or whatever and he just says all this time it's been so good, and Dana questions, like good? And then …

Parks: [he said] "she didn't hate me."

Kayla: Yeah, she doesn't hate me, and he's just saying you know, she could've acted like how she did before Isaac and that's why I think, one of my other points before like, he knows that his conscience is bad, like why would he care what it was like before if she doesn't remember she will love him and then he won't have to rape her, because he doesn't want to rape her. He wants her just to love him naturally and like so he rapes her because she doesn't. So I think he's suggesting from that maybe she kind of like, he knows that it's wrong and he wants it to be the other way.

Kayla's role in this discussion was typical of her participation in class. She frequently challenged the opinions of powerful students in this class, such as Devin, Corey, and Michelle, through direct reference to events in the text. She was willing to challenge others because she had little concern about the social consequences of doing so. She assumed that other students shared her intellectual curiosity and perceptions of the value of classroom debates in which they could test out and modify opinions on literature:

> [I like] just hearing everyone else's opinions about the book. Like if there is something I am unsure of I get to at least get some hints that the book, or the plot, plus like, I don't know, I like expressing my opinion even if it is different. I'm like one of the people who would protest if it was something I was really against because I love voicing my opinion.... The class is definitely always willing to jump in and say "Hey, this is why it is happening," which also goes on when they are against me and willing to tell me I am wrong. But, they can explain to me or if they don't explain they can give me their opinions as to why it is this way or ... I think that there are often times when there is not a right or wrong answer to many things when you are discussing about it, but when it comes out of the text they can give me their ideas and I can form my own opinion.

In reality, other students perceived Kayla as someone with off-base opinions and an aggravating habit of disagreeing with others, a perception mentioned earlier by Corey and Michelle. Kayla was aware that she aggravated other students with her opinions, but she did not really understand why this happened, nor was it enough to stop her from voicing her opinions. She explained,

> Like, certain topics where I have gone against somebody and we have yelled back and forth, and I want to stick to my opinion because that is what I really believe in, like "where do you get that from the text," and they are like, "No, no," and they start yelling at me. I just want to break down. Then, I will see them in the hallway, and they give me dirty looks and I just, all over a book. Which, I mean is, the smallest of, I don't know, things to get mad at somebody else.

Despite the conflict that she often faced from her classmates, Kayla was eager to participate in this class because she felt it was teaching her to be competent at literary analysis on a college level. As did Devin, she responded particularly well to Parks's attempts to teach students the habitus of the college students. Likewise, she was eager to explore unfamiliar discourses and worlds she experienced in the texts. Kayla used Parks's fishbowl metaphor:

I kind of thought that it wasn't necessarily understanding someone else's fishbowl. I think if we did that was a plus. I thought it was more like, just being able to try like the process of doing it. I think that was like the main goal [of the class]. Like the lenses [Appleman, 2001] are the process of understanding it and whether or not you understood it was not what mattered it was just that you could, could try.

She therefore perceived the value of the various critical tools Parks employed in the class in terms of socializing her to adopt the role of future college student.

Summary

Kayla constructed her identity as someone who wanted to be perceived as normal within the school yet who also was critical of the lack of academic engagement in the school given her strong desire to become a successful college student. Some of her critiques of the school reflected the perspective of an outsider who had transferred to Thompson from another school. Though she engaged in various school activities, she did not establish close relationships with peers and was perceived by her peers as a misfit.

In the class, because she had little concern about the social consequences of critiquing her peers' interpretations, she was consistently challenging status quo discourses of masculinity and meritocracy, resulting in backlash responses from other students. She also sought change and transformation in her life, often in opposition to discourses learned at home or at school. She believed that a desire to seek new ideas and to have the courage to change would help her achieve agency associated with her future identity as a college student.

Thus, for both Devin and Kayla, much of their sense of agency was constituted by their anticipation of being college students who need to acquire the academic practices and dispositions operating in Parks's class. Both students' families encouraged them to pursue higher education so that they would acquire more rewarding jobs than their parents. Both students were also willing to engage in institutional critiques of discourses of racism and sexism through valuing their own internally persuasive voices, resulting in their amending or revising their status quo discourses. The fact that they demonstrated change in the course suggests that, as working-class students, they can acquire some of the shape-shifting practices (Gee, 2004, 2006) associated with developing their identities in a new economy.

CHAPTER 8

Identity Construction and Racial Positioning

Kathy and Mai

In this chapter we focus on several critical classroom moments involving students of color in Parks's classroom. Though Parks's class was in many ways structured toward critical conversations about race, class, and gender in literature, students of color did not always find easy spaces to construct agency. Because the culture of this classroom was often dominated by White male students and jock females who supported their opinions, speaking out in class was often difficult for students who disagreed with the discourses forwarded by these popular White students. Opinions based on discourses other than those that dominated the class were often used by the powerful students in this class to position students in particular ways. For some students, refusal to be positioned amounted to refusal to participate in class. For others it meant continually defending their beliefs and positions.

In this chapter we discuss critical moments in class involving two female students of color: Kathy, who is African, and Mai, who is Hmong. We explore how these two students negotiated their places in the classroom as female students of color and how these negotiations were reflected in their stances toward and responses to literature.

Issues Associated with Being a Student of Color in a Multicultural Literature Class

Students of color face a number of challenges in multicultural literature classes, particularly classes in which a majority of the students are White (Beach, 1997; DeBlase, 2005; Easton & Lutzenberger, 1999; Trainor, 2002, 2005). In some cases, these students may be asked by the teacher to share their experiences or to inform their peers about their cultural experiences as the token representative voice for a particular racial or ethnic group portrayed in literature. This assumes that these students can voice the beliefs and attitudes for an entire racial or ethnic group, placing these students in an often awkward, untenable position. Because the main characters of multicultural literature are often portrayed as the victims of oppression, it is often assumed that students of color could share their own similar experiences as victims, when, in fact, they may never have had any such experience.

Assuming that students of color can serve as token representatives for certain racial or ethnic groups also tends to mark these students simply in terms of their racial or ethnic identity, ignoring variations in race according to class and gender (Keating, 2004). In the case of Kathy, other students in the class assumed that she would have some insights into novels about African American characters. However, as a Liberian from a middle-class background (her father was an economist), she had no more understanding of the cultural situations in these novels than did the White students. Although she had experienced discrimination as an African, the assumption that she could explain African American characters' behaviors ignored her own particular cultural heritage. Moreover, setting students up as token representatives or spokespersons for past historical events (e.g., asking African American students to share insights about segregation in the past) assumes that these students have some insights into the past (Lewis, 2000).

A related issue is that White students are often resistant to what they assume are teachers' didactic agendas in using multicultural literature to challenge their racist attitudes (Dressel, 2003). As we noted previously, such an agenda confuses a critique of a discourse of Whiteness with being a White student (Trainor, 2002, 2005). White students may also read this agenda as implying that they need to display positive relationships with students of color. If White students are resentful about being the targets of a teacher's agenda, they may then feel resentment toward students of color (Trainor, 2002, 2005).

As voiced by Mai in Chapter 5, these issues are compounded by the fact that in focusing on critiques of Whiteness, a teacher may ignore or marginalize the perspectives of students of color. If that teacher is White, then these students may assume, as did Mai, that the teacher is not taking their cultural perspectives and experiences with racism into account. In a classroom in which discourses of Whiteness are the primary orienting discourses (Rex, 2002), Mai and the other two Hmong students in the class were not motivated to share their perspectives and participated very little in class discussions. If students of color assume that their cultural perspectives are not valued, they may then have little incentive to share those perspectives.

Theories of Identity Positioning

These issues suggest the need to understand how identity construction in social worlds is shaped by ways in which students are positioned in social contexts. Positionality theory posits that people are positioned in certain ways by cultural notions of difference, discourses, cultural models, and language operating in a certain context or space (Davies & Harré, 1990). Given the ways that differences are culturally constituted, people are positioned accordingly. As Vandenberg, Hum, and Clary-Lemon (2006, p. 15) noted,

> The positions we might occupy in relation to others are defined by the relative status of the differences we exhibit. It seems clear that those differences that are most distant from the cultural ideal, and most difficult to overcome or displace in an effort to approximate the ideal, are most influential on positionality. Rather than simply assume that difference is determined only by race, class, and gender, positionality theory points to the importance of how differences are produced or performed in highly situated ways. Vandenberg, Hum, and Clary-Lemon (2006, p. 373) note that subject positions in specific contexts: mediate our ways of being, knowing, and moving in the world; they shape what we may say, what we can know and write, and what and how we learn ... the structures of authority, power, and privilege that we are bound up with affect the positions from which we speak and write, but positionality is fluid and heavily contextual.

Positionality theory therefore posits the need to go beyond essentialist notions of difference to examine how difference is constructed in particular contexts or spaces. Though the students of color in our study brought race, class, and gender differences to the classroom, what is important is how those differences were perceived and defined, resulting in those students being positioned within a social hierarchy by the dominant discourses operating in the school and classroom. If a discourse of Whiteness is assumed to be the dominant norm in a classroom, then students of color such as Kathy and Mai may be positioned as marginal.

It is also the case that discourses of color-blindness position White students and students of color. White students voice discourses of color-blindness to position themselves as innocent of involvement in racism and to create a false sense of safety (Winans, 2006). The problem with this stance is that it ignores the ways discourses of race are created through social interactions in local contexts such as Parks's class, in which students such as Kathy and Mai were positioned in racial ways that White students do not recognize. As Winans (2006, p. 477) noted,

> White students often assume that racial identity is fixed within and across time and that people of color are the only ones who have racial identities and who are affected by race. They tend not to consider the ways race is created in the context of social relations and how it can be experienced differently by people from moment to moment as a social interaction unfolds.

All of this suggests the need to focus on the complex ways that race is enacted and performed as social practices that position different students in different ways. This chapter examines how two non-White students, Kathy and Mai, were positioned through these social practices in Parks's class and how they responded to this positioning. Both students were aware of the fact that they were being positioned as students of color by their peers' uses of discourses of color-blindness and individualism, particularly in the debates about affirmation action that implied that students like Mai, who depend on these programs, are being given an unfair advantage. And both students adopted countersocial practices to resist this positioning in ways that served to define their agency. Kathy consistently challenges her peers' interpretation as a way of asserting her presence in the classroom. As we previously noted in Chapter 5, Mai adopted a stance of strategic silence (Hartman, 2001, 2006) to consciously choice to remain silent in the face of being positioned as marginal.

Kathy

In Parks's modern literature class students were encouraged to engage in critical discussions of race and in college-level academic discourses of literary analysis. In this critical moment Kathy, a student whose family immigrated to the United States from Liberia when she was seven years old, attempted to engage in these critical race and academic discourses in which Parks encouraged students to participate. Though Kathy actually held very conservative beliefs about race and social class, White students in this class continually perceived her as participating in African American discourses and therefore often assumed that she was "representing," or speaking on behalf of her race in her responses to literature.

The critical moment that we discuss is one of the first in which students began to explore ideas of White privilege in a discussion of *Kindred* (Butler, 1979). Kayla began the discussion by noting that Butler depicts a world in which Whites are clearly central, positioning herself in opposition to White mainstream discourses in the class. Kathy's responses were an attempt to further prove a point that Kayla had argued. However, other students in the class used this as an opportunity to position her as racialized:

Kayla: [In this book] they're like "Whites are better, Whites are better"; it's slavery, and that's the big thing in the whole book, is the slavery and how Whites are better and that's like, they're saying that they're better than anyone else 'cause they're White. It's their group, and their group is White …

Kathy: I agree with what she says because on p. 103, um …

Parks: 103?

Kathy: Yeah.

Kathy: Rufus's mom was telling how Sarah had the white icing [on a white cake] … and I wonder why can't the icing on the cake be any other color but white? Like a couple other times she says White icing on the cake or something and I found that very strange that since white is everything, white is better and even icing on the cake is white. That's very strange …

Sarah: I didn't even think about it. I just thought it was like back then they didn't have food coloring.

[laughter, several comments]

Kathy: But it happened two different times in there so I was like …

Kayla: It's not just white frosting, it's always 'fine white frosting.'

Parks: Fine white frosting?

Troy: That's a baker's term.

[laughter and discussion]

Troy: You can't argue about doughnuts.

Corey: I didn't think that was nothing big; I just thought it was like back then that was the icing they had on their cakes.

[More laughter and discussion]

Parks: So Kathy, you're suggesting that there is deep symbolism in different things, and if you came up with example after example after example …

Kathy: It's in the book twice. Why is it fine white icing? Fine? White? Don't worry about me.

[laughter]

[Several female students] It's a good point.

Parks: Keep an eye out for this. Maybe it is something, it could be … or it could just be icing. Perhaps. Keep throwing that stuff out there, Kathy, because especially if you throw out something that we start latching on to. Don't give up just 'cause everybody is like [whispers], "It's frosting. And the snow's white. Why is snow white?"

In this segment of class discussion Kathy used critical race discourses and academic discourses of interpreting literature through literary devices such as symbolism and imagery to theorize that the descriptions of fine white frosting in *Kindred* may be significant in constructing a world where Whiteness is valued above all else. In developing this idea she made a solid attempt to appropriate and work within discourses that Parks forwarded in the class. She also used the genre of citing the text in her appropriation of academic discourses. However, her theory was flatly rejected by the class. Though the students who responded to Kathy did not blatantly suggest that she was taking a racial stance with her ideas, they did clearly suggest that she was reading too much into this incident.

The first student who responded to Kathy was Sarah, a very popular female student who nearly always supported the opinions of the White male athletes. Troy and Corey, the other students who dismissed her interpretation, were White, male athletes. With the support of Kayla and eventually other soft-spoken female students, Kathy stood her ground against these students.

This segment of discussion was typical of Kathy's participation in discussions of literature and of other students' perceptions of and positioning of Kathy as racialized. Kathy was an assertive student who spoke frequently in discussions. However, she was rarely perceived as agreeing with the views of other students in the class, although she typically did agree with their views.

As they did with Kayla, the dominant students in this class often argued with Kathy almost instantly, regardless of whether they actually disagreed with her. In the following exchange in which students were discussing the merits of affirmative action, Parks actually had to point out to Troy and Kathy that they agreed on a point that Troy tried to argue about with her.

Kathy: Okay, like MEP [Multicultural Excellence Program, which gives students of color assistance with getting into and paying for college. It provides field trips, application assistance, free tuition, etc.], right now, all you have to have is a GPA of 2.5 or something and then you can enter the program and go on to college where you like, at the U or something like that. That doesn't encourage people to go to college! It just tells them that the government will pay for everything.... So, why can't everybody just give people skills instead of giving them money every time like they did something wrong.... It has nothing to do with being Black or White. I think society also has the power to make rules. You don't go into an office dragging baggy pants, Black or White, half down your butt and then say that you can't get a job. And you won't, you won't be respected by anybody. I don't think you even respect yourself ...

Troy: But you still get a scholarship before I do because you're Black and I'm White or you get help. Even if my parents make a lot of money and I'm not living with them, I still don't get any help.

Kathy: I know that. I'm saying, Why do we get help, though? ... Why do we have to keep giving the Black kids help, because it is not encouraging them to do something better. It's like, you know what? 'cause you just got an A then I'm gonna give you money because you are so much better than every other Black person I know, so I'm gonna give you money for being a better Black person who has an A. They shouldn't do that. They shouldn't do that. If you want somebody to be something better, you shouldn't give them money just for being good.

Parks: The two of you are agreeing. You're agreeing.

In this segment, as in many others, Kathy spent a great deal of time trying to make and clarify her point because many students in this class perceived her to be constantly defending her race through discourses that are critical of Whites. In fact, as an African immigrant, Kathy was much more critical of African Americans than Whites. This was apparent in her remarks about norms of dress for African American males.

One of the ways that Kathy established her sense of agency was by resisting her positioning as a student of color through being an outspoken person in this class and in the school on the whole. She was an active member of the school newspaper and was somewhat accustomed to other students questioning her opinions. In part because of her performance as an outspoken girl, Kathy typically did not seem bothered by having to stand up for her opinions and interpretations or by having to restate her ideas. In fact, she often used these moments to clarify and even amend and restate her own opinions. Kathy was also extremely focused on academic achievement and on getting into and attending college so that she could become a journalist. Though Kathy lived with her mother and sister in economic circumstances similar to those of her peers in this class, Kathy's father was a successful, international businessman. He attended a prestigious university in the United States and had for many years pushed Kathy to maintain an academic and extracurricular record that would enable her to attend this same school. As a junior, she already had defined an academic scenario for her future plans. As she wrote in her journal, "Right now I am focusing on trying my best to be able to study political science and mass communication" at the same university her father attended. As was the case with Kayla, the fact that she envisioned herself as a future college student meant that she engaged in those practices associated with what she assumed would best prepare her for college.

Kathy acquired cultural capital from growing up in a middle-class context that differed from the family backgrounds of most of the students in the course. This sort of parental pressure for college attendance was unusual at Thompson, so in many ways Kathy was positioned as an outsider among Thompson students prior to enrolling in this class. The other students in the class therefore tended to either challenge or to dismiss her frequent discussion contributions.

Kathy's middle-class background many times shaped her interpretation of texts. In formulating reasons for Daddy Glen's plight in *Bastard out of Carolina* (Allison, 1993), she framed his downfall in terms of his failure to conform to his family's expectations associated with the need to be "climbing up the ladder":

> Like with Daddy Glen's family is well off in the town, yet he doesn't really follow his parents and go to school or whatever. He ends up having this job and working for his dad and his dad doesn't really like what he does and the people he is with and his whole life he just complains. He is not moving up on the ladder, he is moving down, so … it's kind of hard to say if somebody's social status or money is a road to success. Once you have something, keeping it is the worse part of getting it because if you are getting something then you have nothing to lose, but keeping it is like everything you've ever known and instead of climbing up the ladder you keep coming down, so, that's the hardest part I think.

Kathy often explained in class discussions that much of American culture still seemed foreign to her, particularly African American culture. She once explained that her sister was punished by her mother for using African

American vernacular English. She resented the fact that, even though she was living in a single-parent family with limited resources, she was labeled by her peers as working class because she was believed to be African American. She was also concerned about acquiring markers such as dress and speech consistent with being perceived as middle class. In describing her experience of going to a summer journalism camp, she was initially concerned with being marked as in terms of race and class but found that these markers were less important than how people presented themselves:

> We all had an impression of who we were and like the inner city kids were like, "oh my god, the kids from the suburbs are gonna be like so snotty and everything." But, they represented themselves without talking about their parents, and I think that probably that would change our opinions of them. Because we never once talked about "oh, because you go to a suburban school you like have more stuff." We never talked about the kids who like went to private schools or nothing. We never really talked about race or anything, I think, 'cause we all presented ourselves in a way that we wanted people to see us. So, I think like the way they presented themselves changed my opinion completely.

She therefore adopted a discourse of individualism in which individual authenticity becomes important for success. In responding to a clip from the Public Broadcasting System (PBS) documentary *People like Us: Social Class in America (Alvarez & Kolker, 2001)*, which portrayed a woman receiving lessons in upper-middle-class mannerisms, Kathy was highly critical of such training as ineffectual: "The lady was a fake! If you need someone to tell or teach you how to carry yourself, you are in big trouble." She based her critique on a discourse of individualism that she frequently voiced in responding to texts. She therefore valued the need to "be yourself":

> You can't tell someone how to be worthy of something when they don't think that they are.... When the lady went to the art exhibit and started talking to the guys they could see right through her because she wasn't herself. Even if you are poor or rich, being yourself matters.

In the beginning of the course, she frequently voiced these discourses of individualism in terms of the need for individuals to work hard to achieve their potential. At the same time, based on discussion in the course about institutional barriers, she adopted an ambivalent stance in that she was aware of some of the limitations placed on her by her single-parent family: "You create your own destiny and you deal with the end results, but I also know from my family experience that you don't always get what you want or think you need." Similarly, she was critical of the gender stereotype of the idealized "White woman in her early 20s, with blue eyes, blond hair, and long legs." Yet she believed that these females should exploit their appearance "to their advantage because there will always be someone willing to take care of them."

She also cited an incident in which she and her mother were falsely accused of shoplifting from a K-Mart store by a White police officer who told her mother that she was "stupid for bringing me because she's coming to steal." At the same time, as previously noted, she frequently drew on her father's advice to avoid blaming "troubles in life on a White person," something he attributed to African Americans.

Over time, like Troy, Kathy changed her perspective on issues such as affirmative action, adopting more of a institutional perspective in responding to the later novels. Kathy therefore responded to her positioning by largely ignoring it and focusing on academic and extracurricular achievement and on being and becoming a middle-class American. As was the case with Kayla, she had little interest in fitting in socially at Thompson and had little concern about what other students thought of her. To some degree, she could literally afford to adopt this resistant stance as a middle-class student who had certain resources available to her not afforded to the other students. Thus, the cultural capital derived from her class identification played an important role in her response to positioning.

Mai

Though Kathy remained a vocal student in class discussions despite the fact that she was often racially positioned, Mai, a Hmong girl, used *strategic silence* (Hartman, 2001, 2006) as a means of keeping herself from being racially positioned. Hartman (2001, 2006) used this term to explain the ways that academically successful, working-class girls often chose to remain silent in class rather than risking saying something that might jeopardize their good academic standing. In Mai's case, she chose silence in part because she did not want to risk other students viewing her in racialized ways if she voiced her opinions about race.

The three Hmong students in our study—Mai, Sue, and Pamela—came from a very different cultural background than the other students in the class. And, in contrast to many of the Hmong students in Thompson, these three students were relatively successful. However, as noted in Chapter 2, in the classroom many Hmong students did not assume active roles (Lee, 2001; Vang, 2003, 2005). At the same time, Hmong students and parents strongly believe that attending college is important means of achieving success in American society (Lee, 2001; Vang, 2003, 2005). Like Mai, who ended up attending a public university in her state, Hmong students often are more focused on long-term career needs that could provide a sense of stability rather than their short-term needs such as social status (Vang, 2003). Conversely, as we noted in Chapter 2, Hmong females are often also pulled away from academics by traditional gender role expectations related to early marriage and assuming household responsibilities (Vang, 2003).

These cultural differences in beliefs about the value of schooling function to position Hmong students such as Mai to adopt the social practices of "accommodation and acculturation without assimilation, which is the result of both cultural transformation and cultural preservation" (Vang, 2003, p. 24). The three Hmong students in our study were certainly engaged with the class, but they also tended to isolate themselves socially from the class and school activities, something that Vang (2005) noted can be problematic for these students' future success in college. At the same time, as illustrated by the Winter-Fest event and the female sports program, there were not many supportive events for Hmong students in the school that actively engaged them in school activities.

From Mai's journals, interviews, and other conversations about class, it is clear that she held very complex beliefs about gender and about race. Despite her extensive written journal entries, consistent with previous findings on Hmong students' reluctance to engage in classroom discussions (Vang, 2003, 2005), she rarely contributed to classroom discussions. However, as described in Chapter 5, when Parks and Thein asked her to share her reflections about the topic of White privilege in a conversation with them, she voiced her anger about the focus on White privilege that positioned her and other students of color in the class as the "other."

A few weeks after this conversation, Thein interviewed Mai again about her impressions of class and her responses to literature. At the end of the interview, when asked if she had more to add or had questions of Thein, she wanted to know more about our research and more about what we hoped to learn from students like herself. She asked Thein difficult questions about how her stance as a middle-class, White woman affected this research and even her whole perspective on critical race theories. Mai reminded Thein that her struggles with gender positioning were very different from Mai's because Thein was White. She described the difficulties of being an Asian female and the kinds of pressures she felt. Drawing on Parks's metaphor of hurdles, she explained that she was concerned about her future in terms of being disadvantaged as a Hmong female coping with institutional barriers related to Whiteness and gender:

> I just don't want that to be the reason that I can't be out there, too. Or
> my kids, I don't want them to experience that because they are Asian.
> I want to be equal to White people and do whatever I want to do. Be a
> doctor or anything because I don't want people to judge me because
> I'm Asian and a girl. The male and female thing has to do with all
> societies. I mean, women are, don't get the best positions. If it is a
> female versus a female, I think that puts me at a lower rank because
> I'm female and Asian. I just don't want that to stop me or judge me. I
> want them to allow me to be the best I can be.

She also noted that though she did not often contribute much in discussions, she also did not perceive Parks as himself serving to limit expression
of her thoughts:

> I am really comfortable with what I say, because I know that he isn't
> the kind of teacher that will go against you. I don't know of any
> teachers that go against what the student has to say. But I think, how
> he teaches, we are all comfortable with what we have to say. We don't
> have to hold back.

However, she reiterated her contention that Parks needed to focus more
deliberately on addressing the topic of racism: "If he wants us to learn about
racism, he should tell us. He shouldn't tell us straightforward, but he should
let us know that we will be discussing racism." Her criticism about the need
for a more deliberate framing of the issue of racism reflected her strong
interest in addressing the racism that she experienced in her own life.

In one of the few times we recorded Mai speaking in class, she voiced
her opinion on whether Rufus, in *Kindred,* was a bad person for raping a
slave woman or whether he was generally a good person who was simply
living out the expectations of his historical period. The vast majority of students who were involved in this discussion were White male athletes and
White girls who were supporting their opinions. These students insisted
that Rufus actually loved Alice, the slave woman he had raped, and was
therefore not a bad person. Kayla, as was often the case, was the only person
arguing that Rufus was indeed a bad person and that rape is always wrong.
In this excerpt, Parks pointedly called on Mai to voice her opinion:

Parks: Let me pause there and interrupt because there were a few people
who spoke out strongly that they had some thought on this in
their journal. Mai, would you, I'm sorry to call on you, I don't
normally do that, but you had some thoughts on this from your
journal. Can you express your ideas related to this please?
Mai: Um, about the rape?

Parks: Well, you said that Rufus was bad, and this connects with that idea.

Mai: Just the fact that he tried to rape her is, I mean, that makes him a bad person because rape is, you know, it's not, I don't, it's just ...

Though Mai said very little in this excerpt, we came back to this moment time and again because we were struck by several things. First, Kayla struggled for an extended period of time to try to represent a voice that was different from the dominant students, yet no one supported her. It was easy to assume that no one else agreed with her, especially in such a small class. However, when Parks called on Mai, it became clear that Mai agreed with Kayla, yet she had chosen not to speak out. Second, after this discussion we read Mai's journal and found she was in fact very passionate about her feelings on this topic and had a great deal to say, yet she still chose not to speak in class. When we spoke with her in one-on-one interviews we learned more about why this was. When we asked her about why she chose not to speak in class much of the time she said,

About the whole Asian and White thing, the racism thing. The whole topic. There's so much to say. I guess I know that people know how wrong it [racism] is. If I was just to talk about it, how it happens at the mall and stuff, I'm sure lots of kids would argue with me. Like a lot, like the majority of the class because they are all White. I wouldn't want to see that, and it isn't worth arguing over. I know I'm right. I know it is wrong, and I don't want to argue over it. They just have to realize it themselves. I think if I were like to criticize the White people, they would be really offended, even if the issue was wrong, like racism.

In this quote, Mai suggested that she did not participate in discussions about race because she felt that White students did not respond well to criticism. She clearly did not see a point in arguing about something that was clearly wrong, like racism or rape, with White students whose minds she would not be able to change.

In a discussion that Mai had with Parks, she explained why she specifically chose to remain silent in discussions of books written by and about Asian Americans:

Mai: When it came to like *Obasan* [Kogawa, 1993], maybe for us, the Asian students, we didn't really want to say anything when the other students didn't want to read the book. Even if we did want to read it, we didn't want to say anything. The fact that it was ... I hope you know what I'm saying.

Parks: I do. Can you talk more about it?

Mai: I guess it didn't matter to me if we read the book. But, if I want to, I mean, I thought the book was okay, but everybody was like, "It's not." I guess I didn't want to say anything because the fact that maybe it is an Asian book and the fact that I'm Asian.

Parks: You were thinking that they would think what? Like they say the "book is really slow and this book really sucks" and you had stood up right there ...

Mai: Then they would probably think like I'm being defensive because it is an Asian book and I'm Asian.

In this discussion, Mai explained that although she liked *Obasan* and had ideas to share, she did not speak in class about this book because she anticipated being racially positioned by the White students in this class. Of course in choosing silence, Mai was positioned by White students as a quiet Asian girl, a common way that Asian students were perceived by White students at Thompson. Thus, Mai experienced a double bind as a student of color in this class. No matter how she presented herself she assumed that she would be racially positioned in negative ways by White students.

She was also interested in gaining alternative perspectives from other students in discussions so that she could understand Whites' perspectives about issues such as racism:

> I like to hear what other people have to say and since we are different people; it is interesting to see how differently we think about things. Especially people that are different than me; I'm used to being in a group of all Asian people. I'll be hearing the same thing because we see things the same. But to see, I don't want to say the White opinion, but like what a White person has to say about certain issues, like racism. And to see that it really does exist, is it as hard for them to confront as it is for me.

It's important to note several differences between Mai and Kathy's social and family backgrounds in making sense of their different social negotiations in class. As mentioned earlier, Kathy's family pushed her to be assertive and outspoken at school, and in performing this kind of identity Kathy cared very little about her social position at school. By contrast, Mai was Hmong, popular among her own group of Hmong friends and struggled to find a space for herself within the community of Thompson. She did have some investment in her social standing at school. Also, as a daughter in a traditional Hmong family, Mai's family did not push her to be assertive or opinionated. Rather, she was encouraged to take on a more passive role in social situations. These factors may have played roles to some degree in the ways that Mai and Kathy constructed their positions within this classroom.

All of this suggests that, as Mai was more acutely aware of the discourses of Whiteness operating in Parks's classroom than many of the other students in the class, these discourses positioned her as an outsider in ways that the other students in the class did not fully appreciate. At the same time, she acquired some useful critical tools from the course that assisted her in achieving her long-term goal of becoming a successful college student.

Summary

Both Kathy and Mai were racially positioned by the social practices and discourses of the classroom to adopt defensive (Kathy) or passive (Mai) social identities. However, it may also have been the case that discourses of gender played a role in this positioning. In Parks's classroom students were explicitly asked to critically examine discourses of Whiteness and race in many texts they read. As such, students divided themselves into racialized discourse communities in responding to texts. White girls who identified with the discourse of White, male athleticism did not struggle to find community; they joined the boys. As a result, the females in the class did not create their own countercommunity to support each other's responses. Given the lack of a strong support network among the female students in Parks's classroom, female students often identified, or were positioned as identifying, within racial groups rather than gender groups. The strength of the White community in this classroom left the non-White students, three out of four of whom were female, to fend for themselves in constructing agency in the classroom. Kathy and Mai are examples of two very different ways that girls of color constructed agency and negotiated their positions in this classroom.

These critical moments from Parks's classroom suggest that though this classroom was purposefully structured to be a space for exploring critical issues related to race, this space was sometimes not a supportive environment for female students of color. Again social factors from the larger school culture came into play. This small class was dominated by powerful, White, male students who brought with them often hegemonic discourses from the school and from White, working-class culture. Ironically, Parks's attempts to focus on these White students' racist and sexist discourses often left female students of color, like Kathy and Mai, to experience a sense of marginalization in this classroom.

The chapter raises questions about how students of color are positioned in predominately White classrooms with White teachers. On the one hand, it is essential that non-White students not be positioned as token spokespersons for certain racial perspectives (Keating, 2004). On the other hand, if they are silenced, then there is little expression of alternative cultural views and perspectives essential for creating dialogic tensions. As we demonstrate in the next chapter analyzing classroom discussion, students like Kathy and Mai still provided enough alternative perspectives to least create some dialogic tensions challenging status quo perspectives.

CHAPTER 9

Dialogic Tensions in Classroom Discussions of Three Novels

As we argued in Chapter 3 on responding to multicultural literature, students experience a range of dialogic tensions between competing cultural perspectives and discourses, not only in their responses to texts but also in classroom discussions. That is to say that as students encounter new perspectives and information about a topic or a perspective within a text or classroom exchange, those ideas and information enter into a dialogue with their previously held notions, creating an internal tension until some sort of resolution occurs. Such a tension may also exist as they consider the tensions created by competing discourses and perspectives displayed in texts or in their lives.

Experiencing these tensions portrayed in texts engages students in perspective taking that often leads to self-reflection of their own beliefs and attitudes. For example, in Parks's class, by writing and performing monologues as different characters from the texts students in the class were forced to adopt, even if temporarily, alternative perspectives and discourses grounded in different historical and cultural worlds, leading students to reflect on how different institutional forces shape characters and peoples' perspectives.

Also, adopting different perspectives led students to explore some of the tensions and contradictions between official or idealized versions of reality versus more realistic versions—for example, Rufus's tension between his individual emotional attachment to a slave, Alice, and the systemic norms of how he must interact with her given his position as a White slave owner. By examining how characters coped with these tensions and contradictions associated with status quo worlds resulting in the creation of new worlds (Engeström, 1987) or third spaces (Soja, 1998), students could understand the ways characters came to employ narratives, genres, and language that created new worlds and spaces that addressed the limitations of status quo worlds they had inherited.

Grappling with these dialogic tensions also led students to become aware of and to consider the revision of their own beliefs and attitudes related to race, class, and gender. In this chapter, we examine the dialogic tensions involved in classroom discussions of three novels: *Love Medicine* (Erdrich, 2000), *Kindred* (Butler, 1979), and *Bastard out of Carolina* (Allison, 1993). We demonstrate that through grappling with these competing perspectives and dialogic tensions, students had to formulate, defend, and reflect on their beliefs and attitudes, leading to changes in those beliefs and attitudes for some students. All of this points to the value of classroom discussions about multicultural literature in fostering exploration of alternative perspectives related to race, class, and gender.

Adopting and Voicing Alternative Discourses

Students' literary responses reflect allegiances to competing discourses (Gee, 1996; Rogers, 2004). Though students may not be consciously aware of these discourses, they may react to others' responses based on their sense of the larger ideological stances implied by the other's response. For example, voicing the position that current generations are not responsible for slavery may reflect a discourse of individualism—that individual persons are not responsible for larger institutional forces or events. As they voice competing discourses, students create dialogic tensions reflecting underlying ideological clashes.

In responding to literature, students are also voicing the discourses of characters and narrators whose own voices reflect dialogic tensions operating in text worlds (Knoeller, 1998; Lensmire, 2000; Pearce, 1994). For instance, several male students in our study adopted Rufus's voice in trying to understand his perspective in raping an African American woman he claimed to love; this compelling incident is discussed at length later in the chapter. As in a role play, students sometimes assume another's language and perspective, and in doing so they experiment with alternative perspectives. By voicing these alterative perspectives in discussions, students are publicly acknowledging their temporary or experimental allegiances to these discourses. And in having to defend their stances, they are learning to explore the validity of these stances.

These tensions are most likely to surface in discussions when students can voice and challenge each other's alternative interpretations. In doing so, they are double voice tensions in texts between characters' own voicing of authoritative versus internally persuasive voices (Bakhtin, 1981) associated with characters' development of agency. As characters such as Janie, Esperanza, Dana, and Bone begin to perceived themselves as the objects of racist, class, and gender systems that limit them, they develop their own internally persuasive voices (Bakhtin, 1981) that challenge authoritative voices. From experiencing these challenges to status quo systems, students themselves begin to explore dialogic tensions between status quo and emergent discourses and cultural models in their own lives.

As we noted in the previous chapter, when students adopt certain discourses or cultural models, they position their peers to take up stances of acceptance or rejection of their arguments, creating dialogic tension within the discussions. For example, a student might argue that current generations are not responsible for slavery as a past historical phenomenon. Other students in the discussion may then concur or not concur based on the text, life experiences, or other forms of evidence that they see as useful within the context. Having to defend their beliefs and attitudes may lead some students to reexamine their commitment to those beliefs and attitudes. In addition, student may choose not to speak on the topic given a variety of classroom factors, but the affirming or competing ideas they receive encourages their internal dialogue regarding such perspectives and topics.

Adopting Alternative Identities in Discussions

Within the social world of the classroom, students also take up certain identities based on roles such as interrogator, provocateur, nonparticipant, mediator, dutiful student, class clown, devil's advocate, recorder, facilitator, or feminist critic. For example, for many of the White males, Kayla came to be perceived as someone who continually challenged their perspectives. These males deliberately presented alternative perspectives or critiqued Kayla's words based in part on the interpersonal dynamics related to a perceived threat to their control of the floor.

In his analysis of heterogeneity in classroom discussions, Koole (2003) identified three different types of identities: activity, situated, and transportable, associated with the practices and stances students assume in discussions. Activity identities represent the identities or roles associated with participation in a particular activity. For example, in the activity of a classroom discussion, a teacher assumes the identity of discussion facilitator who positions the students as participants. In discussions, students may also assume the identity of problem poser, which positions the teacher or other students as problem recipients. Parks employed a range of discussion activities that involved students adopting different identities. For example, he selected quotes from each student's response journal and listed them anonymously on a handout for students to read. He then assigned each student a quotation to read aloud. In reading these quotes, students were positioned to temporarily adopt the identities of advocates for the positions represented in the quotes—positions to which they did not necessarily subscribe.

Situated identities refer to how discussion participants situate or position each other in terms of reciprocal roles. A student who adopts the role of challenger or nonparticipant positions the teacher or peers to adopt certain roles, just as the facilitative versus domineering teacher positions students to respond accordingly. Transportable identities cut across different situations or interactions and reflect race, class, or gender identities. The fact that White, male students such as Corey, Devin, and Troy often dominated the class discussions in this study reflects their importing of identities operating in different settings. And the fact that some of the students of color such as Mai believed that they were marginalized or silenced by the teachers' attempts to challenge these White males reflects their own transportable identities as students of color.

Koole (2003) argued that constructing a shared context means that identities are constructed as part of that context. This creates a tension between differences *brought along*—differences students bring to discussions reflecting their transportable identities related to race, class, and gender—and differences *brought about* that emerge within the context of the discussion. In some cases, because participants within a discussion may treat or position someone as having a particular identity, this may mean that the experience or expertise brought along is no longer relevant to how they are perceived or treated in a discussion. For example, though Devin brought an identity as a popular, White, male, athlete to the discussion, an identity associated with alignment to the school's status quo sports culture and hierarchical structure, he also adopted a brought-about identity in the discussions of someone who challenged status quo hegemonic beliefs. Or though Kayla was often reluctant to interact with others in the larger school context, in the classroom discussions she adopted the role of an active participant because she was highly engaged with the topics and issues addressed in the discussions of a college-level classroom.

The fact that students such as Devin and Kayla, as well as Troy and Kathy, assumed active roles in the discussions of points to the need to understand how adopting these active roles and grappling with dialogic tensions leads to critical thinking, construction of alternative stances, and,

Dialogic Tensions Involved in Responding to Literature

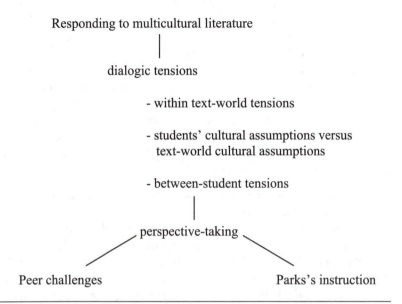

Figure 9.1 Dialogic tensions involved in responding to literature

ultimately, authentic learning. In pinpointing the ways that tensions arose and unfolded in classroom discussions, we identify three types of tensions reflected in students' discussions of multicultural literature.

Types of Dialogic Tensions

Students experienced a number of different types of tensions and contradictions, which are summarized in Figure 9.1.

Within-Text-World Tensions

As we argue in Chapter 3, students experience dialogic tensions among characters' identities, beliefs, perspectives, and discourses operating within a text world. For example, in responding to *Their Eyes Were Watching God* (Hurston, 2000) and *Yellow Raft in Blue Water* (Dorris, 1987), students in our study experienced tensions between patriarchic discourses of male domination of marriage and a rejection of this domination. In responding to *Kindred*, they experienced the tensions between past institutional slavery and contemporary racial attitudes. In responding to *Love Medicine*, they experienced the tensions between the world of Catholicism and the world of Native American spirituality, as well as the tension between hope for a better future and the despair of poverty, alcoholism, and dead-end jobs. In responding to *Bastard out of Carolina*, they experienced the tensions between attempting to maintain the façade of middle-class respectability and the realities of working-class life.

Students construct these tensions by drawing on their experiences with tensions and contradictions in lived-world institutions. For example, one of the tensions inherent in *Bless Me, Ultima* (Anaya, 1995) is that between the practices of organized religion and characters' doubts about organized religion given tensions between religious beliefs—that God is good—and an awareness of evil in the world. In discussing his identification with Tony in *Bless Me, Ultima*, Devin noted that:

> ... I could make a strong relation with Tony in that book because he was kind of caught between the whole issue of religion, of what is right and is there a God. I went through a period real bad like that in my life so I can relate to that book. Like when he is talking about is there a God or should he believe in something else like the whole thing, and I went through the while confirmation thing, but if there is a God, he's not helping me out right now because my family is having a struggle.

Devin constructed the meaning of Tony's grappling with tensions based on his own doubts about his religious belief. At the same time, he used the portrayal of Tony's experiences in the text to frame his understanding of contradictions between a belief in a God and his family struggles.

The texts in the course also invited students to entertain dialogic tensions by portraying different characters' contradictory versions of the same events. In *A Yellow Raft in Blue Water* (Dorris, 1987), three different generations of females—Rayona, Christine, and Ida—formulate totally different versions of events that reflect differences in their beliefs, cultural models, age, and identities. Having to grapple with these characters' competing versions of the same events led students to understand how different interpretations reflect differences in perspectives. And as students encountered an alternative version of the same event from differing perspectives, they had to revise their previous constructions of characters. Devin noted that his negative attitudes about Christine and Ida changed as he was exposed to their perspectives: When "you read her [Christine's] part and you understand what she goes through and then you go, well, I can sort of understand what she goes through and then Ida, she is worse, and then you read that and you go, well, I understand what she's going through."

These textual tensions involve competing uses of narratives. In responding to Ida's autobiographical narratives about her youth in which she raised another woman's baby, as well as narratives acquired from her Native American heritage, students experienced a turn-of-the-century cultural perspective that reflected relatively traditional Native American and gender discourses and power hierarchies through which Ida was willing to make sacrifices to protect others; she was willing to accept a life within a relatively constrained space. As Corey noted about reading *A Yellow Raft in Blue Water,* "You read one person's section and you think man that person is so wrong. Why would you do that? and then you read the next section and you are like oh, that explains the first part and then you are like why would Ida do that and then you read the Ida's part and you are like oh."

Love Medicine also employs a story-cycle genre consisting of multiple stories and shifting, tension-creating narrative perspectives (Cox, 1998). Reid (2000, p. 72) argued that Erdrich deliberately employs multiple perspectives, fragmented narratives, and gaps in *Love Medicine* to involve the reader in constructing the meaning of the novel:

> As readers, we are given access to numerous pieces of information, some of them, like the thoughts that cross June's mind the night of her death, revealed only to us. Moreover, in addition to inducting readers into the tribal community, Erdrich's adaptation of oral narrative techniques—fragmentation and repetition, circularity and interconnectedness—helps teach us how best to construct identities for the characters and communities in her novels. Erdrich thus makes her readers into the mediators ... stories are told in the first-person, events are linked to self-discovery, characters reflect on who they are and where they belong—and require the reader to construct identity within the circular, interconnected pattern common to Native American cultures.

By experiencing alternative narrative constructions, students began to recognize how narrative constructions shape perceptions of social worlds and mediate alternative versions of events. Faced with contradictory narrative versions of the same event invited them to examine issues of truth.

Textual tensions are also created through uses of language categories reflecting social hierarchies in a text world. For example, students noted that Bone in *Bastard out of Carolina* was aware of how language categories such as *White trash* and *nigger* were used to place her within a system of racial hierarchies. As Sue noted:

> Because people call you trash and that is just the same thing you know for a White to be called White trash instead of being called nigger. And I think she took that really like seriously. Plus she is into

that religion and she into her beliefs and that people shouldn't be treated like that and all.

Sue reflected on how the category *White trash* functioned in relationship to *nigger* within the small town's racial hierarchy to equate the poverty and low status of Whites with that of African Americans.

In constructing these tensions between competing perspectives portrayed in texts, students also experienced tensions between their lived-world cultural assumptions and the cultural assumptions operating in the text world. In some cases, given their lived-world assumptions, they had difficulty not simply imposing their lived-world assumptions onto the text—believing that the text world should mirror their own lived world. In doing so, they foreclosed a willingness to entertain tensions between their own cultural perspectives and the perspectives they confronted in the text worlds. For example, in responding to the portrayals of family relationships in *Love Medicine*, some students applied traditional notions of the nuclear family to the novels, expressing difficulty with what they perceived to be dysfunctional family practices given their cultural models of the family.

On the other hand, some students learned to recognize the need to assume a different cultural perspective in entering into a different cultural text world. This was most evident in *Kindred* in which they had to assume Dana's perspective constituted by the world of slavery in 1820s Maryland as contrasted with her experience of 1970s Los Angeles.

This movement across time required them to identify the cultural norms operating within that text world by noting relationships between characters' practices and the consequences of those practices, consequences that suggested the influence of certain norms. Students were more likely to identify these norms when responding to texts with competing norms operating within the same text world. When characters such as Dana are faced with having to cope with different cultural expectations within the same text world, they explicitly reflect on differences between the competing demands of different cultures.

Between-Student Tensions

Students also experienced tensions between each other's perspectives, particularly if they were voicing minority or unconventional perspectives (Pace, 2003). For example, when responding to *Love Medicine*, some students argued that people of color are afforded advantages over Whites through affirmative action programs or school-tuition support, a perspective reflecting political attitudes operating in the larger community. Other students assumed the less popular defense of such programs, creating tensions in the discussion.

These tensions served the valuable purpose of fostering extended stretches of talk (Beach, Eddleston, & Philippot, 2003). As we noted in Chapter 5, the fact that students disagreed with each other on a particular topic or issue served to sustain their focus on that topic or issue. By challenging each other's interpretation, students then had to defend their interpretations, requiring them to provide supporting evidence from the text or to expand on their position. And, in some cases, they recognized the limitations of their own positions, leading to revision of their interpretations.

Given their uncertainty in grappling with dialogic tensions, students may often assume a tentative or hypothetical stance in which they seek out confirmation from others to verify the validity of their stance, inviting others to engage in collaborative interpretations. For example, in response to the movie *Smoke Signals* (Eyre, 1998) viewed in conjunction with *Love Medicine*, Pamela noted that in the movie one of the characters described how their Native American basketball team beat a team of Whites:

He was telling that lady about how they were playing basketball with those Christians, and he said that at least for one day the Indians won. I don't know if he meant that they had won the game, but was he like talking about the war and how they won … I don't know … he just said that …

Framing her interpretation in a tentative, exploratory language—"I don't know if he meant that … " "I don't know,"—invited other students to assist her in determining the symbolic meaning of winning the basketball game.

Devin then responded by recalling one statement about winning related to Hollywood depictions of fights between cowboys and Native Americans:

I remember Thomas saying "the cowboys always win, the cowboys always win." Then Mr. Parks wrote, "They do. Watch all of the old movies." So, I guess that is just the way it was back in the day. Maybe from being put in that situation for so long and from seeing that on TV for so much I guess, the dad was like "one day, we won."

Through these collaborative interpretative efforts, students work together to develop composite interpretations of texts.

At the same time, the students also created groups that opposed each others' interpretations given their shared stances. For example, there were tensions between the shared stances of the White male athletes who adopted a discourse of individualism and competition and other students such as Kayla or Kathy who resisted what they perceived to be an attempt to dominate discussions. Challenges from Kayla or Kathy to these males only further cemented their sense of shared perspectives. As we noted in Chapter 8, because there was no similar shared group stance for the females in the class, they never formed an alternative common bond, splintering instead across differences in race.

Through the process of grappling with these tensions, students learned to accept ambiguity and recognize the limitations of their own perspectives. This is a slow, cumulative process that results from both private writing about texts and public formulation and defense of beliefs and attitudes.

In this chapter we describe the dialogic tensions evident in students' discussions of three novels: *Kindred, Love Medicine,* and *Bastard out of Carolina.* We chose these texts because they were the texts that provided the greatest challenges to the prevailing discourses through which students in this course understood their lived worlds. Though students did not necessarily change their beliefs and attitudes based on these discussions of texts alone, we posit that a close look at these discussions demonstrates that students grappling in authentic ways with the tensions that arose through experimentation with alternative perspectives related to these three texts.

Dialogic Tensions in Discussions about *Love Medicine*

In the novel, at age 14 Marie Kashpaw fights with her teacher, Sister Leopolda, who represents a harsh, imposing, but maternal force. Marie adopts an ambivalent attitude toward religion. On the one hand, she desires to become a devoted Catholic and nun, but on the other hand, she realizes that for her, life in a convent would be challenging. Through her sexual encounter with Nector, she rejects the Catholic image of the Virgin Mary and ultimately achieves a sense of agency through motherhood (Sanders, 1998). When Nector leaves her, she must then redefine her identity through her connections with nature and community associated with her cultural heritage (Sanders, 1998). Her daughter, Zelda, perceives her mother's struggles with Catholicism but still hopes to become a nun.

In discussing this tension in Marie's attitudes toward Catholicism, students struggled to understand her ambivalence toward religion. In the following exchange students disagreed about the strength of both Marie's and Zelda's commitment to Catholicism, and they debated about whether religion can be both practiced and questioned simultaneously:

Pamela: ... In like 1930 or whatever, she, when she was 14, she was almost like daring her to defy ... defy me...Leopolda ... and in 1970 whatever, when she is married to Nector, she seems to be totally Catholic and did whatever they did and she basically wants her children to become Catholic as well, and she goes back to

Leopolda [the nun in the convent], and you were just wondering what happened there? 'cause nothing in that book mentions the transition between when she was 14 and, I don't know, this passage in the book, because it almost sounded like she was evil or something and she did not want to become converted to Catholicism ... and so, just don't know what happened ...

Parks: So, let's throw that out to the group, as with many good questions. How do you make sense of that issue?

Devin: Well, I definitely agree that like at 14, she sort of defied Catholicism, but I don't really see any strong relations later on in the text with her wanting to be a Catholic when she is older. I mean, yeah, she maybe wanted to one, but I don't think those are really huge components of being a Catholic wife. Do you know what I mean? I mean, it's ... they have a passage about Zelda saying that she wants to go to the convent and the mother doesn't really care, but she says that she would rather have her at home, so, I don't think that she gets that much more Catholic when she gets older. She has always defied Catholicism when she was 14, but she was kind of like we are today, just that sort of steam-headed kid that is like, "Oh, I hate school; I hate it so much." Or, "I hate Catholics" and "I'm gonna defy it as much as I can to make my voice heard." You know?

Kathy: So, is it only Zelda who is Catholic ... ? When it says, "I prayed when I was young?"

Devin: She is defying it. She doesn't want anything to do with Catholicism.

Kathy: So, when she talks about that she wants to go to the convent then ...

Devin: That, I don't know. It says later that Zelda wants to become the ... I would imagine so because it says that she wants to become, because she says that one day she will go to the convent, and I know that she gets along with the nuns.

Kathy: 'cause, like at first, I think Zelda was talking to Albertine about her wanting to be a nun before, before she married the Swede Johnson guy. It was in the beginning ... umm ...

Devin: Yeah ... I think that Zelda does end up becoming Catholic.

In this exchange Pamela expressed surprise that despite Marie's mistreatment by Sister Leopolda, she later in life increases her commitment to Catholicism. In expressing an alternative stance, Devin argued that Marie was actually not strongly committed to Catholicism even in later life, as evidenced by her ambivalent response to Zelda's desire to enter the convent. Kathy and Devin also disagreed as to whether Zelda was truly committed to becoming a nun. Kathy noted, "So, is it only Zelda who is Catholic? When it says, 'I prayed when I was young?'" Devin noted, "She is defying it. She doesn't want anything to do with Catholicism."

Parks synthesized the students' discussion of Maria's and Zelda's ambivalent attitudes toward Catholicism by connecting it to potential tensions between practicing religion while at the same time feeling doubts about that practice:

> Is it possible that parents may have rebelled against religion or something earlier in their lives and they don't necessarily tell you, about the rebellion? Maybe they had doubts, and yet they still raise you that way and don't tell you about the doubts.

Mark noted tensions in his own family over religion, explaining that his entire family was Catholic with the exception of his mother who may have rebelled against Catholicism:

Mark: I don't think my parents rebelled. I mean, you gotta, you gotta be ... well, I go to Presention and to be married there you gotta finish all your religion years there. My mom kind of had a problem with that because she is Lutheran and my dad is Catholic. My brother and my sister are Catholic; everybody is Catholic, but my mom. So, I don't know if she really rebelled, but she thinks that I should be able to get married wherever I want.

Parks: Even if you have doubts or struggles with that system, she still wants you to be in it.

Mark: Yeah.

Parks: Which is what we're seeing with Zelda and Ruth.

Mark: It's kind of normal though, growing up, to kind of question your faith. You know, rebel and sometimes you want to do your own thing, which is just a normal kid growing up, basically.

In this excerpt Mark noted that his mother believed that he should not be forced to be married in the Catholic Church. He then applied the idea of the normal process of doubting religion in adolescence to Marie's and Zelda's own religious doubts. By drawing on his own experiences with his lived-world tensions related to religion, he interpreted the within-text tensions about religion in *Love Medicine*.

Students also experienced tensions between their own cultural assumptions and the Native American cultural assumptions they needed to adopt to interpret the symbolic and religious meanings of the novel. Though students were initially confused by many of the events in the novel, Parks encouraged them to try to interpret the novel not through their own cultural assumptions but rather through Native American cultural assumptions. The following excerpt from discussion is an example of two students attempting to use unfamiliar cultural assumptions to interpret a critical yet opaque quote from the novel:

Parks: [Reads quotation] "The snow fell deeper that Easter than it had in 40 years, but June walked over it like water and came home."

Mai: Well, me and Mitch brought this quotation up, and he said that it had something to do with like after death or something. Like when "June came home" it was her spirit was still alive even though she was dead it was still alive. Do you understand? Mitch brought it up, 'cause like Native Americans do believe that your spirit lives in the trees, like Mr. Parks said "animism" is it? And like in trees and rocks and the ground. June, her spirit is still alive ...

Mitch: Like Mr. Parks said, in Native American kind of religion, death is kind of a full circle; therefore, when she comes home, that means her body has died. "The pure and naked part of her" would be her soul. And she didn't lose her sense of direction because her definition was ... umm ... yeah ...

In this example, Mai pointed to this quotation as a textual moment that required her to adopt a different perspective to infer that June's spirit was still alive even though she was dead. She recognized the need to adopt a Native American belief system of animism—that one's spirit lives in trees and rocks and the ground— to fully understand the text. Mitch extended this perspective by noting that, "in Native American religion, death is kind of a full circle; therefore, when she comes home, that means her body has died." Students also noted the symbolic function of water throughout the novel as representing the transforming and purifying force of nature. In recognizing the tensions between their lived-world cultural assumptions and cultural assumptions in worlds, students learned to frame their interpretations of *Love Medicine* terms of Native American cultural perspectives rather than their own cultural perspectives.

In the second day of discussion about *Love Medicine,* students engaged in a debate about whether the novel serves as a valid portrayal of Native American culture. In this discussion, between-student tensions developed as students shared a variety of culturally constructed images of Native American people. Additionally, student-versus-text-world tensions were raised as these same culturally constructed images of Native American people came into conflict with Erdrich's portrayal of the realities of life for many Native American people.

Some argued that the portrayal of alcoholism in the novel served to perpetuate what they perceived as a stereotype of the alcoholic Native American. Others noted that this book did not seem to be about race or an underrepresented culture at all given that the situations in this text "happen in every culture and people gambling, people getting drunk, and things like that." As Pamela noted, "I just thought that the book wasn't really focused on Native American culture, that there is a lot going on with each of the characters, but it does not really provide us with really good insight with what the Native American culture is. Since I'm not Native American, I cannot tell if what is happening in the book is right or not or if it's true or not."

Pamela's comment spurred a discussion about whether *Love Medicine* is an appropriate text to teach, given the minimal experiences that most non-Native American's have about Native American culture. Likewise, students were particularly engaged in discussion related to whether this text serves to stereotype Native American people. The following is an excerpt from that discussion:

Kathy: There aren't a lot of native American Indians in this country, out on the reservations or something like that, so like when the one author writes a book and all the people read it, not the majority, but they are talking about the book or whatever, and the TV shows and they are not great like you said, so I don't think ...

Kayla: You think that they form an opinion off just this one book, though? That that is their whole view?...

Kathy: ... Yeah ...

Michelle: Well, then people do that if they're reading about White people, that we were all slave owners.

Sarah: What's the difference? We were all judged at one point in our lives. We are not gonna judge them all on one thing, right?

Kathy: If it's this one person who is like sleeping with somebody else the whole show is basically about that and getting drunk ... and if there is White TV shows all about the "happy family" or the broken up family or something, and ...

Michelle: See, you're stereotyping White people right there. It's the same thing by basing it off this show. There is a lot of shows with White people where they sleep around and get drunk like *90210* or *Melrose Place,* it's like the same thing. There are comedies about Black people too, and you're basing it off of something you're reading, just like, then basically you're saying that you don't want anybody to read it [*Love Medicine*] because you only take in one viewpoint.

Kathy: But people do do that, though. That's why we have …

Michelle: But then that is what you're doing right now, too, for different people.

Kathy: Yeah, so what I'm saying is based on the whole population … People barely think about that, but if we have like Black and White issues, people don't ignore that because they know there are a lot of Black people and a lot of other people, but if a Native American says something about you or whatever, you basically know that you're not going to be offended by them because there are not a lot of native Americans, there are more Whites than everybody and there are more Blacks than native Americans …

In this segment, Kathy suggested that because Native Americans are a small minority group that is not well understood by the larger culture, the novel perpetuates misunderstandings of Native Americans. Kayla then challenged Kathy by asking whether readers "form an opinion off of just this one book." Sarah shared Kayla's perspective by arguing, "We are all judged at one point in our lives." Kathy defended her position by citing an example of a television program that perpetuates stereotypes of Native Americans whereas most other programs depict White people in a positive light. Next Michelle countered Kathy, this time by suggesting that Kathy was actually stereotyping White people with her comments. Kathy then argued once more for her stance by explaining that the White population does not really take the Native American perspective seriously because they represent a relatively small percentage of the population compared with the more sizable African American population, whose perspective is, she argued, taken more seriously.

There are a number of dialogic tensions in this discussion. Some of these tensions associated with Kathy reflect consistent, long-term attempts by the White students to position Kathy as someone who represented the interests of underrepresented cultures and races, for example, when Michelle suggested that Kathy was stereotyping White people. The students also experienced tensions regarding generalizations about racial groups. As students questioned generalizations and stereotypes, they were also able to identify what they perceived to be some positive aspects of Native American culture, which they then contrasted with various stereotypes and presuppositions. Sue noted that, in contrast to the Hollywood portrayals of Native American, the novel portrays a more contemporary perspective on Native American life. Corey pointed out that despite the conflicts between the characters, "Everyone takes care of each other … even if they might get in fights or get drunk, they always are on the same side. They are never letting anybody get hurt." Following Corey's comments, Troy cited an example of such support in the form of two brothers who after having a fight reassert their bonds to each other.

Students also cited examples from the text suggesting that they acknowledged some of the injustice that has befallen Native American culture. For example, Shelly noted that the portrayal of Gerry's trial demonstrated discrimination against Native Americans in that "they held the trial during pow-wow times and all of the witnesses were gone ... it just didn't seem fair." Shelly's analysis represents an emerging awareness in some students of the institutional forces working against Native Americans, leading her to argue that "I would want people to read this book because it shows how the court system is biased against Native Americans."

Students also noted tensions between their own cultural assumptions and those operating in the novel—their religious beliefs versus the animistic perspective necessary for interpreting the symbolic meanings of the novel versus. They also recognized that their stereotypical presuppositions about Native Americans were challenged by the portrayal of contemporary Native American life in the novel, leading them to recognize how those stereotypes are a function of their White privilege perspectives.

Examining these cultural tensions led some students to reflect on the limitations of binary oppositions related to race, class, and gender as well as binary opposition between the individual self and nature, especially regarding perceptions of death. Though students interpreted a character such as June to have "died," the cultural discourse of the novel purports such a death to be the beginning of June's centrality to the novel. In the novel, the characters frequently perceived themselves as symbolically one with nature, a perception that differs from Western and Judeo-Christian perspectives on opposition between individual and nature.

On the final day of discussion of *Love Medicine,* students' earlier explorations of all three types of tensions led them to draw on both the novel and *Smoke Signals* in further developing an institutional critique of the oppression of Native Americans. To encourage students to explore tensions between White privilege and racial and cultural oppression, Parks provided students with a list of quotations from students' journals and asked them to note those that were the most provocative. This sparked an intense debate about the nature of the American government's treatment of Native Americans and other racial groups. For example, Devin read the following from one of his anonymous classmates: "On the reservation Indians are well to do with free money. Somehow in *Love Medicine* they tend to portray our government as cheap but I don't see it. Indians see us as unfair, but I don't believe it is true in real life." This statement was then challenged by Shelly, who argued, "We are unfair.... We gave away stupid little things in return, but we didn't really do a whole lot for them ... We had nothing to with what our ancestors did, but we are still the one's who have to face the consequences for it." Devin concurred, in a previously cited quote,

> We just kind of came over with all of our oppressionistic views and Catholicism and "this is the way to be" and "this is the way you should be" and "oh yeah, this land is good for cultivating so I'll tell you what; we have guns and you have spears so we will kick you out of here and give you a crappy little plot of land up north." And, "we'll let you sit there for a little while until we need more land, and then we'll take that from you." Then you can live in a more confined area and we'll take some more and then take some more … It was their land in the first place. We had no right to cheat them out of their own land.

Devin had a great deal of social power in terms of pushing the discussion in one direction or another. In this case, Devin's willingness to take on a discourse outside of classroom norms was quite significant in encouraging other students to explore institutional critiques during this discussion. As discussion continued, Devin's continued appropriation of this alternative stance spurred further institutional debate—this time focused on White privilege and affirmative action programs.

Kayla, one of the few students who typically challenged Devin, instigated this new phase of discussion by challenging the notion of White privilege, framing the discussion in terms of a tension between an individualistic discourse of self-sufficiency and a discourse of institutional racism:

> I think that a lot of people, White, Black, Indian, you make what you want out of it. If you are going to have a hard time in life then basically you do it to yourself. If you mess up, it's your fault, then you have a hard life. But if you really don't want to have a hard life, if you want to have an easy life, then you gotta work hard at it and get what you deserve. So, I don't think that … I mean, there's a lot of White people out there that have a hard life, and a lot of Black people who have a great, easy life. It's about what they do now, and how hard they worked before that.

In response to placing this value on hard work, Devin, who often positioned Kayla's opinions as off base, argued that some form of affirmative action is needed given the institutional racism shaping hiring practices:

> You [Kayla] said if you work hard for it you get what you deserve, and that's not necessarily true, because the racism in society is really strong when you try to get a job. There are a lot of jobs out there like business, corporations and building offices that if you have a guy who

goes in there, say a Native American person who is just as qualified as the person if not better, they will always be judged because of their color and because of their background than what a White person would be because they are used to the White person.

Corey, in an unusual and tentative counter to Devin, explained that he understood affirmative action programs as working against his desire to be a police officer: "I want to go to school to be a cop and I was talking to a guy who said that if I really want to be a cop, it would be easier if you were a minority or different color."

Kathy, also taking a stance in opposition to Devin, then cited some instances of these programs as undermining individual initiative:

I think White people don't enjoy that [easiest life], I think Black people and minorities are like [using a low-pitched voice], "you know why? Because Whites did this and they did that and oh they have to pay for it. The government has to pay for it they have to give us money because oohh they kicked us off the land; they took us from Africa and brought us here."

This debate over the issue of affirmative action reflected a tension between the students' adherence to a discourse of individualism and a discourse of institutional racism, a tension that reflected attitudes operating in the community's working-class culture. White students in a number of studies voice limited support for affirmation action programs. One survey study of largely White students in a private, Midwestern high school found that 65% favored affirmation action for college admissions; 30% of the students opposed affirmative action for job hiring and promotion; 10% favored affirmation action; and 18% indicated that it should be revised (Thompson, 2003). Another study found that half of White high school students opposed affirmative action for either college admissions or hiring (Corporate Source, 1998a). Consistent with the fact that the White males such as Corey were opposed to affirmation action, White females are less opposed to affirmative action than are White males (Farley, 2000; Sax & Arredondo, 1996), possibly because White males may perceive their majority status as being threatened by a system that has benefited them historically (Farrell, 1996). Some of the opposition to affirmative action reflects adherence to a color-blind racism that denies institutionalized racial inequality (Farley, 2000). Given attempts by politicians to exploit working-class people's resentment toward people of color, the assumption is that people of color were receiving priorities in terms of job hiring. Kathy also voiced another notion: affirmative action serves to undermine people's motivation to work by rendering them dependent on that support.

Though in the context of this discussion it appears that most students upheld a stance of individual meritocracy in considering issues of White privilege and affirmative action, it is important to note that in focus-group discussions at the culmination of the study, many students cited this as one of the most significant discussions in causing them to reconsider their stances and to recognize the need for affirmation action given the need to rectify the historical institutional advantages afforded Whites over students of color in college admissions and hiring practices. A critical point here is that though little change was seen during the discussion, moments of dialogic tension such as this one created spaces for students to become aware of their stances toward particular issues. This awareness may have ultimately caused students to reconsider or reconstruct some of the cultural and social assumptions that they had normalized through participation in discourse communities and social worlds in their lived experiences.

Each of the three types of tensions we have theorized (Figure 9.1) is reflected in this three-day discussion of *Love Medicine* and *Smoke Signals*. These tensions include those portrayed in the novel between Catholicism and Native American spirituality. Tensions also occurred between students' lived-world cultural assumptions and those operating in the novel—for example, the animistic perspective necessary for interpreting the symbolic meanings of the novel versus students' familiar perspectives. We also point to tensions between students over whether the novel portrayed Native Americans to the American reading public in a positive versus negative light, with some students arguing that the novel's portrayal of alcoholism only serves to perpetuate certain stereotypes about Native Americans.

Dialogic Tensions in Discussions about *Kindred*

In discussing *Kindred*, students encountered a variety of tensions beginning with student-versus-text-world assumptions in trying to understand the culture of slavery and moving to within-text-world tensions and between-student tensions as they grappled with larger moral questions posed by their readings of the text.

In the first two days of discussing this novel, students spent a lot of time negotiating the cultural world of the text in terms of understanding racial and social norms of the antebellum South in ways that are different from how they understood their present-day worlds. In particular, students struggled to understand the norms of sexual relationships between Blacks and Whites in this time period as well as the norms for interracial relationships in 1970s America.

In the novel, after returning home from her first trip to the South, Dana comes across a family Bible with a family tree listed in the front. She notices the names of Rufus Weylin and Alice Greenwood listed as her great-grand-parents. She quickly realizes that it is Rufus whom she encountered on her trip back in time. Dana is upset to discover that her great-grandfather was White. Knowing nothing more about the relationship between Rufus and Alice, the students were initially confused about why this would upset Dana, especially in light of the fact that Dana is married to a White man.

Kathy wondered why it would matter to Dana that Alice had married a White man when she had done the same, especially given that this was in the distant past. Other students also referred to a marriage between Rufus and Alice in discussing this topic. For the first part of the discussion, students failed to consider that this may not have been a marriage but rather a nonconsensual sexual situation, which would have been much more common between an African American woman and a White man at that time.

As the discussion continued, Kayla, tentatively suggested that this relationship might not have been a typical marriage:

> I couldn't get like the time, too. I mean, she [Dana] knows, she figures out that she is in slavery or whatever and there was a lot of like rape and whatever in that time, but there wasn't like somebody White and somebody Black just hitching up and getting married. She could just be questioning that. 'Cause definitely at the time I don't, like know if Kevin is White or whatever then I mean that shows that it is more modern and it is not a big deal, but in slavery, she could just be questioning ... like it even says, "If it even is marriage," you know. Umm ... 'cause, you know then if it is marriage, then why is a White person and a Black person getting married during slavery? And if it isn't, then what happened?

Later in the discussion, students again tried to establish the nature of the relationship between Rufus and Alice, this time by trying to determine whether Rufus is a racist. Troy posed the following theory:

> When Rufus gets mad at her [Dana] for not saying "master" to him. Or not saying like "Master" or "Hey Master" or I don't even know what they said back then "Master." Then he says something like "You want me to call you Black?" And then they go on and like get in a fight about it, and he says, "Nigger" and all these other good words, or bad words back then, but good then, or whatever. But then he like, but then Rufus goes, "It's not for me; it's for my dad." So that kind of surprised me that it was not for Rufus and more for the fact that his dad.... That implies to me that Rufus isn't a racist little guy. Which then in turns means that he could get together with Alice if he is not racist?

Here Troy suggests that Rufus may not actually be racist but that he talks this way to Dana due to his father's, and society's, expectations of him to be called *master*. Because Rufus is portrayed as quite human in this text, initially appearing as a mischievous child, students initially had difficulty perceiving him as a slave owner and as a racist. In this case, given students' lived-world understanding of what a slave owner and a racist might be like (e.g., hateful, coldhearted, uncaring), the very human depiction of Rufus within the world of this text in some ways clashed with students expectation for him. Therefore students' experienced tensions related to student-versus-text world assumptions in discussing this text.

During the second day of discussion students continued to negotiate tensions related to the norms for sexual relationships between African American women and White men. At one point in the novel, Dana's White husband, Kevin, is transported back in time with her. He attempts to protect her by posing as her master. Dana, who usually sleeps in the attic, for a few nights sleeps in the same room with Kevin with no questions asked. The following is an exchange in which one student, Sarah, tried to understand why this is acceptable when a public, mutually consenting relationship between an African American woman and a White man would not be:

Sarah: [laughs] There's one part, where she comes out of Kevin's room and what's-his-name [referring to Rufus's father, the plantation owner] catches him and he winks at him; what the heck is that?
Devin: 'cause he knows that she just gave Kevin some lovin'.
Sarah: Alright, that's what I thought, but I was kind of like "whoa." That's a little weird.

[silence]

Sarah: Yeah, but that's weird, because she's Black and he's White and that was not, that never happened ...

[Devin and Michelle talk over Sarah]

Devin: Actually, that was kind of the norm.
Michelle: Rape did.

[Several other students talk over Sarah inaudible.]

Sarah: All right, I see what you mean.

In continuing to negotiate student-versus-text-world cultural assumptions, the class came to agree that public relationships (e.g., marriage) between African Americans and Whites were not acceptable but that rape of African American women by White men was common. Sarah was not, however, aware that rape in this context was not just common but also socially acceptable and often appeared consensual rather than violent. So Sarah was confused about why a seemly consensual encounter appears to be acceptable. Sarah may have been viewing sex through modern American cultural assumptions in which sex is perceived as either clearly consensual or clearly violent rape. This example represents a tension between an unambiguous, dichotomous way of viewing sexual relationships and violence and the more complex reality of such situations in different social or historical contexts.

In a similar discussion, students negotiated other student-versus-text-world cultural assumptions. This time students were trying to determine why Rufus's father, Tom Weylin, becomes angry with Dana and beats her when he discovers that she has been reading one of his books. Devin began the discussion by suggesting that his anger is related to his feelings for his first wife, who read all the time:

> ... She's [Dana] well educated, she can read and his first wife, all she did was read so he kind of didn't like that ... I think it's something like past aggression he had, and he's like you know, "Finally, someone I can take this out on, someone who could read. I don't like that," so stealing the book gave him a perfect reason to whip her.

Kayla responded to Devin by questioning why Tom would want Dana to teach Rufus, his son, to read if he does not like people who read. Corey offered that Tom probably wants his son to be educated. Kayla continued to express confusion. She responded to Corey and referred to Devin's earlier point: "Yeah, but, like Devin said, that he doesn't like the people that are educated." 'Cause it said earlier in the book if you have educated slaves they get away more easily by writing passes for themselves."

Although Corey offered an economic reason for Tom not wanting Dana to read, Kayla returned again to Devin's point that Tom is expressing aggression related to his first wife. It is at this point that Devin amended his original argument by adding the ideas that Corey formulated:

> I'm not saying that was like the sole reason [anger over his first wife's reading practices], but I think there was definitely some evidence of it there. But I think the reason he has Dana and Kevin teaching his son is because in the book it says when she regularly reads to him Mr. and Mrs. Weylin come in and out but there was a time when Mr. Weylin came in and he said you know, "Look, here, you know, a nigger can read better than you," which is why I think he's trying to get his kid to read, because he's got that resentment toward Dana. He wants his son to be better educated than a Black person.

Once Devin's argument had been amended to include both Tom's anger toward his first wife and his resentment toward Dana for being an African American woman who is more well educated than his son, Sarah further amended the argument to include both of these reasons as well as a gender-related reason:

> Maybe he was mad because he wanted to be married to a wife that wasn't reading all the time. Maybe he doesn't like the power, like girls being able to read better than him, 'cause he's not. And then Black people, which are supposed to be lower, since they're higher in some way, then he must not like that from Black people and women because they are supposed to be lower then men and that's what he is and he doesn't like that. You know what I'm saying? That's a different way to look at it. I think maybe that's the reason he whipped her, cause he didn't like that she had more power in some different way than him? He wants his kid to learn how to read just as good as, you know, you know what I'm saying?

Kayla agreed with Sarah's ideas and added one more reason—she suggested that Tom is also angry with Dana because when he told her that he wanted to buy her, she said she would rather stay with Kevin, her 1970s husband. Kayla suggested that Tom feels snubbed by Dana and is angry that he does not have more power over her.

At the start of this discussion, students struggled to understand why something they viewed as an important and positive skill—reading—was something that caused Dana to be punished. As they explored this tension, they came up against further confusion, the fact that Tom seems not to like those who read yet wants his son to learn to read. However, as students pushed on in this discussion they began first to offer simple explanations and then to synthesize these explanations, arriving at multifaceted, complex, conclusions. In confronting this tension related to student-versus-text-world cultural assumptions, students used discussion to amend their ideas and understand the text world with greater sophistication.

As students continued to read and discuss *Kindred,* they navigated larger issues about morality in reference to whether Rufus was a bad person because he raped Alice or whether he was simply a product of the social worlds that were available to him in this historical period, making decisions that are no different from those that anyone else would make in his situation. Much of the tension in this discussion was a result of some students attempting to hold firm to the binary oppositions of good and bad, while other students struggled to see Rufus as human and neither all good nor all bad.

In the excerpts from student discussion that follow, students experimented with alternative perspectives through voicing Rufus's perspectives and by envisioning themselves in his situation or historical and cultural time period. In doing so, students also learned to judge the limitations of characters' perspectives relative to their cultural contexts, recognizing that characters lacked insights or understandings of their social worlds.

The discussion began with students trying to determine whether any action is universally right or wrong. Of the students who spoke in discussion, all generally agreed that there is little that can be agreed upon as universally wrong. The one exception was Kayla, who firmly insisted that some things, such as rape, simply are wrong. She suggested that one's conscience should be a higher law than any cultural norms or laws. She cited an example from the text to prove that Rufus knew his behavior in raping Alice was wrong. This example led to a discussion of how Rufus might really have felt about Alice and how cultural and historical norms from his social worlds may have motivated his actions.

Kayla: Well, yeah, um, he says, "I'll have her whether you help or not." He's talking to Dana about Alice. Um, "All I want you to do is make it so I don't have to beat her," like right there, like he feels guilty. Like why would he care? You know why would he care about beating her to rape her?

Paul: He loves her.

Michelle: It's because he's shaming himself because he loves her. Because he doesn't want to beat her because he loves her and that's where his conscience comes in.

Kayla: Why would he want to rape her then?

Paul: He does love her.

Michelle: He loves her. That's where his conscience comes in, right there.

Paul: He thinks it's right to rape her, that's why he doesn't ...

Devin: Maybe he raped her, like in a way to show his love. I mean there really is no such a way to show love through rape, but I mean like given his situation, if it's so wrong to love a Black person, maybe he was using rape as kind of an excuse to, you know, to say, "Hey, you know, I just raped her." That was just the norm, but in the subtext he's saying, you know, this is the way I'm trying to show my love for you, but I don't wanna, you know, get any pressure put on me or you, because I know the punishment for you would be a lot worse than it would be for me" ...

Sue: I think he is wrong because when we first meet her she is a free woman and she was in like slavery so she had like [inaudible].

Devin: Put yourself in Rufus's shoes though.

Paul: It doesn't matter; she's Black, he's White, she doesn't have any power.

[Devin continues on for a few minutes explaining how it might feel to be Rufus, loving someone he is not allowed to love]

Sue: I don't think he loves her; I think he's just obsessed with her, 'cause how can he say he loves her if she doesn't love him?

This exchange brought about not only within-text-world tensions but also between-student tensions when we consider how gender and social roles play a part in student responses.

In this discussion, male students actively voiced Rufus's perspective and tried to "put themselves in his shoes." Though these male students, Devin and Paul, were willing to try on this alternative discourse, two of the females in the discussion, Kayla and Sue, were less willing to see rape in any alternative light. Michelle, the one other female student who participated in this discussion, was an exception. She agreed with that stance taken by Paul and Devin. Here we can see how Michelle's situated identity as a female who aligned herself with male friends and her activity identity as Kayla's adversary in discussion likely came in to play. Because she wanted to align herself with the males in the class and against Kayla, Michelle's responses tended to be framed by her social positioning. In general, this discussion was one in which male students were quite dominant, whereas female students remained noticeably more quiet and less willing to entertain alternative view points regarding Rufus's actions. This is likely an example of girls' brought-along tensions regarding rape interacting with boys' brought-about engagement with the character of Rufus.

Tensions in discussions such as this one, as well as Parks's suggestion that students consider the character of Rufus through hypothetical questions, were what led students to the final discussion of this novel through which they examined first what they thought Rufus might be like if he lived today and second what their own actions might have looked like in a different time and place.

Shelley began by saying that she felt that Rufus might be a good person if he had lived today:

I don't know, it's just like his culture says it's wrong to love and right to rape and he just, I don't know, I think that with his racist stuff and everything and all Black people are bad and everything, like Devin wrote that they're subhuman and stuff? Or like, that's how it would be and I think that's his culture. And if he were here, I think he'd be different. Like, like with your fish thing [fishbowl metaphor], that's what he's taken in and that's the way he's been brought up, and I think if he was brought up differently, like raised differently here, that he wouldn't have those views and he'd still love whoever he wanted and he'd be alright.

Considering what Rufus might be like if he lived today led several White students to disclose that they realized that their beliefs and actions are influenced by their cultures and that they might have participated in actions similar to Rufus's or other White people's in the novel if they lived in that cultural setting. Shelley told the class that she could see herself treating other people badly if she lived in the same situation as Rufus's mother, Margaret.

Shelly: I don't think it's really that hard to think about. It's like in my journal I wrote that if I were back there I would compare myself to Margaret Weylin and I could very easily see myself as her. I mean …

Parks: Talk about that a little bit.

Shelly: I don't think I would throw a pot of coffee on anyone, I think that's just cruel, but I think in the right circumstances I might. I don't know, I'd have to be in the circumstances, but like I could see myself like going around, complaining about things just because I have nothing to complain about, 'cause I do that now. And so, if I had slave to complain about, I would, I know I would, and it's, I could just, I could see myself walking around having nothing to do and just complaining because there was nothing else to do.

As with most students, Shelly was willing to try on an alternative discourse, but only momentarily. After stating that she could easily imagine herself behaving like Margaret Weylin, she quickly added the condition that she would not do cruel things like throwing coffee on her slave.

Similarly, Corey inched his way into an alternative discourse but quickly pulled back from it. The following were Corey's thoughts on whether he could imagine himself as a slave holder if he lived in a different time period:

Corey: If I were to go back then I could see myself running a plantation, I mean if I was raised that way, I mean, but I don't, I couldn't see myself hitting somebody with a whip, especially a girl, I mean how could you just sit there and hit a girl with a whip, tied down, defenseless.

Parks: But where would you have gotten the idea that it was wrong? That's what I'm …

Corey: I just couldn't see myself doing it. That's what's hard to think about.

In this segment of discussion, Corey entertained thoughts about what he might have been capable of if he had owned a plantation. First he pointed out that he would have had to have been raised in a certain way (i.e., in a way different from how Corey was actually raised). He then said he would be willing to run a plantation but could not hit his slaves. As he considered this further, he became even more specific: he said he might be able to hit men with a whip, but not women. Finally, he decided that he might be able to hit a woman, but not if she were tied down and defenseless. However, when Parks tried to interject and ask Corey further questions about his beliefs, Corey back-pedaled and firmly stated that he could not see himself doing it, admitting that these issues are hard to think about.

Directly following Corey, Devin voiced an alternative discourse, taking on an appealing discourse of power (Trainor, 2002, 2005):

Devin: I think I could [be a slave holder]. Just because of the ways I'd be raised and the way I am now, I kind of like made a comparison, like I'd definitely have some of the traits I have today that I would back then, and like in some ways when I get mad I get really aggressive, like me and my dad got into it the other night and I was really close to hitting him in the face. I really felt like punching my dad square in the face and knocking him out, cause he ...

Parks: Yeah, yeah you can see it like in your head ...

Devin: 'cause he drove me over the edge and I think, you know, bad as it may seem if a slave you know ran away, and I got really pissed about it, I could see myself doing something like that or you know being a slave owner or what not.

Unlike Shelly and Corey, Devin did not quickly fall back on more familiar and comfortable discourses; rather, he embraced this alternative stance. This may be in part because Devin's transportable identity as a powerful leader seemed to follow him into all of his situated and activity identities at school. He seemed never to worry that his opinions would cast him in a negative light. This social freedom allowed Devin to experiment quite readily with alternative discourses. In other situations he voiced a wide range of social and political views.

In reading and discussing *Kindred* students experienced a variety of tensions. In trying to understand the world of the text, students experienced tensions between the norms of their own worlds and the historical worlds of the text. In constructing the character of Rufus, students negotiated tensions between their differing readings and understandings of the character and his culturally and historically bound social worlds. Finally,

through reading this novel in which a person from the 1970s has to negotiate the world of the antebellum South, students noted tensions between
discourses of individual meritocracy that assume individuals to be responsible for their decisions and actions based on universal norms of morality
versus a discourse that suggests individuals are largely shaped by culture
and context. This challenged students to reconsider their judgments of
others as well as their conceptions of their own morality.

Dialogic Tensions in Discussions about *Bastard out of Carolina*

The primary within-text tensions in *Bastard out of Carolina* are those that
surround poverty and its effects on characters. However, because the students initially had difficulty framing poverty as related to systemic oppression, social class, and cultural expectations, they discussed poverty in this
text primarily in terms of individual characters' lack of money.

For example, in initially theorizing about the causes of the disintegration of Bone's family situation, Mitch suggested that lack of money is the
primary issue of the novel.

Mitch: I said poverty because I kind of pictured them being rich instead of
poor and I couldn't really see the abuse going on really, 'cause
I think it really affected Glen, the fact that the family was mad
at him ...
Parks: You're talking about Glen's family, now ...
Mitch: I'm talking about if Bone's family was rich?
Parks: Oh, oh, oh, keep going with that.
Mitch: I couldn't see the abuse going on because I think it all rooted back
to Glen's feeling of failure and his father and I'm not saying it
doesn't happen in rich families but I'm just saying in this case I
think ....

Even as Mitch posited that Bone's problems are related to money, he also
suggested that these problems are connected to Glen's feelings of failure
in living up to family, social-class expectations. As students continued to
explore the within-text-world tension of the relationship between poverty
and family dysfunction, they began to unravel the shame of generational
poverty that goes beyond individual lack of material goods. For example,
in the following excerpt Pamela offered an alternative perspective that
drew on and extended Mitch's perspectives on poverty as the root of the
problems in Bone's family.

Pamela: That kind of relates to what I chose, to the theme I chose. What I chose was about succeeding in life and I think the reason why Annie abandoned Bone was because she never succeeded in anything in life she was always seen as trash by everyone and the reason why she wanted to marry Glen and stay with him even though he abused her daughter was because um, was simply because she'd always been seen as trash and she wanted to stay with Glen to prove that eventually she had become someone in life and that she had she wasn't a failure, she wasn't a loser, she wasn't trash, like everyone thought she was, and I thought if she had been rich maybe it would not have been that big of a deal, maybe ...

Through this discussion, Pamela was able to take Mitch's idea and add another level of complexity to that idea. Here Pamela suggested that the problems in this family occur because of a sense of shame that Anney feels as a result of a history of poverty in her family. In this sense, poverty can be viewed as contributing to a larger, cultural and systemic sense of shame that comes from being perceived by other groups of people as *trash*. Pamela posited that this may be the real reason why this family fell apart. Anney wanted so desperately for those around her to see her as someone and not trash because she was not willing to leave a man who was abusive to her daughter. However, in agreeing with Mitch she also suggested that had Anney been rich she may not have struggled with the fear of being perceived as trash.

As students continued to negotiate tensions within the text worlds of *Bastard out of Carolina,* they also encountered text-to-life tensions. This was particularly the case as students tried to make sense of the character of Anney and her actions in staying with Glen and in ultimately abandoning Bone.

The character of Anney drew student empathy from the novel's onset. Early, she appears as a naive, pregnant 15 year old. Through the course of the novel she is injured in a car wreck, loses a husband, and fights for her daughter Bone to enjoy a future that is not stigmatized by the label of *illegitimate* on her birth certificate. Anney is a hard-working waitress who wants to make a better life for her children.

Students' journal writings suggested that Anney was a character they supported. For example, in her journal Kathy identified the passage "Glen Waddell turned mama from a harried, worried mother into a giggling, hopeful girl" (p. 35) as important in her understanding of Anney:

This is the reason why Anney married Glen. I can understand that because at 21 she was the mother of two and never had the chance to be a teen where she could have fun and rebel and have a say in her future or not make the same mistakes her mom did.

Alongside this entry, Kathy's journal partner, Corey wrote, "I totally agree with you on this part." These sentiments of support for Anney ran throughout the early discussions as well—Anney was an easy character for students to understand in early sections of the novel, because by working hard to support her children she lives out discourses of meritocracy that students were familiar with in their lived worlds. However, as students read further into the novel, and as Anney's situation became more desperate, students found that Anney's actions and reactions to situations did not fit their cultural models of meritocracy; therefore tensions arose. For example, Anney eventually prostitutes herself to feed her children and ultimately finds herself unable and unwilling to leave Glen, despite the fact that he abuses her children. As these textual situations arise, students were confronted with dialogic tensions between the norms in their lived worlds and those in this text world.

In critiquing Anney's actions, Devin pointed out that she violated norms of meritocracy in terms of not standing up for herself and not doing what was necessary to see that her children succeeded in life. He viewed her as also violating family norms both within the text world and within Devin's lived worlds by failing to be loyal to her children:

Devin: I think family played a huge part in the book. They didn't have the greatest reputation but the always seemed to have each others backs. They're a bunch of drunks but they're a family, I mean they're always behind Bone and like when Earl finds out about what Glen's been doing to Bone and he just goes completely ballistic and goes and beats the crap out of Glen. You know it's kind of going back to the whole loyalty thing, you know, they're loyal to each other but going off what Sue said, the mother and the daughter, I don't know what that's about, that just really I don't see how you could let your child be exposed to that and keep letting it happen time and time again. I know if I were, if I were ever put in a woman's position and my kid kept getting beat by the dad, I wouldn't just bang on the door. I would go grab something and go start beating the guy with it. That's what I'd do. I mean it's a whole lack of trust and loyalty and Bone even says she starts to hate her mother. Kids at the age of 12 aren't supposed to hate their parents, you know. She's got a lot of hate and a lot of feelings that at her age you're not supposed to be exposed to.

Corey: That's why I chose the word trust 'cause who has she got to trust now that her mom's not even on her side. You're supposed to be able to trust your parents to protect you when you're young.

In this excerpt from discussion Devin and Corey both expressed clear statements of what they understand relationships between children and parents should look like. Devin stated, "Kids at the age of 12 aren't supposed to hate their parents"; then he explained what he would do in Anney's situation. Likewise, Corey explained, "You are supposed to be able to trust your parents … " Statements like these demonstrate clear tensions between text worlds and students' lived worlds. In this case Corey and Devin projected norms from their lived worlds onto Anney and her lived worlds rather than understanding Anney's actions as they are related to the norms of her worlds.

Following these comments, Kathy made an attempt to further understand Anney through the text worlds in which she lives:

Kathy: … Like what Devin and Corey was saying, I think because Anney expected Glen to be a perfect gentleman and when he wasn't that she really didn't see anything else. She had an expectation to be young again and when he wasn't doing that and so she still accepted it. So it's all about her expectation for marriage she wanted to prove to her mom that it was good so she kept telling everybody that he loved the kids and stuff so to prove that everything was good.

In discussing the character of Glen, students were equally, if not more, troubled by his actions and reactions to situations in the text. However, Parks challenged students to understand Glen through an examination of possible worlds in his life. In this case, students not only grappled with student vs. text-world assumptions, but also with between-student tensions.

Early in the reading of the novel, Troy suggested that Glen appeared to be a "good guy from a good family" who might do anything to win Anney's affections. Other students chimed in that indeed Glen, like Anney, appeared as a figure of empathy: he is misunderstood and disconnected from his family; he is not prone to anger, drinking, or violence; and he really wants to start a strong family with Anney. Students' early assessments of Glen are aligned with Bouson's (2001, p. 113) analysis of Glen's identity in the novel:

Using a series of class-coded descriptions, the novel presents Glen as an amalgam of middle-class refinement and lower-class brute physicality. He is "a small man but so muscular and strong that it was hard to see the delicacy in him, though he was strangely graceful in his rough work clothes and heavy boots .... Glen Waddell's feet were so fine that his boots had to be bought in the boys' department of the Sears, Roebuck, while his gloves could only be found in the tall men's specialty stores" (34). A man who "didn't drink, didn't mess around, didn't even talk dirty" (35), Glen seemingly offers Anney an escape from her disgraceful White trash family origins and an opportunity to pass as middle class and socially respectable. But, in fact, Glen is attracted to Anney because she is a Boatwright. The Black sheep of the middle-class Waddell family, Glen initially determines to marry Anney because he wants to marry the "whole Boatwright legend" and thus "shame his daddy and shock his brothers."

As the novel unfolds and Glen transforms from a figure of warm empathy into an abuser and pedophile. Devin's initial reaction, for example, was to suggest, "Maybe he's just a pedophile or maybe he's just sick." However, the willingness of some students to explore Glen's motivations was frustrating to other students, leading to some between-student tensions. The excerpt from discussion that follows serves as an example:

Parks: If I told you there was a chapter missing from this book and in that chapter, Daddy Glen goes into great detail about how his father sexually abused him from the time he was young. Would that chapter make a difference in how you view Daddy Glen?

Devin: Yes. Because it, it's almost like it's really easy to judge somebody, everybody is quick to pass judgment on people, you know they only see the bad things, you know but then you gotta look at it from the other point of view that you know, Daddy Glen, he's a person too, dealing with everyday situations, everyday problems, he's got a huge issue with money, he can't make money, he can't keep a job, and this, if there was a chapter that explained why he was the way he was, I think it would completely alter my thoughts about him and kind of give me some sympathy for him, because even though he is like a monster in this book and he's really doing some bad things I mean, he's just, I can't remember who said it earlier in the discussion but he's just following the role of the parents. You know, parents are the greatest influences on kids.

Sarah: I wouldn't give him any sympathy. I would feel the same, because I don't care who a person is or what their parents were like, if they use you, I mean I'm sorry yeah, but if you're gonna take it out on other people you got a problem and he needs some serious help, and he just needs to get the heck out of there.

Paul: Bone's could turn out the same way.

Shelly: I think if he went into detail and there was a chapter missing ...

Devin: I know I've talked three times, but I have to keep going. If he were abused he went through that for at least 12 years. It's a habit, like smoking. There's a lot of hatred and emotions.

Shelly: How can you say that? Have you been sexually abused? How do you know?

Devin: No I haven't.

Parks: I'm with Shelly and Troy, but I also know he's a victim. I understand the dilemma. It's a hard question.

Sarah: He knows he's doing this. Get help! He's ruining a little girl's life because of his problem.

Shelly: He knew it was wrong, or he wouldn't have said he was sorry.

Troy: He enjoyed it. He's sick.

In this contentious discussion, it was Devin and Paul who were willing to explore alternative perspectives. As we noted in our discussion of students' responses to tensions in *Kindred,* as a socially powerful student in this classroom, Devin was often one of the students who seemed most comfortable trying on alternative perspectives. As a close friend of Devin's and a fellow athlete, Paul was often also willing to try on alternative perspectives, as long as this trying on was initiated by Devin. In looking at the between-student tensions in this excerpt from discussion it is worthwhile to note that Sarah and Shelly are two students who rarely disagreed with Devin: Sarah because she is a female jock who typically supports all that Devin says; and Shelly because she lacks social power and remains quiet much of the time to avoid social ridicule. This suggests that though Devin and Mark were willing to explore the possibility of differences between their own and text worlds, Sarah, Shelly, and Troy applied their lived-world assumptions about sexual abuse to condemn Glen's actions.

As discussion of this novel came to a close, students tried to come to a conclusion about a question they had grappled with throughout the reading of this novel: could Bone overcome the shame she feels as a result of living in poverty and suffering abuse at the hands of her stepfather and, as Pamela stated, "become somebody"? Early on in discussions of this novel, students spoke optimistically about Bone's future. Dan shared that his small group believed that Bone's age is what keeps her from overcoming the trauma of abuse, saying "Eventually she'll start to like talk back. As Bone's getting older she's doing that." Paul shared his confidence that Bone can overcome this trauma through the assistance of treatment centers.

Pamela added weight to this optimism suggesting, "Maybe a teacher will be a positive role model." However, as the text and Parks pushed students to understand poverty not just an as individual problem but rather as a systemic issue as well, students began to rethink this discourse of meritocracy and such optimism about Bone's future as someone who is shaped by the systemic, institutional forces of poverty associated with lack of resources and support.

Parks drew a line on the board to represent the continuum of success and asked students to discuss the ways the status of an individual at birth might relate to his or her ability to achieve success in society. This discussion had previously centered around racial stratification but in this session turned toward social class. In this discussion students explored ways that economic and cultural capital (Bourdieu, 1977; 1984) place individuals on a continuum of success. In the following excerpt Corey, Kathy, and Kayla met in a small group and discussed this issue. In this small-group meeting, Corey and Kayla confidently reaffirmed a familiar discourse of meritocracy as he stated that he believed Bone could fulfill her dreams. However, in drawing on the tensions from previous class sessions, Kayla challenged him on this thinking:

Corey: I think she could … if she stayed in school and went to college after, just like anybody else could. But, I don't know, the things that went on in her life might mess her up a little bit. She might need counseling or something, but I still think that she could get probably get through it.

Kathy: I think on p 178, her aunt says, "Trash rises," so she probably sees somebody who has potential. She is always praising her that she does good work and that she keeps coming back, even with all the hurt she's been feeling. Finding out that Reese is also doing the same thing she does [masturbating] just puts her like a step behind. She just had herself to worry about, but now she has herself and Reese to worry about, so it'll probably be hard for her, but if she can get through stuff, she will make it.

Corey: I just think that she has a chance like anybody else. *Anybody* [Corey's emphasis] can, if you do the right stuff and work hard your whole life.

Kayla: In class, Mr. Parks was talking about how everybody doesn't have the same chances.

Corey: Yeah, but … that's probably true, so I don't know. It's hard to say. I think that you can achieve goals in life if you work hard at it.

Kayla: I think that like on the board where somebody starts with success [on the continuum] then, definitely, like Bone and her sister and the whole Boatwright family I think starts behind like just because of their family, like just born as a child. They haven't even had the chance to progress at all, just being born into that, they're starting behind everyone else. They are just gonna have to, if they do want to become something, they would have to work harder to get above, like, right from the start it's really hard. It's a lot harder anyways, somebody who is rich is gonna start farther. Like, even in the book, they are talking about "I wanna be rich, I can be rich someday" it says. Like, that is the thing to be. I don't know, when you are rich, you're kind of already there. You don't really have to do anything, you just have to stay there. It is a lot easier to keep things than to make them.

In this exchange Corey continued to voice discourses of individual meritocracy and hard work acquired through his participation in athletics and in a working-class family and community. However, as Kayla drew on previous class discussions, she challenged Corey to reconsider and even to amend his stance toward these discourses, if only temporarily. Kayla did this not only by double voicing Parks but also by affirming Corey's ideas and then tentatively revising them. In double voicing the working-class myth that "I can be rich someday," Kayla recognized the illusory nature of an economic system in which working-class characters believe that they can easily achieve wealth, in contrast to those who began and remain wealthy. In dialogic exchanges such as this, students did not immediately change their stances but slowly amended text-world assumptions through ongoing discussions.

Student challenges of one another also led to amending and adopting alternative perspectives. In the small-group discussion, Kayla raised the question of whether it was more difficult to move from poverty to wealth when someone has always been poor, such as Bone's family, or to move from wealth to poverty and back to wealth, as with Daddy Glen:

Do you think that because his family started out rich that he's at the same point that is at somebody who is poor. Do you think that it is easier for him to go back to being rich compared to somebody who starts out poor and is becoming rich for the first time?

Corey posited that it would be easier for Daddy Glen because he has previously been wealthy and therefore has the knowledge that a poor person lacks:

Probably ... do I think that it is harder for him to go? No, I think it would be easier for him 'cause he's been there before. Somebody who hasn't been rich before what do they know? They don't know what to do.

Kathy concurred with Corey that Daddy Glen could regain his prior status by changing his behavior and appealing to his father who might give him a job:

> I think that's true 'cause what he has to do basically is like either do what his father tells him to do right now and basically be on his good side and get back into the family business. Instead of him taking orders from people working for his father, then he can give orders to them. Or, everybody knows him in town as somebody whose family is well off, so all he probably has to do is like quit drinking and move back home or something. Probably have to do one other thing. Probably have to go back to school and maybe go back to his dad and apologize or whatever and then he would have a job and so it would not be that hard for him.

However, Kayla challenged the notion that one's family will necessarily assist family members:

> Like what you said, with his family helping him back up, I totally disagree with that. I know that my family is not like "well-to-do," or anything, we just get what we can to pay the rent. If somebody else in our family even that might be lower than us, or not even my family, but any family, that might become lower than us because they go around and stealing and doing drugs and things like that, a lot of times, members of my family that the people who are lower, they'll like push us away because, "oh, you think you're better than us" sort of thing. Or else, other people from my family will be like, "what have you done? Why have you become this?" and I think that there is a certain point where, sure, you know, if it is like life or death, they would help them out, but I don't think that a lot of times family will just make everything all better.

Drawing on her working-class background, Kayla argued that attempts to change or improve one's status would actually bring resentment from other family members, and that one's family status does not necessarily serve to improve individual members. Kayla's assessment reflected her ability to frame issues in terms of power relationships within and between families that serve to challenge Corey's and Kathy's more optimistic portrayals of supportive families. At the same time, students examined how one's cultural capital can play a part in individual success.

Kayla's challenge led Kathy to revise her belief and recognize the more realistic political tensions with Daddy Glen's family:

I guess I agree. The same thing that Daddy Glen is now, his family is acting like they are all high class. He is also pushing them away because if his brother gave him a job, then he wants to find his own way. But, for him, since he wants his father's approval, that is what he wants, he will do what his father wants him to do, so, it isn't like he will get back into the family or whatever, so…

In contrast to her previous rosy scenario, Kathy recognized the more exclusionary aspects of Daddy Glen's high-class family with whom he no longer wants to be associated. Kathy therefore picked up on Kayla's assessment that it is difficult for either poor people or even well-off people such as Daddy Glen to alter their class status because to do so means creating tensions with one's family, a move toward recognizing the power of class.

However, Corey did not pick up on this shift but answered the original question by arguing that poor people have more difficulty changing their status because change in status can only occur through hard work:

Corey: I think that it is true in life that if you do start out poor it will be harder for you to get rich, 'cause you've got to work your way through everything, just like in the book: those are almost the same.

Thus, though Kayla and Kathy moved toward a belief that class structure serves to limit changes in status, Corey still assumed that, though change in status is more difficult for poor people, it can still occur. All of this reflects how dialogic tensions can lead some students to amend their discourses, whereas other students retain their steadfast allegiance to their set discourses.

The novel *Bastard out of Carolina* brought the students into another world where complex factors of shame, poverty, and survival wreak havoc on the Boatwright family. In engaging with the text and with one another, students were forced to consider the role of class structure in the lives of individuals. In the lives and histories of Bone, Anney, and Glen, the students found themselves questioning human behavior and agency. Ultimately, they found themselves questioning the ways in which they judged and assessed others, laying bare their dominant discourses in the arena of classroom discussion.

Summary

Analysis of discussions of these three novels points to the role of different types of dialogic tensions in encouraging students to adopt different perspectives on race, class, and gender.

In responding to *Love Medicine*, students explored within-text-world tensions between Catholicism and Native American spirituality, tensions between their religious cultural assumptions and the animistic perspectives portrayed in the text, and tensions between competing attitudes toward affirmative action reflecting differences between a discourse of competitive individualism and a discourse of institutional racism. This led some students to critically examine the influence of institutional racism.

In responding to *Kindred*, students experienced tensions between different interpretations of the morality of Rufus's role in slavery, reflecting a larger tension between discourses of individual meritocracy and institutional racism related to the system of slavery. Grappling with these tensions encouraged some students to question their adherence to a discourse of individual meritocracy.

And in their responses to *Bastard out of Carolina*, students experienced tensions related to discourses of race, class, and gender hierarchies operating in the small Southern town. These situations led students to focus particularly on the problematic influence of the class system on limiting characters' sense of agency. Some came to voice the ways social class may provide or hinder access for the economic success of individuals.

By interrogating each other's interpretations, students challenged some of their peers' hegemonic discourses, leading some students to reflect on these limitations of those discourses. However, as we noted in the case-study chapters, students varied in their openness to critically reflecting on their discourses. All of this points to the importance of discussions that revolve around conflicting, alternative perspectives and debates that serve to challenge status quo discourses while fostering a variety of dialogic tensions.

CHAPTER **10**

Summary and Implications for
Teaching Multicultural Literature

A change in cultural tools may often be a more powerful force of
development than the enhancement of individuals' skills.

Wertsch (1998, p. 38)

To locate micro-processes of social change, one must look at occasions for, and of, persuasion.

Lindquist (2002, p. 8)

In this final chapter, we summarize some of the overall changes in some of
the participants' responses and discourses, changes we attribute to experiencing dialogic tensions and perspective taking. We then explore three
intersecting factors that we believe served to foster these dialogic tensions
and perspective taking: responses to multicultural texts, participation in
discussions, and Parks's teaching techniques.

Over the relatively short period of six months, we were certainly not
expecting dramatic changes. And consistent with previous research on
the lack of attitude change resulting from responding to multicultural literature (Dressel, 2003; Pace, 2006), we were also not expecting marked
changes in attitudes related to race, class, and gender.

Nor did we define change in terms of enhanced empathy for characters
through responding to literature (Probst, 2004). We assumed that students
were learning to go beyond simply empathizing with characters perceived

as autonomous personalities to focusing on characters as shaped by institutional systems of family, school, peer group, community, or workplace (Engeström, 1999; Vadeboncoeur & Stevens, 2005).

Rather than define change in terms of adopting less racist or sexist beliefs and attitudes, we defined change as the increased propensity to try on, amend, and revise discourses and cultural models of race, class, and gender. Faced with dialogic tensions portrayed in texts and articulated in discussions, students in our study began to examine the limitations of their status quo discourses and cultural models, leading some students such as Troy, Devin, Kayla, Mitch, and Kathy to explore alternative discourses and culture models. At the same time, we noted that some other students such as Corey and Michelle demonstrated less of a propensity to amend or revise their discourses or cultural models given their adherence to status quo discourses and cultural models consistent with allegiances to their social worlds.

In addition to changes in students' willingness to amend or revise their status quo discourses and cultural models, we were also interested in studying changes in students' social and literacy practices reflected in their writing and discussions—their ability to employ new tools to engage in critical analysis, analysis reflecting interrogation of discourses and cultural models. It is difficult to chart any distinct linear improvements in students' interpretive abilities because their ability to interpret often varied with a novel's cultural perspective, difficulty, and appeal. Students found that texts with clearly developed storylines and limited shifts in perspectives were less difficult to interpret that were novels such as *Love Medicine* (Erdrich, 2000) or *Yellow Raft in Blue Water* (Dorris, 1987). Students were also puzzled about characters' motives given their lack of cultural knowledge about certain aspects of Native American culture. And as evident in their journals, students wrote more about novels with a high level of appeal—*Bless Me, Ultima* (Anaya, 1995), *Kindred* (Butler, 1979), *Bastard out of Carolina* (Allison, 1993), and *Yellow Raft in Blue Water*—than those novels with less appeal—*The House on Mango Street* (Cisneros, 1991), *Their Eyes Were Watching God* (Hurston, 2000), and *Obasan* (Kogawa, 1993), although the level of appeal of these novels varied across students.

Changes in Students' Interpretive Strategies

Analysis of students' journal entries and discussion contributions across time demonstrates some changes that reflect influences of instruction in the course.

Use of Supporting Evidence

Over time, students were more likely to cite supporting evidence for their contentions in the form of quotations or descriptions of characters' actions. To some degree, they did so because they recognized that citing supporting evidence was one of Parks's primary criteria in evaluating their entries. However, they may also have acquired a propensity to cite quotations from their experiences in the discussions in which Parks continually asked to provide such support. Corey noted that prior to the course, he only needed to formulate summaries of texts, whereas he now can "form opinions and I will see evidence that I get from the book ... now towards the end [of the course] I have the evidence to support that."

Application of Critical Lenses

Over time, students also became more comfortable applying critical lenses (Appleman, 2000) related to interpreting race, class, and gender differences. In reflecting on the course, the students noted that adopting these lenses meant that they noticed aspects of texts that they would not notice otherwise. Though students were assigned to adopt one lens, they also applied other lenses. As Corey noted:

> I started to find myself taking so much more from books than I usually would like things I would have never seen before ... as the course progressed and we getting familiar with putting on these certain lenses kids were automatically jumping into the conversations and started saying things like that really had some meaning to it. With the *Yellow Raft* book when we were starting to work on our final papers, we were supposed to be looking for issues that dealt with class and like I am just reading and I am specifically looking for issues of class and I am reading through and I kept finding issues with race and feminist view. They were just like popping out at me.

Corey recalled reading *Of Mice and Men* (Steinbeck, 1993), which he noted, in retrospect, he could now interpret in very different ways had he applied critical lenses.

Adopting these different lenses encouraged students to explore perspectives that they may not have subscribed to or that challenged their dominant discourses. By temporarily trying on or amending different lenses, students assumed a critical stance without assuming that this stance represented their own beliefs. For example, Devin adopted a feminist critical lens in responding to *Kindred*, as reflected in his criticism that "women have little to no rights, especially Black women." He explained that the only White woman in the novel, Margaret Weylin, wife of a plantation owner, "doesn't do anything but be bitchy and whine all day." He explained that the Black women in the novel have it even worse in that "White men could come in your home when they wanted and have sex with you and there was nothing you could do." Devin attempted to praise such women as he concluded:

> My hat goes off to the women who survived those horrid times. Now, today you can do just as much if not more than a man. It was those women who survived and gave breed to future men and women who would change it all.

In taking up a feminist lens, Devin assumed a discourse that challenged some of the more traditional gender discourses described in Chapter 6. At the same time, in adopting a feminist lens, he framed female characters only in terms of their roles as victims; he failed to identify any of the numerous instances in which female characters transgress or reject the victim roles. He noted that given his assumption that females are no longer oppressed, females in the past should be remembered as survivors whose ability to breed ultimately connects with the dismantling of the system he believed he was renouncing. Thus, in focusing on women's ability to breed, he perpetuated a focus on sexual objectification fostered by the very system he was attempting to critique. So in trying on some new critical perspectives, Devin still retained some of his traditional notions of female gender discourses.

In applying a feminist lens, students were able to identify instances of gender stereotyping leading some to adopt more complex notions of gender differences. At the same time, as with race and class, students shifted between adopting progressive discourses and then moving back to more traditional gender discourses. For example, in response to the novel *Obasan*, Dan noted that "the women are not being treated as objects but as strong and stern people who have lots of knowledge and get a great deal of respect from men," an analysis that relies on a essentialist binary of women as either traditional—as weak, gentle, lacking knowledge, and respect—or nontraditional—as strong, stern, knowledgeable, and respected—a binary that ignores the complexities of gender (Young, 2003).

Similarly, Devin resisted what he perceived as Sandra Cisneros's feminist perspective on men as perverted, noting, "All men are not like that. On the contrary, in a culture like hers, that is probably common." However, he then subscribed to her agenda of "trying to make the reader aware and sympathetic towards the little girls and the cheap thrills and life they live," a shift toward agreeing with her attitudes.

Students drew on knowledge of feminist lenses for discussing whether Michael Dorris could accurately portray female characters in *A Yellow*

Raft in Blue Water. Michelle argued that it is difficult if not impossible for a male writer to successfully adopt a female perspective. She was critical of what she perceived as the lack of verisimilitude in Dorris's portrayal of Rayona's laconic acceptance of her mother leaving her and Ida's reluctance to express her feelings about having to raise her daughter, Christine. Sarah noted that in describing Rayona, "This guy is not giving much detail about this girl's emotions." Troy contrasted Dorris's characterization of females in *A Yellow Raft in Blue Water* with those in *Their Eyes Were Watching God*, in which Janie "is always analyzing the situation in the book, and like what she can benefit and what she can't, and who is who ... so that is why I think you can tell the difference between male and female authors."

These judgments were based on some relatively essentialist notions of gender differences in language use: males do not keep secrets or are "more simplistic" than females, and "girls just don't tend to accept things that well. They just tend to argue about it and then whatever"; "girls have a tendency to hold a grudge for a long time"; and "guys have a tendency to bond better.... It is easier for guys to get along because they don't measure up against each other."

Another factor in students' engagement with gendered interpretation and discussion may have been that many of the novels highlighted instances of gender discrimination and stereotyping, as well as portrayals of strong female characters who successfully challenged patriarchic systems: Esperanza in *House on Mango Street*; Janie in *Their Eyes Were Watching God*; Ultima in *Bless Me, Ultima*; Dana in *Kindred*; Lulu in *Love Medicine*; Bone and Aunt Raylene in *Bastard out of Carolina*; and Rayona, Christine, and Ida in *A Yellow Raft in Blue Water*. In responding to these characters, students experienced characters' shifts from subject to object (Kegan; 1994; 2000) in terms of their awareness of how gender discourses reflected in the authoritative voices of patriarchic systems were limiting their agency, leading them to develop their own internally persuasive voices that students themselves began to voice.

Students also learned to apply a deconstructivist lens (Appleman, 2000) to critique binary oppositions associated with language categories operating in texts as well as in their own lives. This was evident in their analysis of the categories of *urban, suburban,* and *rural* people associated with meeting students from suburban high schools at the field trip to the university. Though they encountered stereotypical conceptions of themselves as urban students voiced by suburban students, students began to recognize the limitations of their own stereotypical notions of suburban and rural students.

In responding to *Kindred*, students focused on the question of whether Rufus was racist or not. Though students were quick to label him as racist, they came to consider the cultural constructions of the term itself, ultimately leading many students to see that neither term accurately described the character except within sociohistorically constructed definitions; essentialist labels were understood to be too slippery for universal meaning.

The students also grappled with the categories of *good* versus *evil* to describe Rufus's rape of Alice in terms of how to define the meaning of these concepts within particular historical periods. They debated whether they should judge his actions in terms of contemporary or past historical standards. Some of the students recognized the difficulty making these judgments about past historical actions. This recognition raises the historiography issue of *presentism*: the propensity to simply assume that during a past historical period, for example, slavery, people subscribed to certain monolithic beliefs about what constituted good versus bad practices (Power, 2003).

Acquiring these critical lenses therefore provided students with theoretical perspectives for analyzing text meanings in terms of ideological forces operating in texts.

Critiquing Institutional Forces Shaping Race, Class, and Gender Differences

Students also learned to engage in perspective taking; they learned to consider both a character's individual perceptions of their practices and the societal expectations or how other characters perceive those practices (Beach, Appleman, Hynds, & Wilhelm, 2006). They also learned to recognize the limitations of simply imposing their lived-world perspectives onto text worlds.

In the beginning of the course, students such as Michelle and Corey often judged characters negatively for adopting practices inconsistent with their own lived-world expectations, a position Kegan (1994, p. 36) described as a "socializing stance." Students who function in this way are less likely to explore conflicting roles or perspectives in their own lives because they "have trouble coordinating several roles and perspectives when these conflict" (Hammerman, 2005, p. 15).

Other students, such as Devin and Kayla, adopted what Kegan (1994, p. 37) described as a "self-authoring" stance, in which they were more open to exploring competing perspectives rather than simply impose their lived-world assumptions onto texts. Adopting this stance allows students to "understand others' views of them and consider those, but don't feel that other's views' determine their own thinking" (Hammerman, 2005, p. 15). Part of this perspective taking involves what Greer (2004, p. 138) described as "flexible moral realism" in which readers "apply an elastic code of ethics in judging the behavior of characters" based on coping with difficulties in their own lives, a stance she found working-class females adopting in judging female characters' hardships in confessional magazines.

Over time, some students were more likely to acknowledge the impact of institutional forces of discrimination, schooling, employment, and the justice system on characters. Even Michelle noted that students in the class shifted in terms of initially thinking that "we're all the same and we all have equal chances" to an awareness of the various obstacles facing people "because of their race and their culture and how they grew up and all of the things that they had to deal with that I wouldn't being White."

In the beginning of the course, Troy was strongly committed to discourses of individualism, athleticism, and hard work, as reflected in his critique of the McIntosh (1988) essay. However, toward the end of the course he began to shift his beliefs about affirmative action. In his response to *A Yellow Raft in Blue Water*, the course's final novel, he supported the fact that that Ray was hired as a Native American under affirmative action mandates. He noted that historically this program met resistance "because many thought they were losing jobs and those hiring believed that they were losing business—hiring those less fortunate, when that wasn't the case." He came to perceive affirmative action as a tool for addressing patterns of job discrimination, which "helped out a lot when used right." In a focus-group discussion at the end of our study, Troy reflected on changes in his thinking during the course and factors leading to those changes. He noted that on the issue of race and affirmative action, he changed much of his thinking. He said, "Now, at the end of class, my perspective of the whole issue has done a 180. I understand that."

Troy attributed his shifts to an increased awareness of the idea of institutional barriers or, as referred to in class by Parks, the metaphor of institutional *hurdles*. Learning to go beyond framing issues in terms of individual motivation, as well as hearing alternative perspectives on affirmative action, led Troy to alter some of his use of a discourse of individualism. As he noted previously in reference to Parks's use of the hurdles metaphor:

... you understand that people really do have certain hurdles in life, like where they live, the income of their families, siblings, where they go to school, all of that stuff.... That one affected me a lot. That is the one that like changed my opinion about people, about scholarship kind of thing, and ... that is where that plays into that.

Troy may only be momentarily amending his discourses, but he has acquired new ways of thinking critically about his different worlds and his relationships with those worlds.

There were also an increased awareness of institutional aspects of class differences shaping characters and themselves. In the middle of the course,

Thein and Parks collected some responses from three students in the program and three students from another class to the Public Broadcasting System (PBS) documentary, *People Like Us: Social Class in America* (Alvarez & Kolker, 2001), which portrayed vignettes of people defining and reflecting on class differences (see Appendix A for methods and interview questions). In response to one of the vignettes in which a female is receiving training lessons on how to be upper middle class, students expressed the belief that people cannot be trained to acquire class-based markers and that attempts to engage in passing (Bettie, 2003)—assuming that one is a different class—conflicts with the essential notion of identity as not being oneself. And in responding to the portrayal of a poor single mother working at a fast-food restaurant, students framed her situation in individualistic terms of admiring her motivation and hard work, as opposed to larger systemic forces of a low-wage economy. This suggests that at this point in the semester, these students still had difficulty interpreting class differences in terms of larger economic forces.

However, later in the course, as was the case with race, some of the students who had experienced family unemployment and financial struggles began to focus on class hierarchies as unfair systems, adopting a more institutional perspective. One of the appeals of *Bastard out of Carolina* for students was that it realistically portrayed the world of White, working-class poor people consistent with the lives of the students. As Devin noted, "There were points when I wanted to put the book down. I didn't want to read the next word, but I know that is what makes it a strong piece of literature." Interpreting the effects of poverty on working-class Whites in the novel led students to examine the ways a class structure discriminated against Whites, a deviation from the kinds of racial discrimination they read about in the other novels. In having to respond critically to the portrayals of White poverty, the White students in the class could no longer attribute poverty to deficit cultural models based on race. They had to confront the reality of White poverty as a reality that is shaped by institutional forces of class.

At the same time, the students were reluctant to critique middle-class values they were striving to obtain, values that served to define their future trajectories, particularly in terms of notions of the family. As in Seitz's (2004b) research with college students, most of the students in our study perceived little reason to interrogate discourses associated with acquiring middle-class values and job aspirations as a driving force behind their education because they perceived little gain from adopting a critical perspective. They frequently perceived their own future in terms of achieving the ideal of the perfect family, which Paul equated with "middle class, hard working, a lot of love, and that they are always there for each other, both parents and happy family, no problems. I think problems cause dysfunction in families." Some of their resistance to reading and discussing portrayals of dysfunctional working-class families in a novel such as *Bastard out of Carolina* stemmed from their belief in this idealized middle-class family world contrasted with the difficulties associated with poverty and family life. Though both *Love Medicine* and *A Yellow Raft in Blue Water* portrayed similar difficulties of working-class Native American lives, the students were less resistant to *A Yellow Raft in Blue Water* because it also portrayed characters overcoming adversities, something they lauded in *Bless Me, Ultima*.

Students were also challenged by how *Bastard out of Carolina* led them to recognize that race—in this case, Whiteness—was related to issues of class or poverty. In reading about Daddy Glen's abuse of Bone, the students were highly critical of his actions as a White male, which led to critical examinations of working-class versus middle-class White male discourses. Since Daddy Glen was raised in relative affluence yet married a working-class woman, Anney, and lived in utter poverty, they were forced to consider the ways these systems play out in the lives of individual actors. Given Daddy Glenn's Whiteness, however, they had to also attend to the ways Whites in poverty often begin to define themselves in opposition to poor African Americans. Mai noted that she was surprised that they were reading about Whites and the fact that poor Whites are the targets of racism: "There is still racism, even though they are poor White, they still talk about how Blacks are lower. It is different because the characters are White. It criticizes White people. It is something new about this book."

They also noted that the fact that Bone's relatives know that she is being abused by Daddy Glen but have little ability to prevent the abuse reflects the marginalization of women in this culture. And they noted that even when the townspeople looked down on the Boatwright family, they regarded African Americans and Cherokee Native Americans with even greater disdain. Likewise, they learned that despite the marginalization of poor Whites in the novel, those Whites in turn marginalize African Americans. By identifying this hierarchy operating in the town, they interpreted characters within a larger institutional framework shaping the characters.

Students' ability to critique discourses of race, class, and gender varied according to their own race, class, and gender identities and their prior experiences. That is, non-White students such as Kathy and Mai were most likely to recognize instances of institutional racism given their experiences with racial profiling and discrimination. As evident in some Hmong students' challenges to Parks regarding White privilege, these students of color drew on their experiences to critique discourses of race. As students of color, they had to learn to cope with racism in their lives. In contrast, many of the White students, given their sense of power in a school culture built on traditions of White privilege, were less likely to recognize instances of institutional racism. Though some of the White students were able to adopt a critical perspective on race, they had no incentive to critique White privilege that perpetuated their status.

Some of the White students' ambivalence regarding race related to the degree to which they recognized the benefits of increased institutional diversity. Though Michelle was initially critical of affirmative action programs related to college admissions, she also recognized the need for increased diversity on college campuses, adopting the perspective of students of color. Her statement, "I don't know, I can see it from both point of views, and that's what I hate," reflects her sense of the potential benefits to learning in more diverse college campuses, an ambivalence reflecting the experience of living in dialogic tensions.

Some of these shifts in thinking about race are consistent with previous research based on Helms's model of White racial identity (Helms, 1990, 1995; Lawrence & Tatum, 2004; Tatum, 1992). Based on extensive research, this model charts an individual's movement from an initial phase of *abandonment of a racist identity* through *contact* with people from different ethnic and racial backgrounds; *disintegration*, in which people are aware of their Whiteness leading to the experience of anger or guilt; and *reintegration*, in which some Whites adhere to their previous racist perspectives. In a second phase, *establishment of a nonracist White identity*—people in the *pseudo-independence* phase as an alternative to the *reintegration* phase—involves an acknowledgment of the ways that Whites benefit from racism leading to attempts to help people of color without taking action to change the system; *immersion–emersion*, in which people recognize the need to change other Whites and themselves; and *autonomy*, in which people openly embrace the need to learn from others through authentic interactions.

One of the limitations of a development model such as the Helms model is that attempting to label an individual as operating at a particular status or stage fails to consider how people can vary in perspectives or practices associated with a particular status across different contexts or situations. Though Helms (1995, p. 189) certainly recognized that these categories are not definitive and that people often adopt "blends" of different statuses, we did not apply the Helms model to analysis of our students, particularly because a number of them voiced different discourses and cultural models across different contexts, posing a challenge to identifying them as operating at a particular phase. Some of the ideas about development of racial identity from the Helms model, however, appear useful for considering some of the shifts in our participants' discourses and cultural models based on an increased awareness of their complicity in a system of White privilege.

Some of our students' responses to the McIntosh (1988) article reflected the fact that they were still operating at the initial *contact* status of an obliviousness of or resistance to institutional racism. In his critique of McIntosh's analysis of racial profiling, Troy wrote,

> If a traffic cop pulls me over, or if the IRS audits my tax return, I can be sure that I haven't been singled out because of my race. For me, I'm White, I don't worry, but anyone of color, if you do, that's wrong—an overreaction and the threat of racism is too strong. Most people have never been pulled over by a cop for race, and they hear about it so they start to automatically assume things.

Though Troy later amended some of his views, noting that "racism exists and is ever apparent in our country," in this critique of McIntosh (1988), he resisted the idea that racial profiling represents an institutional practice, framing it more in terms of a discourse of individualism, a stance reflecting Helms's initial contact status thinking. At the same time, as we have noted in the last three chapters, Troy's vacillation in his perspectives on race reflected a sense of confusion aligned with disintegration status, which led him to move back to placing the blame for racism on non-White people. For instance, to bolster his argument related to racial profiling, he posited that "statistics show that in [our city], 29% of Blacks get off without a ticket and 23% of Whites do."

In contrast, Devin identified a disconnect between the ideal cultural model of American equality of opportunity and the realities of inequality: "America is the land of the free and we are supposed to believe that if you work, things are easier. Not true." As we described in Chapter 7, in contrast to Troy, Devin moved toward an increasing awareness of institutional racism characteristic of Helms's later statuses of interrogating racism.

Individual Students' Changes During the Course

Students Who Adhered to Status Quo Discourses

It is also the case that, given the limited time period of six months, that there was little or no pronounced change in many of the students' thinking or attitudes, a finding consistent with previous research (Dressel, 2003; Pace, 2006). However, this does not mean that these students did not experience some change. Students often momentarily took up alternative discourses but then often reverted back to fixed, status quo discourses consistent with those operating in their family or school community. We would therefore argue that the change that occurred for some students was less in terms of acquiring new antiracist discourses and more in terms of an increasing willingness to entertain alternative discourses that challenged students' status quo discourses. From having to grapple with dialogic tensions, these students therefore acquired the capacity to engage in perspective taking leading to a less rigid, more flexible orientation toward the world.

The students who demonstrated little change—Corey and Michelle— were less likely to engage in perspective taking because they were largely content with their status quo discourses acquired through family and community socialization and perceived little need to entertain alternative discourses.

One explanation for these differences in students' willingness to entertain alternative discourses and cultural models has to do with their sense of agency related to present and future selves (Moore & Cunningham, 2006). Those students who were more open to amending and revising their discourses and cultural models were more likely to define their agency in terms of their future selves as college students who valued the use of critical practices and dispositions associated with the habitus (Bourdieu, 1984) of a future college student that Parks was modeling in the course. Because they perceived Parks as a working-class student who had been successful in college and graduate school, they assumed that the critical practices and dispositions they were acquiring in his class would help them also be successful in college. Because they wanted to emulate Parks's critical practices as a means of adopting the identity of a future college student identity, they therefore adopted some of his voices as their own "internally persuasive voices" in opposition to the "authoritative voices" (Bahktin, 1981) operating in the school culture and their own social worlds.

In contrast, other students whose sense of agency was located primarily in their present identity based on allegiances to status quo worlds. While he wanted to attend college, as a starter athlete whose status was valued in the school culture, Corey had little reason to entertain alternative discourses and cultural models that challenged his successful status-quo worlds of sports, home and community. Corey was comfortable with his allegiances to a discourse of masculinity/individualism that reified the value of individual competition and "hard work" in sports that he acquired from his father and coaches that was frequently celebrated in the school and community, affording him status within those cultures. He defined himself primarily in terms of traditional masculine practices of being self-assured, authoritative, and "in control" which mitigates against the potential to explore conflicting subjectivities, ambiguities, and complexities (Davies, 2003). Given his adherence to a discourse of individualism, he was reluctant to think in terms of larger institutional perspectives. He was also reluctant to interrogate discourses of White privilege associated with his familiar working-class world, adopting a color-blind stance (Bonilla-Silva,

2001) in which he rejected the structural nature of discrimination (Blum, 2002; Wiegman, 1999) except when he interpreted it as being "unfair" for Whites, as reflected in his attitudes towards affirmative action.

Corey's family was stable and upwardly mobile. For years their discourses and cultural models were supported by those within athletics, church, work, and neighborhood, especially given their new suburban surroundings. Given the success of these discourses in all of those he loves and admires, as was the case with Michelle, Corey had little incentive or reason to question the validity of the discourses that he brought into the classroom. Corey left the classroom as the same student who entered, albeit with new ways of reading and engaging in texts.

Michelle constructed her future identity around the idea of marriage and continued to work with her boyfriend in a fast-food restaurant. She was therefore wedded to familiar roles prevalent in her community that reified status-quo discourses. However, as we argued earlier, while Michelle did not change her general attitudes or goals for life, reading multicultural literature did help Michelle negotiate the parameters for her identity within the roles she would play after high school. For example, she was critically engaged with texts that depicted women negotiating their roles within marriage relationships. Through this engagement, Michelle began to set parameters for the kind of person she hoped to be within a marriage relationship. Because Michelle planned to stay in the East Side neighborhood and did not plan to attend college, it was likely more difficult for her to reject the values, cultural models, and discourses that were tied to this community.

Students Who Questioned Status Quo Discourses

In contrast to Corey and Michelle, students such as Troy, Kayla, Devin, Kathy, and Mai were more open to entertaining alternative perspectives and identities.

Troy had already made some major changes in his own life when he emerged from time in a juvenile detention home and decided to focus on his studies so that he could attend college. While he demonstrated little revision in his voicing of discourses of masculinity, he grew increasingly aware of how discourses of race and White privilege shaped characters and his own perspectives, particularly in terms of his strong interest in discrimination against Native Americans. One primary reason for this was his strong emulation of Parks's critical analyses of White privilege. For Troy, Parks served as a role model of a working-class person who, as Troy noted was "one of us," yet represented someone whose use of critical practices contributed to success at the college level.

It is also the case that Troy's active engagement in his church social world provided him with an arena in which to address race and issues such as affirmative action. While he had initially been critical of affirmative action programs and had engaged in heated arguments with his youth minister's wife on this topic, towards the end of the course, he modulated his view by acknowledging the need for affirmative action. These shifts in his attitudes seemed to have been fostered by engaging in dialogic tensions over issues of institutional racism in his church and in the class.

Kayla perceived herself as operating in her future world of college beyond what she perceived to be the limited high school and community cultures, particularly in terms of traditional gender roles. She therefore did not have close connections with her peers and was willing to challenge others in discussions because she was not concerned about the social consequences of these challenges. In challenging some of the males, she took up feminist perspectives that represented her interest in female characters' development of agency through rejection of patriarchal systems. She responded positively to the critiques of status quo discourses in the course given her future projection of herself as operating in the world of college in which she knew that critical practices were valued. Her willingness to explore alternative discourses contrasts with Michelle; Kayla was engaged in marked transformations which involved interrogating status-quo discourses of the school culture, peer group, and home. In projecting herself into the future as a college student with an interest in academics and ideas, she perceived value in engaging and grappling with ideas as part of her anticipatory socialization into a future world that she valued more than her current worlds, an envisionment that afforded her with a sense of agency (Moore & Cunningham, 2006).

Devin was able to perform, critique, and hybridize the discourses he brought into the classroom, while adopting discourses and cultural models that contradicted those he brought with him. Some of this reflected his strong allegiance to his family and his parent's strong support of his education. The fact that he was open to entertaining alternative discourse may have been a function of his active participation in two integrated sports, football and wrestling, as well as his involvement in youth church trips to Mexico and Native American reservations. And, his classroom identity as provocateur and the "successful student" allowed him to freely engage in a broad range of discourses without clearly displaying lasting change amidst these performances. While Devin vacillated between progressive and traditional discourses, over time, he became increasingly more likely to critique institutional forces shaping characters practices, particularly in response to portrayals of Native American characters and in regard to affirmative action.

Kathy and Mai also changed during the course, but did so in ways that were quite different from White students. As students of color, both struggled with being racially positioned by White students in the course. As a conservative Liberian immigrant, Kathy did not see herself as aligned with African-American students and was in fact quite critical of African-American culture and of affirmative action programs, especially toward the beginning of the course. However, White students in the course continually positioned Kathy as "African-American" and often misinterpreted her opinions as representing those of a critical racial perspective. As a confident, outspoken student, Kathy easily stood up to White students who criticized or questioned her opinions. Her constant need to restate and rethink her opinions in these situations ultimately played a significant role in her willingness to entertain alternative discourses, as reflected in changes in her attitudes about affirmative action towards the end of the course.

Mai, on the other hand, avoided speaking in class discussions, remaining "strategically silent" (Hartman, 2001) as a means of refusing to be racially positioned by White students in the class. However, while silent in class, Mai recorded her strongly held opinions in her response journal and shared them with both Parks and Thein in one-on-one discussions and interviews. As Mai listened to class discussion and adopted the critical practices in the class, in her private journal writing, and in dialogue journal exchanges, she became more vocal about her critiques. However, the fact that she and the other two Hmong students, Sue and Pamela, did not participate to the degree of some of the other vocal students in discussions, represents a challenge in terms of how to involve students who are culturally not accustomed to asserting themselves in public contexts (Vang, 2003, 2005).

Factors Influencing Students' Shifts in the Course

Rationales for the inclusion of multicultural literature into the curriculum as fostering shifts in students' thinking overlook the importance of *how* that literature is taught in the classroom. As we previously noted, the changes that occurred in this study are due to not only responding to multicultural literature, but also to challenges from peers and from Parks's instructional strategies, all of which created dialogic tensions leading to self-interrogation and amending or revising of discourses and cultural models (see Figure 9-1). Based on small-group focus-groups discussions at the end of the course in which students were asked to discuss those aspects of the course that influenced their thinking, we identified a number of influences on their shifts in the course.

Dialogic Tensions with Status Quo Cultural Models

In the course, students experienced tensions between their status-quo cultural models and alternative models of social worlds, leading some to change their cultural models. Parks's use of concrete examples such as the real estate advertisement for a $2,000 house in East St. Louis served to challenge students' cultural models of how economic systemic oppression operates in relationship to racial segregation.

Students also pointed to the presentation by two social workers discussing sexual abuse in relationship to *Bastard out of Carolina* as having a strong influence in challenging some of their notions of gender, power, and abuse. The fact that the social workers cited examples of abuse from familiar settings provided students with information that they then used in analyzing Daddy Glen in *Bastard out of Carolina* and the ways in which his family enabled some of his behaviors.

Students also cited individual examples of specific experiences outside the course that changed their cultural models. As part of one of the course assignments to visit a literary event in the community, Troy described his experience attending a bookstore presentation by a photojournalist, Gwendolen Cates (2001), regarding her experiences taking photos of different Native American tribes that resulted in the book, *Indian Country*. He reported that Cates's primary purpose for doing the book was to disprove the argument that Native Americans were becoming increasingly invisible and to portray Native American's sense of loss given the ecological damage to nature. He also described a presentation by a Native American at the same event, Bill Means, who described the increases in Native American populations and the mistreatment of Native Americans by the United States government, as illustrated by their banning of the Native American languages.

> Acquiring this information had a strong influence on Troy in that it: opened up new perspectives about Natives that made me look back about things I said about Natives and now I am able to see things from different angles. Not to mention that the book showed absolutely breathtaking pictures of Natives to show the nature connection of Natives in a new light for me.

These changes in perceptions demonstrate the importance of providing students with highly concrete materials such as the real estate ad and the Native American photography collection that serve to challenge their often stereotypical cultural models. These concrete materials, along with concrete portrayals in literature referencing aspects of everyday life, function to help students recognize how aspects of everyday life are influenced by racist discourses and cultural models.

Intertextual Connections Across Different Texts

Rather than focus soley on the influence of specific texts, it is also useful to consider the cumulative influence of intertextual connections between multiple texts on students' thinking. Students were encouraged to read across different texts, using what Parks described as "text-to-text" links to illuminate interpretations of a particular text. Rather than perceive tensions between texts, students defined similar themes across texts that represented instances of characters' resistance across different cultures. For example, in responding to *Obasan*, Pamela described similarities in terms of form between *Obasan* and other novels:

> It is like *Love Medicine* in that it seems to have repeating metaphors like the use of rocks to describe things much like *Love Medicine* used water as a metaphor for a lot of things. Also, this book begins with a description of a character who dies in the 2nd chapter, much like June did in *Love Medicine*. The way it's like *Their Eyes Were Watching God* is it starts out with a point about silence and starts in the beginning of the book that I have a feeling the rest of the book is going to follow, like how the first paragraph corresponds to the rest of *Their Eyes Were Watching God* seemed to start out of nowhere and come together at the end.

By describing these similarities in form, Pamela used her previous experience with form to interpret how metaphors and structure are employed in *Obasan*.

She also defined connections between the "fascist nature" of the Japanese internment portrayed in *Obasan* and the Nazi control of Polish ghettos in *Maus* (Spiegelman, 1993):

> In *Maus*, the males and females were split into different camps. In the beginning of Obasan, the males and females were split into separate sleeping quarters. In many cases, people had to get passes to see their families. In addition to having camps split into male/female, some men were sent to labor camps. The labor camps in *Maus* were more severe, but labor camps none the less ... Early in the war, on p. 103, Emily says in her journal, "Mind you, you can't compare this sort of thing to anything that happens in Germany ... Canada is supposed to be a democracy." In fact they were quite comparable. After everything was finished, on the last page in the memoranda sent to the senate, it says the orders were "an adoption of the methods of Nazism."

And, she drew parallels between the internment and the post 9/11 orders "to do what was necessary on the U.S. borders to provide stability and safety."

Pamela used these "text-to-text" links to formulate critiques of "fascist" institutional forces operating in these texts, connections that served to help her define the larger thematic interpretations.

Students also noted that that they needed to assume different cultural perspectives as they moved across different competing social worlds within texts. Moving between these different worlds within texts invited students to reflect on the kinds of perspectives required for interpreting that world and whether they successfully adopted those perspectives. In responding to *Kindred*, Kayla noted that when Dana was transported back to slavery:

> ... she had modern knowledge going back to that time. In a sense, it was like what if I went back would I act the same way she did? But I couldn't really say that because ... it just made me think like this because she is pretty much in the same time I am and what if I got called back somehow like she did. It just kept me wondering ... some books I like when they make me ask questions. This one I really did.

Students also learned to judge the limitations of characters' perspectives relative to their cultural contexts, recognizing that characters themselves lacked historical insights or understandings of their social worlds. This required them to construct the norms, roles, beliefs, and traditions operating in a text world and then to notice how characters are not always consciously aware of the ways in which those norms, roles, beliefs, or traditions influence them. For example, in analyzing Rufus in *Kindred*, Pamela noted that:

> He said his mom told him that the slaves who worked on the plantations were called niggers and that the term nigger used to anger him. I thought it showed that he had no idea what was going on at that time. He thought of the other slaves as niggers as well because he thought they were supposed to be called that. It wasn't because he hated them.

In this excerpt Pamela was interpreting Rufus's perspective as constituted by the institutional discourses and cultural models of slavery, and not simply his own subjective perspective. At the same time, students recognized the importance of having the events of the novel filtered through Dana's perspective as an African-American. When Parks asked students to consider how their perspective would differ if the novel was told from a White person's perspective, Mai noted:

You wouldn't be able to feel the pain as much, like if a slave got whipped, and the main person was a White person, the White person would not have been able to tell you how it felt or you just wouldn't know how bad it was to be a slave. If you were seeing it from a White person's perspective.

Mai then contrasted Dana's point of view with that of Kevin, who had a different perspective as a White male:

There was a part in the book where the kids were playing a big tossing game and Kevin didn't really understand it. But, I guess, his perspective is, I mean, he knows that it is wrong, but he's not able to do anything about it, or maybe he can, but it would cause a fight.... He played the role of the master, like he told Dana what to do. Yes, exactly, he became a part of the culture.

Analyzing the relationships between these characters' perspectives and larger cultural forces shaping those perspectives encouraged students to define perspectives as culturally-constituted, an important step towards distinguishing their own perspectives from others as shaped by differences in culture.

Identity Development within Peers' Community Space

Another important factor influencing change in this course was the amount of time that students spent working with one another—one of the advantages of a block schedule in the school with 90-minute periods. This meant that in addition to reflecting on characters' stances and discourses, they were also reflecting on each others' stances, discourses, and perspectives within the space of a classroom community. As Mai noted:

Since we are different people, it is interesting to see how differently we think about things. Especially people that are different than me. I think I can understand more of what others are going through and compare it to my own life and how different we are and how we live different lives. It is interesting to hear what others have to say.

The mere fact that students interacted with each other in discussions and dialogue-journal exchanges meant that they became increasingly aware of each others' consistent stances, beliefs, and attitudes. As these stances, beliefs, and attitudes solidified, they anticipated how others would respond to them, creating dialogic tensions. Some of the White males knew that their traditional male stances would be challenged by, for example, Kayla's argumentative style which they perceived to be overly persistent: "She just doesn't know when to call it quits and say okay whatever lets move on to the next subject." Anticipating potential critiques of their interpretations encouraged these males to formulate persuasive counter-arguments to her positions. The students therefore positioned each other by adopting "situated identities" (Koole, 2003) associated with the roles of leaders, challengers, facilitators, provocateurs, or non-participants. When, in a journal response to the McIntosh (1988) essay on White privilege, Troy voiced his criticisms of affirmative actions programs and being harassed in the hallways, his journal partner, Sue responded:

> I really disagree with the stereotypes of Blacks, Hispanic, and Hmong. I think that Black people have attitudes because of their hard life, which cause them to be harsher. Hispanics aren't cocky; I guess it's a way of life. Sometimes it seems as if they are harassing you but to them, it would probably be their culture. As for the Hmong, they have a strong sense of loyalty to each other because we all are closely related, not to mention that a lot of guys are in gangs.

And, when Troy cited data to challenge charges of racial profiling, Sue responded in writing to his entry: "I disagree about what you said about racial profiling in traffic cops. Almost all of my friends who drive, about 80%, have been pulled over at least one time. They didn't even break the law." This dialogue-journal exchange served to challenge Troy's stance.

Students positioning in the discussions also varied in terms of the amount of support they received. As previously noted, while the males often bonded together to support each other, the females experienced little such support. For example, on one day of a discussion of *Kindred*, Kathy was actively involved in formulating interpretations because the other females in the class provided her with support. However, in the next discussion of *Kindred*, she assumed only a minor role in a discussion that the males dominated with little female peer support.

All of this points to the role of the classroom community itself in positioning stances and identities, positioning that creates dialogic tensions. Thus, while cooperation and consensus are important aspects of effective group process, students' willingness to challenge and interrogate each other leading to dialogic tensions is a significant factor influencing change.

The Influences of Specific Teaching Methods

Some of the various changes noted above can be attributed to Parks's instructional methods.

Selecting Multicultural Literary Texts

Because students' level of engagement or interest varied across the different texts due to a number of different factors, it is useful to consider each of these factors in selecting multicultural literature texts for high school or first-year college students. One factor is readability or plot complexity. One of the reasons for the popularity of a book such as *Kindred* was that it was relatively easy to read, while the dialect of *Their Eyes Were Watching God* and the complex plot development, use of symbolism, and shifting points of view of *Love Medicine* proved to be more difficult for students, a reaction characterized by other researchers as "aesthetic resistance" (Soter, 1997) or "aesthetic shutdown" (Athanases, 1998). In teaching *Love Medicine*, Parks therefore provided students with additional assistance in interpreting the novel, giving them excerpts of criticism that interpreted symbols, shorter reading assignments between discussions, and a "family tree" of the characters in order to navigate the complex relationships. Given the difficulty level of the language and symbol systems of many multicultural texts, it is important that teachers not forego using these texts and provide students with some assistance in comprehending language and symbols.

Differences in engagement and interest also varied across different students according to race and ethnicity due to differences in background cultural knowledge, findings consistent with Amosa's (2004) research indicating that, as previously noted, Australian ethnic students responded more positively to multicultural literature than did White students. In her study, ethnic students were significantly more likely to adopt characters' perspectives, cite personal relevance of texts, and connect texts with other texts or prior experiences than were White students. They were also more likely to identify instances of prejudice in texts than did White students. In our study, the Hmong students responded more positively to *Obasan* than did the other students in the class.

It was also the case that certain texts such as *Kindred* invited students to employ what AnaLouise Keating (2004) describes as "(de)racialized tactics" (p. 317) by positioning readers in ways that challenged their application of set, permanent racial categories such as "Black" and "White." In responding to *Kindred,* students discovered that Kevin, Dana's husband, was White, as well as the fact that Dana's ancestors were White, a central theme of the novel. Texts such as *Kindred* therefore positioned students to reflect on the limitations of their racial categories, positioning that Parks then expanded on in his analysis of binary categories.

The Teacher as a Text: Parks's Identity and Teaching Style

Parks's own identity was a key factor in shaping students' use of practices and attitudes. By modeling the "habitus" (Bourdieu, 1977; 1984) of an academic and intellectual orientation that most of the students had not experienced in their high school classes, Parks demonstrated what it means to be a college student engaged in a college-level literature course. Consistent with Jacobs's (2005) notion of the teacher as a text, Parks used his own identity as a teacher with a working-class background to model connections between practices associated with working-class life and academic literacy practices so that being "one of us" was linked to assuming the identity of being a college student.

In their recommendations for working with working-class students, Lindquist (1999, 2004) and Sietz (2004a, 2004b) cautioned that in adopting a critical pedagogy approach, it is important to not neglect students' affective experiences associated with working-class experiences. Seitz argued for a need to build on working-class students' affective, insider perspectives of specific local experiences to inductively formulate their own critical theories as opposed to simply accepting deductively imposed theories. Given working-class students' identification with local home spaces and cultures, Parks recognized the importance of referencing links between cultural aspects of texts and similar cultural aspects of students' everyday lives, for example, between the abuse portrayed in *Bastard out of Carolina* and the two school counselors' discussion of abuse in everyday contexts.

Rather than portray himself as an exemplar of academic success, Parks also was willing to share the difficulties and ambivalences with his students about moving between different class worlds related to going to college as a working-class student. As he noted in a postclass reflection:

> I don't know what class I'm in. Clearly, I must be middle class. I can see all of the norms and values. I can see how I've learned them and rejected the one's of my childhood; for example: delayed gratification, thinking in terms of years down the road rather than next week, Honda over Ford, but, I so clearly feel attached to the working-class, it's as if I have two separate registers and codes of behavior, and the longer I live in the middle class, the more experiences I get in that world, the more difficult it is to think of myself in the previous world of working-class.

Knowing the difficulties of adopting a hybrid identity with allegiances to different worlds helped him empathize with his students' experiences of operating within a high school culture defined strongly by working-class values and the college class. As noted in Chapter 5, this led him to explicitly define some of the expectations for the amount, level, and quality of work expected at the college level contrasted with the work expectations and monitoring in high school. All of this points to the centrality of the teacher's identity not simply as a role model but also as a tour guide (Edelsky, Smith, & Wolfe, 2002), who contributes to students' academic socialization by continually metacognitively naming and demonstrating what are often unfamiliar academic practices involved in doing college academic work— ways of formulating arguments, adopting critical approaches and lenses, generating hypotheses, engaging in deliberative discussions, writing academic journal entries and essays, and defining connections between texts. And by making explicit criteria associated with successful use of these practices, for example, the use of supporting evidence in academic journal entries, Parks provided students with ground rules by which they will be assessed at the college level.

Employing Informal Writing

In the course, the students formulated their responses using informal journal writing as opposed to more formal essay responses. Responding through use of informal writing encouraged students to explore their affective responses and some of their contradictory stances evoked by the texts. In contrast to the definitive, prove-one's-point essay mode, informal writing allowed for students to explore alternative, even contradictory, responses related to dialogic tensions in their experiences with texts.

Students also learned to use informal writing to formulate arguments in preparation for discussions and their final formal essay. Parks framed assignments in a manner that encouraged students to adopt a position and defend that position. Several examples of journal prompts are as follows: "Which groups of people (height, weight, religion, gender, race, social class, etc.) have the easiest life in the US? Who is the 'Whitest' character in this novel? Would Rufus be racist if he had grown up in this neighborhood?"

Students who were reluctant to participate in discussions or who had difficulty spontaneously formulating interpretations could fall back on previously articulated responses from their journals. As Troy noted, "The journals for some of the introverts in the class should have become outlets for their ideas that they did not express during class time. I know for a fact that I can get a lot more ideas down on paper than I can if I talk."

The students also noted that having a clear sense of Parks's criteria related to addressing the prompt and citing supporting evidence helped them improve their writing about literature from a critical perspective. As Dan noted:

This class has not only helped my writing skills, but it helped me look at books and other literature as if they were works of art, to be studies and classified through different "lenses." At the beginning of the class, I had a mindset of a regular English class student who only writes how much and what he [sic] wants to write about. Only then did I come to realize that I can't write about whatever I want to but I have to actually do some in-depth thinking about the literature that is assigned to me.

Facilitating Discussions

One of Parks's primary roles was that of facilitator of large-group discussions of the novels. One of the advantages of having large-group discussions is that students can be directed by a teacher who can guide discussions according to a certain agenda or who can model critical strategies (Beach, Eddleston, & Philippot, 2003). At the same time, even with the relatively small group, some of the students in the course rarely participated because they were somewhat intimidated or because they assumed that what they had to say was not worth sharing or was redundant with what had been said. One of the advantages of small-group work is that these students have more opportunities to talk. However, the students noted that when they were in small groups, they lacked a clear sense of direction. As Devin described one of his small-group discussion experiences:

> So when me and Sarah got thrown into the very first student-led discussion, you know, we like just kind of like looked at each other like what are we going to do? I don't know, like, ask questions, or what? Our questions didn't really have anything to instruct people up. It was usually more like we'd ask the question and a couple of other people would have to jump in to help push it along. I'd kind of say things that would kind of strike up a controversy and people would go No, no, no, it's this, so you know, so that's about it.

Students also noted that in the large-group discussions, they perceived Parks as focusing students' attention on analysis of the texts with less attention to autobiographical responses, while in small group discussions, they could discuss autobiographical references consistent with experiences within their age group that were less familiar to Parks.

When leading discussions, Parks regularly avoided privileging some students' interpretations over others or critiquing students' voicing of certain discourses, something that frustrated Mai in terms of Parks's not directly challenging some of students' racist discourses. Though he asked students to expand on their ideas, Parks consistently avoided imposing a particular critical agenda. As Dan noted, "I don't think he ever really tried to force a certain agenda or certain position on us.... So it wasn't like a typical classroom environment where everyday it was like the same routine." In commenting on Parks's role in leading discussions of White privilege, Devin noted that "he just sort of put it out there for us to form our own opinion. He didn't tell us ... basically we understood that he didn't agree with it, but ... he let us form our own opinion about it. Some people never agreed with it and some did."

Role Play and Perspective Taking

Parks also used role-play activities throughout the course to encourage students to assume the language and perspectives of roles or characters distinct from their own identities. Students' use of monologues about specific characters required that they adopt and perform a character's identity as mediated by language use or style. By assuming characters' identities who, as one student noted, are "totally not yourself," students had to use language to construct cultural attitudes and beliefs distinct from their own beliefs and attitudes. For example, when Parks explained to students that they could choose to present an opinion in discussions by saying, "Some people might say ... [insert opinion]," students were more likely to voice alternative perspectives. They therefore learned how language reflects beliefs and attitudes operating in certain cultural contexts or historical period.

Students also created monologues for characters perceived as villains that afforded them with insights into the complexities of their characters. By adopting the perspective of Daddy Glen in *Bastard out of Carolina*, Parks modeled ways of revealing Daddy Glen's possible motives for his abusive actions. As a result, other students then revealed aspects about their characters that helped them understand those characters' motives.

And, as described in Chapter 5, during discussions, Parks employed "what if" hypothetical scenarios that placed students in certain situations in which they had to consider how they would address challenges. For example, as noted in Chapter 9, in discussions of *Bastard out of Carolina*, he asked, "What if I told you that Daddy Glen had been terribly sexually abused as a child. Would that alter your judgments of him in any way?" In another instance, when the students noted their positive response to the Allison novel, he said to students, "What if I told you that I'd received a call from some parents this week who believed that this book was too explicit for readers your age? What would you say to those parents?" Grappling with these hypothetical scenarios served to challenge the students' cultural assumptions.

Teaching Critical Concepts and Lenses

One of the primary challenges facing Parks was his attempt to foster students' critical analysis of institutional forces. One of the reasons for some of the students such as Michelle's and Corey's resistance to adopting critical stances was that they may have perceived little value or purpose in critically analyzing traditional, status quo values. Given the students' reluctance to critique the very middle-class values they are seeking to attain and the limitations of imposing abstract, theoretical critiques (Seitz, 2004a, 2004b), Parks recognized the need to build on students' familiar, current ways of thinking with concrete examples and metaphors that allowed them to inductively formulate critiques consistent with their developmental perspectives. For example, in teaching the Marxist lens to help students understand constraints due to characters' class status, Parks used the metaphor of hurdles on a racetrack to illustrate how some groups of people are afforded certain advantages over other groups. Troy cited Parks's use of the hurdles metaphor related to the institutional obstacles facing people of color as influencial in having "changed my opinion about people, about scholarship kind of thing." Mai recalled Parks's use of the metaphor as useful in her recognition that "women don't get the best positions. If it is a female versus a female, I think that puts me at a lower rank because I'm female and Asian. I just don't want that to stop me or judge me. I want them to allow me to be the best I can be."

To illustrate the idea that characters operate in cultural contexts or worlds influencing social practices, Parks employed the metaphor of the fishbowl to help students think about operating according to certain social norms in a culture. Having asked the students early in the course to consider the quotation, "Water is to a fish like culture is to a person," students used this metaphor to understand the cultural influences of different environments on characters' perspectives. As Troy noted, "You know, Rufus grew up in a different fishbowl than I did; it's tough to say."

And, in teaching the different critical lenses, he modeled the application of the different lenses to analyzing texts. Students had more difficulty applying some lens than others. Students had little difficulty using a reader-response lens to connect their experiences to text interpretations. They also readily learned to apply a feminist lens to analyzing the patriarchal practices of male characters in the novels whose practices were distinctly identifiable given the historical settings of the novels. And some of the students such as Kayla and Michelle applied a feminist critique of the male control of some of the discussions as well as the power of male sports in the school.

However, as fish in water, students had difficulty critically analyzing the influence of working-class culture on characters' practices, preferring, for example, to analyze the characters in *A Yellow Raft in Blue Water* in terms of gender or race. They also had difficulty applying the Marxist lens to critically analyzing the White working-class culture of *Bastard out of Carolina*. And students' ability to apply critical race theory also met with mixed success. For one, whereas the other lenses are based on literary critical analysis, critical race theory is more of a sociological approach requiring the ability to perceive race in institutional terms. Students were able to identify instances of forces of institutional racism shaping slavery, Native American genocide, and the Japanese internment, but they experienced more difficulty with critiquing the institutional dimensions of White privilege. As illustrated by the affirmative action debates, some students became aware of how affirmative action reflects an institutional White privilege, whereas others resisted interrogating White privilege. Some of these difficulties may have been a function of the limited amount of time devoted to learning these lenses; it may also have been the case that applying these lenses required background in sociological and literary critical knowledge the students did not possess.

As noted in the previous chapter, a significant challenge facing Parks was that in engaging White males in the consideration of their privilege, he inadvertently left some Hmong female students feeling marginalized. Even as White students adopted a race-talk discourse to avoid being perceived as racists, the Hmong students—Mai, Pamela, and Sue—were reluctant to address issues of race for fear of being perceived as defensive, doctrinaire, or narrow minded. As noted in Chapters 5 and 8, Mai wanted Parks to more explicitly focus discussions around the topic of racism. This raises important questions as to how a teacher can encourage students of color to express their experiences with racism when the majority of the students in the class are White.

Summary

In this study, we found that the 14 largely working-class students responded to multicultural literature in ways that reflected how they constructed their identities in terms of the discourses and cultural models operating in the social worlds of Parks's classroom: the school, peer group, sports, family, workplace, and community. For some students such as Corey and Michelle, their allegiances to the status quo discourses and cultural models operating in these worlds—for example, the discourses of hard work, control, and athleticism operating in the worlds of the school and sports—foreclosed their exploration of alternative discourses operating in Parks's classroom. These students' sense of agency was constituted by allegiances to these status quo discourses and cultural models.

Other students—such as Troy, Devin, Kayla, and Kathy—who entertained the dialogic tensions between authoritative voices versus internally persuasive voices (Bakhtin, 1981) portrayed in texts and in discussions began to interrogate these status quo discourses and cultural models operating in their social worlds. These students began to amend and revise their discourses and cultural models of individualism operating in the school culture and community by identifying instances of institutional discourses shaping characters' and their own practices. This led to a realization of the need for affirmative action programs to rectify historical institutional advantages afforded Whites in college admissions and hiring. In doing so, they began to adopt critical perspectives on how institutions function to both limit and support characters' and their own development of agency.

These students perceived the value of adopting a critical stance as part of constructing their sense of agency as future college students who would benefit from acquiring the practices and dispositions employed Parks's class. They recognized that Parks's own success as a working-class student was attributed to his ability to employ the practices and dispositions he was modeling in the classroom. It was also the case that some students such as Troy and Devin were also willing to address issues of institutional racism given their exposure to poverty and discrimination through participation in church-related activities.

In conclusion, we believe that engaging students in responding to multicultural literature serves to foster their experience of the dialogic tensions identified in this study, experiences that led some students to shift their perspectives related to their race, class, and gender identity construction. We also believe that the teacher assumes a major role in creating contexts that can foster exploration of these dialogic tensions, suggesting the need to prepare teachers who not only can foster critical responses to literature but also can employ activities designed to challenge students' status quo discourses.

Implications for Teaching Multicultural Literature

The results of this study have a number of implications for teaching multicultural literature at the high school or college level.

Redefining the High School Literature Curriculum

Secondary English teachers often face competing demands shaping their literature instruction. They are asked to teach literary traditions, literary appreciation, formalist readings of texts, literary genre features, self-understanding, critical analysis of language use, critical approaches, and social justice, each of which implies different, often contradictory instructional methods. Mellor and Patterson (2005) identified five different approaches to teaching literature—*heritage, new critical, personal growth, poststructuralist English,* and *critical literacy*—approaches that each involve strengths and limitations. For example, a heritage approach attempts to encourage students to value literary traditions, but may not foster critical analysis of texts. A new critical approach fosters close readings of texts but may not encourage students' engagement with texts. A personal growth approach helps students make connections with texts, but students may not be aware of how those connections are constructed through and by ideological forces. A poststructuralist English approach may encourage critical analysis of language binaries in texts but may not provide students with larger cultural or historical forces constituting those binaries. And a critical literacy approach, which defines "the reader as a social agent with particular capacities—such as that of producing feminist or anti-racist or plural or critical readings of a text" (p. 473), can "produce real changes in students' subjectivities" related to an awareness of social justice issues (p. 471) but may not foster literary critical analysis or appreciation of aesthetic aspects of texts. Though each of these approaches has strengths and limitations, we believe that regardless of the approach being employed, it is important for teachers to define the relationship between what goals they are trying to achieve in their classroom and the approaches best suited to meeting those goals. Parks adopted aspects of all five approaches but focused more on use of poststructuralist English and critical literacy approaches because he was committed to fostering critical analysis through discussions of multicultural literature.

Framing the Value of Multicultural Literature in Terms of Grappling with Dialogic Tensions

In the past, the value of multicultural literature was often framed in terms of a human-relations multicultural education approach of changing students' attitudes related to prejudice and fostering tolerance for diversity, despite research that finds little change in belief and attitudes related to race from reading multicultural literature (Dressel, 2003). It was assumed that by exposing students to portrayals of diverse cultural worlds or characters grappling with racism that students would adopt less prejudiced perspectives. However, this approach assumes that simply exposing students to cultural diversity portrayed in texts not only fosters racial tolerance but also leads to critiques of institutional racism. As we have argued, simply reading portrayals of cultural diversity is a necessary, but not sufficient, method for challenging students' status quo discourses and cultural models of race, class, and gender. What is also needed are instructional activities and peer interaction that allow for challenging these status quo discourses in ways that could lead to amending or revising discourses, particularly in terms of recognizing influences of institutional forces on characters' practices.

Consistent with Mellor and Patterson's (2005) focus on different ways of reading texts, we believe that teaching multicultural literature requires going beyond teaching texts as token representations of particular racial groups or categories, to fostering alternative perspectives on the social and cultural construction of characters' identities in text worlds. Interpreting portrayals of dialogic tensions in multicultural literature texts provides students with a forum rarely found in the school curriculum for discussing complex issues of race, class, and gender differences in ways that lead students to revise and amend their status quo discourses and cultural models. For example, by exploring the ways racism and sexism operated in the working-class neighborhood of *The House on Mango Street*, students began to debate the differential influences of racism, class difference, and sexism on the neighbors' practices. Or by engaging in debate over affirmative action evoked by discussions of *Love Medicine*, students began to explore how college admissions or hiring can be influenced by institutional racism. Or by identifying contradictions in responding to Bone's life in *Bastard out of Carolina*, students struggled to reconcile her abusive upbringing with their beliefs in individualism and autonomy.

Through disagreements fostered by dialogic tensions in literature and discussions, students may voice competing discourses reflecting allegiances to authoritative voices of the school, sports, or community cultures, whereas other students may adopt alternative voices that challenge these voices. In having to defend their allegiances to status quo social worlds, students may examine their assumptions about race, class, and gender constituting their identities in these worlds.

This alternative rationale defines change not as a straight, linear transformation toward enlightened racial tolerance but rather in terms of momentary shifts, revisions, alterations, and regressions in students' thinking that may or may not lead to long-term, substantive change found in other research (Lewis, Ketter, & Fabos, 2001; Lawrence & Tatum, 2004).

Engaging in Perspective Taking   In grappling with the dialogic tensions portrayed in literature, students are identifying disparities between characters' perceptions of their actual practices (i.e., what they were doing) versus their awareness of societal expected practices (i.e., what they are expected to do given their roles or positions within certain social worlds). Having students identify these disparities between actual versus expected practices led them to critique the influence of institutional forces on characters, forces that limit their agency. It also led them to identify differences between main characters' perspectives, other characters' perspectives of main characters, and their own perspectives as reader versus characters' perspectives. For example, in responding to *A Yellow Raft in Blue Water*, students could discuss how the mother, Christine, is expected to assume certain practices associated with her role as mother, a role that is difficult for her to assume given the institutional forces of racism and poverty.

Students could also examine how societal expectations shape characters' and their own perspectives. Rayona, Christine's daughter, expects Christine to be a more conscientious mother, particularly when she contrasts Christine with the middle-class mothers of her peers. As an adolescent, Rayona is not necessarily aware of how these class differences enable certain kinds of mothering. If students judge Christine as neglectful, they could weigh that judgment against the fact that Christine herself was raised by a neglectful, substitute mother and that, as an impoverished woman in a problematic marriage, she was not getting much support in raising Rayona. Students may also consider how their notions of working-class Native American females influence their judgments of Christine.

To engage in this perspective taking, students could address the following questions:

1. How do main characters perceive their own actual practices?
2. How do main characters perceive institutional forces shaping expected practices?
3. How do other characters perceive the main characters' actual practices?
4. How do other characters perceive institutional forces influencing the main characters' expected practices?
5. How do I perceive the main characters' actual practices?
6. How are my perceptions shaped by my own societal expectations?

From all of this, students may learn to entertain alternative perspectives of characters. They may also learn to reflect on how their own beliefs and attitudes shape their judgments of characters and to recognize how cultural and historical contexts constitute characters' practices. They may then recognize differences between their own attitudes about specific social norms and those operating in the textual world.

Addressing Discourses of White Privilege

In interrogating discourses constituting students' literary interpretations, one of the challenges facing Parks was how to address the topic of White privilege associated with issues such as affirmative action without adopting an ideological agenda targeting White students that may only alienate those students. Rather than target White students, an alternative approach involves interrogating the larger discourses of Whiteness constituting the identities of both White students and students of color (Trainor, 2002, 2005). Given Mai's challenge to Parks for focusing primarily on challenging the White students' White privilege, it is also important for the teacher to involve different racial groups in the classroom in discussions of White privilege. And teachers need to address the fact that students of color may be reluctant to participate in these discussions for fear of being perceived as defensive victims of White privilege. Just as Parks sought out individual students to understand their perspectives within those conversations, teachers need to assure these students that their perspectives regarding White privilege contribute to the larger goal of interrogating these discourses.

Part of interrogating the discourses of Whiteness involves encouraging working-class Whites to recognize that they often confront the same institutional barriers as do working-class persons of color within the economic system, leading to reducing tensions between these groups, tensions often promoted by a divide-and-conquer political agendas (Bettie, 2003). Parks provided students with concrete examples of how race and class intersect, leading them to begin to understand how issues of poverty and low wages cuts across racial categories.

Teachers also need to support students in understanding how discourses of White privilege are manifested in institutional forces. For example, in considering affirmative action, examining how institutional forces perpetuated White privilege in college admissions and employment allowed some of the students to perceive the limitations of their individualized conceptions of such programs, leading them to recognize the ways institutional racism operates in society. In grappling with affirmative action, students are dealing with a long history of racism that created institutional inequalities between Whites who benefited from the system and people of color who were disadvantaged by the system.

In grappling with the idea of racial categories based on fixed notions of race in discussions of *Kindred* and *Bastard out of Carolina,* Parks helped students understand how these categories of race are often constituted by economic and political forces that attempt to exploit White, working-class people's fears and prejudices, forces endemic to larger institutional racism.

Using Drama Activities

As noted already, Parks employed drama activities—student monologues based on adopting characters' perspectives—as another tool for fostering perspective taking. Teachers can use drama as a means of having students double voice characters' language use, leading to their analysis of how that character's language reflects allegiances to certain discourses or social worlds (Beach, et al., 2006; Knoeller, 1998). Rather than focus on their subjective identification with characters, students are then examining how language use mediates characters' identity construction, as well as how characters use language in specific contexts for specific rhetorical purposes. For example, by adopting the role of Daddy Glen arguing that he needs financial assistance from his family because he does "not deserve to be poor," students recognized how his discourses of class differences shape his rhetorical stance. And, for some students who are reluctant to voice their own opinions in class, as we found with some of the Hmong students, adopting an alternative voice of a character provides students with a safe arena for expressing themselves in the classroom.

Fostering Intertextual Interpretations

Rather than treating each text as an autonomous entity, teachers can use connections between different texts to help students perceive similar themes that cut across different texts and text worlds, comparing, for example, the practices of internment of Japanese in *Obasan* with practices of slavery in *Kindred* and creation of reservations in *Love Medicine* and *A Yellow Raft in Blue Water*. Students can also consider moving main characters from one text world to another, and analyzing how those characters would operate in a different text world. Comparing how these text worlds constitute characters leads students to examine their own negotiations of identities across different lived worlds.

Students can also go back and reread parts of previously read texts to compare their experiences in one text world with their experiences in another text world (Blau, 2003; Petrosky, 2005). After creating a paper trail of written responses to different texts, students can then reflect on the differences in the portrayal of race, class, and gender across these different worlds.

Implications for Further Research

One of the major limitations of this study was that it focused on students' identity construction for only a six-month period within one semester class rather than on analysis over a longer time period, for example, an eight-year longitudinal study (McLeod & Yates, 2006). Further research needs to examine adolescents' identity construction, particularly in the contexts of participation in literature classes, over a longer period of time. Tracking students' changes in their beliefs and attitudes over a long term reflects the influences of social worlds on their identity construction, as well as how students learn to negotiate differences in the allegiances to different worlds (Beach, Lundell, & Jung, 2002; Phelan, Davidson, & Yu, 1998). Part of this analysis could focus on how adolescents' allegiances to social worlds shift in terms of adopting or rejecting the discourses and cultural models operating in these worlds, as was the previously cited example of Gillian, who learned to adopt the class-based discourses operating in her private school (McLeod & Yates, 2006).

Our study suggests that the students who perceived themselves operating in the future as college students were more likely to challenge their status quo worlds than students who were highly satisfied with their status quo high-school worlds. Further research also needs to examine what experiences contribute to adolescents' development of agency relative to their allegiances to status quo versus future worlds (Moore & Cunningham, 2006). It may be the case that working-class students have difficulty envisioning themselves in the future, as, for example, college students, when they are dealing with everyday economic challenges. It would also be useful to determine what kinds of socializing experiences in high school settings such as the College in the Schools programs serve to provide a sense of future agency (Wahlstrom & Riedel, 2004a, 2004b), as well as how teachers such as Parks function as socializing agents in fostering interest in college academic work.

Further research also needs to examine how adolescents' responses to literature reflect their identity constructions in lived-world contexts. Though recognizing the problem of adolescents imposing their lived-world assumptions onto text worlds, this research could examine how students draw on their construction of specific norms, rules, roles, and purposes operating in their school, peer-group, family, workplace, and community worlds to construct text worlds (Beach & Myers, 2001). It could also examine how students' text world experiences influence their lived-world identity constructions, for example, how adopting alternative cultural perspectives operating in text worlds influences their perceptions of lived worlds.

Further research on teaching multicultural literature needs to examine the intersecting influences of the three components of texts, teaching methods, and peer interactions on students' propensity to amend or revise their status quo discourses and cultural models. We also found that certain texts such as *Kindred, Love Medicine,* and *Bastard out of Carolina* evoked more dialogic tensions in discussions than other texts. Though this may have been due to the particular teaching methods employed with these texts, it also may be the case that certain texts position students rhetorically to reflect on their reading stances. It may also be the case that the uses of certain writing, discussion, or drama methods are particularly effective in fostering certain kinds of critical stance. Or it could be that the dialogic tensions created between students in discussions is itself a key factor in fostering shifts in students' thinking.

References

Alcorn, M. W. (2002). *Changing the subject in English class: Discourse and the constructions of desire.* Carbondale: Southern Illinois University Press.

Allison, D. (1993). *Bastard out of Carolina.* New York: Plume.

Allison, D. (1994). A question of class. In D. Allison (Ed.), *Skin: Talking about sex, class, and literature* (pp. 13–36). Ithaca, NY: Firebrand Books.

Alvarez, L., & Kolker, A. (Directors). (2001). *People like us: Social class in America* [Motion picture]. New York: Center for New American Media.

American Council on Education. (2006). Gender equity in higher education: 2006. Retrieved July 15, 2006, from http://www.acenet.edu/AM/Template.cfm?Section=HENA&TEMPLATE=/CM/ContentDisplay.cfm&CONTENTID=17251.

Amosa, W. A. (2004). *Mooting the mosaic: A study of student engagement with multiethnic literary texts.* Unpublished doctoral dissertation, University of Newcastle, Australia.

Anaya, R. A. (1995). *Bless me, Ultima.* New York: Warner Books.

Anyon, J. (2005). *Radical possibilities: Public policy, urban education, and a new social movement.* New York: Routledge.

Apple, M. W. (2001). *Educating the "right" way: Markets, standards, god, and inequality.* Philadelphia: Falmer Press.

Appleman, D. (2000). *Critical encounters in high school English: Teaching literary theory to adolescents.* New York: Teachers College Press.

Arroyo, C. G., & Zigler, E. (1995). Racial identity, academic achievement, and the psychological well-being of economically disadvantaged adolescents. *Journal of Personality and Social Psychology, 69*(5), 903–914.

Asher, N. (2005). At the interstices: Engaging postcolonial and feminist perspectives for a multicultural education pedagogy in the South. *Teachers College Record, 107*(5), 1079–1106.

Athanases, S. Z. (1998). Diverse learners, diverse texts: Exploring identity and difference through literary encounters. *Journal of Literacy Research, 30*(2), 273–289.

Bailey, R. (2005). Evaluating the relationship between physical education, sport and social inclusion. *Educational Review, 57*(1), 71–90.

Baker, M. P. (1999). The politics of they: Dorothy Allison's *Bastard out of Carolina* as critique of class, gender, and sexual ideologies. Retrieved July 17, 2005, from http://www.radford.edu/~mpbaker/wmst101Allison.htm.

Bakhtin, M. M. (1981). *The dialogic imagination: Four essays.* Austin: University of Texas Press.

Bakhtin, M. M. (1986). *Speech genres and other late essays.* Austin: University of Texas Press.

Barak, J. (2003, March). *Rewriting racism: Whiteness studies in the composition classroom.* Paper presented at the Conference on College Composition and Communication, New York.

Barker, C., & Galasinski, D. (2001). *Cultural studies and discourse analysis.* Thousand Oaks, CA: Sage.

Barnett, T. (2000). Reading "Whiteness" in English studies. *College English 1*(63), 9–37.

Bartholomae, D. (1985). Inventing the university. In M. Rose (Ed.), *When a writer can't write: Studies in writer's block and other composing process problems* (pp. 134–165). New York: Guilford.

Baszile, D. T. (2003). Who does she think she is? Growing up nationalist and ending up teaching race in White space. *Journal of Curriculum Theorizing, 19*(3), 25–37.

Bazerman, C., & Russell, D. (Eds.). (2003). *Writing selves/writing societies: Research from activity perspectives.* Retrieved from http://wac.colostate.edu/books/selves_society/

Beach, R. (1993). *A teacher's introduction to reader response theories.* Urbana, IL: National Council of Teachers of English.

Beach, R. (1997a). Critical discourse theory and reader response: How discourses constitute reader stances and social contexts. *Reader, 37*, 311–26.

Beach, R. (1997b). Students' resistance to engagement with multicultural literature. In T. Rogers & A. Soter (Eds.), *Reading across cultures: Teaching literature in a diverse society* (pp. 69–94). New York: Teachers College Press.

Beach, R. (2000). Reading and responding at the level of activity. *Journal of Literacy Research, 2*, 237–251.

Beach, R., Appleman, D., Hynds, S., & Wilhelm, J. (2006). *Teaching literature to adolescents.* Mahwah, NJ: Lawrence Erlbaum Associates.

Beach, R., Eddleston, S., & Philippot, R. (2003). Characteristics of effective large-group discussions. In C. Bazerman, B. Huot, & B. Stroble (Eds.), *Multiple literacies for the 21st century: Proceedings of the 1998 Watson conference* (pp. 129–150). Cresskill, NJ: Hampton Press.

Beach, R., & Kalnin, J. (2005). Studying value stances in institutional settings. In R. Beach, J. Green, M. Kamil, & T. Shanahan (Eds.), *Multidisciplinary perspectives on literacy research* (pp. 209–241). Cresskill, NJ: Hampton Press.

Beach, R., Lundell, D. B., & Jung, H. J. (2002). Developmental college students' negotiations of social practices between peer, family, workplace, and university worlds. In D. B. Lundell & J. L. Higbee (Eds.), *Urban literacy and developmental education* (pp. 79–108). Minneapolis: Center for Research on Developmental Education and Urban Literacy, General College, University of Minnesota.

Beach, R., & Myers, J. (2001). *Inquiry-based English instruction: Engaging students in literature and life.* New York: Teachers College Press.

Beach, R., & Spicer, D. E. (2004). *Subject/system: Issues in research on identity and agency in developmental transformations.* Paper presented at the annual meeting of the American Educational Research Association, San Diego, CA.

Beach, R., & Thein, A. H. (2006, April). Challenging standardization through place-based critical inquiry. In B. Doecke, M. Howie, & W. Sawyer (Eds.), *"Only connect...": English teaching, schooling and community* (pp. 263–280). Kent Town, South Australia: Wakefield Press.

Bellah, R., Madsen, R., Sullivan, W., Swidler, A., & Tipton, S. (1996). *Habits of the heart: Individualism and commitment in American life.* Berkeley: University of California Press.

Bennett, M., & Fabio, D. (2004). *The development of the social self.* New York: Taylor & Francis.

Bennett, T. (1983). Texts, readers, reading formations. *Literature and History, 9,* 214–227.

Bettie, J. (2000). Women without class: Chicas, cholas, trash, and the presence/absence of class identity. *Signs, 26*(1), 1–35.

Bettie, J. (2003). *Women without class: Girls, race, and identity.* Berkeley: University of California Press.

Blackford, H. V. (2004). *Out of this world: Why literature matters to girls.* New York: Teachers College Press.

Blake, B. E. (1998). "Critical" reader response in an urban classroom: Creating cultural texts to engage diverse readers. *Theory into Practice, 37*(3), 238–243.

Blau, S. (2003). *The literature workshop: Teaching texts and their readers.* Portsmouth, NH: Boynton/Cook.

Bleich, D. (1998). *Know and tell: A writing pedagogy of disclosure, genre, and membership.* Portsmouth, NH: Boynton/Cook.

Blum, L. (2002). *"I'm not a racist, but ...": The moral quandary of race.* Ithaca, NY: Cornell University Press.

Bolgatz, J. (2005). *Talking race in the classroom.* New York: Teachers College Press.

Bonilla-Silva, E. (2001). *White supremacy and racism in the post-civil rights era.* Boulder, CO: Lynne Rienner.

Borkowski, D. (2004). "Not too late to take the sanitation test": Notes of a non-gifted academic from the working class. *College Composition and Communication, 56*(1), 94–123.

Bortolussi, M., & Dixon, P. (2003). *Psychonarratology: Foundations for the empirical study of literary response.* New York: Cambridge University Press.

Bourdieu, P. (1973). Cultural reproduction and social reproduction. In R. Brown (Ed.), *Knowledge, education, and cultural change* (pp. 71–112). London: Tavistock.

Bourdieu, P. (1977). *Outline of a theory of practice.* New York: Cambridge University Press.

Bourdieu, P. (1984). *Distinction: A social critique of the judgment of taste.* Cambridge, MA: Harvard University Press.

Bouson, J. B. (2001). "You nothing but trash": White trash shame in Dorothy Allison's *Bastard out of Carolina. Southern Literary Journal 34*(1), 101–124.

Boyd, R. (1991). Imitate me; don't imitate me: Mimeticism in David Bartholomae's "Inventing the University." *Journal of Advanced Composition, 11*(2), 335–345.

Brown, M. K. (2003). *Whitewashing race: The myth of a color-blind society*. Berkeley: University of California Press.

Brooks, W. (2006). Reading representations of themselves: Urban youth use culture and African American textual features to develop literary understandings. *Reading Research Quarterly, 41*(3), 372–393.

Bruch, P. (2003). Moving to the city: Redefining literacy in a post-civil rights era. In B. McComiskey & C. Ryan (Eds.), *City comp: Identities, spaces, and practices* (pp. 216–233). Albany: State University of New York Press.

Budgeon, S. (2003). *Choosing a self: Young women and the individualization of identity*. Westport, CT: Praeger Publishers.

Burgess, I., Edwards, A., & Skinner J. (2003). Football culture in an Australian school setting: The construction of masculine identity. *Sport, Education and Society, 8*(2), 199–212.

Butler, O. (1979). *Kindred*. Boston: Beacon Press.

Carspecken, P. F. (1996). *Critical ethnography in educational research*. New York: Routledge.

Cates, G. (2001). *Indian country*. New York: Grove Press.

Chouliaraki, L., & Fairclough, N. (1999). *Discourse in late modernity: Rethinking critical discourse analysis*. Scotland: Edinburgh University Press.

Cisneros, S. (1991). *The house on Mango Street*. New York: Vintage.

Cole, M. (1996). *Cultural psychology, a once and future discipline*. Cambridge, MA: Belknap Press of Harvard University Press.

Connell, R. W. (1995). *Masculinities*. Berkeley: University of California Press.

Connell, R. W. (2001). *The men and the boys*. Berkeley: University of California Press.

Corporate Source. (1998). *Attitudes and opinions from the nation's high achieving teens: 29th annual survey of high achievers* (Report No. PS027313). Lake Forest, IL: Who's Who Among American High School Students Survey. (ERIC Document Reproduction Service ED429671)

Cox, K. C. (1998). Magic and memory in the contemporary story cycle: Gloria Naylor and Louise Erdrich. *College English, 60*(2), 150–173.

Daly, B. (2005). Taking whiteness personally: Learning to teach testimonial reading and writing in the college literature classroom. *Pedagogy: Critical Approaches to Teaching Literature, Language, Composition, and Culture, 5*(2), 213–222.

D'Andrade, R., & Strauss, C. (1992). *Human motives and cultural models*. New York: Cambridge University Press.

Davidson, A. L. (1996). *Making and molding identity in schools: Student narratives on race, gender, and academic engagement*. Albany: State University of New York Press.

Davies, B. (2003). *Shards of glass: Children reading and writing beyond gendered identities* (rev. ed.). Cresskill, NJ: Hampton Press.

Davies, B., & Harré, R. (1990). Positioning: The social construction of selves. *Journal for the Theory of Social Behaviour, 20*, 43–63.

Davis, B., Sumara, D., & Luce-Kapler, R. (2000). *Engaging minds: Learning and teaching in a complex world*. Mahwah, NJ: Erlbaum.

DeBlase, G. (2005). Negotiating points of divergence in the literacy classroom: the role of narrative and authorial readings in students' talking and thinking about literature. *English Education, 38*(1), 9–22.

Delaney, D. (2002). The space that race makes. *Professional Geographer, 54*, 6–14.

Delgado, R., & Stefancic, J. (2001). *Critical race theory: An introduction*. New York: New York University Press.

Dews, C. L. B. & Law, C. L. (Eds.). (1995). *This fine place so far from home: Voices of academics from the working class*. Philadelphia: Temple University Press.

Dickson, A. C. (2006). Interchanges: Responses to Richard Fulkerson, "Composition at the turn of the twenty-first century. *College Composition and Communication, 57*(4), 730–738.

Doane, A. W., & Bonilla-Silva, E. (Eds.). (2003). *White out: The continuing significance of racism*. New York: Routledge.

Dorris, M. (1987). *A yellow raft in blue water*. New York: Warner.

Dressel, J. H. (2003). *Teaching and learning about multicultural literature: Students reading outside their culture in a middle school classroom*. Newark, DE: International Reading Association.

Easton, T., & Lutzenberger, J. (1999). Difficult dialogues: Working-class studies in a multicultural literature classroom. In S. L. Linkon (Ed.), *Teaching working class* (pp. 267–285). Amherst: University of Massachusetts Press.

Eckert, P. (1989). *Jocks & burnouts: Social categories and identity in the high school*. New York: Teachers College Press.

Eckert, P. (2001). *Linguistic variation as social practice*. Malden, MA: Blackwell Publishing.

Eddleston, S., & Philippot, R. (2002). Implementing whole-class literature discussions: An overview of the teacher's roles. In J. Holden & J. Schmit (Eds.), *Inquiry and the literary Text: Constructing discussions in the English classroom.* (pp. 49–59). Urbana, IL: National Council of Teachers of English.

Edelsky, C., Smith, K., & Wolfe, P. (2002). A discourse on academic discourse. *Linguistics and Education, 12*(1), 1–38.

Elbert, K. L. (2004, August 14). *Interracial contact and racial attitudes: A comparative study of Asian, Black, Latino, and White youth*. Paper presented at the annual meeting of the American Sociological Society, San Francisco.

Ellison, R. (1994). Battle royal. In M. Meyer (Ed.), *The compact Bedford introduction to literature* (3d ed.) (pp. 286–295). New York: Bedford/St. Martin's.

Engeström, Y. (1987). *Learning by expanding: An activity theoretical approach to developmental research*. Helsinki: Orienta-Konsultit.

Engeström, Y., Miettinen, R., & Punamaki, R. (1999). *Perspectives on activity theory*. New York: Cambridge University Press.

Erdrich, L. (2000). *Love medicine*. New York: HarperCollins.

Eyre, C. C. (Director). (1998). *Smoke signals* [motion picture]. United States: ShadowCatcher Entertainment.

Erickson, F. (2004). *Talk and social theory*. Cambridge, England: Polity Press.

Fairclough, N. (2001). *Language and power* (2d ed.). London: Longman.

Fairclough, N. (2003). *Analysing discourse: Text analysis for social research*. New York: Routledge.

Fairclough, N. (2003). Semiotic aspects of social transformation and learning. In R. Rogers (Ed.), *New directions in critical discourse analysis: Semiotic aspects of social transformation and learning* (pp. 225–235). Mahwah, NJ: Erlbaum.

Farley, J. E. (2000). *Majority–minority relations*. Upper Saddle River, NJ: Prentice Hall.

Farrell, C. S. (1996). Is racism a male thing? *Black Issues in Higher Education, 13*(16), 22–25.

Faulkner, W. (1997). Barn burning. In P. Lauter (Ed.), *The Heath anthology of American literature* (pp. 1553–1565). Lexington, MA: Heath.

Faust, M. (2000). Reconstructing familiar metaphors: John Dewey and Louise Rosenblatt on literary art as experience. *Research in the Teaching of English, 35*(1), 35–65.

Feagin, J. (2000). *Racist America: Roots, current realities, and future reparations.* New York: Routledge.

Feagin, J. R., & O'Brien, E. (2003). *White men on race: Power, privilege, and the shaping of cultural consciousness.* Boston: Beacon Press.

Fecho, B. (1998). Crossing boundaries of race in a critical literacy classroom. In D. Alvermann, K. Hinchman, D. Moore, S. Phelps, & D. Waff (Eds.), *Reconceptualizing the literacies in adolescents' lives* (pp. 75–101). Mahwah. NJ: Erlbaum.

Finders, M. (1997). *Just girls: Hidden literacies and life in junior high.* New York: Teachers College Press.

Fine, M., & Weis, L. (Eds.). (1999). *Unknown city: Lives of poor and working-class young adults.* Boston: Beacon.

Fine, M., Weis, L., Powell, L., & Wong, L. (Eds.). (1997). *Off white: Readings in race, power, and society.* New York: Routledge.

Fishman, S. M., & McCarthy, L. (2005). Talk about race: When student stories and multicultural curricula are not enough. *Race, Ethnicity & Education, 8*(4), 347–364.

Frank, T. (2004). *What's the matter with Kansas? How conservatives won the heart of America.* New York: Metropolitan.

Freeman, C. (2004). Trends in educational equity of girls and women. Retrieved July 14, 2005, from http://nces.ed.gov/pubsearch/pubsinfo.asp?pubid=2005016

Galda, L., & Beach, R. (2001). Theory and research into practice: Response to literature. *Reading Research Quarterly, 36*(1), 64–73.

Gallagher, C. (1995). White reconstruction in the university. *Socialist Review, 24,* 165–187.

Gallagher, C. A. (1997). Redefining racial privilege in the United States. *New Jersey Project Journal, 8,* 28–39.

Gass, W. (1971). *Fictions and the figures of life.* Boston: David R. Godine.

Gee, J. P. (1996). *Social linguistics and literacies: Ideology in discourses.* New York: Falmer.

Gee, J. P. (1999). *An introduction to discourse analysis: Theory and methods.* New York: Routledge.

Gee, J. P. (2004). *Situated language and learning: A critique of traditional schooling.* New York: Routledge.

Gee, J. P. (2006). Self-fashioning and shape-shifting: Language, identity, and social class. In D. E. Alvermann, K. A. Hinchman, D. W. Moore, S. F. Phelps, & D. R. Waff (Eds.), *Reconceptualizing the literacies in adolescents lives* (pp. 165–185). Mahwah, NJ: Erlbaum.

Gee, J. P., Allen, A., & Clinton, K. (2001). Language, class, and identity: Teenagers fashioning themselves through language. *Linguistics and Education, 12*(2), 175–194.

Gergen, K. J. (1994). *Realities and relationships: Soundings in social construction.* Cambridge, MA: Harvard University Press.

Giddens, A. (1979). *Central problems in social theory.* New York: Cambridge University Press.

Giddens, A. (1991). *Modernity and self-identity: Self and society in the late modern age.* Stanford, CA: Stanford University Press.

Goffman, I. (1981). *Forms of Talk.* Philadelphia: University of Pennsylvania Press.

Greer, J. (2004). "Some of their stories are like my life, I guess": Working-class women readers and confessional magazines. In P. P. Schweickart & E. A. Flynn (Eds.), *Reading sites: Social differences and reader response* (pp. 135–165). New York: Modern Language Association.

Griffin, C. (1989). *Typical girls?: Young women from school to the job market.* New York: Routledge.

Griffin, R. S. (1998). *Sports in the lives of children and adolescents: Success on the field and in life.* Westport, CT: Praeger.

Grobman, L. (2004). Rhetorizing the contact zone: Multicultural texts in writing classrooms. In P. Schweichkart & E. Flynn (Eds.), *Reading sites: Social difference and reader response* (pp. 256–285). New York: Modern Language Association.

Guerra, J. (1997). The place of intercultural literacy in the writing classroom. In C. Severino, J. Guerra, & J. Butler (Eds.), *Writing in multicultural settings* (pp. 248–260). New York: Modern Language Association.

Guinier, L., & Torres, G. (2003). *The miner's canary: Enlisting race, resisting power, transforming democracy.* Cambridge, MA: Harvard University Press.

Gushue, G. V., & Carter, R. T. (2000). Remembering race: White racial identity attitudes and two aspects of social memory. *Journal of Counseling Psychology, 47*(2), 199–210.

Gutierrez, K. D., Baquedano-Lopez, P., & Tejeda, C. (1999). Rethinking diversity: Hybridity and hybrid language practices in the third space. *Mind, Culture, and Activity, 6*(4), 286–303.

Gutierrez, K. D. and Rogoff, B. (2003). Cultural ways of learning: Individual traits or repertoires of practice. *Education Researcher, 32* (5), 19–25.

Hammerman, J. K. (2005). The several wisdoms of groups. *ReVision, 27*(4), 12–19.

Harklau, L. (2001). From high school to college: Student perspectives on literacy practices. *Journal of Literacy Research, 33*(1), 33–70.

Hartman, P. (2001). *Academically successful working-class girls constructing gender and literacy.* Unpublished doctoral dissertation, State University of New York, Buffalo.

Hartman, P. (2006). "Loud on the inside": Working-class girls, gender, and literacy. *Research in the Teaching of English, 41*(1), 82–117.

Hawkins, M. R. (2004). Researching English language and literacy development in schools. *Educational Researcher, 33*(3), 14–25.

Helms, J. E. (Ed.). (1990). *Black and White racial identity: Theory, research, and practice.* Westport, CT: Greenwood Press.

Helms, J. E. (1995). An update of Helms's white and people of color racial identity models. In J. G. Ponterotto, J. M. Casas, & C. M. Alexander (Eds.), *Handbook of multicultural counseling* (pp. 181–197). Thousand Oaks, CA: Sage.

Hemphill, L. (1999). Narrative style, social class, and response to poetry. *Research in the Teaching of English, 33*(3), 275–302.

Henry, S. E. (2005). A different approach to teaching multiculturalism: Pragmatism as a pedagogy and problem-solving tool. *Teachers College Record, 107*(5), 1060–1078.

Hicks, D. (1996). Learning as a prosaic act. *Mind, Culture and Activity, 3,* 102–118.

Hicks, D. (2001). Literacies and masculinities in the life of a young working-class boy. *Language Arts, 78*(3), 217–226.

Hicks, D. (2002). *Reading lives: Working-class children and literacy learning.* New York: Teachers College Press.

Hicks, D. (2005). Class readings: Story and discourse among girls in working-poor America. *Anthropology and Education Quarterly, 36*(3), 212–229.

Holland, D., & Eisenhart, M. (1990). *Educated in romance: Women, achievement, and college culture.* Chicago: University of Chicago Press.

Holland, D., & Lave, J. (Eds.). (2001). *History in person: Enduring struggles, contentious practice, intimate identity.* Santa Fe: School of American Research.

Holland, D. C., Lachicotte, W., Skinner, D., & Cain, C. (Eds.) (1998). *Identity and agency in cultural worlds.* Cambridge, MA: Harvard University Press.

Holland, D., & Leander, K. (2004). Ethnographic studies of positioning and subjectivity: An introduction. *Ethos, 32*(2), 127–139.

hooks, bell. (1992). *Black looks: Race and representation.* Boston: South End.

hooks, bell. (2000). *Where we stand: Class matters.* New York: Routledge.

Hum, S. (2006). Articulating authentic Chineseness: The politics of reading race and ethnicity aesthetically. In P. Vandenberg, S. Hum, & J. Clary-Lemon (Eds.), *Relations, locations, positions: Composition theory for writing teachers* (pp. 442–470). Urbana, IL: National Council of Teachers of English.

Hurston, Z. N. (1994). How it feels to be colored me. In N. Baym (Ed.), *Norton anthology of American literature* (4th ed., Vol. 2) (pp. 1425–1428). New York: W. W. Norton.

Hurston, Z. N. (2000). *Their eyes were watching God.* New York: McGraw Hill.

Hyland, N. E. (2005). Being a good teacher of black students? White teachers and unintentional racism. *Curriculum Inquiry 35*(4), 429–459.

Ibsen, H. (1992). *A doll's house.* New York: Dover.

Indiana University Center for Postsecondary Research (2005). *NSSE 2005 annual report: Exploring different dimensions of student engagement.* Retrieved August 6, 2006, from http://nsse.iub.edu/NSSE_2005_Annual_Report/index.cfm.

Jacobs, W. (2005). *Speaking the lower frequencies: Students and media literacy.* Albany: State University of New York Press.

Jensen, B. (2004). Across the great divide: Crossing classes and clashing cultures. In M. Zweig (Ed.), *What's class got to do with it* (pp. 168–183). Ithaca, NY: Cornell University Press.

Jordan, S., & Purves, A. (1993). *Issues in the responses of students to culturally diverse texts: A preliminary study.* Albany, NY: National Research Center on Literature Teaching & Learning.

Jung, H. J. (2007). *Learning to be an individual: Emotion and person in an American junior high school.* New York: Peter Lang.

Karolides, N. (2000). *Reader response in secondary and college classrooms.* Mahwah, NJ: Erlbaum.

Kashima, Y. (2002). Culture and self: A cultural dynamical analysis. In Y. Kashima, M. Foddy, & M. Platow (Eds.), *Self and identity: Personal, social, and symbolic* (pp. 207–226). Thousand Oaks, CA: Sage.

Keating, A. (1995). Interrogating "whiteness," (de)constructing race. *College English, 57*(8), 901–914.

Keating, A. (2004). Reading "whiteness," unreading "race": (De)racialized reading tactics in the classroom. In P. P. Schweickart & E. A. Flynn (Eds.), *Reading sites: Social difference and reader response* (pp. 314–343). New York: Modern Language Association.

Keeter, S., & Smith, G. A. (2006). *In search of ideologues in America: It's harder than you may think.* Retrieved July 25, 2006, from http://pewresearch. org/obdeck/?ObDeckID=17.

Kegan, R. (1994). *In over our heads: The mental demands of modern life.* Cambridge, MA: Harvard University Press.

Kegan, R. (2000). What "Form" Transforms?: A constructive-developmental approach to transformative learning. In J. Mezirow (Ed.), *Learning as transformation: Critical perspectives on a theory in progress* (pp. 35–70). San Francisco: Jossey-Bass.

Kehily, M. (2005). *An introduction to childhood studies.* Berkshire, U.K.: Open University Press.

Kent, T. (1993). *Paralogic rhetoric.* London: Associated University Press.

Ketter, J., & Lewis, C. (2001). Already reading texts and contexts: Multicultural literature in a predominately White rural community. *Theory into Practice, 40*(3), 175–183.

Kingston, M. H. (2000). *Woman warrior.* New York: Vintage.

Knoeller, C. (1998). *Voicing ourselves: Whose words we use when we talk about books.* Albany: State University of New York Press.

Kogawa, J. (1993). *Obasan.* New York: Anchor.

Koole, T. (2003). The interactive construction of heterogeneity in the classroom. *Linguistics and Education, 14*(1), 3–26.

Kozol, J. (1992). *Savage inequalities.* New York: Harper Perennial.

Kumashiro, K. (2000). Toward a theory of anti-oppressive education. *Review of Educational Research, 70*(1), 25–53.

Lacan, J. (1978). *The four fundamental concepts of psycho-analysis.* New York: Norton.

Lave, J., & Wenger, E. (1991). *Situated learning: Legitimate peripheral participation.* Cambridge, England: Cambridge University Press.

Lawrence, S. M., & Tatum, B. D. (2004). White educators as allies: Moving from awareness to action. In M. Fine, L. Weis, L. P. Pruitt, & A. Burns (Eds.), *Off White: Readings on power privilege and resistance* (2d ed.) (pp. 362–372). New York: Routledge.

Leander, K. M. (2001). "This is our freedom bus going home right now": Producing and hybridizing space-time contexts in pedagogical discourse. *Journal of Literacy Research, 33*(4), 637–680.

Leander, K. M. (2002). Polycontextual construction zones: Mapping the expansion of schooled space and identity. *Mind, Culture, and Activity, 9*(3), 211–237.

Leander, K. M. (2004). "They took out the wrong context": Uses of time-space in the practice of positioning. *Ethos, 32*(2), 188–213.

Leander, K. M., & Sheehy, M. I. (2004). *Spatializing literacy research and practice.* New York: Peter Lang.

Lee, C. D., & Ball, A. (2005). All that glitters ain't gold: CHAT as a design and analytic tool in literacy research. In R. Beach, J. Green, M. Kamil, & T. Shanahan (Eds.), *Multidisciplinary perspectives on literacy research* (pp. 101–132). Cresskill, NJ: Hampton Press.

Lee, C. D., Spencer, M. B., & Harpalani, V. (2003). "Every shut eye ain't sleep": Studying how people live culturally. *Educational Researcher, 32*(5), 6–13.

Lee, S. J. (1996). *Unraveling the model minority stereotype: Listening to the voices of Asian American youth.* New York: Teachers College Press.

Lee, S. J. (2001). More than "model minorities" or "delinquents": A look at Hmong American high school students. *Harvard Educational Review, 71*(3), 505–528.

Lee, S. J. (2002). Learning "America": Hmong American high school students. *Education and Urban Society, 34*(2), 233–246.

Lee, S. J. (2004). Up against whiteness: Students of color in our schools. *Anthropology & Education Quarterly 35*(1), 121–125.

Lee, S. J. (2005). *Becoming racialized Americans: Hmong American high school students in the Midwest.* New York: Teachers College Press.

Leer, E. B. (2003). *Multicultural literature in a homogeneous setting: Teacher beliefs and practices in one small-town English department.* Unpublished doctoral dissertation, University of Minnesota, Minneapolis.

Lensmire, T. (2000). *Powerful writing, responsible teaching.* New York: Teachers College Press.

Lesko, N. (2000). *Masculinities at school.* Thousand Oaks, CA: Sage.

Lewin, T. (2006, July 9). At colleges, women are leaving men in the dust. *The New York Times,* p. 1.

Lewis, C. (2000). Limits of identification: The personal, pleasurable, and the critical in reader response. *Journal of Literacy Research, 32*(2), 253–266.

Lewis, C. (2001). *Literacy practices as social acts: Power, status, and cultural norms in the classroom.* Mahwah, NJ: Erlbaum.

Lewis, C. (2006). "What's discourse got to do with it?": A mediation on critical discourse analysis in literacy research. *Research in the Teaching of English, 40*(3), 373–379.

Lewis, C., & Ketter, J. (2003). Learning as social interaction: Interdiscursivity in a teacher-researcher book group. In R. Rogers (Ed.), *An introduction to critical discourse analysis in education* (pp. 117–146). Mahwah, NJ: Lawrence Erlbaum.

Lewis, C., Ketter, J., & Fabos, B. (2001). Reading race in a rural context. *Qualitative studies in education, 14*(3), 317–350.

Lewis, C., & Moje, E. (2004). Sociocultural perspectives meet critical theories: Producing knowledge through multiple frameworks international journal of learning. *International Journal of Learning, 10,* 1980–1995.

Lewis-Charp, H. (2003). Breaking the silence: White students' perspectives on race in multiracial schools. *Phi Delta Kappan, 85*(4), 279–285. Retrieved from http //www.pdkintl.org/kappan/k0312le0311.htm.

Lincoln, Y. S., & Guba, E. G. (1985). *Naturalistic inquiry.* Thousand Oaks, CA: Sage.

Lindquist, J. (1999). Class ethos and the politics of inquiry: What the barroom can teach us about the classroom. *College Composition and Communication, 51*(2), 228–247.

Lindquist, J. (2002). *A place to stand: politics and persuasion in a working-class bar.* New York: Oxford University Press.

Lindquist, J. (2004). Class affects, classroom affectations: Working through the paradoxes of strategic empathy. *College English, 67*(2), 187–209.

Maher, F., & Tetreault, M. K. (1997). Learning in the dark: How assumptions of whiteness shape classroom knowledge. *Harvard Educational Review, 67*(1), 321–349.

Majerus, R. (1996). *Discourse communities: High time high school teachers take note.* Retrieved July 16, 2006, from http://www.engl.niu.edu/wac/majpap.html.

Mayo, C. (2004). Certain privilege: Rethinking white agency. *Philosophy of Education Yearbook*, 308–316.

McBride, J. (1996). *The color of water: A Black man's tribute to his White mother.* New York: Penguin.

McCarthy, C. (1994). Multicultural discourses and curriculum reform: A critical perspective. *Educational Theory, 44*(1), 81–118.

McDermott, M. (2006). *Working-class white: The making and unmaking of race relations.* Berkeley: University of California Press.

McCoy, B. A., & Jones, J. M. (2005). Between spaces: Meditations on Toni Morrison and whiteness in the classroom. *College English, 68*(1), 42–71.

McIntosh, P. (1988). *White privilege and male privilege: A personal account of coming to see correspondences through work in women's studies.* Wellesley, MA: Wellesley College Center for Research on Women.

McLeod, J., & Yates, L. (2006). *Making modern lives: Subjectivity, schooling, and social change.* Albany: State University of New York Press.

McRobbie, A. (1978). Working class girls and the culture of femininity. In: Centre for Contemporary Cultural Studies Women's Group (Ed.), *Women take issue* (pp. 97–108). London: Hutchinson.

Mead, S. (2006). *Truth about boys and girls.* Retrieved July 14, 2006, from http://www.educationsector.org/analysis/analysis_show.htm?doc_id=378705.

Mellor, B., & Patterson, A. (2005). Critical literacy: Theory, pedagogy and the historical imperative. In R. Beach, J. Green, M. Kamil, & T. Shanahan (Eds.), *Multidisciplinary perspectives on literacy research* (pp. 455–448). Cresskill, NJ: Hampton Press.

Miller, S., & Legge, S. (1999). Supporting possible worlds: Transforming literature teaching and learning through conversation in the narrative mode. *Research in the Teaching of English, 34*(1), 10–65.

Moje, E. B., Ciechanowski, K. M., Kramer, K., Ellis, L. C. R. & Callazo, T. (2004). Working toward a third space in content area literacy: An examination of everyday funds of knowledge and discourse. *Reading Research Quarterly, 39*(1), 38–70.

Moje, E. B., & Helden, C. V. (2005). Doing popular culture: Troubling discourses about youth. In J. A. Vadeboncoeur & L. P. Stevens (Eds.), *Re/constructing "the adolescent": Sign, symbol, and body* (pp. 211–248). New York: Peter Lang.

Möller, K. J., & Allen, J. (2000). Connecting, resisting and searching for safer places: Students respond to Mildred Taylor's the friendship. *Journal of Literacy Research, 32*, 145–186.

Moore, D. W., & Cunningham, J. W. (2006). Adolescent agency and literacy. In D. E. Alvermann, K. A. Hinchman, D. W. Moore, S. F. Phelps, & D. R. Waff (Eds.), *Reconceptualizing the literacies in adolescents lives* (pp. 129–146). Mahwah, NJ: Erlbaum.

Morris, E. W. (2005). From "middle class" to "trailer trash": Teachers' perceptions of white students in a predominately minority school. *Sociology of Education, 78*, 99–121.

Morrison, T. (1972). *The bluest eye*. New York: Pocket.

Moses, C. (2000). *Dissenting fictions: Identity and resistance in the contemporary American novel*. New York: Garland.

National Center for Education Statistics (2003). *Remedial education at degree-granting postsecondary institutions in fall 2000: Statistical analysis report*. Washington, DC: U.S. Department of Education.

Nayak, A. (2003). Boyz to men: Masculinities, Schooling and labour transitions in de-industrial times. *Educational Review, 55*(2), 147–159.

Newkirk, T. (2002). *Misreading masculinity: Boys, literacy, and popular culture*. Portsmouth, NH: Heinemann.

Ng-A-Fook, N. (2003). A curriculum behind the *boys'* locker room doors: Bodies, desires, and perpetuating patriarchy. *Journal of Curriculum Theorizing, 19*(4), 65–72.

Ngo, B. (2002). Contesting "culture": The perspectives of Hmong American female students on early marriage. *Anthropology & Education Quarterly, 33*(2), 163–188.

Orfield, G., & Lee, C. (2006). *Racial transformation and the changing nature of segregation*. Cambridge, MA: Civil Rights Project at Harvard University.

Nixon, S. (1996). *Hard looks: Masculinities, spectatorship and contemporary consumption*. London: UCL Press.

Pace, B. (2003). Resistance and response: Deconstructing community standards in a literature class. *Journal of Adolescent and Adult Literature, 46*(5), 408–412.

Pace, B. G. (2006). Between response and interpretation: Ideological becoming and literacy events in critical readings of literature. *Journal of Adolescent & Adult Literacy, 49*(7), 584–594.

Parker, W. C. (2002). *Teaching democracy: Unity and diversity in public life*. New York: Teachers College Press.

Pearce, L. (1994). *Reading dialogics*. New York: Edward Arnold.

Perry, P. (2002). *Shades of white: White kids and racial identities in high school*. Durham, NC: Duke University Press.

Perry, W. G. (1998). *Forms of ethical and intellectual development in the college years: A scheme*. San Francisco: Jossey Bass.

Petrosky, T. (2005). *The reading difficult text example*. Unpublished report. Pittsburgh: University of Pittsburgh.

Phelan, P., Davidson, A. L., & Yu, H. C. (1998). *Adolescents' worlds: Negotiating family, peers, and school*. New York: Teachers College Press.

Plucker, J. A., Wongsarnpigoon, R. L., & Houser, J. H. (2006). Examining college remediation trends in Indiana. *Education Policy Brief, 4*(5). Bloomington: Center for Evaluation & Education Policy, Indiana University. Retrieved August 5, 2006, from http://ceep.indiana.edu

Pollock, M. (2004). *Colormute: Race talk dilemmas in an American school*. Princeton: NJ: Princeton University Press.

Power, C. L. (2003). Challenging the pluralism of our past: Presentism and the selective tradition in historical fiction written for young people. *Research in the Teaching of English, 37*, 426–466.

Powers, P. (2002). A ghost in the collaborative machine: The white male teacher in the multicultural classroom. In B. TuSmith & M. Reddy (Eds.), *Race in the college classroom: Pedagogy and politics* (pp. 28–39). New Brunswick, NJ: Rutgers University Press.

Pratt, M. B. (1995). Dorothy Allison, lesbian author, interview. *The Progressive, 59*(7). Retrieved August 2, 2006, from http://www.findarticles.com/p/articles/mi_m1295/is_n7_v59/ai_17105308.

Prior, P. (1998). *Writing/disciplinarity: A sociohistorical account of literate activity in the academy.* Mahwah, NJ: Erlbaum.

Probst, R. E. (2004). *Response & analysis, Second Edition: Teaching literature in secondary school.* Portsmouth, NH: Heinemann.

QSR International. (2005). *NVivo* (research software). Cambridge, MA: QSR International.

Quantz, R. A. (1999). School ritual as performance: A reconstruction of Durkheim's and Turner's uses of ritual. *Educational Theory, 49*(4), 493–513.

Quinnipiac University Polling Institute (2003). *Voter attitudes towards affirmative action.* Hamdem, CT: Author.

Rabinowitz, P. (1998). *Before reading: Narrative conventions and the politics of interpretation.* Columbus: Ohio State University Press.

Raby, R. (2004). There's no racism at my school, it's just joking around: Ramifications for anti-racist education. *Race Ethnicity and Education, 7*(4), 367–383.

Reason, R. D., Scales, T. C., & Rossa-Millar, E. A. (2005). Encouraging the development of racial justice allies. *New Directions for Student Services, 110,* 55–66.

Reid, E. S. (2000). The stories we tell: Louise Erdrich's identity narratives. *Melus, 25*(2), 65–78.

Reid, K. S. (2004). Survey probes views on race. *Education Week, 23*(36), 1–4.

Reiman, J. (1995). *The rich get richer and the poor get prison.* New York: Allyn & Bacon.

Reisigl, M., & Wodak, R. (2001). *Discourse and discrimination: Rhetorics of racism and antisemitism.* New York: Routledge.

Rex, L. (2001). The remaking of a high school reader. *Reading Research Quarterly, 36*(3), 288–314.

Rex, L. (2002). Exploring orientation in remaking high school readers' literacies and identities. *Linguistics and Education, 13*(3), 271–302.

Rich, M. D., & Cargile, A. C. (2004). Beyond the breach: Transforming white identities in the classroom. *Race Ethnicity and Education, 7*(4), 351–365.

Rivera, T. (1992). *And the earth did not devour him.* Houston: Arte Publico.

Roediger, D. R. (2002). *Colored white: Transcending the racial past.* Berkeley: University of California Press.

Rogers, R. (2004). (Ed.). *A critical discourse analysis of family literacy practices: Power in and out of print.* Mahwah, NJ: Erlbaum.

Rogers, R., Malancharuvil-Berkes, E., Mosley, M., Hui, D., & Joseph, G. (2005). Critical discourse analysis in education: A review of the literature. *Review of Educational Research, 75,* 365–416.

Rosenblatt, L. (1970). *Literature as exploration.* London: Heinemann Educational.

Rosenblatt, L. (1978). *The reader, the text, the poem: The transactional theory of the literacy work.* Carbondale: Southern Illinois University Press.

Roth, W. M., Hwang, S. W., Lee, Y. J., & Goulart, M. I. M. 92005). *Participation, learning, and identity: Dialectical perspectives.* Berlin: Lehmanns Media.

Rowan, L., Knobel, M., Bigum, C., & Lankshear, C. (2002). *Boys, literacies and schooling.* Buckingham, England: Open University Press.

Rushdy, A. H. A. (1993). Families of orphans: Relation and disrelation in Octavia Butler's kindred. *College English, 55*(2), 135–157.

Russell, D. (1997). Rethinking genre in school and society: An activity theory analysis. *Written Communication, 14*(4), 504–554.

Ryan, J., & Sackrey, C. (Eds.). (1996). *Strangers in paradise: Academics from the working class.* Lanham, MD: University Press of America.

Rymes, B. (2001). *Conversational borderlands: Language and identity in an alternative urban high school.* New York: Teachers College Press.

Salinger, J. D. (1996). *The catcher in the rye.* New York: Bantam.

Sanders, K. (1998). A healthy balance: religion, identity, and community in Louise Erdrich's *Love Medicine. Melus, 23*(2), 129–144.

Sadowski, M. (2003). Adolescents in school: Perspectives on youth, identity, and education. Cambridge, MA: Harvard Education Press.

Sax, L. J., & Arredondo, M. (1996, April). *Student attitudes toward affirmative action in higher education: Findings from a national study* (Report No. HE029163). Paper presented at the annual meeting of the American Educational Research Association, New York, NY. (ERIC Document Reproduction Service No. ED394467).

Schechner, R. (2002). *Performance studies: An introduction.* New York: Routledge.

Schneider, B., & Stevenson, D. (1999). *The ambitious generation: American's teenagers motivated but directionless.* New Haven, CT: Yale University Press.

Schweickart, P. P, & Flynn, E. A. (Eds.). (2004). *Reading sites: Social difference and reader response.* New York: Modern Language Association.

Scott, J., & Leonhardt, D. (2005, May 15). Class in America: Shadowy lines that still divide. *The New York Times.* Retrieved August 5, 2006, from http://select.nytimes.com/gst/abstract.html?res=F00E1FF935540C768DDDAC0894DD404482.

Seitz, D. (2004a). Making work visible. *College English, 67*(2), 210–221.

Seitz, D. (2004b). *Who can afford critical consciousness? Practicing a pedagogy of humility.* Cresskill, NJ: Hampton Press.

Shepard, A., McMillan, J., & Tate, G. (Eds.). (1998). *Coming to class: Pedagogy and the social class of teachers.* Portsmouth, NH: Boynton/Cook.

Silko, L. M. (1977). *Ceremony.* New York: Penguin.

Smagorinsky, P. (2001). If meaning is constructed, what is it made from? Toward a cultural theory of reading. *Review of Educational Research, 71*(1), 133–169.

Smith, M., & Strickland, D. (2001). Complements or conflicts: Conceptions of discussion and multicultural literature in a teacher-as-readers discussion group. *Journal of Literacy Research, 33*(1), 137–168.

Soja, E. W. (1998). *Thirdspace: Journeys to Los Angeles and other real-and-imagined places.* Malden, MA: Blackwell.

Solorzano, D., & Yosso, T. J. (2001). From racial stereotyping and deficit discourse toward a critical race theory in teacher education. *Multicultural Education, 9*(1), 2–8.

Soter, A. O. (1997). Reading literature of other cultures: Some issues in critical interpretation. In T. Rogers & A. O. Soter (Eds.), *Reading across cultures: Teaching literature in a diverse society* (pp. 213–230). New York: Teachers College Press.

Spiegelman, A. (1993). *Maus: A survivor's tale: My father bleeds history/Here my troubles began.* New York: Pantheon.

Steinbeck, J. (1993). *Of mice and men.* New York: Penguin.

Strong, M. (2001), October 2). *Talking trash: The interview: Dorothy Allison.* Retrieved April 1, 2007. http://earthlink.net/~uur/trash.htm.

Sumara, D. J. (2002a). Creating commonplaces for interpretation: Literacy anthropology and literacy education research. *Journal of Literacy Research, 34*(2), 237–260.

Sumara, D. J. (2002b). *Why reading literature in school still matters: Imagination, interpretation, insight.* Mahwah, NJ: Lawrence Erlbaum.

Tatman, A. W. (2004). Hmong history, culture, and acculturation: Implications for counseling the Hmong. *Journal of Multicultural Counseling and Development, 32,* 222–233.

Tatum, B. (1992). Talking about race: Learning about racism: The application of racial identity developmental theory in the classroom. *Harvard Educational Review, 62,* 1–24.

Tatum, B. (2003). *Why are all the Black kids sitting together in the cafeteria? And other conversations about race: A psychologist explains the development of racial identity* (rev. ed.). New York: Basic Books.

Taylor, D. M. (2002). *The quest for identity: From minority groups to generation Xers.* Westport, CT: Praeger Publishers.

Thompson, F. T. (2003). The affirmative action and social policy views of a select group of White male private high school students. *Education and Urban Society, 36*(1), 16–43.

Thorne, B. (1993). *Gender play: Girls and boys in school.* New Brunswick, NJ: Rutgers University Press.

Townsend, J. S., & Fu, D. (1998). Quiet students across cultures and contexts. *English Education, 31,* 4–19.

Townsend, J. S., & Fu, D. (2001). Paw's story: A Laotian refugee's lonely entry into American literacy. *Journal of Adolescent and Adult Literacy, 45,* 104–114.

Trainor, J. S. (2002). Critical pedagogy's "other": Constructions of Whiteness in education for social change. *College Composition and Communication, 53*(4), 631–650.

Trainor, J. S. (2005). "My ancestors didn't own slaves": Understanding White talk about race. *Research in the Teaching of English, 40*(2), 140–167.

Trepagnier, B. (2001). Deconstructing categories: The exposure of silent racism. *Symbolic Interaction, 24*(2), 141–163.

Vadeboncoeur, J. A. (2005). The difference that time and space make: An analysis of institutional and narrative landscapes. In J. A. Vadeboncoeur & L. P. Stevens (Eds.), *Re/constructing "the adolescent": Sign, symbol, and body* (pp. 121–152). New York: Peter Lang.

Vadeboncoeur, J. A., & Stevens, L. P. (Eds.). (2005). *Re/constructing "the adolescent": Sign, symbol and body.* New York: Peter Lang.

Vandenberg, P. Hum, S., & Clary-Lemon, J. (Eds.) (2006). *Relations, locations, positions: Composition theory for writing teachers.* Urbana, IL: National Council of Teachers of English.

Vang, C. T. (2003). Learning more about Hmong students. *Multicultural Education, 11*(2), 1–14.

Vang, C. T. (2005). Hmong-American students still face multiple challenges in public schools. *Multicultural Education, 13*(1), 1–35.

Villaneuva, V. (1993). *Bootstraps: From an American academic of color.* Urbana, IL: National Council of Teachers of English.

Vinz, R., Gordon, E., Lundgren, B., LaMontagne, J., & Hamilton, G. (2000). *Becoming (other)wise.* Portsmouth, NH: Boynton/Cook.

Vygotsky, L. (1978). *Mind in society: The development of higher psychological processes.* Cambridge, MA: Harvard University Press.

Vygotsky, L. S. (1986). *Thought and language.* Cambridge, MA: Harvard University Press.

Wahlstrom, K. L., & Riedel, E. S. (2004a). *College in the schools: Follow-up student survey.* Center for Applied Research and Educational Improvement, University of Minnesota. Retrieved July 20, 2006, from http://education.umn.edu/CAREI/Reports/default.html

Wahlstrom, K. L., & Riedel, E. S. (2004b). *Analysis of college in the schools (CIS) surveys: Program impact survey.* Center for Applied Research and Educational Improvement, University of Minnesota. Retrieved July 20, 2006, from http://education.umn.edu/CAREI/Reports/default.html

Walkerdine, V. (1990). *Schoolgirl fictions.* New York: Verso.

Weis, L. (1990). *Working class without work: High school students in a de-industrializing economy.* New York: Routledge.

Weis, L. (2004). *Class reunion.* New York: Routledge.

Wenger, E. (1998). *Communities of practice: Learning, meaning and identity.* New York: Cambridge University Press.

Wertsch, J. (1998). *Mind as action.* New York: Oxford University Press.

West, C. (2001). *Cornel West: A critical reader.* Malden, MA: Blackwell.

West, T. R. (2002). *Signs of struggle: The rhetorical politics of cultural difference.* Albany: State University of New York Press.

Wiegman, R. (1999). Whiteness studies and the paradox of particularity. *Boundary, 2*(26), 115–150.

Willis, P. (1977). *Learning to labor: How working class kids get working class jobs.* New York: Columbia University Press.

Willis, S. (1998). Teens at work: Negotiating the jobless future. In J. Autin & M. N. Willard (Eds.), *Generations of youth: Youth cultures and histories in twentieth-century America* (pp. 347–357). New York: New York University Press.

Winans, A. E. (2005). Local pedagogies and race. *College English, 67*(3), 253–273.

Wortham, S. (2001). *Narratives in action: A strategy for research and analysis.* New York: Teachers College Press.

Wortham, S. (2006). *Learning identity: The joint emergence of social identification and academic learning.* New York: Cambridge University Press.

Yon, D. A. (2000). *Elusive culture: Schooling, race, and identity in global times.* Albany: State University of New York Press.

Young, J. (2003). Cultural models and discourses of masculinities: Being a boy in a literacy classroom. In R. Rogers (Ed.), *An introduction to critical discourse analysis* (pp. 147–171). Mahwah, NJ: Erlbaum.

Zandy, J. (Ed.). (1990). *Calling home: Working-class women's writing, an anthology.* New Brunswick, NJ: Rutgers University Press.

Appendix A
Methods

Researchers

Each of the three authors participated in different ways in this study. Richard Beach, professor of English education at the University of Minnesota, brought a background of conducting research on responses to literature in the 1970s and 1980s, with a more recent focus on experience on studying responses to multicultural literature (1997, 2000). He also applied theoretical perspectives on literary response drawn from sociocultural activity theory (2000, 2002) and critical discourse analysis (1997, 2004).

Amanda Thein, a former high school English teacher, at the time of the study was a doctoral student in literacy education at the University of Minnesota, with an interest in multicultural literature, gender, and critical ethnography. She was primarily responsible for observing classroom discussions, conducting postobservation reflections with Daryl Parks, interviewing students, and conducting ethnographic analyses of the school culture. She is assistant professor of education at the University of Pittsburgh and continues her work on high school students' social and cultural literary response practices. She has also been awarded a 2007 Promising Researcher Award by the National Council of Teachers of English.

Daryl Parks, the teacher of the class, was the third member of the research team. He was a doctoral student in literacy education at the University of Minnesota at the time of the study and, as of fall 2004, assistant professor of English education at Metropolitan State University in St. Paul, Minnesota. Parks, a popular English teacher at the school who has won several teaching awards, was open to sharing how his working-class background experiences shaped his own responses to literature.

Data Collection: Phase I

Data collection occurred in the academic year of 2001–2002. The 14 Thompson High School students enrolled in Parks's College in the Schools multicultural literature course served as participants. Participants were asked to grant their consent to participate in the study by signing consent forms approved by the University of Minnesota Human Subjects in Research Committee. Consistent with the consent agreements, the school and all participants are identified by pseudonyms.

Large- and small-group discussions were audiotaped and transcribed, generating approximately 30 hours of student discussion data. Thein also took field notes of the discussions, noting which students participated and stances they adopted. For dates in which Thein was not taking field notes, Parks wrote reflections in a journal about class sessions.

After most of the class discussions, Parks and Thein met after class and discussed the classroom activities and student interactions, with Parks recording their reflective comments on a laptop. Then, on a weekly basis Parks, Thein, and, occasionally, Beach met to discuss their different perceptions of the week's discussions as a means of triangulating the perceptions of the discussion.

The students wrote journal entries three to four days per week as part of the evaluation for the course. The journal entries were responses to their readings, class discussions, handouts, peers' journals, or topics provided by the teacher. The journals provided insight into the students' thoughts and perspective separate from the discussions. Selected journal entries were typed and incorporated into the database.

The researchers interviewed each student at least twice during the course in a semistructured fashion (see interview questions). Questions were also drawn from students' discussion comments or journal writing.

Interview Questions for Students' Responses to the Novels

1. What was your reaction to the novel?
2. In reading the novel, what were some things about how it was written that made it easy to comprehend or understand? What were some things about how it was written that made it difficult to comprehend or understand?
3. How would you describe the cultural world or worlds portrayed in the novel? What were some things about the cultural world that were familiar or easy to understand? What were some of the things about the cultural world that were puzzling or difficult to understand?

4. What were some of the rules or norms as to appropriate behavior operating in the world of the novel? What are some specific things in the novel that suggest these rules or norms? What are some of the beliefs and attitudes operating in this world? What are some specific things in the novel that suggest these beliefs or attitudes?

5. How do you perceive the world of this novel as similar or different from the worlds of the other novels in this course? In what ways are they similar or different?

6. Did the characters, conflicts, situations, or resolutions portrayed in the novel remind you of any experiences in your own world? How are these experiences similar to or different from those portrayed in the novel?

7. What do you perceive to be some of the key issues or problems portrayed in the novel? What are some reasons why you may consider these issues or problems important to you?

8. In studying the novel, what were some classroom activities that were helpful for you in understanding the novel and why?

9. What are some reasons why other students may have been resistant to reading this novel? To what parts of this novel, if any, did you find yourself feeling resistance? How did your own response differ from other students' responses?

10. What were your favorite topics/issues to discuss in class in relation to the text? Which did you enjoy the least? Why?

Focus-Group Interviews

At the end of the course, students participated in six hours of focus groups. Beach and Timothy Lensmire, a professor at the University of Minnesota and colleague of the researchers, conducted these interviews; as adults whom the students did not know, we hoped to avoid bias that could result from the teacher's and researcher's relationships with the students, particularly in terms of addressing issues related to evaluating the course. Thein and Parks also conducted other focus-group interviews with students about the course that did not involve course evaluations.

Students were asked questions (see following) designed to foster their reflection on their beliefs and attitudes espoused in group discussions, differences between beliefs and attitudes espoused in the class and those held by persons outside of the class, changes in beliefs and attitudes during the course, what they learned from the course, applications of what they learned to their own experiences, and ways they might teach a multicultural literature course if they were the teacher:

1. If an outsider had listened to a typical discussion from the course, for example, a discussion of affirmative action or McIntosh's essay on white privilege, what would they have said the class clearly valued or thought was important? Did the class as a group agree on what they valued; why or why not? What would an outsider have thought that the teacher valued?
2. Are you aware of individuals or groups in your world(s)—peers, teachers, family members, community members—who hold different values than those displayed during the classroom discussions? In what ways do these individuals or groups' values differ from your own values?
3. Did taking the course cause you to change you mind about anything that you believe or think? What specific things in the course challenged to think further about something or change your mind about something? What were some things that you got out of or learned in the CIS class? In what ways have any of these things been useful in your current courses and/or your own life experiences?
4. If you were to teach your own multicultural literature course for seniors at Thompson High School, what would be some things you would do in this course and for what reasons?

Interview with Parks

Beach conducted an interview with Parks based on the following questions about his role as a teacher in the course, his beliefs about teaching, and his perceptions of positive and negative aspects of the course:

1. How would you describe what you believe is most important in terms of teaching literature?
2. What do believe is that primary purpose for teaching literature? Where or how did you acquire these beliefs?
3. What were some things that you hoped your students would learn from taking your course?
4. What types of social practices did you emphasize given those hopes?
5. What were some of the critical lenses that you were teaching? What were some strategies that you used to teach those strategies?
6. One role that you played was that of mediating or negotiating differences between different worlds—the course versus school; the students' worlds and the world of academic work; the students' worlds and the cultural worlds portrayed in the novels? How do you perceive yourself engaged in this process and how did you do this?

7. You also played the role of tour guide/modeler of critical approaches and interpretive strategies? How would you describe that process? How did you determine the level or students' zone of proximal development at which to model practices for students?

8. One of the instructional strategies that you employed could be described as "orienting" related to value stances towards literature. What are some things that you valued about literature or learning in classrooms that you tried to directly or indirectly convey to students? How did you attempt to "orient" students in certain ways?

9. How to you cope with or accommodate for individual differences in your students' attitudes, beliefs, abilities, performance?

10. You also assumed the role of facilitating discussions. How would you describe what you believe to be an ideal discussion? What specific strategies did you employ to foster discussions? Which of these worked well and which, less well?

11. How would you describe your identity as being constituted as "working class." What are some of the practices that mark the school's and/or your students' working-class culture? How did you use that background experience in building a link between your own and your students' working class culture identifications?

12. You also served in the role of evaluator? What is your philosophy of evaluating students? How did you evaluate the students? On what basis? Do you believe that your evaluations functioned effectively in fostering learning?

All of these interviews, in addition to students' formal discussion groups in the course, were recorded for transcription and data analysis. Similarly, the teacher's journal and the researchers' discussion journal were transcribed and entered into the database.

Data Collection: Phase II

A second phase of the data collection occurred after the course was completed. During the following semester, Parks conducted additional interviews with former graduates and community leaders to gain a better sense of community influences. Parks also analyzed selections from 80 years of high school yearbooks to gain a sense of the changing student body over time, school events and clubs, and the involvement of the community in the high school. He held additional meetings and interviews with students and corresponded via e-mail and telephone with these students.

To gain an understanding of the school culture, Thein conducted field observations of a variety of classrooms, several lunch periods, athletic events, and a student assembly, as well as writing general observations of the hallways during passing periods and physical descriptions of the building. She also interviewed three of the students from the original study—Corey, Michelle, and Kayla—in more detail about the ways that they had constructed their identities at Johnson.

In this work, she addressed the following questions:

1. On what traditions is the culture of Johnson High School based?
2. How does the school work to maintain these traditions?
3. How do school traditions influence student social group construction?
4. How do school traditions influence individual identity construction?
5. How do all of these factors play out in classroom discourse?

She also observed classrooms, taking field notes in which she noted the nature of the students' social interactions in class discussions.

In conducting her ethnographic study of Thompson High School, she employed a critical ethnographic methodology (Carspecken, 1996), which emphasizes:

1. Generation of monologic data through observing social interactions
2. Generation of dialogic data through interviews with participants
3. Discovery of systems relationships through examining relationships between the immediate social context and other social sites that interact with the immediate context

In the first stage of data collection Thein focused on monologic data collection through detailed field notes of classrooms, the lunchroom, sports events, and school ceremonies such as the Snow Daze event. Also, general descriptions of the hallways during passing periods and physical building were written. These field observations were conducted primarily over the course of one school year.

This passive observational phase of data collection aims toward an understanding of the culture being studied, prior to disrupting the culture through later dialogic data collection designed to examine the underlying structures operating in the school culture. According to Lewis (2001, p. 71), it is these small everyday interactions that school ethnographers should focus on rather than more unusual events (e.g., dances, awards ceremonies):

School ethnographers should examine how students and teachers perform their identities and their politics" (Quantz, 1999, p. 509) in the seemingly mundane ritualized activities that make up school life.

As Quantz (1999) pointed out, "[It is] in the smaller, daily rituals, we are likely to find the real stuff of cultural politics. It is there that we are able to see how power is skillfully applied and just as skillfully resisted" (p. 509).

As part of the dialogic stage of data collection, interviews were held with students in the course after completion of the course as a means of providing the participants an opportunity to verify or challenge some of the researchers' preliminary perceptions and theories, dialogic data analysis designed to democratize the research process (Carspecken, 1996, p. 155). Students were asked to reflect on their experiences at Thompson High School, their involvement in the East Side community, and their thoughts on early patterns that we saw arising from preliminary analysis of the monologic data. Additionally, Thein interviewed faculty and staff members at the school about their experiences at Thompson High School.

In the final phase of research, Thein and Parks engaged in an analysis of the "systems relationships ... the relationship between the social site of focused interest and other specific social sites bearing some relation to it" (Carspecken, 1996, p. 42)—the other cultures operating within the East Side community at large. They attended community events, interviewed community members and leaders, and researched the history of the neighborhood. The data collection continued throughout the two years following our initial study of the classroom.

Data Collection: Phase III: Students' Learning in the Course

To examine what students were learning in the course, we examined changes across time in their thinking, the focus of Chapter 10. We also compared the perceptions of three students from the course with perceptions of three students who did not take the course related to the subject of class differences. We did not perceive this in any way as representing a control-group comparison because we were looking at only three students, and individual differences in students' ability, knowledge, or attitudes may have shaped any comparisons. Because students in the course had been discussing issues of class differences, we were simply interested in examining how some of those discussions may have influenced the three selected students from the course versus students who had not been involved in those discussions.

Of the three students from the course, Devin and Kathy are case-study participants. A third student, Mitch, a White male who identified as middle class, was also selected. Three students outside of the class were Jessie, a White female who identified as lower middle class; Ron, a White male who identified as middle class; and Brendon, a White male who identified as middle class.

Students were asked to write about themselves and their families for homework the day before the start of the study. The goal of this writing was to gain information to help paint an accurate portrait of the respondents for the reader. The students were given the following prompt:

Tell us a little bit about yourself and your family.

1. How do you see the world? What are your goals and values? How do you picture your future occupations and educational experiences?
2. What kinds of things do your parents and family value? What are some of your family's goals? What have been your parents' experiences with occupations and education?

On completion of the first prompt, Parks and Thein met with the students in two separate groups. Students were asked to write about social class in society and in their own lives based on the following prompt and questions:

"I was talking to this guy at the mall and I mentioned that I was a teacher in the city. He was like, "really, what kind of school and students is that?" I said, "what do you mean?" He said, "Are the students working class, middle class or upper class?" So I asked, "you mean the whole school or the individual students?" and he said, "Either one." So, I said, "umm ... I don't know, why don't I ask the students?"

1. What are your thoughts about the importance of "class differences" in this country?
2. Think about yourself and your individual world. If forced to do so, how would you describe or categorize the "class" you are in?
3. What reasons would account for this description?
4. How might people try to figure out what "class" someone else is in?
5. How might people switch from one class to another?

Next, students viewed and responded, in writing, to the following four short segments from the Public Broadcasting System (PBS) documentary *People Like Us: Social Class in America* (Alvarez & Kolker, 2001).

1. Four-minute introduction to "Bourgeois Blues": focuses on the idea that everyone believes himself or herself to be middle class.

   Student writing prompt: What are your thoughts about the people in this section, what they said, and what they experienced?

2. "How to Marry the Rich": focuses on the idea of passing for a different class based on the direct instruction of class codes and norms.

   Student writing prompt: "What are your thoughts about the people in this section, what they said, and what they experienced?

3. "Tammy's Story": focuses on the challenges faced by an impoverished, underemployed mother and her children who have different ideas about class and identity.

   Student writing prompt: What are your thoughts about the people in this section, what they said, and what they experienced?

4. "Don't Get Above your Raisin": considers the challenges of a young Appalachian woman who went away to the big city, then went back to visit her Father, raising the question, "Can you go home again?"

   Student writing prompt: What are your thoughts about the people in this section, what they said, and what they experienced?

Data Analysis

Selected classroom discussions, student interviews, focus-group discussions, and the interview with Parks were coded using NVIVO™ QSR International, 2005 qualitative software. Employing a grounded theory perspective (Lincoln and Guba, 1985), codes were generated inductively through extensive discussions among the three researchers. The researchers devoted multiple meetings to sharing their perceptions of the transcripts, noting consistent themes related to student identity construction, social practices, discourses, stances, and norms operating in the classroom, school, community, family, and workplace cultures. The researchers generated a tentative set of codes, which was then applied to samples of the data. Comparisons of the three researchers' coding of the data to determine reliability led to further revisions and refinements of the coding system. A final version of the coding system (Table A.1) was again used in coding a sample of the data to determine inter-judge reliability and a relatively high level of agreement (more than 75%) was achieved.

Table A1 Coding System

Coding Categories
1. Participant
2. Text
3. Teacher Techniques
    3.1 Modeling/Demonstrating Own Responses/Direct Instruction ("tour guiding")
        3.1.1 Critical Lenses
        3.1.2 Interpretive Strategies (e.g., "go to the text," critical concepts)
    3.2 Framing Discussion Topics, Eliciting Student Response
    3.3 Seeking Clarification/challenging Student Response
    3.4 Solidarity/Support with Students
4. Student Discussion, Positioning Strategies
    4.1 Challenging or Disagreeing with Other Students, Group
    4.2 Affirming Others' Stances, Shared Thinking
    4.3 Making Connections to Other Texts, Personal Experiences, Previous Discussion
    4.4 Formulating Lengthy, Original Interpretation
    4.5 Voices Teacher Words or Actions or Displays Instructional Strategies
5. Voicing, Adopting Stances, Lenses, Identity Related to Discourses of:
    5.1 Gender
    5.2 Class
    5.3 Race
    5.4 Sports, Athletics
    5.5 School, Education, Socialization
    5.6 Historical, Cultural Analysis in General
    5.7 Psychological
    5.8 Religious, Spiritual
6. Contextualizing, Constructing Text Worlds in Terms of:
    6.1 Norms, Conventions, Beliefs, Values in the Text
7. Categorizing, Defining Perceptions of Self, Others, and Characters
    7.1 Categorizes Self or Others or Describes Perceptions of Self and Others in Terms of Identity, Role, Ability, Status, Beliefs
    7.2 Categorizes or Describes Perceptions of Characters in Terms of Identity, Role, Ability, Status, Beliefs

---

These codes include an analysis of Parks's use of different teacher techniques (3 and 4), drawing on some of the analysis of a teacher's strategies in Edelsky, Smith, and Wolfe (2002), as well as the students' challenging or disagreeing versus affirming others' stances or shared thinking. This focus on classroom discussions also examined students, making connections to other texts, personal experiences, previous discussion; formulating lengthy, original interpretation; and voicing the teacher words or actions or displays instructional strategies—how students were internalizing and adopting the teacher's discourses, genres, stances, and heuristics over time.

Drawing on critical discourse analysis (CDA) (Fairclough, 2003; Gee, 1996, 1999; Rogers, 2004; Rogers, Malancharuvil-Berkes, Mosley, Hui, & Joseph, 2005), we identified some of the discourses voiced by students (category 5). Lewis (2006, p. 374) described CDA as "both a theory and a method that examines how social and power relations, identities, and knowledge are constructed through written, visual, and spoken texts and the contexts of their production and consumption." She posited the need to use CDA to address specific research questions or problems. For example, her six-year study of White teachers' discussion of multicultural literature required the use of CDA to examine how "our talk about texts worked to inscribe particular racial identities and how the social and political context of the community was constructed through our talk" (p. 374). She also notes that CDA can be useful when combined with Activity Theory (Engström, 1987) in terms of analyzing the ways power operates social worlds or activity systems, as well as for "analyzing agency when it occurs—how and when subjects are able to make and remake themselves, discursively, within the system" (p. 376). Based on her analysis of the White teachers' discussions of multicultural literature in ways that were "disrupting fixed discourses," CDA was useful for examining "how the teachers worked to make and remake themselves through their talk…" (p. 377).

In our analysis, we focused on students' use of different discourses related to race, class, gender, athleticism, schooling, historical-cultural contexts, psychology-family, and religion. Based on the idea of discourses as particular ideological orientations related to knowing and thinking about the world (Gee, 1996, 1999), we selected these particular discourses because the participants consistently used language reflecting these discourses in their writing and discussions. Or they double voiced (Bakhtin, 1981) characters' uses of language reflecting those characters' discourses. Adopting certain discourses also functioned as identity tool kits (Gee, 1996) to constitute participants' allegiances to the status afforded by adopting a certain discourse within a specific social world. For example, in discussing their participation in sports, some of our participants, both male and female, voiced a discourse of athleticism that celebrated an ideological commitment to the values of competitiveness, achievement (i.e., winning), training (i.e., hard work), physical toughness and prowess, and self-control.

We also drew on positionality theory (Davies & Harré, 1990) to analyze how discourses position or orient (Rex, 2001; 2002) students to adopt certain identities in social worlds, particularly the classroom. For example, the discourses of masculinity functioned to position Troy to adopt certain traditional sexist perceptions of female characters. We also examined how discourses and cultural models contributed to interactional positioning (Wortham, 2001, 2006) to enhance others' status or to silence others, as well as how participants such as Mai adopted strategic positioning (Hartman, 2001) by deliberately remaining silent.

We were also interested in how certain discourses operated across different social worlds so that certain ideological orientations are transferred from one world to another. For example, we found that some of the same language used to describe sports was used by some of the Thompson administrators in describing the school culture in which control was a primary metaphor. As we found in the study, the discourses of athleticism are evident in discourses of schooling celebrating physical control (Weis, 1990, 2004) that constitute the meaning of disciplinary rules and practices in the school.

Our analysis of discourses of race drew on critical race theory (Bonilla-Silva, 2001; Delgado & Stafancic, 2001; Guinier & Torres, 2003; hooks, 1992, 2000; Roediger, 2002; West, 2001). This analysis identified participants' voicing of discourses and cultural models related to these various topics, for example, adoption of discourses of individual prejudice or race talk (Bonilla-Silva, 2001) related to discussions of race. We were particularly interested in how discourses of Whiteness operating in the school and classroom functioned to control or exert order or rationality against what is assumed to be disorder and irrationality associated with the "other" (Barnett, 2000).

Sociocultural, Activity Theory Analysis of Constructing Social Worlds We also developed a set of codes related to ways students constructed text worlds (category 6) and perceptions of their identities, roles, abilities, status, or beliefs in lived worlds (category 7) (Table A1).

This analysis drew on previous research by Phalen, Davidson, and Yu (1998) on high school students' perceptions of conflicting identities across different worlds of school, peers, family, and community, as well as perceptions of the borders and barriers between these worlds. Then, consistent with the literary response model of parallel processing of interpretations between lived and text worlds, we analyzed students' perceptions of characters' identities, roles, abilities, status, or beliefs (Beach & Myers, 2001).

Our analysis also drew on sociocultural theory of sociocultural, Activity Theory of learning regarding how culturally constituted practices and tools are acquired through participation in cultures or social worlds (Bazerman & Russell, 2003; Cole, 1996; Engeström, 1987; Engeström, Miettinen, & Punamaki, 1999; Lee & Ball, 2005; Lee, Spencer, & Harpalani, 2003) as well as in responding to literary texts (Beach & Kalnin, 2005; Brooks, 2006; Galda & Beach, 2001; Smagorinsky, 2001). A sociocultural perspective on literary response assumes that students learn to interpret literature as part of acquiring and engaging in certain social practices—ways of talking about, valuing, using, interpreting, or believing in texts, valued in certain social contexts (Gee, 1999).

In our analysis, we focused on examining how participants acquired certain tools such as language, discourses, and cultural models that mediate participation in social worlds or activity systems. Russell (1997, p. 510) defined an activity system as "any ongoing, object-directed, historically conditioned, dialectically structured, tool-mediated human interaction. Some examples are a family, a religious organization, a school, a discipline, a research laboratory, and a profession." The meaning of these tools depends on how they are used to achieve certain objects or outcomes driving a social world or system, objects or outcomes that often involve changing or improving an activity, creating a motive for achieving that object or outcome (Engeström, 1987). People acquire uses of tools through social interaction in which they internalize others' voices and discourses connects by appropriating and double voicing others' language as they move through these worlds (Bakhtin, 1981, 1986; Vygotsky, 1978, 1986). We considered how, as our participants acquired these various tools, they moved from peripheral to insider status in these social worlds (Wenger, 1998, p. 154), as well as how learning of tools in one social world as transfers to learning in another world (Prior, 1998).

Analysis of California high school students from lower socioeconomic homes found that some acquired genres that helped them bridge gaps between the middle-class culture of the high school and their home cultures of their homes (Davidson, 1996; Phelan, Davidson, & Yu, 1998). Based on high school students' perceptions of participation in different worlds, Phelan, Davidson, and Yu (1998, p. 16) identified six different types of relationships between family and peer group and school worlds: "congruent worlds/smooth transitions; different worlds/border crossings managed; different worlds/border crossings difficult; different worlds/border crossings resisted; congruent worlds/border crossings resisted; different worlds/smooth transitions." When worlds are perceived as incongruent, students perceive these borders as insurmountable barriers between worlds, particularly when they assume they lack the social or cultural capital valued in academic worlds (Beach, Lundell, & Jung, 2002). We therefore noted instances in which there was congruency between students' social worlds, for example, between students' home world and the school world, as well as instances of or incongruent relationships, for example, between the "culture of control" (Weis, 1990) of the school world and Parks's classroom world.

Cultural Models   We also analyzed the data for individual participants' voicing of certain specific cultural models defined as participants' adoption of hierarchical value systems in which certain practices or dispositions are valued over other practices or dispositions (Beach & Kalnin, 2005; D'Andrade & Strauss, 1992; Holland & Eisenhart, 1990; Holland, Lachicotte, Skinner, & Cain, 1998). Identifying these cultural models involved noting certain consistent patterns in students' writing and discussions that suggested commitment to certain value hierarchies. For example, in the analysis of Kayla in Chapter 7, we identified one of her cultural models as that of appearing to be involved in hegemonic white culture that creates the appearance of white, middle-class normalcy and happiness, "regardless of how one actually feels." Adopting this cultural model reflected Kayla's high priority on appearing to be normal and happy to her peers within the school culture through contributing to the school newspaper. Fostering this appearance took priority over expressing the fact that she felt somewhat alienated from the school culture which she contrasted with the culture of her previous suburban school; she also reported being bored in many of her classes. Thus, fostering the appearance of normalcy took priority over expressing her actual feelings.

Case-Study Analyses

Based on the data analysis, seven students were selected for case-study analyses, students who represented differences in race (five White, one African, and one Hmong) and their stances toward institutions adopted in the course. Troy, a white student who was featured in Chapters 1 and 2, began the course with relatively traditional discourses of individualism but shifted to adopt discourses of institutional analysis toward the end of the course. Corey and Michelle (both White) adopted discourses of individualism and were reluctant to challenge the school culture or hegemonic institutional forces portrayed in the novel. Devin and Kayla (both White) adopted a more critical stance, challenging some of the institutional practices operating in the school culture, although they were not always consistent in their stances. Kathy (African) and Mia (Hmong) also adopted relatively more critical stances, although they were ambivalent about their perceptions of race and their stances shifted over time.

In conducting these case-study analyses, drawing on the coded data, we analyzed consistent patterns in the students' perceptions of different worlds and the texts as well as shifts in their thinking during the course. We identified certain themes, discourses, and cultural models constituting their stances and identities, as well as their negotiations of identities across different worlds.

Summary Descriptions of Case-Study Participants The following are summary descriptions of our seven case-study participants. To describe some of these participants from working-class, low-income families, we draw on Bettie's (2003) distinction between settled-living working-class students whose parents have relatively stable earnings and housing versus hard-living working-class students whose parents lack stable earnings and may often be struggling with issues of unemployment, crime, health, or drug use.

Corey: White, settled-living working-class, male student from a two-parent home of long-time community residents; co-captain of the hockey and football teams; works in sports-training facilities and assists his father with construction after school; struggled to voice or adopt new discourses or perspectives that would question the status quo.

Devin: White, settled-living working-class male from a two-parent home of long-time community residents; outstanding athlete and leader in wrestling and football; wildly popular student on campus; works after school in a nearby gas station/convenience mart; regularly adopted alternative perspectives and discourses in ways that would support his classroom success.

Kathy: Black, first-generation female from Liberia; lives with single mother who struggles financially; involved in journalism and theater; a talkative student, Kathy regularly participated in all conversations while displaying a wide range of discourses and perspectives.

Kayla: White, working-class student from a hard-living, single-parent family who served as an editor for the school yearbook; worked as a telemarketer; adopted an active role in the class by voicing critical analyses of peers' interpretations.

Mia: U.S. born, Hmong, female student; active in Asian Culture Club, badminton team, and senior class politics; engages in all aspects of the course, but struggles to convey her perspectives given their potential to create conflict; cites increased understanding of racial and social class dynamics as occurring in the course.

Michelle: White female from a settled-living working-class family; editor of the school newspaper; works at a nearby Dairy Queen; regularly confronts student hierarchies within the school; regularly disputes claims of students that she doesn't like; speaks of numerous changes to her perspectives as a result of the course.

Troy: White male who lives on his own; hard-living, working-class family background; when younger, but has not participated in sports in high school; outspoken, he shies away from few students or conflicts; cites how his faith has helped him turn from early life rebellion; cites meaningful changes to his racial discourses and perspectives due to the course.

Appendix B
Literature Used in the Course;
Recommended Literature

Books Read in the Course

Allison, D., *Bastard out of Carolina*
Anaya, R. A., *Bless me, Ultima*
Butler, O., *Kindred*
Cisneros, S., *The house on Mango Street*
Dorris, M., *Yellow raft in blue water*
Erdrich, L., *Love medicine*
Hurston, Z. N., *Their eyes were watching God*
Kogawa, J., *Obasan*

Recommended Multicultural Literature Titles for College in the Schools Literature Courses (in addition to those listed above):

Achebe, Chinua, *Things fall apart*
Alexie, Sherman, *The Lone Ranger & Tonto fistfight in heaven*
Al-Shaykh, Hanan, *The story of Zahra*
Alvarez, Julia, *In the time of the butterflies*
Baldwin, James, *Giovanni's room*
Benitez, Sandra, *A place where the sea remembers*
Cao, Lan, *Monkey bridge*
Chopin, Kate, *The awakening*
Collins, Billy, *Picnic, lightning*
Conrad, Joseph, *The heart of darkness*

Dangarembga, Tsitsi, *Nervous conditions*
Danticat, Edwidge, *Krik? krak?*
Deloria, Ella Cara, *Water lily*
Divakaruni, Chitra, *The mistress of spices*
Doty, Mark, *Heaven's coast*
Ellison, Ralph, *Invisible man*
Emecheta, Buchi, *The joys of motherhood*
Erdrich, Louise, *tracks*
Faqir, Fadia, *Nisanit*
Farah, Nuruddin, *Sweet & sour milk*
Faulkner, William, *As I lay dying*
Frazier, Charles, *Cold Mountain*
Gaines, Ernest J., *A lesson before dying*
Garcia, Christina, *Dreaming in Cuban*
Gilman, Charlotte P., *The yellow wallpaper*
Goldberg, Myra, *The bee season*
Guterson, David, *Snow falling on cedars*
Haruf, Kent, *Plainsong*
Hegi, Ursula, *Stones from the river*
Hemingway, Ernest, *In our time*
Hogan, Linda, *Solar storms*
Holthe, Tess Uriza, *When the elephants dance*
Howe, Leanne, *Shell shaker*
Jin, Ha, *Waiting*
Jordan, June, *Kissing God goodbye*
King, Thomas, *Green grass, running water*
Kincaid, Jamaica, *My brother*
Kingsolver, Barbara, *The poisonwood bible*
Kingston, Maxine H., *Woman warrior*
Kushner, Tony, *Angels in America*
Lorde, Zamy, *A new spelling of my name*
Marquez, Gabriel, *One hundred years of solitude*
Mahfouz, Naguib, *The journey of Ibn Fattouma*
Martel, Yann, *Life of Pi*
Monette, Paul, *Becoming man*
Morrison, Toni, *Sula, beloved*
Mukherjee, B., *The middleman and other stories*
Naylor, Gloria, *Mama day*
Ninh, Boa, *The sorrow of war*
Nye, Naomi Shihab, *19 varieties of gazelles*
O'Brien, Tim, *Going after Cacciato*
O'Brien, Tim, *The things they carried*

Otsuka, Julie, *When the emperor was divine*
Paley, Grace, *Enormous changes at the last minute*
Power, Susan, *Grass dancer*
Roy, Arundati, *The god of small things*
Rulfo, Juan, *Pedro Paramo*
Senna, Danzy, *Caucasia*
Sijie, Dai, *Balzac and the little Chinese seamstress*
Silko, Leslie M., *Ceremony, The gardens in the dunes*
Tan, Amy, *The joy luck club*
Tan, Amy, *Kitchen god's wife*
Troung, Monique, *The book of salt*
Watson, Larry, *Montana 1948*
Wicomb, Zoe, *You can't get lost in cape town*
Winterson, Jeanette, *Oranges are not the only fruit*
Yamamoto, Hisaye, *Seventeen syllables*

Index

A

Academically motivated students, 43
Academic discourse community,
    problem with model of, 118
Academic socialization, 271
Activity Theory, 309
Adolescents, consistent beliefs of, 6
Advanced placement (AP) class, 3, 10,
    138
Affirmative action, 3
    church social world and, 262
    college admissions and, 228
    competing attitudes toward, 248
    debate over, 177, 198, 228, 275, 278
    job discrimination and, 255
    merits of, 200
    opposition to, 101, 102, 110, 178
    programs
        critiques of, 11, 18
        discrimination against White
            students under, 115, 146, 218
        need for, 25, 262, 276
        reverse discrimination of, 16
        support for, 228
    White privilege and, 15, 275, 279, 280
African American(s)
    control of, 178
    culture, 202
    marginalized, 257
    students, hallways behaviors of, 157
Agency
    alternative discourses and, 260
    alternative family world and, 24

athletic performance and, 143, 145
boyfriend and, 160
character acquisition of, 70–71
character development of, 213, 262
classroom, 209
class system limiting, 179
college student, 171, 184, 190, 260
countersocial practices and, 198
development of, 21, 25, 31, 282
future selves and, 54, 141
gender differences, 29
institutional forces limiting, 70
marriage relationship, 99
motherhood and, 220
peer emulation and, 38
peer relationships and, 151
personal decision and, 22
poverty and, 76
practices defining, 7
reflective language and, 77
resistance of school culture, 40
self-determination and, 22
sexism limiting, 83
sports and, 61
status quo and, 142, 149, 165, 276
subordinate roles undermining, 96
value of, 24
way of establishing, 201
American equality of opportunity,
    cultural model of, 259
Anger, feelings related to, 232
Animism, 223
Antipoverty government programs, 3
AP class, see Advanced placement class

319